The dominant and deceptively simple theme of this book is the relationship between the moral environment of the courtroom and that of the society in which the court is situated.

Like other *Past and Present* edited collections the volume ranges widely across time and space, from ancient Greece to twentieth-century Africa. As a consequence, it encompasses not only the highly professional legal systems of the Roman, later medieval and modern worlds, but also the relatively unprofessionalised courts of classical Athens and of the early middle ages and the alien, imposed legal systems of colonial Rhodesia and Kenya.

PETER COSS is Professor of Medieval History, School of History and Archaeology, Cardiff University.

Past and Present Publications

The Moral World of the Law

Past and Present Publications

General Editor: JOANNA INNES, *Somerville College, Oxford*

Past and Present Publications comprise books similar in character to the articles in the journal *Past and Present*. Whether the volumes in the series are collections of essays – some previously published, others new studies – or monographs, they encompass a wide variety of scholarly and original works primarily concerned with social, economic and cultural changes, and their causes and consequences. They will appeal to both specialists and non-specialists and will endeavour to communicate the results of historical and allied research in the most readable and lively form.

For a list of titles in Past and Present Publications, see end of book.

The Moral World of the Law

Edited by
PETER COSS

CAMBRIDGE UNIVERSITY PRESS

PUBLISHED BY THE PRESS SYNDICATE OF THE UNIVERSITY OF CAMBRIDGE
The Pitt Building, Trumpington Street, Cambridge, United Kingdom

CAMBRIDGE UNIVERSITY PRESS
The Edinburgh Building, Cambridge CB2 2RU, UK http://www.cup.cam.ac.uk
40 West 20th Street, New York, NY 10011–4211, USA http://www.cup.org
10 Stamford Road, Oakleigh, Melbourne 3166, Australia

First published 2000

Printed in the United Kingdom at the University Press, Cambridge

Typeset in Monotype Times New Roman 10/12 pt *System* QuarkXPress™ (SE)

A catalogue record for this book is available from the British Library

Library of Congress cataloguing in publication data
The moral world of the law / edited by Peter Coss.
p. cm. – (Past and present publications)
Includes index.
ISBN 0 521 64059 8 (hardback)
1. Law and ethics – History. 2. Justice. Administration of – Europe – History. 3. Justice, Administration of – Africa – History.
I. Coss, Peter R.
K247.6.M67 2000
340′.112–dc21 99-15978 CIP

ISBN 0 521 64059 8 hardback

Contents

Contributors

PAUL BRAND is a Fellow of All Souls College, University of Oxford. His publications include *The Making of the Common Law* (1992) and *The Origins of the English Legal Profession* (1992). He has recently edited *The Earliest English Law Reports, volumes I and II* (1995 and 1996).

PETER COSS is Professor of Medieval History at Cardiff University. His books include *Lordship, Knighthood and Locality: A Study in English Society c.1180–c.1280* (1991), *The Knight in Medieval England* (1993) and *The Lady in Medieval England* (1998).

WENDY DAVIES is Professor of History at University College London and Pro-Provost (European Affairs). Her books include *Small Worlds: The Village Community in Early Medieval Brittany* (1988) and (with Grenville Astill) *A Breton Landscape* (1997). She has edited (with Paul Fouracre) *The Settlement of Disputes in Early Medieval Europe* (1986) and *Property and Power in the Early Middle Ages* (1995).

CAROLINE FORD is Associate Professor of History at the University of Columbia. She is the author of *Creating the Nation in Provincial France: Religion and Political Identity in Brittany* (1993). She is currently completing a book on the feminisation of religion in nineteenth-century France.

PAUL HYAMS is Associate Professor of History at Cornell University. He is the author of *King, Lords and Peasants in Medieval England* (1980) and of numerous essays exploring the mutual impact of medieval English law and society. He is currently completing a book entitled *Rancour and Reconciliation in Medieval England.*

MARTIN INGRAM is Senior Tutor and Fellow of Brasenose College, and Lecturer at the University of Oxford. He is the author of *Church Courts,*

Sex and Marriage in England, 1570–1640 (1987) and of essays on crime and the law, sex and marriage, popular customs and religious culture. He has also published on the history of climate.

DIANA JEATER is Senior Lecturer in African History at the University of the West of England. She is the author of *Marriage, Perversion and Power: The Construction of Moral Discourse in Southern Rhodesia* (1993). She is currently working on a book entitled *Law, Language and Science: The 'Civilising' Project of the White Administration in Southern Rhodesia, 1890–1930*.

THOMAS KUEHN is Professor of History at Clemson University. His publications include *Law, Family and Women: Towards a Legal Anthropology of Renaissance Italy* (1991) and *Emancipation in Late Medieval Florence* (1982). He is currently completing a book on illegitimate children in fifteenth-century Florence.

ANDREW LEWIS is Senior Lecturer in Laws at University College London and editor of *The Journal of Legal History*. He has published essays on the history of Roman law in Europe and has edited (with D. J. Ibbetson) *The Roman Law Tradition* (1994). He has recently completed an edition (with I. Cox) of Montesquieu's *Collectio Juris*.

JOHN LONSDALE is a Fellow of Trinity College and Reader in African History at the University of Cambridge. Past editor of the Cambridge University Press African Studies Series, he has written widely on the political, social and intellectual history of Africa, and of Kenya in particular, and has co-authored (with Bruce Berman) *Unhappy Valley: Conflict in Africa and Kenya* (1992).

STEPHEN TODD is Senior Lecturer in Classics at the University of Keele. His books include *The Shape of Athenian Law* (1993) and *The Oratory of Classical Greece, volume 2: Lysias* (1999). He is co-editor (with P. A. Cartledge and P. C. Millett) of *Nomos: Essays in Athenian Law, Politics and Society* (1990).

CHRIS WICKHAM is Professor of Early Medieval History at the University of Birmingham. His books include *Land and Power: Studies in Italian and European Social History, 400–1200* (1994), *Community and Clientele in Twelfth-Century Tuscany* (1998) and *Law, Custom and Community* (1999).

Preface

All but one of the essays presented in this volume are based on papers delivered to a Past and Present conference on *The Moral World of the Law* held at the University of Birmingham on 12 and 13 July 1996 and organised jointly by Chris Wickham and myself. The one exception was specially commissioned from Andrew Lewis and I am most grateful to him for stepping in to plug a potential gap in the volume's coverage. I owe him a second debt of gratitude for suggesting the very apt cover illustration. I would like to take this opportunity of thanking, on behalf of myself and my co-organiser, all those who gave papers to the conference, whether represented here or not, and of thanking both them and the many other participants whose lively and informed discussion helped to make the conference a notable success. Special thanks are due to Chris Wickham for his aid and generosity during the editing of this volume, to Joanna Innes for her helpful criticisms, to Charles Philpin for his ever welcome advice, and to my wife, Angela Coss, for compiling the index.

P. R. C.

1. *Introduction*[1]

PETER COSS

Any historian of the law or of legal records is bound to confront, sooner or later, the question of the autonomy of the law. In its crudest form, the notion of autonomy suggests that the law possesses internal structures which operate independently of the society within which it is situate.[2] These structures may have the capacity to act as a separate causal agent.[3] In recent years legal historians have been moving away from this approach. Historians of the English common law, for example, have been much concerned to enlarge the scope of their inquiries and to shift from the 'legal functionalism', or 'evolutionary functionalism', of the common-law mind which has long dominated the subject. Exactly how the legal historian should now proceed is problematic. The general widening of the project of legal history has been accompanied by a stark realisation that the subject of *law in history* involves more than the juxtaposition of 'law and society', 'law and economy' and so on; more than the setting of text within context.[4] Yet few serious scholars of the subject would be happy to subscribe to the antithesis of autonomy, the idea of law and legal practice as mere reflexes or expressions of social value and social change; still less with the law as constitutive, mechanistically, of an ideological superstructure. Most would have at least some sympathy with the manner in which E. P. Thompson voiced his famous reaction against this:

> I found that law did not keep politely to a 'level', but was at *every* bloody level; it was imbricated within the mode of production and productive

[1] I would like to thank Joanna Innes and Chris Wickham for their helpful comments on a first draft of this introduction.

[2] For the practical, legal consequences of this view see below, Andrew D. E. Lewis, 'The autonomy of Roman Law', p. 37.

[3] For a recent collection of essays on the subject see R. George (ed.), *The Autonomy of Law* (Oxford, 1996).

[4] See, in particular, David Sugarman, 'Writing "Law and Society" Histories', *Modern Law Review*, 55 (1992), pp. 292–308, this being a review of W. R. Cornish and G. de N. Clark, *Law and Society in England, 1750–1950* (London, 1989).

> relations themselves (as property-rights, definitions of agrarian practice) and it was simultaneously present in the philosophy of Locke; it intruded brusquely within alien categories, reappearing bewigged and gowned in the guise of ideology; it danced a cotillon with religion, moralising over the theatre of Tyburn; it was an arm of politics and politics was one of its arms; it was an academic discipline, subjected to the rigour of its own autonomous logic; it contributed to the definition of self-identity both of rulers and of ruled; above all, it afforded an arena for class struggle, within which alternative notions of law were fought out.[5]

Not surprisingly, revisionist theses tend to take a two-way traffic as axiomatic: 'law shapes society and its social activities, while its rhetoric, structure and procedures can be regarded as a reflection of society's own perceptions of (and attempts to reproduce and change) social reality'.[6] For some this hardly goes far enough. In the USA the so-called 'Critical legal writers' or 'Critical scholars' in their reaction against the traditional legal discourse – in both its 'formalist' and its 'realist' manifestations – have dismissed even the idea of the 'relative autonomy' of legal structures as insufficiently theorised.[7] For them, law and society are so inextricably mixed, so deeply imbricated with one another, to use Thompsonian phraseology, as to render such a conception otiose. In short, law is 'omnipresent in the very marrow of society'.[8] In consequence the debate around how best to pursue historico-legal inquiries is a long way from being resolved.

Meanwhile, social and cultural historians have been turning to legal records with a new agenda, the reconstruction of the mental world of their chosen subjects. Most spectacularly in early modern studies, involvement in the law, and the language deployed in that involvement, has been seen to forge a direct entrée into the lives of individuals and of their communities.[9] The new accent upon language, in the wake of the so-called linguistic turn, has shown that it is not only in the words themselves that one can perceive the interpenetration of law and society but in the narrative and linguistic strategies employed.[10] It is here that critical theory has been brought

[5] E. P. Thompson, *The Poverty of Theory* (London, 1978), p. 96. At the same time, Thompson was perfectly well aware that the law operated formally under its own rules, rules which could be difficult for the outsider, even an upper-class outsider, to penetrate. See *Whigs and Hunters* (London, 1975), ch. 10, section iv.

[6] Anthony Musson, *Public Order and Law Enforcement: the Local Administration of Criminal Justice, 1294–1350* (Woodbridge, 1996), p. 1.

[7] See Robert W. Gordon, 'Critical Legal Histories', *Stanford Law Review*, 6 (1984), pp. 57–125. [8] Ibid., p. 109.

[9] Perhaps the widest known example is C. Ginzburg, *The Cheese and the Worms: The Cosmos of a Sixteenth-Century Miller* (London, 1982).

[10] See, for example, the recent studies of rape narrative in England: Miranda Chaytor, 'Husband(ry): Narratives of Rape in the Seventeenth Century', *Gender and History*, 7, no. 3 (1995), pp. 378–407, and Garthine Walker, 'Rereading Rape and Sexual Violence in Early Modern England', *Gender and History*, 10, no. 1 (1998) pp. 1–25.

effectively into play. For historians employing the historical record of the law in new, or for that matter in the old, ways it is clearly a vital matter that the relationship between what went on in the courtroom and what went on in the society outside of that courtroom should be properly understood.

For these, and other, considerations, therefore, it seemed to Chris Wickham and myself that the time was ripe for a direct confrontation with the issue of the courtroom and society, and that this was an ideal theme for a *Past and Present* conference of the classic type, ranging across historical time and across space, and complementing the earlier and highly successful conference on the study of disputes and settlements.[11] A conference on *The Moral World of the Law* was duly held at the University of Birmingham on Friday 12 and Saturday 13 July 1996. The idea of a separate moral world, with its Thompsonian overtones,[12] seemed to us to offer the most direct approach to the issues which we wished to confront, that is to say it offered the most immediate prospect of entering into the legal experiences of people in the past. Accordingly, our speakers and discussants were given a specific brief, which was to look at some of the following issues:[13] how legal rituals, and the culture of the courtroom itself (including the modes of discourse permissible in it), differ from those of the rest of society; how these rituals are generated (whether by legal theory, legal practice, the cultural assumptions of the ruling class, or all three); whether they are internally consistent – for there are often several, competing, legal systems in a given society (canon versus civil law, Roman versus local law, 'native' versus colonial law, and so on), all of which may be more or less opaque to outsiders; and how much coercive power they really have. We were also interested in whether periods of sharp institutional change could be identified, when the relationship between law and everyday morality gets particularly out of sync, and in the ways in which access to the practical knowledge of the law may be gendered or class bound.

Not all of these issues were addressed, at least not to an equal degree, and the conference took us in some unexpected directions. The theme itself, if not an aunt sally, was slightly tongue in cheek in that it tended to presuppose the issue in question, i.e. whether or not there were indeed such separate moral worlds and whether or not we should approach the legal record in this way. As is normal with such proceedings, the essays published here do not represent all of the papers and discussants' rejoinders that were delivered. Several represent fuller and further thoughts on the part of the

[11] John Bossy (ed.), *Disputes and Settlements: Law and Human Relations in the West* (Cambridge, 1983).

[12] See, especially, E. P. Thompson, 'The Moral Economy of the English Crowd in the Eighteenth Century', *Past and Present*, 50 (1971), pp. 76–136.

[13] What follows is taken from the advance notice of the conference in *Past and Present*, 146 (February, 1995), pp. 188–9.

discussants and one, by Andrew Lewis, was specially commissioned to help produce, as it were, a more rounded volume. At the conference Roman law, if not exactly the spectre at the feast, was at least an absent presence. Most speakers referred to it, none directly addressed it. We are most grateful that Andrew Lewis and Paul Hyams have significantly filled this gap.

The volume begins, as did the conference, with Stephen Todd's paper on 'The language of law in Classical Athens'. Todd takes us directly into the question of the autonomy of legal language which, he points out, has two distinct though related dimensions. On the one hand there is 'a technical legal vocabulary which non-lawyers are in danger of mis-using', while, on the other, there is language used in legal contexts which 'has autonomy of meaning over the intention of its users'. Athenian law lacked the formalism of Roman and other ancient legal systems; indeed, it lacked even the degree of formal linguistic usage present in modern civil- and common-law systems. There are a number of reasons for this. Essentially, Athens lacked the means by which precise legal terminology could arise. The necessary preconditions were simply not present. Statutes tended to be imprecise in their meaning, a profession of jurists failed to develop, and the fact that most cases were decided by the verdict of several hundred *dikastai* – without discussion and by majority vote – left no room for authoritative rulings to which one might subsequently appeal. In a carefully nuanced essay, to which a brief précis is in danger of doing violence, Todd takes us through the use of language by litigants, or more precisely by the logographers or ghost-writers who produced speeches for them, showing how the system worked through the art of persuasion rather than the reception of established interpretation and rules. The language and the rhetoric, however sophisticated, needed to be comprehensible by an essentially non-professional court, where litigants spoke on their own behalf. However, this is not to say that the language of the court and the language of the street were mutually exchangeable. Ordinary words did develop specialised meanings in the courts. What they did not do was to develop autonomous meanings which carried independently of their users' intentions.

The lack of a specialised legal profession did not mean, however, that people were not advantaged or disadvantaged before the courts. Participation – as *dikastai*, as witnesses and as public officials, and of course as litigants – was wide in democratic Athens; or it was for adult male citizens. As large numbers of *dikastai* were required, many male citizens would have become quite experienced in the ways of the court. This inevitably created difficulties for others, whatever the level of transparency in the proceedings. Strangers, for example, could be significantly disadvantaged. Metics, the free non-citizens who were resident in Athens, enjoyed only limited participation while women, who could not testify, were represented by male citizens when litigants and rarely seem to have been present in court. We find that those who had social influence outside of the court are likely to have had distinct advantages inside the court too. Rich men who had financed public works had reason to feel that they were in credit with the citizens who would be giving their verdicts. The drama of the court had much in common with Athenian theatre, not least in that the cases were judged by non-experts: 'what made the process "democratic" was not that poor contestants would have stood an equal chance if pitted against rich ones, but that it was the *dêmos* (common people) which was allocating the prizes among the elite'.[14] Just as the Athenians lacked the autonomy of legal language, so they appeared to have lacked the notion that the operation of the law was autonomous from outside pressures. Indeed, this appears to have been a Roman construct, and has been traced to Cicero in the first century BC.[15] One might also reflect that as far as the law courts are concerned the practical advantages possessed by the rich and otherwise socially advantaged in human society are not necessarily dependent upon access to legal counsel and other professional expertise. In some societies the relationship between power and influence inside and outside of the courtroom can be much more direct.[16]

When we turn to Roman law we are, needless to say, in a radically different world. Andrew Lewis, in 'The autonomy of Roman law', elegantly re-examines the development of legal autonomy from the time of Cicero in the first century BC through the classical period in Roman law, from the first century AD to the beginning of the third. In so doing he tells us a great deal about the relationship between jurists, advocates and judges and their respective relationships to the law. Two principal factors combined to promote autonomy. One was the separation of the roles of jurist and advocate. The other was the primacy of procedure. The jurists, the legal specialists whose writings were transmitted to posterity through Justinian's codification of the law in the sixth century, developed 'a highly specialised framework of peculiarly juridical argument'. Consequently, it was 'no longer sufficient to present a court with a series of arguments drawn from commonplaces about honesty, justice and piety'.[17] The advocates (orators, not lawyers), who represented their clients in court, became detached from the legal consequences of their pleading, while the judges, who were laymen or officials and generally lacking in legal training, were required to pay

[14] Todd, below p. 24.

[15] B. W. Frier, *The Rise of the Roman Jurists: Studies in Cicero's* Pro Caecina (Princeton, 1985); Todd, below p. 22.

[16] It is also the case that the richer Athenians had greater access not only to logographers but also, presumably, to the 'interpreters' who offered advice to litigants: Todd, below pp. 21, 28.

[17] Lewis, below p. 40.

attention to the detailed arguments of the law according to criteria presented, via a rather complex mechanism, by jurists. The outcome of cases was much dependent upon precedent with only marginal interaction with 'general moral and ethical thought'. The situation is encapsulated in an anecdote by Aulus Gellius in his *Attic Nights*, written during the first century AD. Called upon to act as judge in a case of debt, he found that his instincts favoured the creditor as opposed to the debtor, who was of ill repute. However, the failure of the plaintiff, without witnesses, to make a *prima facie* case meant that he should find for the defendant. Gellius consulted a philosopher, Favorinus, who urged him to proceed on moral grounds. But this did not help him. As he would have no option but to reach his decision upon formal grounds as directed by the jurists and their rules Gellius asked to be relieved of his case. The dictates of conscience were thus external to the court and should not intrude upon its peculiar moral world. Nevertheless, there must always have been ways in which external pressures could bend the law. Most interestingly, Cicero's speeches reveal that advocates sought to obfuscate the issues in such a way as to impede the application of the law.

Justinian's reification of the writings of the jurists in his *Digest* led the way to their magisterial treatment during the legal revival that began in the late eleventh century. In his 'Due process versus the maintenance of order in European law: the contribution of the *ius commune*', Paul Hyams examines the decisive moment in the appropriation of Roman legal thinking by the medieval world. He shows how the West's 'highly significant differentiation' – from ancient Athenian and early medieval law, for example, as much as from non-western systems – 'came as a result of choices made in the period between the eleventh and thirteenth centuries'.[18] As a result of the legal revolution of the period 1175 to 1215 lawyers came to refer to the principles they knew to be common to western Christendom as the *ius commune*. Hyams outlines the characteristics of this *ius commune*, concentrating on its concept of natural rights and its protection of the individual in the courts through the *ordo iudicarius*, the high medieval equivalent of 'due process', itself a term coined in fourteenth-century England. He points out, however, that procedures were not employed uniformly in the middle ages but varied according to gender, social status and reputation, and he adds the cautionary note that 'mere notions of fairness, however attractively packaged in maxims, are likely to be ineffective until they are provided with procedural teeth'.[19] The long reach of medieval principles into the modern world is illustrated through the Fifth and Sixth Amendments to the US Constitution. The principal long-term significance

[18] Hyams, below p. 62. [19] Hyams, below p. 75.

of the *ius commune*, arguably, is that the notions of human rights that we see as 'self-evident' are so 'engrained' in our culture as to give 'the illusion of their indisputable rightness', and it is this illusion which underlies much of the conflict between western and non-western ideas in the modern world.[20]

Hyams also points out that we seek two barely compatible goals from our legal system; both safeguards for ourselves under the law, and protection against the criminal activities of others. The tension between these two desires was as present in the early centuries of the *ius commune* as it is today, and he traces the development of summary process alongside 'due process' from the formation of the 'persecuting society', as R. I. Moore famously put it, in the thirteenth century onwards.[21] One of the most absorbing features of this discussion is the frequent use of legal maxims. Their usage here reflects the fact that they were in themselves 'one of the routes by which the teachings of the *ius commune* passed into the legal culture of the west'. In an appendix Hyams examines why legal maxims should have so developed and have carried the legal weight that they did. But their significance is greater even than this. Some of them passed from the law into other dimensions. Hence their appearance in literary texts. In a call for further research on the subject, he suggests that those maxims that reached a general public 'must have contributed in many ways of which we currently know very little to inform ordinary folk (those whom lawyers call laymen) what law was about'.[22] Maybe they were assimilated to the general compendium of proverbs, to be deployed in similar ways. Here, perhaps, is a novel way of approaching 'the boundaries of the law's autonomous domain within western culture',[23] of examining what Robert Gordon calls its 'positive feedback loop'.[24]

In 'Local participation and legal ritual in early medieval law courts', Wendy Davies examines the situation in western Europe from the seventh to the tenth centuries, prior that is to the legal revolution which Hyams describes. She finds that there were considerable similarities across time and space and across language groups. In those we can designate rulers' courts litigants usually spoke through advocates, and women necessarily so, although these advocates (Ireland excepted) were not generally professional lawyers. There was a heavy emphasis upon correct procedures and courts were highly ritualised. Although many of the rituals may appear to the twentieth-century observer as quaint, and the language arcane, below the surface there was broad consistency in practice and much of what went

20 Hyams, below p. 62.
21 R. I. Moore, *The Formation of a Persecuting Society* (Oxford, 1987).
22 Hyams, below p. 90. 23 Hyams, below p. 84.
24 Gordon, 'Critical Legal Histories', p. 60.

on was in essence mundane. It was the 'emphasis on right order' which 'proclaimed both the existence of a distinctive system and its separation from "everyday life"'.[25] Tellingly, Davies points to the existence of contempt of court – for producing false written evidence, for example, or for sending a substitute to answer a charge – which in itself indicates 'systems with their own rules and own logic'.[26] In this sense, the courts constituted a world apart, but they tended nevertheless to be large public gatherings and, as in ancient Athens, this appears to have added rather than detracted from the courtroom as the scene of dramatic performance. Some of the drama took place, in fact, outside of the court as a designated space; in the highly ritualised walking of the boundaries, for example.

Rulers' courts were often political instruments, and there is no necessary separation between judicial and political functions. However, it was not only rulers who manipulated courts for personal ends. They tended to be seen by litigants as 'an instrument for securing personal advantage'.[27] Participation in the law courts may have been wide, but it was restricted to only a proportion of the population – those who were adult, male and free. As in the ancient world, the unfree played little or no part. Serfs are to be found at rulers' courts claiming free status. When they did so they were likely to be defeated. Unfamiliarity with the courts and inexperience in the use of evidence generally told against them. They could be defeated by superior witness or on the basis of written texts. Peasants seeking fairer treatment would often fare no better. Even where, as at Fiesso in the ninth century, a group of peasants challenged a written text in a fairly sophisticated way, they were defeated by the greater ingenuity of their monastic opponents. Written evidence, 'part of the special apparatus of the world of the law',[28] was highly selective in the benefits it conveyed.

Most importantly, Davies contrasts rulers' courts with local courts. The latter differed in important respects. The litigants tended to speak for themselves, and there was less formality, less emphasis upon procedure. Perhaps the greatest difference, however, was the much stronger emphasis upon settlement. At the village level, in particular, the drive to settle was born from practical necessity. What was at stake was the social harmony of the small community. Male, free peasants were solving their own problems in the courts. 'At this level', Davies points out, 'the world of the law does not seem to have been so morally distinct.'[29]

Paul Brand's 'Inside the courtroom: lawyers, litigants and justices in England in the later middle ages' gives us a picture of a highly professionalised court at work. This is the English Common Bench, the royal court

[25] Davies, below p. 54. [26] Davies, below p. 53. [27] Davies, below p. 58.
[28] Davies, below p. 61. [29] Davies, below p. 61.

which specialised in civil pleas. From around 1270 the formal records of the court, the plea rolls, are supplemented by unofficial law reports, produced for the most part by law students (apprentices) who were present in the court. Unlike the plea rolls which are in Latin and in indirect speech, the law reports are in French, the language actually spoken in the court, and are in direct speech. They afford us the kind of access into the deliberations of a law court which we lack for almost any previous time or place. Rarely did litigants speak for themselves in this court, although they were not formally barred from doing so. Most employed attorneys to act on their behalf. Attorneys, however, did not plead for their clients but acted as intermediaries between them and the court. Anyone could be appointed attorney but increasingly it became the preserve of the 'exclusively male, professional attorneys'. What the reports reveal in detail is the pleading dominated by highly experienced professional lawyers, the serjeants at law. Generally speaking, the litigants were thus at two removes from the court, separated by the attorneys who handled their cases and then serjeants who spoke on their behalf. Litigants (or their attorneys) could be asked to avow (that is, confirm or deny) what was said on their behalf, but as often as not those litigants were not even present in court. In one respect, Brand argues, the employment of professional serjeants could have been of particular value to lower-class litigants: 'For a man of lower social standing engaged in litigation with a man of higher social standing, it may have been valuable to have someone speaking for him whose very appearance and way of speaking was not a constant reminder to the court of the relative position of the two sides in the case.'[30] The rich, of course, could be advantaged through their personal contacts with the professionals. On one occasion we learn of a judge inviting himself to sit alongside the judge who was presiding over a case, as a 'well-wisher' of one of the parties, a fact that was the subject of a later complaint.

It was partly the language itself that made much of the pleading inaccessible to lay people. It was not just that it was in French – although by 1300 it could no longer be relied upon that even members of the gentry automatically spoke French – but because the vocabulary had become technical and specialised. The law reports reveal the phenomenon once again of words bearing meanings in a legal context which they did not possess outside. There is little wonder that the court was a classroom as well as a court of law.

In common with other contributors, Brand reflects on the resemblance between litigation and dramatic performance: serjeants spoke as if playing a part; people, including judges, made entrances and exits; props were

[30] Brand, below p. 95.

brought in; the demeanour of a litigant might be noted – one defendant was said to be 'sighing' and 'in tears'. The court was not the sedate forum suggested by the formal plea rolls, but a lively, even rowdy place. Above all, everyone had their role to play. The judges intervened in a variety of ways. After a man admitted that he was of unfree condition, a judge directed his lord to 'take him by the neck, as your villein'. Part of a judge's role seems to have been to introduce a note of humour into the proceedings. Brand suggests that they may have been the only people who were truly at their ease in the court. The coarseness of some of the reported humour may reflect the fact that this was a drama in which all the parts were played by men.

In 'Moral and legal conflicts in a Florentine inheritance case of 1422', Thomas Kuehn argues that 'the historian needs to come to grips with specific and not generic forms of moral and legal dilemma'.[31] The case in question arose from the will of ser Viviano di Neri Viviani, one of Florence's wealthiest citizens. Two issues were contested between one of Viviano's eight sons, Giovanni, and the hospital of the Innocenti, testamentary beneficiary of Giovanni's brother, Ludovico. One of the issues revolved around the legal technicalities resulting from the several types of substitution. It was effectively decided by the Florentine jurist, Benedetto Barzi, and his fellows. In a fascinating display of verbal dexterity and specialised learning – combining acute clausal analysis and centuries of juristic commentary – they resolved the issue in favour of the hospital. The second issue went to arbitration, but in practice the arbitrators sought resolution, once again, from the jurists: this time the college of jurists of Genoa. The underlying conflict was born of tensions between brothers and between the demands of the family and the demands of the soul. What the jurists contributed to the dispute, however, was not 'a perception of conflict or of the interests at stake'. 'They brought a professional expertise that could determine what rules to apply, a presumed impartiality even when retained by litigants, a type of charisma captured in their wax seals and textual citations, and a certainty of judgement.'[32] The parties themselves, however, were not entirely ignorant of the law and its potentialities. The law itself contained ambiguities to be exploited by those parties and their professional counsel. They could do so because of another set of ambiguities, those surrounding the contemporary ideology of inheritance. Both family interests and individual rights warranted protection. It is the potentiality for conflict here which demands that the modern commentator should view a case such as this from an anthropological as well as a legal perspective. In short, what we see is a complex interaction between

[31] Kuehn, below p. 113. [32] Kuehn, below p. 131.

familial and charitable expectations and the law. It was an interaction in which the law 'in its technical richness and complexity gave shape to the moral and legal claims' of the parties.[33]

As with inheritance in fifteenth-century Florence so with slander in sixteenth- and seventeenth-century England. In his 'Law, litigants and the construction of "honour": slander suits in early modern England', Martin Ingram takes a broad sweep in which he illustrates the constant dialogue between 'the arcane laws that constrained would-be litigants' and 'the streetwise strategies that enabled plaintiffs and defendants to exploit these rules to their own advantage'.[34] A major complication here was the existence of rival systems of law, comprising the church courts as well as a variety of secular jurisdictions. As a result, 'the lines of demarcation cut across the realities of argy-bargy on the streets, in the fields, and wherever else that people quarrelled and fought'.[35] In the highly litigious society of Tudor and early Stuart England there were many possibilities open to litigants seeking to save themselves from ignominy, but they had to know which court provided the best means of redress in their particular circumstances. They had to know, for example, which words were actionable in common law and which were not. If, in broad terms, the law reflected the social needs of the time, it also helped to shape that society, and not least in its gender relations. What is apparent is that defamation cases need to be interrogated extremely carefully if they are to be brought to bear effectively in understanding the sexual mores of society. Ingram shows, for example, that the incidence of female agency in matters of sexual reputation is exaggerated if one takes the suits at face value. In many cases women were attempting to clear the names of both themselves and their husbands, or indeed acting on the man's behalf. Controversially, again, he argues that in Tudor England there were slanderous words to denote a sexually lax man which approached that of 'whore' in their acerbity: 'whoremaster' and 'whoremonger', for instance, 'knave', and, sometimes, 'rogue'. In the late sixteenth century the secular courts decided that such words as 'knave' and 'rogue' were 'words of choler', without definite meaning, and hence were not actionable. As a consequence of legal decisions the sexual connotations of these words atrophied. The double standard in sexual matters was not constant in its intensity but varied, with legal considerations playing a major role in determining those variations. The decline in the communal regulation of morals in post-Restoration England, and after, may well have liberated male sexuality more than female, intensifying the differences in how their respective reputations were defined. The ensuing partly 'deregulated' world was also one in which 'the construction

33 Kuehn, below p. 121. 34 Ingram, below p. 135. 35 Ingram, below p. 142.

of honour or reputation was less dependent on the moral world of the law'.[36]

Caroline Ford turns to close examination of the actual narratives presented in court. As she points out, story-telling is a normal part of any legal system, and these systems seek to formalise the conditions under which the stories are told. Nevertheless, the study of such narratives 'provides a window on to the social and moral categories of a given society as well as hidden and sometimes unspoken cultural codes and societal fears'.[37] In 'Story-telling and the social imagery of religious conflict in nineteenth-century French law courts' she examines the case of the nun, Jeanne-Françoise Le Monnier, who in 1845 brought a case over her incarceration within her convent and subsequently in an insane asylum, seeking both damages and the right to re-enter her order. Her story was presented by her lawyer in the form of a *mémoire judiciaire*, a phenomenon inherited from the Old Regime which became a type of popular pamphlet literature and a major factor in the formation of popular opinion. Such *mémoires judiciaires* were written with a wide, popular audience in mind as well as the court. Ford shows how the *mémoire* of Jeanne-Françoise drew on the widely read claustral literature of the eighteenth and nineteenth centuries. We see its familiar plots and its characteristic imagery, we see its strategy of narrative constructed in the first person to enhance the 'immediacy and pathos' of the story, and we see direct references to popular works of literature; in short, we see 'the devices of theatrical melodrama'. Jeanne-Françoise Le Monnier is presented to the court as the romantic heroine of a Gothic novel. As her lawyer taps into the anticlericalism, even anticlerical hysteria, of contemporary France, what opens up in front of us is not only the social stereotype of the cloistered nun but also what Ford calls the 'collective fantasies of claustration'. This nun's story, mediated through the skilful constructions of her lawyer, an anticlerical republican male with his own political agenda, both appeals to and draws its inspiration from the popular imagination.

Ford presents the historian of court narrative with three dimensions: the manner in which those narratives draw on pre-existing moral categories and assumptions, whose origins are external and anterior to the court; the constraints imposed by the social and political, as well as the legal, contexts in which they are told; and the historical moment as determinant not only of the types of case that come prominently before a court but also of the manner in which they are presented. In consequence, such cases 'are often themselves markers of social, political, or moral preoccupations that in turn shape the way in which stories are ultimately told in legal courts'.[38]

[36] Ingram, below p. 160. [37] Ford, below p. 162. [38] Ford, below p. 177.

Passing now to the world of colonial studies, Diana Jeater in '"Their idea of justice is so peculiar": Southern Rhodesia 1890–1910' takes us directly into the clash of legal systems and the worlds they represented or, more accurately in view of what has gone before, of the moral worlds of which those legal systems formed a part. The cases that came before the District Magistrate and the local Native Commissioner at the town of Melsetter in the late nineteenth and early twentieth centuries indicate an almost unbridgeable gap between the Roman-Dutch criminal law administered by the British South Africa Company on the one hand and native law on the other. The decision to leave the latter intact as 'civil law' meant that the administrators were forced to confront a moral world very different from the one they understood as 'civilisation'. The crux of the problem was that African law was 'restorative', that is to say it functioned in terms of 'recompense and reparation' and knew no distinction between criminal and civil law, while European law was 'retributive' on the criminal side and 'contractual' on the civil side. Which jurisdiction a case would be brought to was often a matter of choice. However, the problems went far deeper than the choice of process. In observing the outcome we are brought face to face with the European sense of 'self-evident' and 'engrained' principles to which Paul Hyams has referred. While the Africans found the idea of retribution 'futile and unpleasant', the notion of compensation for crime was 'actively abhorrent' to white administrators. In fact, they frequently conflated the Africans' notion of compensation with the (for them) *mere* payment of a fine. Through a close examination of cases deriving from the custom of bridewealth (*lobola*) – the means by which the prospective husband or his family compensated the wife's in return for her person – Jeater demonstrates the utter incomprehension of the white administrators when faced with an alien worldview. Since for them marriage was 'an event not a process', the bridewealth could be understood only in terms of the singular, one-off, purchase of a bride. Any infringement of the custom was consequently seen as a breach of contract. In short, the 'entire African bridewealth system was viewed through contract and tort-tinted spectacles'.[39] This could lead to judgements that were incomprehensible in African eyes, as for example when a widow was allowed to return to her own family but only if *they* paid the *lobola* to get her back. When the whites experienced abhorrence at 'barbaric' practices they were viewing, it was often in their own misinterpretation of those practices that their abhorrence chiefly lay. Thus the 'sale' of women was found distasteful because the 'complex web of patronage and kinship which the bridewealth relationship encompassed was crudely misinterpreted as the open-ended transfer of disposable goods'.[40]

[39] Jeater, below p. 188. [40] Jeater, below p. 192.

In 'Kenyatta's trials: breaking and making an African nationalist', John Lonsdale shows white inability to comprehend the moral world of a colonial people being displayed in full view of the world's press. The trial of Jomo Kenyatta and five others opened at Kapenguria on 3 December 1952. The charges were management of an unlawful society, conspiracy to forcibly administer oaths, incitement of disaffection and the promotion of ill-will and hostility between different classes. The aim was to convict Kenyatta after due process. As the British press later reported on the verdict, he was to enjoy all the advantages of British justice in 'a trial of scrupulous fairness'. The world would then appreciate Kenyatta's guilt which would be open for all to see. The trial reveals, *inter alia*, a deep trust in the autonomy of the law on the imperial side: 'The legal cement of the empire-commonwealth was the common law, based on the universal validity of judicial precedent and respect for the liberties of individuals who are deemed to be equal. It was more of a tie than parliamentary democracy, the crown or even cricket.'[41] This was a political trial, sure enough, but it was not a show trial. Notwithstanding the deep presumption of Kenyatta's guilt, there was always the *possibility* of Kenyatta's acquittal, an eventuality much feared in certain quarters within Kenya.

The ideological force of autonomy was shown at the trial itself. One fascinating episode was when the presiding magistrate insisted that the leading defence counsel be tried for contempt for asserting to British MPs and the press that the handicaps he faced amounted to a denial of justice on the part of the British government. As Lonsdale points out, contempt was a lawyer's issue, turning on English precedents. It was not of great interest to the African defendants. For them, the resulting delay in their trial amounted to 'a Christmas break'. The contempt issue failed to reinforce the principle that politics had no place in the court; on the contrary, its effect was to bring the political nature of the trial into sharper relief. Due process was supposed 'to produce forensic fact by shutting politics out'. In reality, politics constantly intruded. How could they not in the circumstances of the trial? Nor is it surprising that, in practice, the proper rules of procedure were not adhered to. Unproven prior knowledge was allowed and the magistrate proved to be a player not an independent arbiter. As Lonsdale says, the 'majesty of the law did not beyond doubt cast out partisan white interest with pedantic procedure'.[42]

While much revolved around supposed understanding of the African way of life, the trial actually revealed profound ignorance on the part of the magistrate and the respective counsel. Why was this? At the heart of Kenya's agrarian problem there lay a clash of moral worlds, in the classic

[41] Lonsdale, below p. 215. [42] Lonsdale, below p. 215.

Thompsonian sense: the one was peasant, the other capitalist. In essence, for the white settlers the Kikuyu squatters were – or at least they should have been – a rural proletariat, for whom they had no responsibility beyond the payment of a wage. This attitude tore at the heart of African understanding of the relationship between land and labour. For them their very presence on the land conferred rights: 'To African farmers land was people and authority, land was labour and obedience. The equation was reversible. People were land, obedient labour deserved land from a patron.'[43] The problem lay much deeper, however, than a clash between legal perceptions. In any case, the notion of 'customary law' was itself a difficult one, closely bound up with colonial politics. The fundamental clash was between legal and moral memory. If the imperial power failed to understand this, it equally failed to understand the deep divisions within African society on how the community's rights to land should be understood. On one level this was a division between political theories; on another it was a rift between chiefs and juniors, between 'elderhood' and 'impatience'. It was this rift which gave rise to Mau Mau. How could the authorities understand when the basic colonial official on the ground, the district commissioner, saw his role as a civilising one? As Lonsdale puts it, they were 'Trustees of their African wards, they were schoolmasters in modernity'.[44]

At his trial Kenyatta's responses were often unintelligible to the court or wholly misunderstood. On one level he was perhaps content that they should be. Many of the contributors to this volume have affirmed the dramatic nature of court proceedings. In this case the drama unfolded in a global arena. Kenyatta probably realised at the outset that by fully participating in the trial he would ultimately win through. Not that he would be acquitted – which was always unlikely despite the paucity of genuine evidence against him – but because the global audience would make him the star of the show. This show became a contest between 'nationalism' and 'imperialism'; the Kapenguria trial 'dramatised the decline of empire'.[45]

In his Conclusion to the volume, Chris Wickham characterises the 'three rough categories of legal practices' in relation to civil society as they emerged at the conference: *the relatively unprofessionalised legal system*, where the moral world of the law is analogous to that of society though by no means synonymous with it, *the professional legal system* whose crucial feature has been shown by several contributors to this volume to be not so much the written law itself as the role of its legal professionals, and *the imported legal system*, where the law had no roots in the society to which it was being applied. Even within the second and the third of these categories, however, it is rare for the law to remain impervious to the moral values

[43] Lonsdale, below pp. 204–5. [44] Lonsdale, below p. 199. [45] Lonsdale, below p. 231.

of at least some sections of its laity. As Wickham observes, the interpenetration between law court and society, its circumstances and its consequences, is likely to remain a focus of research, both specific and cross-cultural, for some time to come. Drawing on recent work in the anthropology of law as well as the studies presented in this volume, he suggests some specific lines of future inquiry, focusing on the strategies deployed by litigants and lawyers, the specific ways in which their narratives actually functioned in court, and the relationship between the strategies chosen by them and the dominant power relations within their respective societies. At the same time he conveys some of the flavour of the lively, rich and intellectually generous debate which characterised the conference.

2. *The language of law in Classical Athens*[1]

S. C. TODD

I. HUMPTY DUMPTY AND THE MEANING OF WORDS

One distinguishing feature of an independent legal system is the power to define the meanings of words. This point was brought home to me by personal experience a few months prior to the conference for which this paper was written. I had been spending the previous academic year on a visiting research fellowship at the Center for Hellenic Studies in Washington DC. When I went to the US, I naively thought I was covered by Article 20(1) of the US/UK income tax treaty, which exempts from US income tax those university teachers from Britain who are in the USA for less than two years to engage in teaching or (as in my case) research, and I expected to be taxed by the UK authorities when I got home on the basis of my combined US and UK income over the period.

It subsequently transpired, however, that the US authorities define 'research' in somewhat narrow terms, which served to exclude what I was doing (and I suspect most humanities research), apparently on the grounds that the Hellenic Center was deriving no financially quantifiable benefit from my activities: 'The US Internal Revenue Service views this provision [Article 20(1)] as being limited to situations where compensation is being paid for teaching or research services – keying on the phrase "remuneration for such teaching or research". Scholarship or fellowship grants, where services are not provided for the benefit of the grantor, are not deemed to constitute such compensation.'[2]

1 My thanks are due to the organisers of the *Moral World of the Law* conference and also to those who hosted preliminary versions of the paper at Yale and Brown Universities. Various Classical colleagues have made useful comments on successive drafts, for which I thank Paul Cartledge, Carolin Hahnemann, Andrew Lewis, Josh Ober, Robin Osborne, and especially my respondent Rosalind Thomas, who because of the pressure of other commitments has been unable to contribute an essay of her own to this book, but has generously encouraged me to incorporate a number of her suggestions.

2 E-mail message from G. Poppe, Office of the Harvard University Advocate, 21 February 1996 (quoted by permission).

The right of the US courts independently to define the meanings of words is of course partly a function of the sovereign power of the modern state, which can only be limited to the extent that national governments enter into treaties and commit themselves to resolve their differences by arbitration, and such arbitration has ultimately no more than persuasive authority over national legal systems. Admittedly the British tax authorities have offered me a discreetly coded rejection of the American interpretation of the treaty – 'I will not comment on how the IRS [the US Internal Revenue Service] has interpreted Article 20. If you were an American coming to Keele for less than 2 years in the same circumstances, I would be inclined to allow exemption from UK tax'[3] – but a British court does not have the jurisdiction to impose its interpretation on the USA, nor vice versa.

To include a piece of autobiography in an academic paper is of course gratuitously self-indulgent, but the story is for me an interesting one, not simply for personal reasons, but because it highlights the technical nature of legal language in modern jurisdictions. This paper began with the proposition that one distinguishing feature of any independent legal system is the right within its own jurisdiction to define the meanings of words, which is illustrated here by the different interpretations that the UK and US authorities put on the same text. What the story further illustrates, however, is that such legally defined meanings may bear little relation to the meaning which the same words would bear in non-legal contexts – with the effect that the duties of a person on a 'research fellowship' can be deemed in law not to constitute 'research'. In the face of legal language, the naive amateur sometimes feels as frustrated as Alice: '"When *I* use a word," Humpty Dumpty said in rather a scornful tone, "it means just what I choose it to mean – neither more nor less."'[4]

Defining the meaning of words in the specific context of legal statutes is a bigger issue in some legal systems than in others. Traditionally this has been less important in continental European systems of civil law than in common-law systems such as obtain in England and the USA: a leading English textbook points out that the civil-law 'absence of method' in this area is notorious, at least to common lawyers,[5] and the authors of a German textbook on comparative law remark on the 'dense web of rules and principles engendered by statutory construction in England', and liken the more flexible civil-law interpretations of statutes to the flexibility with

[3] Letter from T. Ward, UK Inland Revenue NW office, 3 April 1996 (quoted by permission).
[4] L. Carroll (= C. L. Dodgson), *Through the Looking Glass, and What Alice Found There* (Macmillan edn), p. 114.
[5] F. R. Bennion, *Statutory Interpretation: a Code*, 2nd edn (London, 1992), p. 1.

which English courts interpret not statutes but cases.[6] Even within the common law, however, there are differences. The relative prominence of textbooks on the subject suggests that more attention is devoted to statutory interpretation in England than in the USA:[7] one possible explanation may be the preoccupation of the US Supreme Court with interpreting the Constitution, for which there is no British equivalent.[8]

At first sight, then, the question of what words mean might seem to be a peculiar characteristic of English law. But the example of the income tax treaty suggests that questions of interpretation are not unique to the UK. And there is perhaps a wider issue here, that of the autonomy of legal language, or the principle that certain formal phrases used in particular formal contexts can take on a significance that may not have been intended by the people who used them: a phenomenon which is common to many if not all jurisdictions. Such linguistic autonomy is particularly characteristic of certain ancient legal systems, for instance Roman law, as illustrated by the famous story of the orator Gaius Albucius Silus, who made the mistake of speculating out loud the terms of an oath which he might challenge his opponent to swear in resolution of the case: when the opposing orator Lucius Arruntius accepted the challenge on behalf of his client, the centumviral court refused to accept Albucius' plea that he had been speaking figuratively rather than dictating the terms of the challenge.[9]

Although modern civil- and common-law jurisdictions, by contrast, rely much less on the observance of legal forms, nevertheless 'in all modern legal systems there are some transactions which have to be in a special form if they are to receive legal recognition'.[10] And in this context the choice of words can be very important. A good illustration of this is found in a speech placed by the detective novelist D. L. Sayers in the mouth of one of her characters (the barrister Mr Towkington, speaking to Lord Peter Wimsey):

6 K. Zweigert and H. Kötz, *Introduction to Comparative Law*, Engl. tr. by A. Weir, 2nd edn, 2 vols. in 1 (Oxford, 1992), pp. 273–8 (the quotation is from p. 276).

7 E.g. (all on English law, and in addition to Bennion, cited in previous note): J. Bell and G. Engle, eds., *Cross on Statutory Interpretation*, 2nd edn (London, 1987), and P. St.J. Langan, ed., *Maxwell on the Interpretation of Statutes*, 12th edn (London, 1969).

8 On the special status of the Constitution within US law, see A. Scalia, *A Matter of Interpretation: Federal Courts and the Law* (Princeton, 1997), at pp. 37–41 (a perceptive if committed critique of post-1940s liberal trends in constitutional interpretation by a Supreme Court Justice).

9 Suetonius, *On Orators*, §6, and in more detail Seneca, *Controversiae*, book 7, preface, §§6–7. (The rule was that if a challenge was offered and accepted, the party challenged would win the case if he swore and lose it if he refused.) For linguistic formalism generally in Roman law, see B. Nicholas, *An Introduction to Roman Law* (Oxford, 1962), pp. 61–4.

10 Zweigert and Kötz, *Introduction to Comparative Law*, p. 392.

> Then again, words which are quite meaningless in ordinary conversation may have a meaning in law. For instance, I might say to a young man like yourself, 'You wish to leave such-and-such property to so-and-so?' And you might very likely reply, 'Oh yes, absolutely' – meaning nothing in particular by that. But if you were to write in your will, 'I leave such-and-such property to so-and-so absolutely,' then that word would bear a definite legal meaning, and would condition your bequest in a certain manner, and might even prove an embarrassment and produce results very far from your actual intentions.[11]

The example is of course fictitious on all levels, but is accurate as a statement of English law, and it is worth highlighting two of the assumptions involved: first, that there is a technical legal vocabulary which non-lawyers are in danger of mis-using, and secondly, that such language used in legal contexts has autonomy of meaning over the intentions of its users.

II. AUTONOMY AND THE COURTS

The question at the heart of this essay is the extent to which Athens in the classical period (the fifth and fourth centuries BC) did or did not have a technical or an autonomous vocabulary of law, but it may be useful to set this in context by first considering the question of autonomy more broadly: to what extent was law in Athens perceived as autonomous from society as a whole, or to put it another way, to what extent was it felt that decisions in law courts should be made without reference to social and political considerations?

To understand the working of the law at Athens, it is important to consider the political and social framework within which the courts operated. What is significant here is that the system relied on the participation of private individuals from among a citizen body that was small both in absolute numbers (modern estimates for the fourth century are of some 20,000–30,000 adult male citizens) and also in the sense that it excluded women, slaves, and metics (free non-citizens resident in Athens). The vast majority of litigants and witnesses in the surviving cases, for instance, are citizens operating as private individuals. It was admittedly possible for metics to testify, but women could not, and the evidence of slaves could be given only under torture; similarly, metics could be litigants, and so in a few types of case could women, though a metic possibly and a woman certainly would have been represented by a male citizen speaking on his/her behalf (indeed, as we shall see, such a woman may not even have appeared in court).[12]

[11] D. L. Sayers, *Unnatural Death* (New English Library edn), p. 162.

[12] On legal capacity, see S. C. Todd, *The Shape of Athenian Law* (Oxford, 1993), at p. 187 (slaves), p. 196 and p. 198 (metics), and pp. 201–4 (women). On women in court, see further section IV.

Citizen litigants were expected to speak for themselves, because this was part of the duty of a citizen: Athenian law is notable for the virtual absence of advocates and barristers on the one hand, and of public prosecutors on the other. Paradoxically, this principle gave rise to the unofficial profession of ghost-writer or logographer, whose speeches were commissioned by litigants wanting to deliver them in court in their own names and in their own persons. (The majority of the ten 'Attic Orators', including Lysias and in his early career Demosthenes, were logographers, and their speeches are our leading evidence for the law of classical Athens.) Moreover, the fact that there was no office of public prosecutor meant that the term 'public prosecution' is used with reference to Athenian law to denote not cases brought by a public official, but cases brought by private individuals – often politically active individuals prosecuting their political rivals – in which the aggrieved party was not so much the individual prosecutor but the community as a whole.

The reliance on private individuals rather than public officials is seen also in the judging of trials. The majority of cases – there were some exceptions, most notably homicide – were heard by what are known as 'dikastic' courts. The word *dikastês* (pl. *dikastai*) is awkward to translate, because it corresponds simultaneously both to 'judge' and to 'juror'. Like the modern juror, the *dikastês* was an ordinary private individual, and to be eligible you had simply to be a male citizen, aged at least thirty, and to have been one of the panel of six thousand[13] who volunteered at the start of each year for jury service by swearing a special oath. There was no judge in the modern sense: each court was presided over by a public official, but he was not legally trained, and his authority was little more than that of non-voting chairman, with no power to advise the *dikastai* on points of law or to sum up. Indeed, whereas in Anglo-American law we differentiate between the tasks of the jury (to decide matters of fact) and those of the judge (to decide matters of law and to pass sentence), in an Athenian court all these functions belonged to the *dikastai*, who delivered a single verdict, and then if necessary passed sentence, in both instances by simple majority vote.

Perhaps the most important contrast between the modern Anglo-American jury system and the Athenian dikastic court, however, is one of numbers. The Athenian dikastic jury was not a small body of twelve citizens, chosen to serve once or twice in a lifetime, and entrusted with the task of reaching an ideally unanimous opinion by secret discussion; instead, it was a mass meeting of several hundreds – two hundred or four hundred in private cases, depending on the sum at issue, and five hundred (or

[13] A large fraction of the total citizen body, estimated at 20,000–30,000 for the fourth century (above).

occasionally multiples of five hundred) in public cases, which were normally political in nature – who voted by secret ballot but without formal opportunity for discussion. (The large size was intended presumably to prevent intimidation or bribery, which was also apparently the reason why trials were completed within a day, and why dikastic juries were selected afresh by lot on the morning of the trial.) Taken together, all this will have created a very different atmosphere from that with which we are familiar: a deliberate rejection of professionalism in the sense of technical legal training, combined with the fact that individual *dikastai* will have been much more experienced than modern jurors.[14]

The idea that it is desirable for law to be autonomous from political and social pressures is closely associated in the modern mind with the concept of the rule of law, and the question of how (if at all) the latter concept was regarded at Athens has been much debated over recent years. It is certainly true that there is a lot of language about the rule of law in our texts. In the law-court speeches of the Attic Orators, the rule of law is routinely described as a good thing, and is associated with Athens rather than with non-democratic regimes.[15] However, we should be wary of assimilating such language to our own. We are conditioned, mainly by lawyers, or at least by those lawyers who are not critical legal theorists, to regard the statue of justice as blind: that is, to believe that extraneous social pressures should have no influence on the practice of the courts. But Frier[16] has argued that this view of the courts as ideally autonomous from society is a Roman construct – he traces its origins to Cicero in the first century BC – and there is no reason to believe that Athenians three centuries earlier would have thought in the same way. There is certainly no systematic attempt at Athens to distinguish between those bodies which undertake political deliberation and those which exercise legal judgement (that is, to construct a doctrine of separation of powers).[17] What is significant here is

[14] Various questions glossed over in this account (e.g. the treatment of homicide cases, and how a mass jury can decide a sentence by majority vote) are discussed in my *Shape of Athenian Law*.

[15] E.g. Demosthenes, 24.5; Aeschines, 1.4 (repeated at 3.6), and 3.196; Lycurgus, 1.3–4. The leading proponents of the rule of law as a constitutional doctrine at Athens are M. Ostwald, *From Popular Sovereignty to the Sovereignty of Law: Law, Society and Politics in Fifth-Century Athens* (Berkeley and Los Angeles, 1986) and R. Sealey, *The Athenian Republic: Democracy or the Rule of Law?* (Philadelphia, 1987).

[16] B. W. Frier, *The Rise of the Roman Jurists: Studies in Cicero's* Pro Caecina (Princeton, 1985).

[17] Sealey, *The Athenian Republic* at p. 43 seeks to find a doctrine of separation of powers at Athens, but see the criticisms made by Todd and Millett, 'Law, Society and Athens', in P. A. Cartledge, P. C. Millett, and S. C. Todd, eds., *Nomos: Essays in Athenian Law, Politics and Society* (Cambridge, 1990), pp. 1–18, at p. 16 n. 33.

not simply that the same bodies of government could fulfil both political and judicial functions, such that the *Boulê* or Council of Five Hundred was not only the executive committee for the Assembly but could also hear some cases and impose fines in its own right, and such that the Areiopagos was simultaneously the main Athenian court for homicide and also at times a deliberative body. What is more significant is that nobody in antiquity thought to complain about this.

One of the characteristic features of Athenian law is the overlapping range of procedures and penalties available against a particular offender. This has been well analysed by Osborne, on the basis of a passage in Demosthenes, which implies that social grounds determine the choice of how to prosecute for instance a thief.[18] (It is important to remember here that Athenian prosecutors were typically private individuals, not public officials.) Demosthenes says that a powerful man who feels confident (at least vis-à-vis the prospective defendant) could afford to select *apagôgê* (summary arrest), which was a particularly high-profile, high-penalty and high-risk strategy, rather than the alternatives of *ephêgêsis* (denunciation), *graphê* (public prosecution), or *dikê* (private prosecution): he classifies each of these procedures as successively less risky for the prosecutor but correspondingly involving lower penalties for the defendant. Of course we have only Demosthenes' word that social factors like confidence were the reason for the overlapping procedures, but this was presumably plausible to the *dikastai* who heard him say it.

This assumption that social and indeed political criteria will influence a law court is reflected in many other aspects of Athenian law-court oratory.[19] One of the most striking illustrations arises out of a distinctive feature of public finance at Athens, which was that the role of the public treasury was kept to a minimum. Services which might have involved state expenditure, most notably the financing both of civic festivals and of warships, were instead imposed on rich individual sponsors as what are conventionally called 'liturgies' – though the Greek word *leitourgia* (lit. 'public work') has none of the religious overtones of its English derivative. The system had elements of compulsion, in that rich men who could not find an excuse were obliged to undertake the liturgy, and had to spend a fixed minimum; but those rich men who were politically active could deliberately overspend, and this was a recognised way of investing in the *kharis* (or 'gratitude') of the public, which you could then cash in the form of political support. Athenian litigants, or at least those litigants who were rich

[18] R. G. Osborne, 'Law in Action in Classical Athens', *Journal of Hellenic Studies*, 105 (1985), pp. 40–58, at pp. 42–3, citing Dem. 22.25–7.

[19] Politicisation of the law courts at Athens is discussed in more detail in Todd, *Shape of Athenian Law*, pp. 154–63.

enough to commission the speeches which survive as our sources, routinely mention the liturgies which they have undertaken and those which their opponents have skimped, in the belief that this will affect not only the penalty but also the verdict. The phenomenon is so common as not to require detailed citation, but one example perhaps deserves mention. This is taken from the first of a group of speeches, the so-called *Tetralogies*, which are attributed to Antiphon, the earliest of the ten Attic Orators: the *Tetralogies* are not real speeches, but artificial specimens, perhaps designed as models for the teaching of rhetoric. What is significant here is first that this is a fifth-century text, which implies that the *topos* was familiar enough to be imitated even at this early date, and also that it is written as if for a homicide trial, in which there was at Athens a special rule obliging speakers to stick to the point.[20]

The mention of liturgies provides a convenient bridge between the law courts and the theatre. Greek plays in the classical period were a characteristically Athenian phenomenon; the genre originated there, and is found only at Athens, or later at cities under Athenian influence. Each play or group of three plays was written for a single performance at a religious drama festival: this festival took the form of a competition (*agôn*), at which a small number of productions would be judged for a prize by a group of festival judges selected by lot from among the population at large. Several recent scholars[21] have highlighted a wide range of important parallels (seating, etc.) between drama and the law court. There are of course differences between the two types of competition. For instance, the number of competing productions at a festival was typically three, whereas in a law court the choice was between prosecutor and defendant. Similarly, the number of judges voting at the drama festival was typically five (though they would presumably be influenced by the audience's reaction), whereas most lawsuits would be judged, as we have seen, by several hundred *dikastai*, the number depending on the nature of the case. But in both contexts they judged without expert guidance: what made the process 'democratic' was not that poor contestants would have stood an equal chance if pitted against rich ones, but that it was the *dêmos* (the common people) which was allocating the prizes among the elite.[22]

[20] Antiphon, *Tetralogy*, 1.2.12. For the rule on relevance, see Aristotle, *Rhetoric*, 1.1.5 = 1354a22–3.

[21] J. Ober and B. S. Strauss, 'Drama, Political Rhetoric and the Discourse of Athenian Democracy', in J. J. Winkler and F. I. Zeitlin, eds., *Nothing to do with Dionysos? Athenian Drama in its Social Context* (Princeton, 1990), pp. 237–70; E. Hall, 'Lawcourt Dramas: the Power of Performance in Greek Forensic Oratory', *Bulletin of the Institute of Classical Studies*, 40 (1995), pp. 39–58.

[22] J. Ober, *Mass and Élite in Democratic Athens: Rhetoric, Ideology and the Power of the People* (Princeton, 1989), p. 309.

Now of course there are dramatic elements in many modern systems of justice. The gowns and wigs of British law courts are supposed to dignify and to isolate justice from other fields of life, and although the purpose of televising American law courts is allegedly to make legal proceedings accessible to a wider public, it could be argued that the effect of television is in fact to dramatise and therefore to isolate what goes on. There are at Athens some elements of isolating drama in law-court ritual, most notably the daily allocation of *dikastai* to courts. An unpublished paper by Bers emphasises the way in which the selection (by lot) of jurors on the morning of a trial, and their organisation into the various law courts, was for the most part arranged by *dikastai* themselves rather than by bailiffs. Those selected then went to the appropriate court, each carrying colour-coded batons, in a procession which will have set them apart from their fellow-citizens while at the same time emphasising the non-professional nature of the system.[23] Moreover, there is evidence to suggest that a group of buildings in the north-east corner of the Agora (market place/civic centre), dating from the mid-fourth century, may have formed a complex of courts with restricted entrance:[24] the aim will presumably have been to reduce the chance of the *dikastai* being nobbled between selection and arrival in court, and it will have had the effect of isolating the *dikastai* still further, but possibly also of removing their activities from the public mind, by rendering the procession invisible.

Despite these signs of isolating drama, however, the scale of the parallels noted by recent scholars between law court and drama festival[25] suggests that isolation may have been only a small part of the story, and that the emphasis should once again be on the extent to which the law was embedded within other aspects of society – not as implying that the one was modelled on the other, or vice versa, but as suggesting that experience in judging the one would be conditioned by experience in judging the other.[26] The idea of performance, both in law court and in the theatre, is important here: Aristophanes depicts a group of young men admiring the technical skill of a law-court orator, and although they are not meant to be typical citizens, nevertheless the passage implies that such language could be used about the law courts as early as the 420s.[27]

[23] V. Bers, 'The Jury in Rhetoric, Theory and Spectacle' (unpublished paper delivered to the American Philological Association in December 1995).

[24] A. L. Boegehold, *The Athenian Agora: Results of Excavations Conducted by the American School of Classical Studies at Athens*, vol. xxviii, *The Lawcourts at Athens: Sites, Buildings, Equipment, Procedure, and Testimonia* (Princeton, 1995), pp. 14–15.

[25] Hall, 'Lawcourt Dramas' discusses similarities of context (daylight setting, etc.), relationship between speaker and audience (applause, etc.), attention to performer's appearance (costume, demeanour, etc.), and other elements of stagecraft.

[26] Thus Ober and Strauss, 'Drama, Political Rhetoric, and the Discourse', at p. 238.

[27] Aristophanes, *Knights*, 1375–80.

III. THE LAW COURTS AND THE DEFINITION OF LANGUAGE

We have seen that although there is a degree of isolation in the drama of the law courts, there is nevertheless little sign of autonomy in the way in which law courts were constructed within society at Athens. It is now time to consider more specifically the question of language as promised by the title of this essay: how far did this form a specialist, technical, or autonomous legal vocabulary?

It is at first sight difficult to see how Athens could have developed a truly technical vocabulary of law, because of the absence of mechanisms by which words could have been authoritatively defined as having a legal meaning that was different from their meaning in everyday usage. The three ways in which this could have been done would be: for statutes to have given authority to particular interpretations by defining their own terms, or for jurists to have developed a system in which their opinions about the meaning of legal terms would be accepted as authoritative by the courts, or for judges to have issued reasoned rulings which could have been regarded in subsequent cases as authoritative interpretations of the law. But as will be seen from the following discussion, none of these three conditions applied.

In the first place, Athenian statutes were notoriously vague in their use of terms. The most famous example of this is the law of *hubris*, where the law appears simply to have said 'if somebody commits *hubris* [undefined] against either a boy or a woman or a man, either of those who are free or of those who are slaves, or does anything unlawful against any of these, let anybody who wishes bring a *graphê* [public prosecution] against him.'[28] It is fairly clear that *hubris* denotes a type of aggravated assault, but scholars are quite unable to agree whether the aggravation lies in the psychology of the attacker or in the sociology of the victim.[29] More importantly, in the absence of any established legal definition, the question of whether the defendant's behaviour in a particular instance constituted *hubris* was open for discussion in each case on the basis of general principles rather than legal ones: what made it *hubris* was not that it fulfilled certain statutory criteria, but that it was a serious assault. This is presumably why the prosecutor in at least one case of *aikeia* (non-aggravated assault) asserts that friends and bystanders had tried to persuade him to bring a case for *hubris* – not to prove that the case fulfilled statutory criteria, but to heighten the outrageousness of the opponent's behaviour.[30]

[28] Demosthenes, 21.47, cf. Aeschines, 1.15.

[29] See most recently D. M. MacDowell, *Demosthenes Against Meidias (Oration 21), edited with introduction, translation and commentary* (Oxford, 1990), at pp. 18–22 (psychology of attacker); and N. R. E. Fisher, *Hybris* (Warminster, 1992), pp. 36–82 (sociology of the victim).

[30] Demosthenes, 54.1, with another possible example in Isocrates, 20.2–3.

To take another example, that of justifiable homicide. Euphiletos, the defendant and speaker in Lysias 1, claims justification for having summarily killed Eratosthenes after finding him in bed with Euphiletos' wife. We cannot unfortunately be sure of the precise wording of the statutes which Euphiletos quotes in his defence, because (like most such documents) they are not preserved in the manuscripts of the speech. We can however make a plausible if cautious reconstruction of these laws, on the basis of what Euphiletos and other orators say about them. One of the allegations that Euphiletos seeks to rebut is that he has enticed Eratosthenes into his house, and scholars often claim that this would have been illegal.[31] It is not clear, however, that we can go as far as this, because there is no sign that justification was statutorily defined in terms more precise than 'or [having found him] beside his wife or mother or sister or daughter or concubine kept for the purpose of free children'.[32] Nothing is said about the absence of enticement here, and the point of Euphiletos' discussion is surely not that enticement was statutorily unlawful, but that the court would be likely to regard it as an improper exercise of his statutory rights.

Admittedly not all Athenian statutes were as general as the *hubris* law, and some did try to set out the limits of their own applicability. But such attempts were not always successful. Athenian inheritance law, for instance, permitted a man to make a will only in very restricted circumstances, and in particular allowed the court to annul it in favour of his next-of-kin if he were found to have acted when 'mad or drugged or under the influence of a woman'. Critics of democracy protested that this clause gave too much scope to the *dikastai*, and the short-lived oligarchy of 404/3 temporarily abolished it, but this was annulled by the restored democracy, and the inheritance speeches of the fourth-century orator Isaeus make extensive and sometimes creative use of it.[33] The crypto-oligarchic pamphlets of his contemporary Isocrates maintain a curious ambivalence towards the question of whether precise drafting was desirable to tie the hands of the *dikastai*: while insisting that law is a good thing and *epieikeia* ('equity', i.e. giving the court a wider scope) was a bad one, Isocrates nevertheless claims that proliferation of laws and the search for *akribeia* ('precision') was to miss the real function of law, which was to be general and morally educative.[34]

The second possible method of definition would have been by jurists, or legal experts whose opinions were accepted (as they were by Roman courts)

[31] Thus most recently C. Carey, *Lysias. Selected Speeches* (Cambridge, 1989), pp. 60–4.

[32] Demosthenes, 23.53–5, cf. also Lysias, 1.30–1.

[33] For criticism of the clause, see e.g. *Ath.Pol.*, 9.2; its abolition by the oligarchs is mentioned by *Ath.Pol.*, 35.2. We know of one case in which the clause was used to attack a man's adoption of his brother-in-law, on the grounds that he had been influenced by his wife (Isaeus, 2.19–20).

[34] Isocrates, 7.33 and 7.39–40.

as authoritative, but it is striking that such a profession failed to develop at Athens. We do admittedly meet a rather shadowy group of individuals known as the *exêgêtai* or 'interpreters', who gave advice in cases of homicide to individuals, including potential litigants. (Homicide was regarded as an area of religious law, and the *exêgêtai* appear to have been primarily concerned with the ritual aspects of legal procedure.) However, they never developed into anything resembling the Roman jurists, not least because their opinions were not regarded as binding on a court. Indeed, with one possible exception they are never cited in terms which suggest an expectation that the court would be interested to hear what they had had to say.[35]

The final possibility would have been for legal definition by judges but, as we have already seen, verdicts in Athenian dikastic courts were decided by *dikastai* by simple majority vote and without formal discussion. A recent book by Carawan presupposes extensive discussion of cases by the members of the Areiopagos and other homicide courts, but we do not know whether there was opportunity for this, and there is certainly no evidence of judicial intervention on points of law even during homicide trials.[36] At any rate, since Athens had no appeal courts, there was no opportunity for judges there to deliver a reasoned judgement. That is not to say that those who voted in Athenian courts were as inexperienced as modern jurors. In the case of homicide in particular, the Areiopagos certainly, and possibly also the ephetic courts which dealt with cases of e.g. non-deliberate killing, consisted of men who had served for a year as one of the Nine Archons, and who remained members of the court for life, which would have given them considerable experience and consequently expertise in deciding such cases. Even in the dikastic courts, the individual *dikastai* are likely to have acquired some expertise as a result of hearing repeated cases. But the fact that the *dikastai* voted without discussion means that however much they will have observed each other's reactions during the speeches, or however much they may have chatted while lining up to vote,[37] they will have had no formal opportunity to share their expertise; and at any rate, such expertise may have consisted mainly of experience in spotting certain types of plausible lying.

It is certainly true that Athenian litigants sometimes appeal to the spe-

[35] The exception is Demosthenes, 47.68–73 (explaining the speaker's failure to prosecute for homicide), though note his insistence that after consulting them he went and checked that their advice corresponded with the inscribed text of the law.

[36] E. M. Carawan, *Rhetoric and the Law of Draco* (Oxford, 1997). There is no sign in speeches before the Areiopagos of the court ever intervening to rule out of order those litigants who ignored their statutory obligation to stick to the point (for which cf. n. 20 above).

[37] For both possibilities, see V. Bers, 'Dikastic *thorubos*', in P. A. Cartledge and F. D. Harvey, eds., *Crux: essays presented to de Ste. Croix, G. E. M. on his 75th birthday* (Exeter, 1985), pp. 1–15, at pp. 13–14.

cialist knowledge of their hearers: this however is not for knowledge of law but for knowledge of facts which 'the older ones among you will remember'.[38] Demosthenes does on one occasion recount a series of previous cases in order to show that behaviour like that of his opponent Meidias has always been regarded as heinous – the climax is the case of Euaion, narrowly convicted for killing because of the provocation he had received from his victim, which allows Demosthenes to emphasise that the insult offered to Euaion by Boiotos was far less than the insult offered by Meidias to himself – but he is telling these stories to the court, rather than relying on his hearers' knowledge.[39] The nearest we get to a doctrine of precedent at Athens is the *topos* that other potential criminals are watching the court's verdict to see whether the Athenians are going to punish crimes in future,[40] and that is hardly the basis for developing a system of case law.

The absence of formal mechanisms for the authoritative definition of legal terms does not of course mean that questions of definition cannot be raised in an Athenian court. It simply means that they cannot be answered by means of an appeal to authority, and that all such definitions must therefore remain informal, in the sense that they represent occasional attempts by an individual litigant to explain the meaning of a crucial term to a particular audience of *dikastai*. Sometimes these informal definitions are simply tendentious, as when Aeschines explains that *phêmê* ('common report') is the type of rumour that he is putting forward, which is entirely different from the *diabolê* ('defamation') being peddled by his opponent;[41] in all cases they are potentially competitive, in that the aim is to persuade the court to follow the speaker's interpretation of the law in preference to any interpretation put forward by the opponent.

Given the linguistic obscurity of some Athenian laws – particularly in the case of early laws, like those dealing with homicide, where the archaic phrasing can render the meaning highly ambiguous – it is at first sight odd that such informal definition by litigants is not more common. Two factors may account for this. The first is the general tendency of ancient readers (not simply readers of legal texts) to focus on the broad meaning of a text rather than the details of its wording.[42] But the second, which may be more important here, is that statute in Athenian law plays a rather different role from that with which we are familiar. It is notorious, for

38 E.g. Antiphon, 5.71 (the story of Sosias and the Hellenotamiai) and Demosthenes, 59.30 (the dissolute lifestyle of Phrynion). 39 Demosthenes, 21.71–6.

40 For variations on this *topos*, see Lysias, 1.36; Isocrates, 18.42; and Lycurgus, 1.7–8.

41 Aeschines, 2.144–5, cf. 1.125–31.

42 R. Thomas, *Oral Tradition and Written Record in Classical Athens* (Cambridge, 1989), p. 47.

instance, that ancient rhetorical theorists classify laws as a form of evidence, whereas we would tend to speak of evidence being used to demonstrate matters of fact and laws being the rules on the basis of which those facts are to be judged;[43] and it is striking that whereas a modern court is deemed to know the law, at Athens this did not apply, and it was the privilege (not the duty) of the litigant to produce in evidence the text of any legal statutes which he thought would strengthen the general rightness of his case.

There is however one example in our texts of highly sophisticated legal interpretation, which deserves to be discussed because it represents not simply the interpretation of individual statutes, but the creation of a general theory of statutory interpretation. This is Lysias 10, in which the speaker discusses a series of ancient and possibly obsolete laws on a variety of subjects, in order to prove the general principle that the hearers should mentally substitute modern equivalents for archaic words: thus 'stocks' (*xulon*) for 'foot-retainer' (*podokakkê*, which was no longer a meaningful term), 'swear' (*omnumi*) for 'abjure' (*epiorkeô*, which in classical Greek meant 'commit perjury'), and the like.[44] But the unusual nature of the argument here can perhaps be explained by considering its function within a trial for defamation, and the fact that the Athenian law of defamation made illegal the use of certain statutory insults (the so-called *aporrhêta*, 'things which may not be said'). Lysias' unnamed client is the prosecutor, and his opponent Theomnestos has put forward an intriguing argument: while admitting that he had made an allegation of parricide, Theomnestos denies liability on the grounds that he had not used the prohibited word *androphonos* ('man-slayer'). It is to counter this highly sophisticated and sophistical argument that Lysias puts forward his equally sophisticated general theory of statutory interpretation, and this speech should therefore be taken not as evidence for the level of legal definition that was normal, but rather as evidence for what was conceivable.

Other examples of legal definition are notably rare. There are a few cases of what might be called systematic exposition, where a litigant will systematically interpret an area of law for his hearers. Thus Andocides, for instance, lists exhaustively the various types of *atimia* (deprivation of citizen rights); and Lycurgus on two separate occasions classifies things in threes, such that there are three safeguards to the constitution, and three types of *dokimasia* (or judicial scrutiny).[45] Given that Andocides' speech belongs in 400 BC, and those of Lycurgus in the 330s and 320s, it is tempting to suggest that the extent and the systematic nature of such classifica-

[43] Aristotle, *Rhetoric*, 1.15.2 = 1375a24–5. [44] Lysias, 10.16–19.

[45] Andocides, 1.73–6, on *atimia*; Lycurgus, 1.3–4, on safeguarding the constitution; Lycurgus, frag. *On his Administration* (*dioikêsis*), on the *dokimasia*.

tion may increase during the period covered by our speeches (broadly speaking the century from 420 to 320), which would be striking, because this is precisely the period when philosophers like Plato in the world outside the law court were raising questions of language and of systematic definition. But this is too small a sample from which to generalise, and there may be reasons either of rhetorical strategy or of personal preference in each instance. In Andocides' case, for instance, his problem is that whereas *atimia* (deprivation of citizen rights) has in general been pardoned under the decree which he quotes, Andocides' own status is rather exceptional. By cataloguing all the different types of *atimia*, he distracts the audience from the awkward question, where does Andocides' own *atimia* (if it is really *atimia*) fit into this analysis?

It is interesting that each of three passages cited in the previous paragraph comes from those few speeches which were written by a politically active orator to be delivered in his own person as litigant, rather than being ghost-written by a logographer for delivery by a client. Well-known politicians could probably get away with looking knowledgeable about the law, in the way that was risky for Nikomakhos, the minor civil servant who is accused in Lysias 30 of overstepping his powers as legislative commissioner: one of the rhetorical strategies of Lysias' prosecution speech in this case is that Nikomakhos knows the law too well.

Attempts to define or to systematise the law remained at all times a persuasive strategy, and remained rare perhaps because of the risk of distancing yourself as a legal specialist from the audience as amateurs. The *topos* of 'I have been forced to study the law because of the wiles of my opponent' is not uncommon,[46] and may be characteristic of those litigants who are trying to look like private individuals. It is worth bearing in mind here the advice offered by Aristotle in his rhetorical handbook: if the written law is against you, emphasise considerations of 'general law' and 'fairness'; if it favours you, tell the court that their job is to apply it.[47] Discussions of law in the orators are competitive attempts at persuasion[48] precisely because citing the law was not the court's responsibility but the litigant's privilege. If an orator wished to define or to systematise, that was his prerogative, but the wheel had to be reinvented on every occasion, so that a technical vocabulary could not easily be developed.

[46] E.g. Demosthenes, 54.17; Hyperides, *Against Athenogenes*, §13.

[47] Aristotle, *Rhetoric*, 1.15.4–12 = 1375a27–b25. There is one case in which fellow prosecutors appeal to the court to do opposite things: 'you need to be not simply *dikastai* but lawgivers' (Lysias, 14.4) and 'you have come here not to be lawgivers but to vote according to the established laws' (Lysias, 15.9).

[48] E.g. Lysias, 22.6: 'let him demonstrate that there exists a law which orders him [to act as he did], . . . because we have shown one which forbids it'.

IV. THE CONSTRUCTION OF A SPECIALIST VOCABULARY: A PALINODE

Given the absence of juristic writings, of case law, and of self-defining statutes, it is tempting simply to conclude that Athens could not have had a technical vocabulary of law. I have myself said in print both that 'the language of the street was the language of the law', and also more assertively that 'the language of the law was the language of the street'.[49] This is a good sound-bite, but I now believe that it was a misleading exaggeration, because it focuses too much on one part of the picture – the absence of mechanics or formal definition – while tending to distract attention from another and equally important aspect of the question, which is that Athenian law certainly has a specialist vocabulary, if not an autonomous one, in that ordinary words when used in law courts take on special meanings.

It is difficult to be sure how and why the various elements in this specialist vocabulary have developed, and it may be that the explanation is different in different cases. The use of the terms *ho pheugôn* ('the pursuer') and *ho diôkôn* ('the one who flees') to denote respectively the plaintiff and the defendant, for instance, suggests the use of a hunting metaphor, and it is easy to imagine that the repeated use of such language could have become routine, just as we tend to use metaphors from sport when speaking about politics: British politicians 'play with a straight bat' when asked awkward questions, whereas American penal policy is defined in terms of 'three strikes and you're out'. But this type of explanation does not work so well for other words, because there is often no obvious metaphor. Indeed, one of the things which makes Athenian law initially inaccessible, even to those who know a fair bit of ancient Greek and are widely read in Greek literature, is that legal sources like the Attic orators use Greek words in senses that are not immediately clear from their normal use in non-legal contexts, or indeed from their etymology; so rather than spending time considering how the various words have acquired their special meanings, it may be more profitable simply to illustrate the point, and then to consider some of its implications.

Take for example the word *graphê*: literally a 'writing', and hence in common usage a 'written document', and so by extension a 'written prosecution' – but it is not immediately clear to the non-specialist scholar, and it may not have been immediately obvious even to a native Greek speaker inexperienced in the law, why the word should serve to denote a public pros-

[49] Respectively in Todd and Millett, 'Law, Society, and Athens', at p. 17; and in S. C. Todd, 'Lysias Against Nikomakhos: the fate of the expert in Athenian law', in L. Foxhall and A. D. E. Lewis, eds., *Justifications not Justice: Greek Law in its Political Setting* (Oxford, 1996), pp. 101–31, at p. 121.

ecution, in other words one which could be brought by anybody or at least by any citizen, as opposed to a *dikê* (private prosecution) which could only be brought by the aggrieved party. Or take the word *paragraphê*, literally an 'alongside-writing', which in normal Greek means a marginal note in a document: there is nothing obvious in the etymology of the word which would allow the first-time hearer to predict that in legal contexts this should denote a counter-prosecution brought by the original defendant, alleging that his opponent's indictment had been brought illegally, and seeking to punish the original plaintiff for such illegality.

We need to be careful here, because part of the impression of verbal technicality may be an illusion created by the tendency of English translators (and it is hard to see how we can avoid doing this) to use nouns to describe things which Greek writers will often express by means of (for instance) cognate verbs. For example, the law on *hubris* was discussed in section III of this essay, but the law does not actually say (as quoted there), 'if somebody commits *hubris*, let anybody who wishes bring a *graphê* against him.' What it says is, 'if somebody *hubrisêi* ['hubrisises'], let anybody who wishes *graphesthô* ['cause to be written'].' The lexical point is a simple one, but it may have been significant psychologically for those involved: Greek, with its mixture of nouns and cognate verbs, is much less formulaic than our English translations of such texts.

Indeed, in sharp contrast to what we know of early Roman law, it seems that legally binding actions at Athens, like selling land or freeing a slave, at no time required the use of a particular form of words in order to be valid. There are some formulae, such as the phrase 'for the ploughing of legitimate children' which typically accompanies betrothal in Menander's comedies, but even here the verbal variants imply that no set form of words was required.[50] There is also one case where the Eleven as presiding officials refuse to accept an *apagôgê* (summary arrest) until it contains the standard but in this case false declaration that the accused has been taken *ep'autophôrôi* ('in the act'),[51] but this is probably less a question of validity, and more an attempt to make the prosecutor responsible for the falsehood, and so to protect themselves against a subsequent accusation of overstepping their powers.

The only possible counter-example here is the argument of Theomnestos in Lysias 10, discussed in section III of this essay, that what matters in the law of defamation is the use of particular words rather than the intentions of those who use them, and this (as we saw) is an exceptional argument which Lysias was able to present as highly sophistic. To put it another way,

[50] See A. W. Gomme and F. H. Sandbach, *Menander: a commentary* (Oxford, 1973), p. 531, on *Perikeiromene*, 1010.

[51] Lysias, 13.86.

Athenian law may have a specialist vocabulary, but it does not have an autonomous vocabulary, in that the absence of legal formalism means that words do not take on meanings independent of the intentions of their users.

We have already touched on the question about how the language of *graphê*, *paragraphê*, and so on would have appeared not simply to the modern non-specialist reader of the orators, but to their original hearers. This is not a question that we can resolve, though it may be worth drawing attention to certain considerations. In the first place, *dikastai* like public officials had to be male citizens aged at least thirty. The contrast is with the Assembly, for which the membership age was eighteen. (It is possible that you could not speak until you were twenty, but this will not have affected attendance.) Probable mortality patterns suggest that about half of the eighteen-plus population will have been aged under thirty, so that the courts will have tended to appear at least middle-aged when compared to the Assembly. (This may be part of the reason why Aristophanes' comedy the *Wasps* caricatures the typical *dikastês* as old and cantankerous, though some scholars believe that jury service will have been particularly attractive to those past the age of active work.[52]) Unlike the Assembly, however, the courts seem to have had no formal ban on the presence of bystanders, including not only citizen males but possibly also foreigners, though social pressures may have discouraged the presence of women.

It is therefore possible that people who intended or expected to get involved as *dikastai* or as litigants or as witnesses or even as public officials – the majority of whom were appointed by lot, and had the task of presiding over a dikastic court – would have been able to go along first as spectators, and so gain confidence in the rituals and the language of the courts.[53] This may not, however, have been possible for everybody.

Women, for instance, are not generally found as actors in Athenian courts: a judicial oath by a woman would be sworn not in the court itself but in a temple,[54] and her claim to a disputed inheritance would typically be pleaded by her husband, probably in her absence. But we do hear of a few instances of women being prosecuted, normally in cases where the

[52] My own views on this question are set out in S. C. Todd, '*Lady Chatterley's Lover* and the Attic Orators: the social composition of the Athenian jury', *Journal of Hellenic Studies*, 110 (1990), pp. 146–73.

[53] Spectators at Athenian trials have not previously attracted much attention from scholars, but the evidence is well set out in a paper by A. M. Lanni, 'Spectator Sport or Serious Politics? *hoi periestêkotes* and the Athenian lawcourts', *Journal of Hellenic Studies*, 117 (1997).

[54] This point has recently been emphasised by S. D. Goldhill, 'Representing Democracy: women at the Great Dionysia', in S. Hornblower and R. G. Osborne, eds., *Ritual, Finance, Politics: Athenian democratic accounts presented to David Lewis*, pp. 347–69 (Oxford, 1994), at pp. 357–8.

penalty was death or enslavement. Presumably under such circumstances they will still have been defended by their male relatives, but it is possible that in such a case the defendant will herself have been present in court to await the sentence, and the novelty of the proceedings will presumably have had a psychological impact on her. The most explicit evidence for the presence of a woman is the story that the orator Hyperides, seeing that he was about to lose his defence of the courtesan Phryne (who was his mistress) on a charge of impiety, won the sympathy of the judges by stripping her naked in court, but the earliest attestations are post-classical[55] and the story may not be authentic. The abortive arrest of Zobia, however, for which there is contemporary evidence, does imply that she was present at least when the public officials determined whether there was a case to answer.[56]

The other category of people who would be likely to be lacking in experience and therefore confidence when dealing with the language and ritual of an Athenian court is non-Athenians, and in particular non-residents of Athens. We may wonder about the case of Euxitheos, the Mytilenean who is defending himself against a homicide charge in Antiphon 5. Clearly this is a very rich man, who can afford a speech by Antiphon and (presumably) private tuition in coping with stage-fright, but if he was indeed arrested and imprisoned the moment he got to Athens to answer the charge, he may not have had the prior opportunity to observe what if anything was distinctive about the language and the ritual of an Athenian as opposed to a Mytilenean court. And although this is the only person in this situation that we can identify by name, we know that Athens during the period of the fifth-century empire insisted on cases involving serious penalties being transferred from the courts of the subject-allies to be heard at Athens: so there are likely to have been others, who may not have been able to afford the services of a logographer like Antiphon.

All this is rather speculative, so let me close by considering something about which we can perhaps be more specific: the linguistic reception of the Attic orators in antiquity, and the comparison with other literary genres. The obvious example to use as a contrast is Athenian tragedy, because for a modern reader, the language of tragedy (particularly Aeschylus) is quite as abstruse as the language of any of the orators. Indeed one of the orators, Lysias, is syntactically so easy that he is regularly used as the first Greek author read by modern students, notwithstanding the legal terminology. Both tragedy and oratory were frequently glossed in later lexica, but there is an important difference between the reception of the two genres. The tragedians are glossed for the most part in general lexica like Photius or the

[55] Athenaios, 13.590e, [Plutarch], *Life of Hyperides*, 849e. [56] Demosthenes, 25.57–8.

Souda, both of which also gloss the orators. Most of the fragments of the orators, however, come from specialist lexica. The most important of these is Harpocration's *Lexicon to the Ten Orators*: a significant title, though Harpocration also includes quotations from historians and from tragic and comic poets. Many fragments from the orators are also to be found in a group of five lexica, published by Bekker in 1814:[57] these include the *Lexeis Rhêtorikai* (literally 'Readings from the Orators') and the *Dikôn Onomata* (literally 'names of *dikai*', i.e. of prosecutions, or more broadly of legal procedures). What is significant here is not so much the absolute linguistic difficulty of the texts, but the perception in antiquity that the language of the Athenian orators and of Athenian law belonged to a world of its own.[58]

[57] They are often collectively known as 'Bekker's *Anecdota*' (lit. 'unpublished things').

[58] Despite the fact that much of Greek literature is laced with legal allusions: for examples, see Todd, *Shape of Athenian Law*, pp. 8–10.

3. *The autonomy of Roman law*

ANDREW D. E. LEWIS

Modern legal theorists disagree about the extent to which a legal system and its rules can be viewed as independent of the social structure in which it operates. This is the question of autonomy.[1] Whilst those, legal positivists, who adhere to a strong position on the autonomy of law can acknowledge an interrelationship between a system's rules and their social application, they are committed to an idea of law which enables them to speak about law's operation without commenting on its social effects.[2] Most legal practitioners in all times and places will take the same view, whether on the principle that eschewing contemplation of the results of one's action is economical or on the surgeon's principle that speculating on long-term consequences may hamper short-term efficiency. The question of autonomy is more than a matter of theory, however; as well as being a way of looking at the world, it can also affect it. A judge who subscribes to autonomy is far less likely to be swayed in his reasoning by appeals to the social consequences his decision may bring about than one who harbours doubts whether the practice of law can be systematically justified other than by its effect in practice.

What was the position in Roman law? We have first to decide which of the many phases of development of Roman law to address. The period usually called by Romanists the classical period (of law) stretches from the first century AD to the beginning of the third century AD. There are reasons for this choice and nomenclature which it is needless to enter into here.

[1] There is a large literature. See, for a recent collection of views, R. George, ed., *The Autonomy of Law* (Oxford, 1996). For a recent attempt to rehabilitate positivism from a philosophical perspective see Tom D. Campbell, *The Legal Theory of Ethical Positivism* (Aldershot, 1996).

[2] The most widely respected theorist in this tradition is the late H. L. A. Hart, whose *The Concept of Law* (first published Oxford, 1961), elegantly re-established the English positivist tradition on a surer footing than its sovereignty-based beginnings with Bentham. Although fortified with sociological insights and acknowledging contingent requisites of the human condition the theory remains unashamedly descriptive of what it supposes actually goes on in legal systems.

Suffice it that although not perhaps the most interesting period of legal development in Rome it is the one about which we can claim to know most, whether from lay or legal sources. Even for this period we lack an important source of information for assessing the degree of autonomy Roman law enjoyed in practice. Our sources of law include largely the views of lawyers, the jurists, as preserved in later texts: but the structure of the Roman legal profession meant that lawyers were not normally judges. As a result we know little about the way judges decided cases in practice. Furthermore jurists rarely appeared in court as advocates. Of advocates we know more than judges owing to the habit of some rhetors publishing their successful speeches for posterity, though chance has only preserved substantial remains from one orator, Cicero, who was active a century before the juristic classical period.

I. JURISTS

The Roman jurists were a self-perpetuating clique of experts. Originally in the Roman Republic drawn from amongst the upper social class of those who had no need to work for their living, they perceived the acquisition of legal skills as a civic duty which could have personal benefits in terms of private patronage and political prestige. The skills were developed by personal attendance upon existing acknowledged masters who would in turn recognise the talents of a young newcomer by citing his opinions.[3] Republican jurists had offered their services free to those who required them, magistrates (that is politicians), lay judges or potential litigants, as well as advising less formally on the making of wills, contracts, etc.[4] Such advice formed the basis of more or less public discussion in which differing opinions might be expressed by other jurists, engendering a dialectic debate which remains the foremost legacy of Roman law in the form of free forensic exegesis. Under the Empire some attempt was made by the emperors to harness or restrict the public giving of legal opinions, though the details are obscure in our sources.[5] Although some jurists now required employment, not being from the traditionally wealthy class, there remained an inhibition against the giving of legal opinions for reward. Many jurists took administrative positions in the running of the Empire, as provincial governors or members of the emperor's council. The leading members of the last great generation of Roman jurists at the

[3] Gellius' *stationes ius publice docentium aut respondentium* indicates that both teaching and practice were carried out informally: *Noctes Atticae,* xiii.13.1.

[4] Cicero, *de oratore,* i.212.

[5] The basic material is the account by Pomponius, a jurist of the second century AD, preserved in *Digest*, ii.2.48–9.

beginning of the third century AD, Papinian, Paul and Ulpian, seem all to have served as praetorian prefect, in effect the emperor's chief minister.[6] Importantly, even for this last generation of independent jurists, full time imperial service did not exclude continued private juristic practice, though social change and the pressures of public business meant that consultations seem to have been carried out in writing rather than by personal attendance. Especially in their writings these high officials functioned in the law, for all the respect in which their opinions were held, as private individuals.[7]

It is the writings of these jurists, transmitted to us via the codification of the law under Justinian in the sixth century AD, which serves as our major source for the reconstruction of Roman legal history. We have already noted how this perspective limits our understanding of the role of the judge. More importantly it also masks the role of the advocate. Occasionally acknowledged jurists appeared as advocates, orators, representing clients before the courts, but in general the roles were seen as distinct.[8] The most famous of all Roman orators, Cicero, was not a jurist, for all his interest in and (limited) knowledge of the law. That he read the jurists and enjoyed scoring points off his legal colleagues appears from his correspondence.[9] He himself tells the story of a client who approached his contemporary, the jurist Aquilius Gallus, for an opinion. Gallus examined the problem, and perceiving that it turned on a matter of evidence, observed: *nihil hoc ad ius, ad Ciceronem* (There is no law in this, it's one for Cicero).[10] Not only does this anecdote show Cicero's perception of himself as a presenter of argument rather than a master of legal doctrine, it simultaneously reveals that this distinction, which lies at the heart of the autonomy of a

[6] Historia Augusta, *vita Heliog.*, 16.4; *vita Niger*, 7.3; *vita Alex.*, 26.5; Aurelius Victor, *Caes.*, 20.34; 24.6; *Digest*, xii.1.40pr. T. Honoré, *Ulpian* (Oxford, 1982), pp. 43, 191–2 doubts Paul's being a praetorian prefect.

[7] The conflict in roles that this produced is occasionally to be found reflected in the surviving literature as when Ulpian, who rose to be the emperor's right hand man, writes that on a certain occasion when advising the urban praetor, the supreme legal executive in the Republic and still in Ulpian's time of judicial importance, the praetor acted in a particular way *me adsidente*, 'with my assistance': *Digest*, iv.2.9.3. For an account of the succeeding generations of jurists working as full time officials in the imperial bureaucracy see T. Honoré, *Emperors and Lawyers*, 2nd edn (Oxford, 1994).

[8] The separation was more or less established before the end of the Republic. A clear example from the Principate of a jurist who was also an orator is Aristo: see W. Kunkel, *Herkunft und soziale Stellung der roemishen Juristen*, 2nd edn (Weimar, 1952), pp. 326–8.

[9] At dinner one day he insisted against the jurist Trebatius that Brutus and other jurists of the middle of the second century BC had wondered whether an heir could bring an action for theft against someone who had abstracted property from an estate before the heir had succeeded to it. Next day, having checked his legal sources, he sent a joyful note to Trebatius confirming his claim 'that Sextus Aelius, Manius Manilius and Marcus Brutus had held a view which you said no one had held': *ad fam.*, vii. 22.

[10] Cicero, *Topica*, 51.

legal system's rules, was already developed in the middle of the last century BC when many of the classical rules were as yet unformulated. It is the capacity to separate the discussion of legal rules from their possible application in actual circumstances that characterises autonomy.

Two factors were critical in the development of autonomy in Roman law, one social, the other juridical. The social factor was the separation of the roles of advocate and jurist, already noted. Until the last century of the Republic (the first century BC) it was possible, and may even have been common, to combine both functions. Of the leading jurists in the first half of this period Q. Mucius Scaevola (*ob.* 82 BC) was both an orator and a jurist.[11] His much younger contemporary Servius Sulpicius Rufus (*ob.* 43 BC), adjudged by Cicero to be the greater lawyer in that he not only knew the law but treated it as a science (*ars*), was trained as an orator and would in Cicero's judgement have been amongst the leaders in that profession had he not opted for the law.[12] This choice, which might in other circumstances appear a personal one, coincides with the quickening process of development of the civil law in the late Republic which was to flower into the systematic exposition of the rules of the law in the writings of the jurists of the Principate.[13] The separation was viewed with mixed feelings: although, as we have just seen, Cicero praises Servius Sulpicius for his greater juristic gifts, Quintilian a generation later still regards jurists as poor relations.[14] Perhaps there is some truth in the view that Quintilian, whose examples are nearly all from an earlier time, hankered after a lost relationship between law and advocacy.[15] Like it or not the jurists, starting from the middle of the first century BC, had developed a highly specialised framework of peculiarly juridical argument. It was no longer sufficient to present a court with a series of arguments drawn from commonplaces about honesty, justice and piety. Although this need persisted and can be documented,[16] the judge was increasingly bound to pay attention to the detailed arguments of law or else lay himself open to a charge of 'making the case his own'.[17]

The second factor, linked intimately to the causes of the first, is the dependence of the substantive legal rules upon their origin in procedure. This is a complex matter which can only be sketched here. The Roman civil judicature system, from the end of the Republic until the middle of the Principate,

[11] Cicero, *Brutus*, 39.145. [12] Cicero, *Brutus*, 41.151.

[13] On this process in the Republic see B. W. Frier, *The Rise of the Roman Jurists* (Princeton, 1985). [14] Quintilian, *inst. or.*, xii.3.2–3.

[15] But see Crook's defence of Quintilian: J. Crook, *Legal Advocacy in the Roman World* (London, 1995), pp. 167ff., pointing out that an age in which both Tacitus and Pliny were at the bar cannot have been all that poor in skills.

[16] See, for example, the fragments of arguments made before the emperor Caracalla in a case at Antioch in 216 AD, preserved in an inscription *SEG* xvii. 759. See the discussion by Crook, *Legal Advocacy*, pp. 91ff. [17] On this see below, n. 29.

was dependent upon the jurisdiction of the urban praetor. This magistrate, elected every year as were all the major magistracies, was responsible for setting in motion all legal proceedings between individuals. This he did on the basis of his edict, a procedural document which announced the range of remedies which he would grant to aggrieved plaintiffs. The case itself would be heard by one or more lay judges, appointed by the praetor, the scope of whose deliberations and judgement was predetermined by a document, the *formula*, which the praetor issued at the conclusion of the hearing before him. The *formula* was itself a product of the edict. The skills of the jurists lay first in the formulation of the edict itself, for the praetor being an annual magistrate need have little juridical knowledge himself, and then in its interpretation, first for the benefit of the litigants and the praetor in an instant case and secondly for the instruction of the judge or judges called upon to hear that case. The intricacies of edictal interpretation provided little scope for arguments based upon justice and honesty and although there were constant efforts to free up the system by the insertion of fresh terms into the *formula*, the need, above all the need of the judge, for certainty, constantly drove the jurists to interpret and define these in precise terms.[18] The net effect was the creation of a wholly new body of knowledge of which the jurists were masters. Although this knowledge was applied to control the world and to remedy injustices arising in the world it was itself an independent set of criteria with only the most marginal of interactions with general moral and ethical thought.

II. ADVOCATES

As we have seen, advocates in Rome were not lawyers. Their role was to represent clients in court rather than to give legal advice. In the case of jury courts, the criminal courts and the centumviral court which heard inheritance cases, the nature of the proceedings, requiring declamation before a large body of jurors who were as likely to decide the case on appearance and presentation as on any detailed assessment of the evidence or the law, necessitated some representation. But it appears that advocates were also to be found appearing in cases heard by a single judge, though, perhaps significantly, we do not have so much information about these, despite the fact that most Roman trials in our period were of this type.[19]

[18] On this whole development the best starting point is Frier, *Rise of the Roman Jurists*.

[19] This is a controverted matter. There was an intermediate type of tribunal, the *recuperatores*, usually five or seven in number. Our knowledge of this body, which appears to have been appointed *ad hoc* for each occasion just like single judges, is flimsy. Obviously, like the modern English jury, the social dynamics of this small body offers more scope for genuine oratory than the single judge. It has been argued that it was a normal method of trial at

It is no accident that *patronus* is the normal Latin word for one who represents another in court.[20] By the last century of the Republic the leaders at the Roman bar had mastered a range of professional skills which made it difficult for the merely socially superior to compete successfully in the courts.[21] The prestige associated with a successful defence of interests in court, however, remained and attached itself to those whose advocacy was learned as a specialism. In this way representation in court became a powerful route to political dominance by the socially disadvantaged.[22] Cicero himself was a *novus homo*, a new man who was the first of his family to rise to the supreme magistracy, the consulate. One of his early rivals at the bar was Julius Caesar who was later to adopt a more direct path to power.

The advocate was therefore detached from the legal consequences of his case in two ways: he had no necessary personal interest in the outcome and he had no detailed knowledge of the appropriateness of the result in terms of the law. From the evidence of Cicero's civil law speeches we can judge that an advocate was not above presenting the evidence in such a way as to make it difficult to apply the law to the facts in such a way as to harm his client's interests, in a word to obfuscate the issue.[23] But Cicero lived in a period before the detailed elaboration of the civil-law rules in the juristic classical period and we cannot always be sure that his muddiness is not a genuine reflection of an as yet undeveloped law. We have no comparable material from the classical period itself, lacking the speeches of the younger Pliny. More strikingly we have from that later period rhetorical exercises which purport to be reports of the sort of training given to young advocates: Seneca's *Controversiae*. Despite attempts to argue the contrary it is generally recognised that the legal substance of these exercises is not Roman, and is probably entirely fictional.[24] The point is that it was possible, and arguably desirable, to teach rhetoric in a fashion which removed the irrelevancies of the formal law.

footnote 19 (*cont.*)
Rome in the classical period and earlier with the single judge as the exception: J. Kelly, *Studies in the Civil Judicature of the Roman Republic* (Oxford, 1976). The recently discovered legislation governing judicial proceedings in the provinces, the *lex Irnitana*, throws doubt on Kelly's suggestion without clearly refuting it: see, generally, P. Birks, 'New Light on the Roman Legal System: The Appointment of Judges', *Cambridge Law Journal*, 47 (1988), p. 36.

20 On which see Crook, *Legal Advocacy*, pp. 146ff. against W. Neuhauser, *Patronus und Orator* (1958).

21 See, for example, the reference to advocates' wiles in Seneca, *Controversiae*, ii.4.11–12.

22 In the early imperial period advocacy even became open to those who needed paying for their services, though the fiction that they were not to be remunerated persisted, see Crook, *Legal Advocacy*, p. 39.

23 Indeed he himself boasted of the fact: Quintilian, *inst. or.* ii.17.21.

24 On this see Crook, *Legal Advocacy*, pp. 163ff.

III: JUDGES

Judges were either laymen chosen as arbitrators or jurymen to determine a single case, or officials who acted judicially as a part of their administrative functions. In either case judges were not expected to be legally trained (though the social context of the Empire resulted in many jurists taking office as administrators under the emperors, they were numerically insignificant).[25] Although official judges, Roman provincial governors and the like, kept records, *commentarii*, of their proceedings including judicial business, from which surviving records we can glimpse the judge at work, these official records give us little or no insight into the judge's thinking about a decision.[26] There is very little information at all about how lay Roman judges went about their task: there is but one account in our sources from the hand of someone appointed judge. In the first century AD the author Aulus Gellius composed an entertaining pot pourri of anecdotes and reminiscence under the title *Attic Nights*. In it he recalls the one time when he was called upon to be a judge.[27]

Gellius tells us nothing about the way he came to be appointed, though from other personal reminiscence in his book it appears that he studied law for a time and he shows an unusual interest in legal antiquities and anecdotes. New evidence from Spain, though of texts designed to govern provincial and not metropolitan practice, gives us some greater insight than hitherto into the appointment of judges in first-century Rome.[28] There was an official list, the *album*, of citizens allocated to judicial duties. Litigants could choose a judge from this list to hear their case or, if they preferred, a citizen not upon the list. In the latter case the rules permitted the individual

[25] Some, e.g. R. Feenstra, 'La preuve dans la civilisation romaine, rapport de synthèse' in *Recueils Jean Bodin XVI, i 'La preuve (antiquité)'* (Brussels, 1964), p. 635, would place the emergence of a regular salaried judiciary as early as the first century AD, but the evidence is thin on which to base any opinion. Others suggest that as the majority of those single judges whose identity is known to us from the Republic turn out to be jurists perhaps the practice of appointing juridically qualified judges to act was more prevalent at that time than might appear from the formal evidence: P. Collinet, 'Le rôle des juges dans la formation du droit romain classique' in *Recueil d'études sur les sources du droit en l'honneur de François Gény* (Paris, 1934), p. 23, cited by Crook, *Legal Advocacy*, p. 175.

[26] A papyrus from Egypt (whence much of the surviving material comes) shows one Roman governor's view of an institution of his own system. The case before him concerned a limitation period, after which no proceedings could be brought. The law in question was native Egyptian law and the plaintiff disputed the governor's ruling. 'Look here,' said the governor, 'in our law it's only one year!': *P. Strassb.* 22. The reference is to the Roman law of *usucapio*: Justinian lengthened the period and his *Institutes* draws indirect attention to the surprisingly short period the old law presents: *J.Inst.* ii.6pr.

[27] Gellius, *Noctes Atticae*, xiv.2.

[28] J. González, 'The *Lex Irnitana*', *Journal of Roman Studies*, 76 (1986), p. 147; P. Birks, 'New Light on the Roman Legal System: the Appointment of Judges', *Cambridge Law Journal*, 47 (1988), p. 36; E. Meztger, *A New Outline of the Roman Civil Trial* (Oxford, 1997).

to excuse himself on certain grounds, including age and public duties. If the litigants could not agree on a judge to hear their case, perhaps the most likely event, then the rules obliged them, alternately, to reject those on the list whom they were unwilling to have until but a single name remained: this one, the least disliked by both, would be appointed to determine the matter. We may suppose that Gellius was chosen in this way rather than that the litigants chose him directly for his personal qualities. In the latter case we might, perhaps, have expected him to boast about it.

The case Gellius heard was one of debt, in technical language a *condictio* brought by the supposed creditor against his debtor. As on many such occasions there were no witnesses and it was the word of the one litigant against the other. From his legal advisers Gellius learned that the plaintiff creditor was expected to make out a *prima facie* case and that in this sort of situation therefore the plaintiff should lose if there were no reason to prefer the one's testimony to the other. But Gellius was unhappy as he was minded on extrinsic grounds to believe the creditor and discount the word of the supposed debtor, a known rogue. He therefore consulted a philosopher, Favorinus, to ask whether he was not in conscience bound to find for the one he believed, albeit without firm evidence. Favorinus advised that he could properly, on moral grounds, decide in favour of the juster cause. In the end unable to satisfy the jurists' requirements of proof but equally unwilling to give judgement against his conscience, Gellius applied to the magistrate to be relieved of his liability and withdrew from the case. To be permitted to do this he had to swear that he was unable to decide the case – *non liquet* – and this has given rise to an idea that in Roman practice a judge had three options: to condemn, absolve or declare *non liquet*. But this is myth. Gellius' decision was to escape entirely from the case which would in all probability have been transferred to another judge. The implication of his oath was that he could not decide it, not that it could not be decided. Unable to form a firm opinion he needed to be formally released from the obligation to give judgement as judges could be made personally liable for wrong judgements by an action brought against them by the losing party.[29]

The Gellius anecdote shows that it was perfectly possible for a Roman to form a moral opinion about the law and the legal outcome of a case. Nothing could be clearer than Gellius' desire to find in favour of the party whom he found credible. But it is all the more significant therefore that Gellius felt unable to risk making a decision in his favour which lacked

[29] Knowledge of the way in which lay judges could be made liable for 'making a case their own' (*litem suam facere*) is limited and controverted: see, most recently, P. Birks, 'A New Argument for a Narrow View of *litem suam facere*', *Tijdschrift voor Rechtsgeschiedenis*, 52 (1984), p. 373; F. Lamberti, 'Alcuni riflessioni in tema di "litem suam facere"', *Labeo*, 36 (1990), p. 218 and T. Giménez-Candela, *Los llamados cuasidelitos* (Madrid, 1990).

formal evidence to support it and which he would therefore find difficulty in justifying were he himself to be sued by the disappointed debtor. The legal system itself did not favour the giving of legal decisions on other than formal and justifiable legal grounds.

Gellius was exercised to get his decision right, though whether moved by justice or a fear of personal liability is unknowable. But for all his care and consideration of extra-legal opinion the overall impression left by the anecdote is that the world of the law was one apart: one indeed from which it might be preferable to step aside if troubled by conscience. It is perhaps fortuitous that this, our sole insight into the mind of a classical Roman judge, should so clearly reveal the autonomous nature of the system. But we have no good reason to think that this example is not, in this regard, typical, and that the majority (at least) of Roman judges were constrained to adjudicate in accordance with the rules elaborated by the professional jurists.

Such evidence as we have of other legal judgements supports this conclusion. The *commentarii* and other records from provincial courts reveal arguments from precedent: the principle that a case should be decided in accordance with the way previous such cases were decided.[30] Reliance upon precedent is characteristic of many judicial and bureaucratic systems and there may be many causes of it. What all such systems necessarily share is commitment to certainty and regularity and the appearance of a doctrine of precedent is a sure sign of a preference for formal over substantive justice.

Both in the practice of its courts and the opinions of its legal experts therefore, Rome subscribed to the view that law occupied an autonomous sphere. This, it is important to stress, was a practical result and not a philosophical position. The Roman jurists, for all that they lacked the professional apparatus of the modern lawyer, were first and foremost practitioners and had the typical customary lawyers' distrust of theorising about law. Their attitude to philosophers of the type of Favorinus is neatly summed up in an imperial rescript of the early third century which deals with the exemptions from burdensome duties which could be granted to various classes of municipal worthies: physicians, teachers of rhetoric and orators. Philosophers, the emperor's bureaucracy announces, are a doubtful case: they ought in principle to be prepared to expend their patrimony in public service; moreover, adds the lawyer-author in the emperor's name, if they presume to object, they only show how unphilosophic they are![31]

[30] R. Katzoff, 'Precedents in the courts of Roman Egypt', *Zeitschrift Savigny-stiftung für Rechtsgeschichte*, 89 (1972), p. 256. Although the jurists did not discuss the role of previous decisions, the advocates recognised their importance: Quintilian, *inst.or.*, v.2.1.

[31] Rescript of the emperor Antoninus Pius quoted by Modestinus in *Digest*, xxvii.1.6.7.

IV. THE LATER HISTORY OF ROMAN LAW

The image of Roman law as an impartial structure of rules is enhanced by the history of the transmission of its remains to medieval and modern Europe. In sixth-century Byzantium the emperor Justinian responded to a long-felt need for a consolidation of the sources of the law: his law commissioners produced the *Digest*, an encyclopedia of much earlier juristic writings dating from between the late Republic and the third century AD, the *Code* of edited imperial legislation and the introductory *Institutes*. The publication of the *Digest* rendered the original texts of the earlier jurists otiose and indeed unusable for legal purposes and gave these literary products of earlier ages the status of legislation. As these private texts from diverse hands and different centuries naturally revealed different conceptions of the rules it was imperative that those who compiled the *Digest* should have power to edit and amend the texts: their task was to produce not merely a historical monument but a living law-book. The result was a more-or-less homogenised product which was issued as an act of imperial will.[32] This sanitisation of the jurists' work was further enhanced when, in the eleventh-century revival, the *Digest* again became a major source of legal rules. Doubly divorced, first by the compilers and then by the medieval jurists, from their original context, the jurists' writings now became *ratio scripta*, written reason, the acme of positivistic imaginings of law. Only in the period since the humanist revival of the sixteenth century, and intensively only in this century, has scholarly endeavour attempted to deconstruct the *Digest* into its component parts to support a history of Roman law. For much of the intervening period legal scholarship was devoted to the eliciting of a set of harmonious legal regulations for practical application from material which, both because of its origins and of its imperfect redaction, was often opaque and difficult. The very effort required, though attracting scorn from the more radical humanist historians,[33] added its weight to the positivistic tradition. Nothing requiring so much expenditure of labour could be lightly dismissed: rather it should be all the more valued.

The moral indifference of the Roman jurists to the substance of their system engendered a formality which enabled it to be all the more easily absorbed into the very different social and political structures of medieval Europe. It can be doubted whether a more engaged legal practice could have been so effectively transformed. The form in which that practice was

[32] For an account of the process of compilation see T. Honoré, *Tribonian* (London, 1978).

[33] Following the lead of scholars like Lorenzo Valla, Rabelais famously compared the accumulation of medieval scholarship in the Gloss accompanying the printed editions of the *Corpus Juris* to dung surrounding a cloth of gold: *Pantagruel*, ch. 5.

transmitted created a scholarly community in medieval and early modern Europe whose very efforts appeared to testify to the intrinsic importance of the material. This in turn supported, in the various European countries of the civil law tradition, a philosophic commitment to the independence of the legal system from the social and political context of which it necessarily formed a part.

4. *Local participation and legal ritual in early medieval law courts*

WENDY DAVIES

When I thought about the questions posed by the organisers of the *Moral World of the Law* conference, my immediate reaction was that the early middle ages did not fit into their framework at all. This was, first, because early medieval courts were places for much more than legal and judicial business: most strikingly, they were occasions as well as places, occasions when friends were entertained, visitors were received and 'policy' was discussed and determined; settlements were negotiated and business was done. Hence, to suggest that the court was in opposition to everyday life makes no sense. Secondly, law itself was often a mixture of the customary, the prescriptive and the academic; hence, to pose questions about conflict between custom and written legislation is meaningless (or, at least, it is at one level). Thirdly, early medievalists do not normally expect to find professional lawyers manipulating courtroom drama and hogging the public stage. The image seems to sit too squarely in the twentieth century, in the world of mass media, global entertainment and vast audiences.

On the other hand, it is not too difficult to think of rules and rituals in the context of early medieval law and courts; and, on deeper reflection, some of the assumptions behind the framing of the questions do become surprisingly appropriate.

This is not the place to provide a full description of the early medieval context, but the points that immediately follow provide some essential briefing for those who may be unfamiliar with early medieval western Europe. The cultures with which we are concerned in the early middle ages had levels of literacy that were exceptionally low by modern, western standards, even if we nowadays recognise that there was a higher degree of literacy than once thought.[1] Partly as a consequence of the limited place of writing in everyday life at that time, anyone investigating the period in the late twentieth century has to confront considerable problems of evidence:

[1] R. McKitterick, *The Carolingians and the Written Word* (Cambridge, 1989), *passim.*

there are very many things that we do not and cannot know – about life, about events and about courts; there are few accounts of court proceedings that could remotely be described as 'impartial'; we are nearly always dependent on a single record for our knowledge of what happened in a case;[2] and although some of these records have a formal status, drawn up at the conclusion of a case, they are nothing like as full as a modern recorder's transcript and are even farther from the objective. We are extremely dependent upon the eyes and ears of a single scribe, who frequently came from a church or monastery with an interest in the outcome; documents produced by beneficiaries were common.[3] However, despite the obvious problems which that circumstance creates, the repetition of elements of procedure in a multiplicity of recorded cases can be as valuable a guide to procedure, if not more, as a mass of well corroborated detail on a single incident. Useful, usable, material does exist.

Law texts themselves, that is the texts which we depend on for statements of the content of law, may in fact be records of cases rather than anything approaching legislation; and they are often found embedded within conveyancing documents and estate surveys. A body of case law may therefore be our only guide to the principles of a legal system. Where principle is stated, there is frequently a pronounced customary element, being descriptive of what was believed to be normal practice. The texts sometimes include new rules, whether deriving from a ruler's commands or a council's deliberations; they often include elements of new rules as well as custom; and both rulers and lawyers confirmed and modified custom as well as made provision for completely new situations. The fact that we have any texts at all can be for varied and different reasons: kings ordered records to be made (and distributed); lawyers collected and copied material to assist with professional practice, creating both the library reference work and the pocket book for journeys; others (usually clerics) had a scholarly habit of studying law; and others had a personal interest in 'being in the know'.[4]

The early middle ages are a long period, eight hundred years or so, and cover a multiplicity of cultures and language groups, from the Near East to

[2] Although, for example, some Spanish cases generated two or more documents per case; cf. a case held at Empuries in Catalonia in 843 and others in León in the tenth century; R. Collins, '"Sicut lex Gothorum continet": law and charters in ninth- and tenth-century León and Catalonia', *English Historical Review*, 396 (1985), pp. 492–4, 498–502.

[3] W. Davies and P. Fouracre, eds., *The Settlement of Disputes in Early Medieval Europe* (Cambridge, 1986), pp. 211–12; P. Chaplais, 'The origin and authenticity of the royal Anglo-Saxon diploma', *Journal of the Society of Archivists*, 3 (1965–9), pp. 55–61; cf. S. Keynes, *The Diplomas of King Æthelred 'The Unready' 978–1016* (Cambridge, 1980), p. 28.

[4] Pocket books: see D. Jenkins, *The Law of Hywel Dda* (Llandysul, 1986), pp. xxi–xxiii. Early medieval law texts: P. Wormald, '*Lex scripta* and *verbum regis*: legislation and Germanic kingship, from Euric to Cnut', in P. H. Sawyer and I. N. Wood, eds., *Early Medieval Kingship* (Leeds, 1977), pp. 105–38.

Ireland, and the Mediterranean to Iceland. It makes no sense to generalise across the lot. In order to make some sort of sense, and keep this essay graspable, it will focus on western Europe (including Ireland, but not Scandinavia) and on the period from the seventh to the tenth century, *c.* 650–950. It would be valid, and relevant to the issues considered in this volume, to discuss the eleventh and twelfth centuries but one would make quite different points and suggest different emphases: the issue of competing systems, for example, would become much more prominent.

I. PROCEDURE

Perhaps surprisingly, given the range of cultures, the surviving records of court cases suggest that there were considerable similarities of procedure across time, space and language group. Although, of course, there were differences, the degree of similarity is striking, as is the familiarity of some aspects of procedure (evidential aspects especially).

Legal cases were virtually always heard at public meetings, often involving a large number of people, whether they occurred in Celtic, Germanic or Latin cultures. The numbers attending could easily reach fifty or a hundred and sometimes ran into several hundreds; more than fifty might be listed by name. More than 55 individuals were mentioned as present at Valenciennes in northern France in the 690s; over 40 witnessed an inquest about mill and shipping rights at Cremona in the Po valley in 841; about 90 were present at *Clofesho* (England) in 824 – including 'the whole ecclesiastical and political "establishment"', as Patrick Wormald put it (Anglo-Saxon charters are especially notable for their long lists of witnesses who attended public meetings).[5]

Another common feature is that some person, or some group of people, presided over the meeting: there was a chairperson (sometimes literally using a special seat). In Carolingian Europe there could well be two people sharing the position, like the count and bishop who presided at Empuries (Catalonia) in 843 or the duke and bishop at Lucca (northern Italy) in 847.[6] This position of president or chair might be held by a king, or royal or other officers, or a bishop,

[5] P. Fouracre, ed., appendix no. 6, in Davies and Fouracre, eds., *Settlement of Disputes*, pp. 244–5; C. Manaresi, ed., *I Placiti del 'Regnum Italiae'*, 3 vols. (Rome, 1955–60), vol. I, Inquisitiones no. 7, pp. 576–81; W. de Gray Birch, ed., *Cartularium Saxonicum*, 4 vols. (London, 1885–99), vol. I, no. 379, pp. 519–22, on which by P. Wormald, 'Charters, law and the settlement of disputes in Anglo-Saxon England', in Davies and Fouracre, eds., *Settlement of Disputes*, p. 152.

[6] P. de Marca, *Marca Hispanica sive Limes Hispanicus*, ed. S. Baluze (Paris, 1688), appendix 16, pp. 779–80; Manaresi, ed., *Placiti*, vol. I, no. 51, pp. 169–73. For all aspects of procedure in Italy, see now F. Bougard, *La justice dans le royaume d'Italie de la fin du VIIIe siècle au début du XIe siècle* (Rome, 1995).

or the holder of an immunity (where the immunist had personal political power and in effect ruled his own patch of land), and it demanded especial respect.

Plaintiffs and defendants did not usually speak for themselves, for there was often an advocate to speak on behalf of the principal parties (necessarily so for women and for churches). Advocates did not have to be professional lawyers (and probably were not usually so), but they were likely to have been literate and may well have been very experienced in 'the law'; in Ireland, by contrast, a land noted for its distinctive class of high status professional lawyers, they were likely to be lawyers.

It was common for the accused to be required to make a formal denial, perhaps on oath, perhaps supported by other people. For example, at Nogent-sur-Marne in the 690s Abbot Ermenoald had to deny formally the accusation that he had failed to make good his pledge to pay oil and good wine to Chaino, abbot of the monastery of St Denis, or, failing that, to pay a fine; and at Chasseneuil in Poitou, in 828, the advocate for the monastery of Cormery denied the accusation that increased rents had been required from peasants by using the written evidence of an estate survey.[7] Records of court cases place an emphasis on the formal act of denial and its place in the procedure.

The oath was also a major recurrent element of procedure: oaths of denial, like that made at the Nogent case cited above, or others taken on the Gospels, are but one form. Oaths were also taken to underline evidence of fact: in the Loire valley in 857 (within the immunity of St Martin, Tours) nine local peasants swore to the truth of disputed facts in a case, swearing by God, their christianity, their good faith, and the relics of the saints there present.[8] Oaths might also be sworn to reinforce written evidence, as required in the case of Helmstan's claim to property in England in the early tenth century.[9] Oath-helping, essentially the procedure of making public statements of confidence in the character of one of the parties to a dispute, could also play a part: at Langon in eastern Brittany in 801, in default of evidence, the accused had to swear to the truth of his defence himself, but also had to associate twelve 'suitable' men with his oath; in Canterbury in 844 men from the three Kentish monasteries of Dover, Folkestone and Lyminge swore on behalf of the archbishop, in addition to those of his household at Christchurch, in a dispute about a grant to Christchurch.[10] In

[7] P. Fouracre, ed., appendix no. 5, in Davies and Fouracre, eds., *Settlement of Disputes*, pp. 243–4; L. Levillain, ed., *Recueil des actes de Pépin I et de Pépin II, rois d'Aquitaine (814–848)* (Paris, 1926), no. 12, pp. 46–7.

[8] M. Thévenin, ed., *Textes relatifs aux institutions privées et publiques aux époques mérovingienne et carolingienne* (Paris, 1887), no. 89, pp. 120–3.

[9] F. E. Harmer, ed., *Select English Historical Documents of the Ninth and Tenth Centuries* (Cambridge, 1914), no. 18, pp. 30–2.

[10] A. de Courson, ed., *Cartulaire de Redon* (Paris, 1863), no. 191, pp. 147–8; Birch, ed., *Cartularium Saxonicum*, vol. II, no. 445, pp. 22–5.

these texts the oaths sworn were Christian oaths, although early Irish material shows traces of pre-Christian oath-swearing.[11] The Christian character of the oath could well be emphasised by reference to explicitly Christian objects, such as the Gospels, the altar, or relics; one well-known thief who was denying a charge in Gwynllŵg in south-east Wales, some time in or before the eleventh century, was threatened with having to take an oath on St Cadog's holy knife: on hearing this threat, he immediately confessed.[12]

The taking of evidence was also extremely common. It was taken from written texts and also from personal witnesses to fact or to the past, and it could be provided by accuser and accused or by an independent panel. At the Chasseneuil case, it was a written estate survey that was produced as evidence against the peasants; in the Catalan case of 843 cited above the judges made a point of asking for proof, written or oral; in the Pavia case of 880 discussed below, the court asked repeatedly for a *notitia*. At one of the ruler Salomon's courts, in eastern Brittany, *c*. 857, Salomon gave the machtiern Ratfred (a petty aristocrat) ten days to produce proof and witnesses (who had to be 'law-worthy' local men) at another court; Ratfred was required to demonstrate at this second hearing that the abbot of the monastery of Redon had given him property in Bains; this he failed to do and thereby lost the case.[13]

The characteristics mentioned so far were norms. Not quite so common but still common were the use of pledges, the making of a record and the invocation of penalties for contempt. Using pledges or sureties to guarantee some part of the procedure (especially to guarantee that parties would present themselves at a deferred hearing) is particularly well evidenced in Italian material, although not exclusive to Italy, with plenty of narrative detail of comings and goings to different hearings. Pledges (both persons and things) were also used to guarantee that the judgement or settlement that terminated a case would be carried out. Making a record of the outcome of a case, listing some or all of the witnesses to the occasion, could be ordered by kings (as Pippin I of Aquitaine did for the monastery of Cormery) or requested by successful parties (as Norbert the priest did at the conclusion of the Loire valley case); the victors often generated such records in England, but public notaries did so in ninth-century Spain.[14]

[11] F. Kelly, *A Guide to Early Irish Law* (Dublin, 1988), p. 198.

[12] 'Vita Sancti Cadoci', ch. 33, in A. W. Wade-Evans, *Vitae Sanctorum Britanniae et Genealogiae* (Cardiff, 1944), pp. 94–6. See further below, pp. 56–7, on oaths and judgement.

[13] See above, nn. 7, 2; Manaresi, ed., *Placiti*, vol. I, no. 89, pp. 318–22; de Courson, ed., *Cartulaire de Redon*, no. 105, pp. 79–80. For machtierns, see W. Davies, *Small Worlds. The Village Community in Early Medieval Brittany* (London, 1988), pp. 138–42, 175–83.

[14] Cf. Levillain, ed., *Recueil des actes*, no. 12; Thévenin, ed., *Textes relatifs*, no. 89; cf. above, n. 3.

Heavy penalties could be invoked for 'contempt' of court: for producing false written 'evidence' in tenth-century Castille, for example, or for sending a substitute to answer the charge at the Valenciennes case.[15] The articulation of the idea of contempt (*contemptio ordo racionis*) in itself emphasises that these were systems with their own rules and own logic.

If one turns from consistency of procedure to its rituals, some descriptions of cases include ritualistic elements that appear decidedly quaint; on the surface what went on in these courts looks strange. Hence, in courts in Aquitaine, Francia and Italy, people grasped a *festuca* (symbolic rod) to indicate acceptance of the judges' decision; and in Spanish León, a witness to fact was submitted to the ordeal of grasping two or three stones from hot water with his right hand; in order to demonstrate the truth of his evidence, his undamaged hand had to be exposed to public scrutiny three days later. While the need for witnesses to go to the ordeal could be set aside (as it was in 940 when water rights for their mill were judged to Sancho and Nuño Gómez, after they produced twelve witnesses and three sureties), its application to innocent witnesses is very well evidenced on other occasions.[16] The value of submitting witnesses to the ordeal may be difficult for the late twentieth-century reader to grasp. However, use of the hot iron ordeal as a verification procedure for witness evidence was clearly common in late eleventh-century England too: such practices were obviously deemed appropriate in the early middle ages.[17]

Some of the procedures are described in language which will also strike the late twentieth-century reader as odd: the second formal stage of pursuing a case in eighth-century Ireland, according to the tract *Cóic Conara Fugill*, was for the plaintiff's advocate to choose the proper 'path of judgement', that of 'truth' or 'entitlement' or 'justice' or 'propriety' or 'proper enquiry', each with its own appropriate procedures; if he chose the wrong path, he was fined.[18] However, despite the unfamiliarity of the concepts here, neither odd actions nor odd language alter the similarities in what was actually done; rather, they serve to conceal the broad consistencies of practice.

Although, then, it is true that elements of the court ritual can be selected that sound alien, in fact the most essential qualities of the ritual are much more mundane (as they are also very familiar). These essentials lay in

[15] L. Serrano, ed., *Becerro Gótico de Cardeña* (Valladolid, 1910), no. 210, pp. 224–5; Davies and Fouracre, eds., *Settlement of Disputes*, pp. 244–5.

[16] Davies and Fouracre, eds., *Settlement of Disputes*, pp. 29, 39, 271; A. Ubieto, ed., *Cartulario de San Millán de la Cogolla (759–1076)*, vol. I (Valencia, 1976), no. 27, pp. 44–5; Collins, '"Sicut lex Gothorum continet"', pp. 503–4.

[17] R. Fleming, *Domesday Book and the Law: Society and Legal Custom in Early Medieval England* (Cambridge, 1998), Index rerum *s.v.* 'ordeal'.

[18] Kelly, *Guide to Early Irish Law*, pp. 191–2.

repetition, in doing things in the correct order, in having the correct type of person perform particular actions, and in the respect accorded (as now) to oath. Denying or ignoring the right order (both spatially and temporally) was contempt; it amounted to insult, not just to the president of the court but to the whole system: in Merovingian Francia court presidents could in theory be executed for failing to follow the proper procedure.[19] The formulaic nature of the records serves to emphasise this attitude: things had to be done in the right way and the right things had to be said, using the correct words. People consciously acted within the framework of ancient and long-established legal traditions: they used the words of formularies of the sixth and seventh centuries, even in the eighth and ninth centuries; they referred explicitly to (classical) Roman law as their standard in ninth- and tenth-century charters from Burgundy and Aquitaine; and they cited Visigothic law of the sixth and seventh centuries in Spanish charters of the ninth to thirteenth centuries, where the earlier law is often quoted verbatim.[20]

This emphasis on right order thereby proclaimed both the existence of a distinctive system and its separation from 'everyday life'. To that extent, at least, early medieval law courts are entirely within the framework of issues posed by the conference organisers, even if we cannot perceive all the rules and all aspects of the system from the present distance. As for courtroom drama: dramatic public performance is clearly indicated by some texts and is emphasised by the sometimes lengthy quotations of who said what, especially in records of Italian cases;[21] documents could be dramatically thrown on the altar, or pierced right through, or even burnt; judges could themselves walk disputed boundaries (with kings, abbots, bishops striding beside the locals), taking the court outside the courtroom. Even without particular incidents of this kind the court meeting was so insistently public that there was necessarily a performance element to the procedures.

II. THE ACTORS

The examples and elements discussed above occur overwhelmingly in rulers' courts, although they are not confined to those arenas. The courts were rulers' courts in the sense that not just a king but his officers or an

[19] Davies and Fouracre, eds., *Settlement of Disputes*, p. 216.

[20] W. Davies, 'The composition of the Redon Cartulary', *Francia*, 17 (1990), pp. 79–80. 'Lex Romana (e)docet . . .': for example, M. Deloche, ed., *Cartulaire de l'abbaye de Beaulieu (en Limousin)* (Paris, 1859), nos. 20, 104, pp. 45, 157, and A. Bernard and A. Bruel, eds., *Recueil des chartes de l'abbaye de Cluny*, vol. I (Paris, 1876), no. 81, p. 91; Collins, '"Sicut lex Gothorum continet"', p. 493.

[21] Cf. C. J. Wickham, 'Land disputes and their social framework in Lombard-Carolingian Italy, 700–900', in Davies and Fouracre, eds., *Settlement of Disputes*, p. 107.

immunist, lay or clerical, presided. The law court was often, therefore, an explicitly political instrument: it was the occasion when the ruler (or his agent) was seen to preside; since it was very public, it reinforced the place of the ruler in the world *ordo* and served to extend his practical political power. The fact that courts could meet in many locations, with no single special meeting place – royal or aristocratic palaces, within or beside churches, villages, fields – contributed to that extending power; the ruler or his agents moved about the area they ruled.

The law court could also be the place where the ruler himself gave judgement and, in extreme cases, like that against the Breton machtiern Ratfred, exercised the separate functions of presiding, judging and punishing.[22] Presiding at court could thereby be a means of controlling aristocracies. There are late ninth-, tenth- and eleventh-century cases of this overtly political combining of separate functions in south Wales, exercised through the immunity of the bishopric of Llandaff; there are tenth- and eleventh-century examples of the duke presiding and giving judgement in Aquitaine; and there are tenth-century cases of Anglo-Saxon royal intervention in disputes in clearly political contexts: both King Edwy and King Edgar intervened with reference to the disputed estate of Sunbury in the mid-tenth century, and King Edward the Elder earlier in the century forfeited Goda's properties in favour of Eadgifu.[23] Even seventh- and eighth-century Ireland sometimes fits this pattern, despite the prominence of the learned legal class: Tírechán related that people went to King Loíguire for judgement on matters of inheritance.[24]

Clearly, all rulers' courts were not political instruments in the latter sense, and these cases may be exceptional. Just how exceptional is difficult to assess, given the language of the records: in southern Europe (Italy, Spain,

[22] Salomon, *princeps*, asked Ratfred in court why he had threatened to burn the monastery of Redon if some property was not handed over to him; when Ratfred said that the property had been given to him freely, Salomon asked the abbot why he had made such a fuss, confiscating the property and asking Ratfred to produce proof of his claim. Ratfred could neither do that nor find witnesses. Salomon therefore restored the property to Redon; de Courson, ed., *Cartulaire de Redon*, no. 105, pp. 79–80.

[23] *The Text of the Book of Llan Dâv*, ed. J. G. Evans with J. Rhys (Oxford, 1893), nos. 212, 214, 223, 244, 245, 255; cf. W. Davies, 'Adding insult to injury: power, property and immunities in early medieval Wales', in W. Davies and P. Fouracre, eds., *Property and Power in the Early Middle Ages* (Cambridge, 1995), pp. 138–40. J. Martindale, '"His special friend"? The settlement of disputes and political power in the kingdom of the French (tenth to mid-twelfth century)', *Transactions of the Royal Historical Society*, 5 (1995), p. 47. A. J. Robertson, ed., *Anglo-Saxon Charters* (Cambridge, 1939), no. 44, pp. 90–2; Harmer, ed., *Select Documents*, no. 23, pp. 37–8.

[24] 'Tírechán', ch. 15, in L. Bieler, ed., *The Patrician Texts in the Book of Armagh* (Dublin, 1979), p. 134. See D. A. Binchy, ed., *Críth Gablach* (Dublin, 1941), ch. 41 and p. 37, and F. Kelly, ed., *Audacht Morainn* (Dublin, 1976), for judgement as exercised by kings; cf. M. Gerriets, 'The king as judge in early Ireland', *Celtica*, 20 (1988), pp. 29–52.

the Byzantine Empire) it was usual for panels of judges to make judgements, under the presidency of count, duke, bishop or whomever; the judges were local men and they clearly took some real part in the decisions. But in England and Francia, and by implication in Wales, it is very common for texts to say that 'the court' gave judgement, or king and magnates, or a council, or 'all': in 1023 in England 'all the shire granted him'; in 926 in Aquitaine judgement was by Count Ebles and his *fideles* 'with the counsel and consent of all present'.[25] Here our understanding is dependent on the language used by the recorder and the formulaic influences conditioning his writing: when he used such phrases as 'the court' or 'all', did he mean that the whole court (maybe hundreds of people) shouted out guilty or not guilty (as reported of Pontius Pilate's judgement)? Or did he mean that the president, having taken due notice of all evidence, made a judgement on behalf of the court? Or that a panel of judgement-finders made the decision, which was then announced by the chair? We usually have no way of knowing, although all three may have happened. Recourse to the notion of 'collective decision-making' does not help with the real problem since it does not tell us who in practice made the decision. There is therefore a crucially important procedural aspect of rulers' courts of which we are often unsure: who actually made the judgement?

Now for local courts. Discussion so far has focused on procedure in rulers' courts. There were other courts in Europe at this period, which did not depend on king or state apparatus (or immunist), although they are much less frequently evidenced. In eastern Brittany, for example, law courts met in most villages in the ninth century, with a local person of status presiding (sometimes sitting on a three-legged seat), in a range of possible locations (in church, in front of the church, in the president's residence, and so on). Many of the local male population would be present. Plaintiffs made accusations and the accused made denials, speaking for themselves. Evidence was provided to support the denials, by documents or by witnesses to fact giving evidence on oath; and evidence was also sometimes produced to support accusations. A panel of very local judges – as few as three and as many as fourteen members are recorded – made a judgement (failing settlement), on the basis either of the evidence produced or of their own knowledge of the parties, of the locality and of the past. Where the evidence was not decisive the judges sometimes conducted an inquest and sometimes ordered oath-helpers to swear in support of the accused. Much is made of the 'suitability' of the judges and witnesses, that is of their 'law worthiness', and sometimes formal investigation of the judges' suitability

[25] Robertson, ed., *Anglo-Saxon Charters*, no. 83, pp. 162–4; Martindale, '"His special friend"?', p. 28; cf. the involvement of the 'whole synod' in judging southern Welsh kings, Evans with Rhys, ed., *Book of Llan Dâv*, no. 244.

to judge was made: they had to be free, male, propertied, and of good repute.[26]

In other words, although the scale and the interests were much smaller, there is plenty here that parallels the essentials of procedure in rulers' courts: the public meeting, the chairperson or president, accusation and denial, the production of evidence, the use of oaths. What is different is the fact that people spoke for themselves; and there is rather less emphasis in the records on procedures surrounding the oath and on 'right order'. As might be expected, there was less formality, although the process was nevertheless referred to as *in lege*, going to law.

What is also different in records of these cases from procedure in rulers' courts is the fact that many local court cases ended in settlement, obviating the need for judgement.[27] And even when the judgement was that there should be an oath, this could be dispensed with (as it was in one late tenth-century English [not so parochial] shire court, in order to maintain 'friendship').[28] The drive to settle was clearly extremely strong in the villages (if for no other reason than the practical necessity of social harmony within a small community). Disputes were settled out of court too, with evidence used in a similar way to arrive at the settlement and a record sometimes being kept. Such occasions did use quasi-judicial procedures but they are differentiated from what went on in local courts: they were even less formal, had fewer procedures, are recorded in different language, and had no judges.

The Breton corpus is a particularly full and rich set of texts. There are not many other sets of material from so basic a social level, but isolated cases certainly occur in collections from all over the Carolingian world. Estey's work on the Mâcon area of Burgundy and on Languedoc in the ninth century provides a number of examples; so does the eighth- and ninth-century St Gall material from Switzerland.[29] By implication, south Wales was similar: the 'surexit' memorandum, from the region near Llandeilo Fawr, records the initiatives of *degion*, literally 'good men' (cf. *boni viri* in continental texts), in the mid-ninth century; no rulers or their representatives are mentioned in the course of this famous settlement.[30] It

[26] Davies, *Small Worlds*, pp. 146–60.

[27] I am not suggesting that there were never settlements in rulers' courts; cf. the 806 settlement made by the abbot of St Gall, witnessed by 42 people, P. J. Geary, 'Extra-judicial means of conflict resolution', *Settimane di Studio*, 42 (1995), pp. 579–80.

[28] Robertson, ed., *Anglo-Saxon Charters*, no. 66, pp. 136–8.

[29] F. N. Estey, 'The *scabini* and the local courts', *Speculum*, 26 (1951), pp. 119–29 (cf. G. Duby, 'Recherche sur l'évolution des institutions judiciaires pendant le Xe et XIe siècle dans le sud de la Bourgogne', *Le Moyen Age*, 52 (1946), pp. 149–94, and 53 (1947), pp. 15–38); R. Sprandel, *Das Kloster Sankt Gallen in der Verfassung des karolingischen Reiches* (Freiburg, 1958), and McKitterick, *Carolingians and the Written Word*, pp. 79–126.

[30] D. Jenkins and M. Owen, 'The Welsh Marginalia in the Lichfield Gospels, Parts I and II', *Cambridge Medieval Celtic Studies*, 5 (1983), p. 51, and 7 (1984), pp. 91–120.

therefore seems reasonable to propose that the existence of small-scale, local courts was widespread in western Europe in at least the eighth to tenth centuries, even if they understandably do not feature as prominently in the record as do rulers' courts.

While serfs sometimes went to rulers' courts to claim free status, they cannot be found as judges or witnesses there;[31] nor are they found in these roles in local courts at this period. Although serfs moved about the peasant community, had households and families, and paid dues to peasant masters, they do not appear to have participated in community business in public:[32] if they went to meetings they did not speak at them; there is therefore no sign that they participated as members of the society in meetings which were constituted as courts. These people were pre-eminently 'unsuitable' as witnesses, sureties and judges. Hence, although the material allows us to perceive the operation of the legal process at a level far below that of rulers and high politics, it certainly does not show us a society in which people had equal status and participated in the rural community on equal terms. At local level participation in legal process was limited to the free, to those of good reputation and – overwhelmingly – to males: 'citizenship' was exclusive. This was a world that was a long way from the peasant idyll of equality for all at the heart of rural society.

III. WORKING THE SYSTEM

Reflecting on the questions posed at the outset, it is evident that early medieval courts did have their own rules and their own internal logics. What went on in an early medieval court could certainly be different from what went on in everyday life (insofar as we can perceive everyday life). It was different in the sense that the world of the court was for the most part only open to a proportion of the population, adult, male and free. Courts could be used to secure personal or institutional property rights, like the suits of the bishop of Freising in the late eighth century, and were thereby an instrument for securing personal advantage.[33] Courts could certainly be manip-

[31] For serfs in rulers' courts see, for example, the Italian cases discussed below, p. 60, and the peasants who went from Mitry in 861 to the court of Charles the Bald at Compiègne to protest that the monastery of St Denis was trying to force them to 'inferior service' when by right they were free *coloni*; J. L. Nelson, 'Dispute settlement in Carolingian West Francia', in Davies and Fouracre, eds., *Settlement of Disputes*, pp. 50–2. In such cases the peasants were clearly protagonists, not members of the court; and they clearly were of the view that they were *not* serfs.

[32] I am using 'serf' here to refer to the unfree; they could easily be classified as a type of slave, even if they were slaves who had their own households and control of their own labour on a day-to-day basis. See further W. Davies, 'On servile status in the early middle ages', in M. L. Bush, ed., *Serfdom and Slavery. Studies in Legal Bondage* (London, 1996), pp. 245–6.

[33] P. Fouracre, 'Carolingian justice: the rhetoric of improvement and contexts of abuse', *Settimane di Studio del Centro Italiano di Studi sull' alto Medioevo*, 42 (1995), p. 785:

ulated for political ends, at least to the extent that rulers' courts could be a means of expressing, and organising, political power.

Using the court for personal interest not only happened in rulers' courts. At local level in Brittany it is noticeable that members of a judgement panel could also act for the parties in a case: in 801 at Langon the six judgement-finders judged that the accused should clear himself with his own oath and with those of twelve oath-helpers; after that, three of those judgement-finders themselves stood as oath-helpers. Forty years later, at Avessac, six local elders provided evidence about property ownership (that is, they acted as independent expert witnesses in a case) and then two of them stood as sureties for the future payment of dues by one party. At about the same time, in Guer, four judgement-finders judged that a man had no claim on property and then two of them stood as surety that the man would make no further claim. A generation later, in 867 in Peillac, four men agreed to the future payment of rent after a dispute, and then three of them stood as guarantors for two of their own number: in other words, although they were parties to the dispute it was nevertheless acceptable for them to stand as sureties for each other.[34] None of this need constitute evidence of manipulation but it certainly indicates that some people knew how to play the system. A different though comparable point might be made of the witnesses of an earlier transaction called to appear at the Loire valley case of 857, who were persuaded to assert on oath that the document they appeared to have formerly witnessed had neither been confirmed by them nor properly corroborated.[35] By the time we reach the very well documented Domesday inquests of late eleventh-century England, we can see rival gangs of witnesses 'willing to swear on oath or undertake the judicial ordeal' and lords openly using their men as jurors. As Robin Fleming says, this material 'allows us a glimpse at the real-world politics that must have operated at every court in the tenth and eleventh centuries'.[36]

The world of the court was also different in the sense that what was 'just' to the court did not always meet the deepfelt sense of injustice of plaintiffs: the court *did* have its own, different, moral framework. Although peasants could cross the boundary between local courts and rulers' courts, and enter the higher arena, they could not necessarily work the system when they got there. The twenty-three peasants from Mitry who travelled sixty km to take their complaints about status to King Charles the Bald in 861 (along with eighteen women and their children, making a group of at least sixty-one

'Freising's use of courts to defend its interests may well have amounted to an abuse of judicial privilege.'

[34] De Courson, ed., *Cartulaire de Redon*, nos. 191, 61, 180, 96, pp. 147–8, 49, 139–40, 72–3.

[35] Nelson, 'Dispute settlement', p. 56, and Davies and Fouracre, eds., *Settlement of Disputes*, p. 234.

[36] Robin Fleming has some substantial new work on the nature and use of juries in Domesday England: Fleming, *Domesday Book and the Law*, ch. 1.

people), patently felt a deep sense of injustice. But they did not succeed in their complaint because they were defeated by the landowner, who marshalled counter witnesses. When Maurinus and his son went to the count's court in Pavia in 880 to protest that the monastery of Novalesa had reduced them to servitude, it was argued that they had been given a chance earlier in the year to produce witnesses to their freedom, but had failed to do so. Though the two men maintained insistently that they had been enserfed by force, the court judged that in default of witnesses or papers they were servile; a document to that effect was then prepared for the monastery.[37]

In other cases when peasants queried a monastic landlord's powers, texts were used against them, like the written estate survey produced in 828 to demonstrate conclusively that Cormery's peasants from Antoigné in Aquitaine were paying the customary rate, as established twenty-seven years previously, when the peasants maintained that rents were much too high and had recently been increased.[38] When a couple of years earlier ten men from Fiesso in Italy, led by a man called Martin, questioned the right of the abbot of Nonantola to exclude them from fisheries and pasture on the borders of Reggio, the monastery's advocate Reginald argued that the monastery had held exclusive rights for a long time and brandished documents recording a judgement by King Desiderius in the monastery's favour (*c.* 758). Martin and his fellows proclaimed the document false, but others testified that it was true and enquiries were then made of local men about amounts assigned to Fiesso. It was demonstrated that, despite King Liutprand's earlier grant of limited pasture rights to Fiesso men, Desiderius had subsequently granted exclusive rights to the monastery.[39] This case is interesting because the peasants did try to argue on the basis of text (they even took their own notary with them); but they were outmanoeuvred by superior dexterity with written evidence: their own document was invalidated by the later one.

In a world in which written evidence was admissible, it could be used against people who had neither the skill nor the experience to retaliate or who had insufficient skill to use the resource conclusively; if, like the *servi* of Limonta (near Lake Como) between 882 and 957, they made some attempt to influence the record and thereby limit the growing weight of exactions, they had very little chance of success.[40] The written text thereby

[37] Manaresi, ed., *Placiti*, vol. I, no. 89. Cf. the cases in the Trita valley in the territory of Valva in the Apennines in the late eighth century: C. Wickham, *Studi sulla società degli Appennini nell'alto medioevo* (Bologna, 1982), pp. 20–8.

[38] Nelson, 'Dispute settlement', pp. 49–50.

[39] Manaresi, ed., *Placiti*, vol. I, no. 36, pp. 109–13.

[40] R. Balzaretti, 'The monastery of Sant'Ambrogio and dispute settlement in early medieval Milan', *Early Medieval Europe*, 3 (1994), pp. 7–12; and *passim* for using writing as a weapon.

became part of the special apparatus of the world of the law. In cultures like the Irish the written text was so special that it could not reveal its meaning without professional elucidation: lawyers were essential for the understanding of legal text, which became ever more elaborately and arcanely glossed; legal language was so distinctive it was almost secret.[41]

In all of these ways the early medieval legal experience fits the framing, and does so very clearly. But the framing does not invariably suit every situation: at aristocratic levels it does so strongly; but at peasant levels it is much less so. At local, community level the procedures look as if they were accessible to anyone qualified to participate and seem to have been freely used by them (though we should remember that the qualified did not include all people of the locality). The world of these local courts did not have so distinctive and internal a logic (just as the drive to settle took precedence over the drive to operate the rules and proceed to judgement). Everyday life was not so different; and male, free peasants clearly used the court as a means of solving their own problems. At this level the world of the law does not seem to have been so morally distinct.

[41] The glossing of Irish law texts, and the nature of those glosses, is a clear demonstration that the language of law was not accessible to all; Kelly, *Guide to Early Irish Law*, pp. 225–35; cf. K. Hughes, *Early Christian Ireland: Introduction to the Sources* (London, 1972), pp. 44–6.

5. *Due process versus the maintenance of order in European law: the contribution of the* ius commune

PAUL HYAMS

It was one of the quirks of an otherwise marvellous, well-balanced conference programme, that Roman law was conspicuous mainly by its absence. Somehow this made its centrality to the western tradition all the more evident. It soon became obvious that early medieval law, even the law of ancient Greece, had much more in common with many non-western systems than the law of the modern West. The West's highly significant differentiation came as a result of cultural choices made in the period between the eleventh and thirteenth centuries which saw the revival of academic legal analysis for the first time since the end of the Roman Empire.

This bears closely on one of the lasting problems of international politics today. We increasingly experience confrontations between western nations and those of the so-called Third World over notions of human rights, corruption etc., which we in the West see as self-evident but which they sometimes characterise as western impositions unsuited to the conditions of their states. These misunderstandings are firmly rooted in formulations of the issues inherited from Roman law.[1] Not just the specific content of these rights but their whole orientation is very largely owed to legal ideas expounded by the classical jurists of the first centuries of our era, codified under Justinian in the sixth century, then taken up and developed in European law schools from the eleventh century onwards. They are now so deeply engrained into our culture that I for one frequently espouse the illusion of their indisputable rightness as passionately as anyone else and experience angry frustration at the inability of outsiders to see the

[1] Kenneth Pennington, *The Prince and the Law, 1200–1600: Sovereignty and Rights in the Western Legal Traditions* (Berkeley, CA, 1993), p. 90, cites Brian Tierney making very much this point. My interest in this topic and the written form of this essay owe much to my friend Ken Pennington and his admirable book. He has been trying to 'civilise' my thoughts on the law over the more than twenty years since our first meeting in the bowels of Boalt Hall Law School in Berkeley CA. Two other friends, David Seipp and Marie DeFalco, have been good enough to read drafts and make comments and suggestions that have certainly also improved the final product.

truth. So hard is it to see them for what they are, as context-dependent as any other aspect of our culture.

This essay traverses a wide and very diverse territory on a kind of armed pilgrimage. Its route will resemble most one of the great popular crusades of the thirteenth century that travelled far but got nowhere. It might be as well, then, to start by mapping the sometimes convoluted road to be travelled and some of the contours of the land through which we shall pass. I first sketch some of the main lines along which that 'civilian' influence (as insiders call Roman law) flowed into our laws and ways of thought. This is of quite as much significance to the United Kingdom and our Anglo-American common law as it is to continental Europe with its civil-law systems.[2] The *ius commune* of the twelfth to sixteenth centuries was the common inheritance of all westerners, a common standard of excellence against which all vernacular law was to be measured. I show how the medieval West acquired its *ius commune*, and outline its main characteristics (including its important and idiosyncratic theory of rights) and some of its consequences. In the second part of the essay, I turn to consider the confrontation of emerging western notions of due process with an at times equally strong sentiment in favour of law and order, the repression of crime. In conclusion I try to draw a few morals for the 'moral world of the law'. At every stage of the essay, I draw on appropriate legal maxims that encapsulate many of the points contemporaries thought worthy of special note. Because the legal maxim was so important a route for the transmission of ideas such as those treated here from the *ius commune* into the general legal culture of the West, I devote a final appendix to a sketch of its history and significance.

1. THE EVOLUTION OF THE *IUS COMMUNE*

The revival of law in written and thus analysable form began in the eleventh century. The goal of the newly revived schools was to teach and expound the law as it had appeared to the compilers of the *Corpus Iuris Civilis*, not to update it for the changed circumstances of the medieval day. In this they

[2] The arguments here are either European in scope or they are nothing. They need testing against German, French and, especially, Italian data. I illustrate them mostly from the English materials with which I have reason to be familiar. The common-law test has the merit of making the case for the importance of the *ius commune* in western law from the least promising of materials. And that is good scientific method. See on the origins of the 'Common Law' label F. Pollock and F. W. Maitland, *The History of English Law before the Time of Edward I*, 2 vols., 2nd edn reissued by S. F. C. Milsom (Cambridge, 1968), I, pp. 176–8, and further R. H. Helmholz, 'The Learned Laws in "Pollock and Maitland"', in J. Hudson, ed., *The History of English Law: Centenary Essays on 'Pollock and Maitland'* (London, 1996), pp. 145–70.

were quite successful. Thus no system of courts implemented Roman law directly in its pure schools form. The point, to demonstrate how law should ideally work, was most fully taken up by the Church's canon lawyers, who did have from the second half of the twelfth century courts and a whole programme of reform and discipline to implement in them. The canonists, indeed, adopted civilian principles and ideas so wholeheartedly as to justify our seeing medieval canon law as *ius scriptum* in action. This is the more important, since canon law developed powerfully in its classical period, from about 1140 into the fourteenth century, as much through the ingenuity of individual lawyers in the schools and courts as through the better known papal and conciliar legislation. Many secular laws were almost as enthusiastic recipients, the more successful coming from those southern areas (especially Italy and the French Midi or '*Pays de droit écrit*') where compatible legal customs already existed. A substantial degree of fusion resulted, especially of the two 'learned laws', but including also various borrowings from Italian and other practice. Lawyers came to refer to the principles they knew to be common to Christendom and the two learned laws as the *ius commune*.[3] This represented the Roman law legacy not merely as an organisational structure and a standard for other laws but also as a treasury of modular solutions to legal problems ready, as we shall see, to be slotted into receptive vernacular legal schemes. Despite some initial hesitations, canonists of the later twelfth century and after enthusiastically solved their problems with the help of civilian texts and insights. Quite soon the civilians too showed themselves happy for the most part to return the compliment and borrow canonistic ideas from the flood of innovation proceeding from the *ius novum* of papal and conciliar lawmaking.[4] The Italian cities, which used a law already deeply impregnated with Roman devices and institutions, naturally followed suit. Even the *droit coutumier* from north of the Alps swiftly felt the new influences and began a process of reshaping with Roman terminology and conceptual organisation, whose depth is perhaps not yet fully acknowledged.[5] Treatises like the so-called

[3] Pennington, *The Prince and the Law*, p. 6 and James A. Brundage, *Medieval Canon Law* (London and New York, 1995), pp. 59–61, 176–7 give brief characterisations of the *ius commune*. The most accessible and comprehensive account of the legal revolution in continental Europe is now Manlio Bellomo, *The Common Legal Past of Europe, 1000–1800* (Washington, DC, 1995), esp. chs. 3–5, 7. Bellomo provides for the inexpert like myself not only a good guide to Italian law but also, unfortunately, to the character of Italian legal historiography which appears, alas, to be almost as ill-informed about the Anglo-American Common Law (and other secular laws) as common lawyers are of the *ius commune*.

[4] See Brundage, *Medieval Canon Law* and Bellomo, *Common Legal Past,* on borrowings between the two laws and the emergence of *doctores utriusque iuris*.

[5] Bellomo, *Common Legal Past*, pp. 152–3 makes the point that most – he says all – writing about norms was done in Latin and so inevitably drew minds towards the formulations of the *Corpus Iuris Civilis*. This suggests a working hypothesis which I think I owe to my friend

'Bracton' in England, *c.* 1220, and a succession of *coutumiers* in thirteenth-century France could not have been written and cannot now be assessed without a daunting degree of learning in the learned laws. Such learned borrowing was much easier for jurists and legal writers than for lawyers in courts run by men dedicated to the maintenance of the customs of their fathers.[6] So substance lagged behind form on the southern side of the Channel as much as in England, where the gap between native practice and law-school learning progressively widened from the late thirteenth century on. Even so, it must have been unanswerably obvious in the later middle ages to any ambitious young man, hoping to use skills acquired at law school as his route to fame and fortune, that he must acquire not just one learned law but both. In a word, professional advancement and the chance to rise in the world came from mastery of both laws (*doctor utriusque iuris*) and of the *ius commune* as a whole.

All this legal learning rested on the foundation of a revolution in the teaching of legal principles and the organisation of court procedure commenced, and more or less completed, between 1075 and 1215. This encompassed a great deal more than the mere assimilation of Roman law texts for dissection in the schools. Its ramifications touch most corners of the European medieval experience. I confine my scope on this occasion to the impact of the *ius commune* on the lives of the mass of the people through the secular legal systems under which they had to live, and which could either guarantee or trample upon their individual civil rights. Roman law as the middle ages knew it was the law of a (Christian) empire. It is not immediately obvious what use this could be in medieval Europe. The (German) emperor was frequently at odds with the Church and patently incapable of playing any dominant role as sole sovereign of Christendom.

For the *ius commune* to contribute in any important manner to the

F. L. Cheyette. It seems likely that people first adopted from the Roman legal vocabulary impressive terms for existing legal institutions. In due course their successors better educated in the learned laws began to notice and question the dissonance between usage in 'real' written law (i.e. the *ius commune*) and that of their own customs under the same labels. This in turn set the scene for a further and more profound assimilation of learned legal concepts into local law. The inquiry to test this view, similar to that called for by R. J. Aubenas, 'Quelques réflexions sur le problème de la pénétration du droit romain dans le Midi de la France au moyen âge', *Annales du Midi*, 76 (1964), pp. 371–7, remains to be done, as far as I can tell. My own 'The Charter as a Source for the Early Common Law', *Journal of Legal History*, 12 (1991), pp. 173–89 examines the comparable changes in practice of property dispositions in England but quite ignores the possibility of law-school influence.

6 An excellent illustration is the refusal of the English barons in 1236 to accept the canonical rule for the legitimation of children by a subsequent marriage of their parents. Their rationale is said to have been that *nolumus leges Angliae mutare*. The classic account of F. M. Powicke, *Henry III and the Lord Edward* (Oxford, 1947), I, pp. 150–2 now needs some updating. See also D. J. Seipp, 'The Reception of Canon Law and Civil Law in the Common Law Courts Before 1600', *Oxford Journal of Legal Studies*, 13 (1993), pp. 397–8.

political environment, medieval jurists had first to recognise the political realities of their time.[7] The minimum requirement was some way to apply the legal powers, which Roman lawyers had ascribed to their emperor, to the secular rulers who exercised real authority in the kingdoms and city states of the middle ages.[8] Roman law treats government and authority at length. Its texts often say what the *princeps* can or cannot legitimately do. Some statements like 'the prince's will has the vigour (or force) of law' or 'the prince is loosed from the laws' were widely known in the middle ages far beyond the ranks of specialist lawyers and scholars. Many laymen could cite fragments of this kind to promote, perhaps, the supremacy of the king's sovereign will. In the schools matters were a trifle different. The *Corpus Iuris Civilis* was always read by minds convinced in advance that rulers held their offices on condition of good behaviour and subject to the pre-existing rights of their citizens and subjects.[9] But just who was this 'prince'?

Jurists long debated the applicability of texts concerning the *princeps* to contemporary figures. When the *Corpus Iuris Civilis* was compiled the reference was naturally intended for the Roman emperor alone. The great canonist Hostiensis was in the second quarter of the thirteenth century the first to apply *princeps*, not merely to the pope, which was not unprecedented, but also to contemporary kings, princes and even the podestàs of Italian cities. The acceptance during the second half of the century of this position, sealed in the maxim *Rex in regno suo imperator est*,[10] constitutes a notable recognition of the rising status of the emerging European nation-state.[11]

II. NOTIONS OF RIGHTS

This significant absolutist strand in thirteenth-century thought[12] was matched by a countervailing scrutiny of the limits of that authority. Kings had rights, and so did their subjects, both kinds of right demanding careful

7 Bellomo, *Common Legal Past*, ch. 4, '*Ius Proprium* in Europe', surely over-argues the case when he steps beyond Italy.

8 Pennington, *The Prince and the Law*, chs. 2–3.

9 Brian Tierney, '"The Prince is not Bound by the Laws": Accursius and the Origins of the Modern State', *Comparative Studies in Society and History*, 5 (1963), pp. 378–400.

10 Pennington, *The Prince and the Law*, pp. 31, 35 warns that there were other lessons drawn from this maxim besides the obvious one that a king should enjoy the same authority within his realm as an emperor in the empire. Cf. Bellomo, *Common Legal Past*, pp. 157–9.

11 This surely influenced the contemporary analyses of justice which were just at this time separating *haute justice* from lower forms to reserve it for princes and higher powers. On this subject, I still rely for the main lines on A. C. F. Koch, 'L'origine de l'haute et de la moyenne justice dans l'ouest et le nord de la France', *Tijdschrift voor Rechtsgeschiednis*, 21 (1953), pp. 420–34.

12 Pennington, *The Prince and the Law*, chs. 1–3 traces the fascinating way that the phrase *potestas absoluta* was transformed from a theologian's distinction concerning the nature of God's powers into a description of the absence (in principle) of limits to royal authority.

examination. Two lines of schools thought thus responded to such great issues of the thirteenth-century day as the challenge of heresy, and the difficulty of proving who were the heretics, with the aid of the same novel natural rights theories.

The notion that all individuals have by the fact of their live existence certain rights is not to be taken for granted. Historians traditionally regarded it as post-medieval. Most took it for granted that the central premises of western civilisation not already apparent in antiquity were to be sought in the Renaissance. Thus the search for the origins of western doctrines of subjective rights inevitably concentrated on the early modern period. The demonstration that we really owe our rights to high medieval lawyers is quite recent and came, I am proud to say, very largely from my Cornell predecessor and colleague, Brian Tierney.[13] He notes that the notion of subjective rights inherent in human beings *qua* human beings is 'a distinctively western invention'. The Greeks had nothing like it. Nobody could realistically suggest that the Ten Commandments conferred or recognised any such rights. Roman law, it is true, accepted the existence of an 'objective natural law', but never took the short step from treating dominion as a right to the recognition of a 'doctrine of subjective natural rights'. That most of the characteristic arguments of modern natural rights language can already be found in the middle ages is due almost entirely to canon lawyers. The process nicely demonstrates, indeed, the way that canon law functioned as a learned law that dealt with the real world, and so adapted civilian doctrine to the real-life situations that faced them in court and confessional.

'Medieval society was saturated with a concern for rights,' declares Tierney. Common sense (that most unreliable of guides) finds it hard to envisage an age when people in the West did not think and argue about rights. Men and women certainly talked on occasion about royal rights and their own property and ownership, to give just the obvious examples.[14]

[13] For the rest of this paragraph, I follow Brian Tierney, 'Origins of Natural Rights Language: Texts and Contexts', *History of Political Theory*, 10 (1989), pp. 615–46, collected with other pertinent papers into Tierney's *Rights, Laws, and Infallibility in Medieval Thought* (Brookfield, VT, 1997). The same author's new book, *The Idea of Natural Rights, 1150–1625* (Atlanta, GA, 1997) was not yet available.

[14] Latin words like *rectitudo* are used in context in coronation *ordines* and the like that imply something very like a right back into the tenth and ninth centuries. Most experts in the medieval vernaculars would concede that Old French *dreit*, Middle High German *Reht*, Old English *riht* and, probably also, the Italian predecessor to *diritto* could mean at least property rights back into the very early twelfth century, which may be as early as the vernaculars can take us. Susan Reynolds, *Fiefs and Vassals: The Medieval Evidence Reconsidered* (New York, 1994) constantly talks of property and other rights in her discussion of the early middle ages. Tierney's accomplishment makes a historical study of the lexicography of rights language a real priority.

There may, indeed, be little novel in the twelfth century about assertions of old rights or claims to new ones. But the previous arguments were usually oral and always short on analytical base. When a lord was faced with a decision between claimants petitioning for admission to his land as tenant around 1100, for example, men often said that he was determining the right (Old French *dreit*) to hold his land. But no one ever declared that his chosen tenant was the sole person with any right to hold that land. Instead he selected, with God's help (i.e. by a judicial duel), the claimant with the greater right (*maius ius*).[15] Here and elsewhere in everyday discourse Latin *ius* meant a subjective right, but not one easily susceptible of either real analysis or unaided human decision in court. The schools brought these vernacular notions of right into much sharper focus, to render feasible the more precise analyses now felt necessary. Canonists, in particular, were clearly aware of the major currents of schools humanism regarding individual intention and individual consent and brought these to bear for the first time on rights. The semantic muddle on *ius naturale* bequeathed to them by Gratian in his *Decretum* (1140/50) swiftly compelled them to make the effort to distinguish between the multiple meanings of key words like *ius*. These decretists (as those who lectured on Gratian are known) quite quickly engineered 'a decisive shift of emphasis' to an understanding of *ius naturale*, apparently for the very first time, as 'a subjective force or faculty or power or ability *inherent* in humans'. Aware of the centrality of free will in Christian life, they analysed their rights in terms of free choice exercised by individual human beings. Yet these were not atomised individuals licensed for the ruthless pursuit of their own interests. 'The first rights theories were . . . derived from . . . reflection on the right ordering of human relations in' an all too changeable world. One fruit of this Christian approach was the deduction from the duty of the rich to aid the poor a poor man's right to expect such aid. But in truth, by 1250 individual subjective human rights were so commonplace among canonists that natural rights analysis is everywhere in not just their writings but those of theologians and philosophers too. They sought their rights in every field of law and life, rights to property, to political consent and to marriage, but also rights to legal protections including a day in court for trial and due process while there.

[15] *Liber Eliensis*, ed. E. O. Blake (Camden 3rd ser., xcii, London 1962), p. 89 says of a female land litigant that, as against her husband and his heirs, she had *maius rectum . . . alterius viri coniugium*. When she arrived to finance a sale to the abbey of Ely, a claimant to part of the land turned up, and a complex set of negotiations ensued. While the text in this form comes from the twelfth century, it is known to follow at this point word for word an earlier Latin text, the *Libellus Æthelwoldi* which is itself translated from a lost Old English original. This probably takes the evidence back into at least a time in the early eleventh century when multiple rights to land were patently very much conceivable in eastern England.

III. PROTECTION FOR THE INDIVIDUAL

The profound 'legal revolution' effected between 1075 and 1215 encompassed a whole new set of legal procedures felt at the time to offer substantially greater rationality on account of their high, ancient and Roman authority.[16] This *ordo iudiciarius* was not drawn up in any way at random. It rather coalesced as part of the Church's struggle to liberate itself from the control of secular rulers and their barbaric legal systems. For all their Roman inspiration, the real point of the rules was originally to protect churchmen from the inequities of the thug justice of the lay courts. (*Curia a cruore* was the twelfth-century clerical quip; they call them 'courts' because of the blood, *cruor*, those laymen spill there!) The *ordo iudiciarius* was, therefore, intended both to defend churchmen from simple violence and to supersede irrational lay procedures, 'vulgar' proofs like the ordeals. The emphasis could be selective. Ordeals were, as befitted the judgements of God, sometimes appropriate to help convict those who resisted reform, while remaining always impermissible in trials of good clerics. The overall flavour of the new judicial order was, however, unmistakeably Roman, though including perhaps more trial rights than the classical jurists had allowed and thus enabling litigants to influence or even control the conduct of their trials.[17]

In the 1160s, the canonist, Stephen of Tournai, summarised the minimum requirements for the first time as follows.[18]

> That a defendant be called before his judge; that he be lawfully summoned to the case by 3 [normal] edicts or one peremptory edict;[19] that once summoned, he be permitted lawful delays; that the accusation be made with due formality and in writing; that lawful witnesses be produced; that no judgement be pronounced unless he is convicted or confesses; that the judgement must be in writing, unless the litigation be short and especially nasty.

One can measure the extent of progress made during the high middle ages by a comparison of this account with the fuller position of the later middle ages as stated in the early fourteenth century. Johannes Monachus (*ob.*

[16] Pennington, *The Prince and the Law*, p. 134.

[17] Ibid., pp. 135–6, 144 summarises the conclusions of Linda Fowler-Magerl, *Ordo Iudiciorum vel Ordo Iudiciarius* (Repertorien zur Frühzeit der gelerhten Rechte, Ius Commune, Sonderhefte 19: Frankfurt am Main, 1984).

[18] Stephen of Tournai gl. ad C. 2. 1 *an in manifestis*, cited in Pennington, *The Prince and the Law*, p. 143, n. 87 from Fowler-Magerl, pp. 27–8, n. 76.

[19] This was 'an official summons addressed to a defendant who refused to appear in court warning him that the trial would be conducted even in his absence', Adolf Berger, *Encyclopedic Dictionary of Roman Law* (Transactions of the American Philosophical Society n.s. 43.2, Philadelphia, 1953), p. 449.

1313) was, in his influential commentaries and glosses, the first canonist to subordinate even the pope to the full range of due process restraints.[20] He acknowledged that the pope was above positive law – he certainly made new law in his decretals – but was subject like anyone else to the precepts of natural law, which included many of the procedural regulations. 'Citation [i.e. summons] is from natural law and consequently the pope cannot proceed against anyone without a previous citation,' he asserted. So he cannot condemn without summons; even God had been prepared to summon Adam to trial in the Garden of Eden despite His omniscience which must have entailed foreknowledge both of the facts of the case and of Adam's guilt. This held even under the summary process for notorious cases, like that of the men of Sodom (Gen. 18.22–33), and in cases where the pope or his cardinals were in possession of private information proving the accused's guilt.[21] Johannes proclaims the presumption of innocence in almost modern terms ('Again everyone is presumed innocent **[innocens]** unless he is proven guilty **[nocens]**')[22] and goes on to assert that 'the law is more prompt to absolve than to condemn'.[23] So trial before an open-minded court must also precede condemnation. Even the Devil (so it was commonly said) had a right to his day in court.[24] To put it another way, there could be no default judgements in criminal cases.[25] The willingness of a loyal canon lawyer to subject the head of his Church and his legal system, God's vicar on earth, to such rules is really very remarkable. Sauce for such

20 Jean Lemoine was trained at Paris and died as bishop of Meaux. Pennington, *The Prince and the Law*, pp. 61–3 quotes the texts I paraphrase and cite.

21 Yet another maxim lies behind this, that 'a judge should judge according to the pleadings and not from his own knowledge'. Knut Nörr, *Zur Stellung des Richters im gelehrten Prozess der Frühzeit: Iudex Secundum Allegata Non Secundum Conscientiam Iudicat* (Munich, 1967) studies this much debated notion in detail.

22 See generally Richard M. Fraher, '"Ut nullus describatur reus prius quam convincatur": Presumption of Innocence in Medieval Canon Law', in S. Kuttner and K. Pennington, eds., *Proceedings. of the 6th International Congress of Medieval Canon Law, Berkeley 1980* (Monumenta Iuris Canonici, Series C. 7: Vatican City, 1985), pp. 493–506. A complete history of the presumption of innocence will need to treat also the parallel maxim from *Digest*, 48. 19. 5 which quotes Trajan as saying '*satius enim esse inpunitum relinqui facinus nocentis quam innocentem damnari*'. In some form such as that 'it is better that a guilty man . . . escape than that an innocent man be condemned', this tag worked against condemnation on suspicion without proof into the days of Voltaire and Blackstone. Rather few prosecutors and judges are likely to have been convinced by the presumption in this sharp form.

23 It is unlikely that we ought to take this statement quite at face value. The likely inspiration is the maxim *Semper in dubiis benigniora praeferenda* (*Digest*, 50. 17. 56), for which see also below at nn. 31–2.

24 Pennington, *The Prince and the Law*, pp. 151, 163, 192 cites some instances.

25 The prohibition of default judgements may not be absolute. Cf. above at n. 19, for the peremptory edict whose threat is precisely judgement in default of appearance. But the prohibition is entailed by the confrontation clause, as below, and mostly followed in secular practice, on which see for example Pollock and Maitland, II, pp. 594–5. A prohibition of default judgements on civil litigation would just about bring the courts to a standstill today.

a goose could give hope to even the meanest gosling, and efforts were made to implement the rules against the highest persons in even the most high profile, 'political' cases.[26]

Modern common lawyers know many of the very same rules and devices for the protection of accused people before their conviction. But where medieval lawyers mostly referred to the *ordo iudiciarius*, we talk of 'due process'. The origin of this phrase is not very well known. Its story is worth rehearsing here, even at the risk of a small digression, for one may extract from it some constructive contributions to our theme.[27] The familiar phrase first appeared in a 1354 statute of Edward III.

> That no man of what estate or condition that he be shall be . . . taken nor imprisoned nor disinherited nor put to death without being brought in answer by due process of law (*par due proces de lei*).[28]

What this meant at the time can be established with some confidence from other statutes that do and do not use the phrase. This seems to have been no more than 'the process [meaning legal procedures] which the person involved is entitled to receive'. The phrase itself may seem tautological. It certainly amounts to significantly less than the thrust generally given it today, although we must not forget that 'due process' remains living law still evolving in case law on both sides of the Atlantic.

The medieval phrase was already less simple than it seems at first glance. It grants rights to the generality of all inhabitants of the realm, all subjects of the king, but it does so through language focused on individuals and allowing room for individual or group differences in treatment. This seems to contradict the very premise of modern due process, that all share the same procedural rights. But modern law too discriminates, not explicitly between different categories of individual but in terms of some very subtle distinctions between differing situations analysed as to life, liberty and property. A great deal hangs on context. Nothing in either modern or fourteenth-century understanding of the phrase 'due process' prohibits the limitation of procedural privileges to those accused of notorious or manifest offences under the summary procedures to be discussed below. In the middle ages, everyone was entitled to the *ordo judiciarius*, but not

[26] Pennington, *The Prince and the Law*, chs. 5, 7 deal with this kind of *cause célèbre*, whose issues and the documents they generated, he argues, had an exceptionally wide and powerful effect on legal thought and practice.

[27] Pennington, *The Prince and the Law*, pp. 5–6 brought this to my notice, including the citation of Keith Jurrow, 'Untimely Thoughts: A Reconsideration of the Origins of Due Process of Law', *American Journal of Legal History*, 19 (1975), pp. 265–79, from whom (p. 265) comes the 1910 definition I quote in the text.

[28] Stat. 28 Ed III, ch. 3, *Statutes of the Realm* (London, 1810), I, p. 345. David Seipp tells me that the first Year Book reference he has found is *Liber Assisarum*, 42 Edw. III, pl. 5, fol. 258 from 1368; it instances indictment, suit of a party or 'other due process'.

necessarily at the same level. In the extremely hierarchical world of the earlier middle ages it seemed unnatural to suppose that everyone had the same dues, whether to process or anything else. So much turned on one's status. Clerics are the clearest case. Their *privilegium fori* exempted them from various kinds of process to which laymen were subject. Like exemptions, entitlements to favourable proofs, too, varied with gender, social status and previous reputation. In earlier secular contexts the word used for process or proof had been *lex*, as in the phrase to be worthy of one's 'law'. A man accused of grave offences for the *n*th time could not expect gentle treatment. His *lex* might be to carry the hot iron, while his co-defendant might be allowed to clear himself much less uncomfortably by a mere oath, as a first-time offender or a cleric.

This may well be, as some guessed long ago, the real context behind those most famous guarantees against arbitrary arrest and maltreatment in clause 39 of the 1215 Magna Carta. 'No free man is to be arrested or imprisoned or disseised or outlawed or exiled or in any way destroyed . . . except by legal judgement of his peers *vel per legem terre*.' This rule, that judgement had to be by one's peers and *per legem terre*, should arguably be read as a reference to appropriate proof, a real step in the direction of 'due process'. Magna Carta declared that the standard was thenceforth at least to be national not personal.[29] It applied within the realm (*terra*) to all free men alike. In future all free men within the realm – but not serfs – were to enjoy the protection of the 'law of the land'. This genuine advance in liberty must itself owe something to canonist thought on the *ordo iudiciarius* over the previous half century or so.[30]

Legal analysts trained in the common law often declare a belief that there is little 'real' law in crime. If they were right, we ought to depreciate the traditional applause for clause 39 as one of the great foundations of English liberty. Magna Carta only influenced subsequent law where the clauses were drafted (or redrafted) so as to enable lawyers to use them in the courts. *Ex hypothese*, criminal courts that lacked genuine legal argument can have made little out of the bare cloth of clause 39. Legal historians have always held that the rules of pleading already, well before the sixteenth century, gravely restricted the right of those accused of crime to plead in their own defence, and excluded them from access to legal counsel for help. David Seipp has, however, recently shown from the Year Books that this rule was

[29] I first assembled the relevant evidence in my *King, Lords and Peasants in Medieval England* (Oxford, 1980), pp. 128–30. What the consequences of the view in the text are for the unfree villein I am unsure. J. C. Holt, *Magna Carta*, 2nd edn. (Cambridge, 1992), pp. 6, 10, 327–31 is the best general discussion of Magna Carta and due process.

[30] A draft by R. H. Helmholz on 'The Origins of Magna Carta (1215) and the European *Ius Commune*', traces many canonistic influences behind other clauses of Magna Carta, but has nothing on cl. 39.

not yet law in the later middle ages. He has found many criminal cases reported there replete with legal arguments apparently pleaded in court by judges, prosecutors and defence counsel.[31]

Professor Seipp further believes that he finds 'a pro-defendant sentiment' running through the reports of criminal cases. This again goes against the weight of past opinion, which is prone to see on the English criminal bench not bleeding hearts but hanging judges and wretches hurriedly condemned that jurymen might dine. Seipp's suggestion is, of course, as he well knows, much less a comment on court practice than a deduction from texts never intended to enable their readers to take the temperature of law enforcement. As a professional literature designed exclusively for internal consumption, the Year Books most likely just reflect the self-image of the lawyers of their day. Their pious hope, for example, that the defendant should get the benefit of any doubt surely derives from such maxims of the *ius commune* as *benigniora praeferenda*.[32] However this may be, Seipp's revelation that there was indeed legal argument about process and procedural rights in fourteenth-century criminal cases lends a newly plausible context to the statutory recognition of 'due process'.

Many parts of the *ordo iuris* were in essentials much older than the twelfth-century revival of legal learning which first generated educated lawyers able to hammer them into appropriate shape for routine implementation in court. Two examples that nicely illustrate the lasting impact of the *ius commune* upon western legal culture are to be found within the US Bill of Rights, as parts of the Fifth and Sixth Amendments respectively to the Constitution.

The privilege against self-incrimination is much the better publicised of

31 D. J. Seipp, 'Crime in the Year Books', in Chantal Stebbings, ed., *Law Reporting in England* (London and Rio Grande, 1995), ch. 2, pp. 15–34. Seipp, pp. 22–4 cites the three early but widely separated cases (1302, 1406, 1469) that have been seen as implying the later rule. He also argues that the accused was first compelled to plead as to guilt before receiving access to counsel, so that the judges could gain an impression of his character and demeanour. If right, this is virtually a corollary to the thrust of the 'confrontation clause' discussed below.

32 Of course, good judges seldom do doubt the guilt of the lower-class villains who come up before them for dispatch. Yet they also argue in appropriate cases for the presumption of innocence. David Seipp pointed out to me a unique early example in *The Earliest English Law Reports*, ed. Paul Brand (Selden Society, vol. 111: London, 1996), 1283. 6, pp. 128–31 where different reports give the honour to different pleaders and judges! I have myself argued for a degree of procedural purity in the comparably prejudiced trials of personal freedom during the thirteenth and fourteenth centuries in my *King, Lords and Peasants*, ch. 12. This common-law *favor libertatis* was also demonstrably a matter of self-image engendered by Roman law texts and infiltrated into practice in maxim form by Bracton and other treatise writers. The same maxim from the *Digest* ('*Semper in dubiis benigniora praeferenda sunt*', *Digest*, 50. 17. 56) that may lie behind both trends was well enough known in England to be cited on occasion in the Year Books. On the whole subject, see Berger, *Encyclopedic Dictionary of Roman Law*, pp. 333–809, s. vv. *Benigne, Favor, Favor libertatis* etc.

the two but may be less central to our wider story. In the form, *nemo tenetur prodere seipsum*, the privilege certainly began its medieval currency at the very heart of the *ius commune* in the *Glossa Ordinaria* (or standard commentary) to Gregory IX's official collection of *Decretales* of 1234.[33] It seems to have been derived from a patristic text included by Gratian in his *Decretum* to the effect that no one is obliged to uncover his own shame.[34] Canonists mostly felt that the requirement could be by-passed in appropriate cases such as heresy accusations or where the prosecutor claimed reform rather than punishment as his goal.[35] The contention that this privilege is 'one of the great landmarks in man's struggle to make himself civilized' may need adjustment given that it is far from universally followed even among civilised western nations outside the United States.[36]

The English history of the maxim is both instructive and a little mysterious. It was certainly known and available for citation and use in the church courts of the fourteenth and fifteenth centuries. Yet the first actual citation in a royal court does not come until 1568.[37] The explanation is not the ignorance of the common lawyers but the fact that bare ideas, even clothed in maxims, carried no weight until they found their right context. 'Mightier than the sword', said Churchill, 'is the idea whose time has come.' John Langbein has argued persuasively for a long time lag. 'The true origins of the common law privilege', he contends, 'are to be found . . . in the rise of adversary criminal procedure at the end of the eighteenth century.'[38] He makes the powerful point that the procedure in criminal trials of the early modern period would have made any recourse to the privilege a virtual

[33] R. H. Helmholz, 'Origins of the Privilege Against Self-Incrimination: The Role of the European *Ius Commune*', *New York University Law Review*, 65 (1990), pp. 962–90 at 967, n. 26. M. R. T. MacNair, 'The Early Development of the Privilege Against Self-Incrimination', *Oxford Journal of Legal Studies*, 10 (1990), pp. 66–84 independently reached a similar conclusion about the canonical origins of the privilege (pp. 70–3) by a different and more summary route, with useful detail on the post-Reformation persistence of the canonical doctrines in England.

[34] Helmholz, 'Origins of the Privilege Against Self-Incrimination', pp. 981–2.

[35] Ibid., p. 985; H. A. Kelly, 'Inquisition and the Prosecution of Heresy: Misconceptions and Abuses', *Church History*, 58 (1989), pp. 439–51 at 447. The confrontation clause, discussed below, was also regarded as less than mandatory.

[36] The remark was made in 1955 by E. Griswold and is quoted without special comment by Helmholz (1990), p. 962. The relevant part of the Fifth Amendment runs, 'No person . . . shall be compelled in any criminal case to be a witness against himself,' and then goes on to echo cl. 39 of Magna Carta. England recognises no privilege in comparably absolute language; a judge may comment on an accused's choice not to testify and the jury may draw unfavourable inferences, David M. Walker, *The Oxford Companion to Law* (Oxford, 1980), p. 1129.

[37] Helmholz, 'Origins of the Privilege Against Self-Incrimination', p. 962. David Seipp supplies a second instance in 1587 (74 Eng. Rep., 645) in which the court adds 'yet in criminal cases he shall answer'.

[38] J. H. Langbein, 'The Historical Origins of the Privilege Against Self-Incrimination at Common Law', *Michigan Law Review*, 92 (1994), pp. 1047–85 at 1047.

guarantee of the accused's conviction. This is because the courts treated accused persons as a source, almost the sole source, of testimony. Much of the trial turned on the way that the accused was perceived to bear himself in 'altercation' with his accusers. He was permitted neither to summon witnesses on his own behalf nor to hire counsel to make legal arguments for him. Silence, whatever the dangers of self-incrimination, was procedurally suicidal. Not until the late eighteenth century did the various elements of the modern criminal trial come together in such a way to enable claims to the privilege to make sense to accused persons and their advisers. One important element of this, the requirement for proof beyond reasonable doubt, is especially noteworthy here. With hindsight that rule seems a mere reformulation of the maxim that enshrines the presumption of innocence. The step from the maxim to the rule appears to be very small, but until it was actually taken expectations of security were illusory.

Langbein's story has the ring of truth about it. It is, for example, very much congruous with the evidence about criminal law in colonial America.[39] It nevertheless remains a hypothesis awaiting test and proof, beyond reasonable and unreasonable doubt, and a twist or two may remain to be discovered. One potentially weak link in the straightforward narrative concerns the transition from middle ages to modernity. Criminal procedure in the fourteenth and fifteenth centuries may have differed from the norms under Tudor and Stuart monarchs. We have seen that some accused persons at least did have access to counsel. We cannot be quite certain that such cases approximated to Langbein's too simple 'Accused Speaks' model. Probably not. And with counsel able to make a case on the accused's behalf, his refusal to respond to accusations could have made strategic sense. One cannot therefore quite exclude the possibility that an occasional litigant might not have chosen to plead even with success the maxim *nemo tenetur prodere seipsum*. But this remains a relatively academic point in the present state of knowledge. The more important message of the episode is to underline the fact that mere notions of fairness, however attractively packaged in maxims, are likely to be ineffective until they are provided with procedural teeth.

The Sixth Amendment contains what is known as the Confrontation Clause. This enshrines the principle that nobody should be put to his defence without an opportunity to see and confront his accuser.[40] The

[39] Eben Moglen, 'Taking the Fifth: Reconsidering the Origins of the Constitutional Privilege Against Self-Incrimination', *Michigan Law Review*, 92 (1994), pp. 1086–1130.

[40] I take most of my account from Frank R. Heermann and Brownlow M. Speer, 'Facing the Accuser: Ancient and Medieval Precursors of the Confrontation Clause', *Virginia Journal of International Law*, 34 (1993–4), pp. 481–552. A Resident Alien myself, I recognise that readers may need to be reminded of the text: 'In all criminal prosecutions, the accused shall enjoy the right . . . to be confronted with the witnesses against him.'

underlying premise is pretty ubiquitous in learned as much as vernacular laws. The New Testament (Acts 25.16) shows that it was already Roman custom if not actual *ius* in the first centuries of our era. Scholars have been able to trace the progressive strengthening of formulation through Roman law, canons, and secular legal texts into the thirteenth century. The biblical authority often cited in support during the middle ages was the story of the woman taken in adultery (John 8.10–11).[41] No person should be compelled to defend his or her body unless an accuser appears to make the charge. Clause 38 of Magna Carta 1215 echoes this principle while adding two very important provisos: that an accuser must not simply be present but (a) show that he has a *prima facie* case (offer suit) and (b) put himself and perhaps his body at risk in the same way as the defendant is forced to do.[42]

But by 1215, the principle itself was, as it were, on the defence. The twelfth-century rise of public prosecution in both Church (*ex officio* by prelates) and State (e.g. indictment, presentment and the grand jury in England) seriously weakened the force of the principle, and the process continued during the penal revolution of the thirteenth century.[43] Obviously, the whole inquisitorial process, for example, was designed almost entirely to ensure that accusers did *not* have to confront their enemies in public. Ironically, the first known appearance of the word 'confront' (in Latin), to denote a face-to-face meeting, is in a late fourteenth-century inquisitor's handbook.[44] Secular laws certainly retained the principle that an accuser should be present in court but only too often breached the norm they claim to honour.

IV. PROTECTION FOR SOCIETY

Protections against arbitrary treatment by law and government are central to the western view of civilisation. Most of us (outside the US with its Second Amendment) are nevertheless uneasily aware that governmental power, with its claim to a near-monopoly of the means of violence, is also our guarantee of freedom. There are villains out there whose freedoms

[41] The intriguing aspect of this particular story is its absence from the other Gospels and even the original Greek text of John. Medieval scholars were aware of and grappled with the difficulty.

[42] I deal with Magna Carta, cl. 38 in context and at length in my forthcoming book, *Rancour and Reconciliation in Medieval England*, ch. 6. Helmholz, 'The Origins of Magna Carta (1215) and the European *Ius Commune*' also devotes a couple of sensitive and learned pages to the clause.

[43] Richard M. Fraher, 'Conviction According to Conscience: The Medieval Jurists' Debate Concerning Judicial Discretion and the Law of Proof', *Law and History Review*, 7 (1989), pp. 23–88 sees Thomas de Piperata (*ob.* 1282) as the pioneer; see also Helmholz, 'Origins of the Privilege Against Self-Incrimination', pp. 976–7.

[44] Heermann and Speer, 'Facing the Accuser', p. 536.

threaten those of the respectable residue. It is no accident that law is so often associated with order in popular parlance. Most ordinary folk are quite uninterested in the glories of legal science and have no understanding of what 'black letter' technicalities are about, beyond perhaps to mystify and defraud us honest folk. But all of us who possess even a modicum of property and position, want to keep them. We then seek two almost incompatible goals. We want vigorous prosecution of crime for the maintenance of good order, against 'them' to protect 'us', our families, our possessions and way of life. But we also expect the kinds of safeguards that I have just been discussing for our own liberties and innocence against mistaken or false accusations. We demand in short a level playing field in the American sense.[45] We want proper arrangements for us to get redress for our wrongs through our day in court, not to mention the occasional chance to get our own back (preferably with interest) on the perpetrators. We also expect our legislators occasionally to load the dice yet more heavily against groups we regard as a threat. Our emphasis can swing to and fro. When the talk turns to the need for quasi-military action against anti-social threats, then society favours the suspension of the kinds of due process protections we have been talking about, the lowering of requirements for successful prosecutions in the interests of some war against crime or heresy.[46]

The ruling minority had similar feelings over long periods of the middle ages. One of their number in the thirteenth century included among his definitions of *ius* (right) the wages you have earned, as one may say of a thief hanging on the gallows that he has had his due, his right.[47] The longings of the propertied classes for 'law and order' lie behind the pledges of good justice extracted from kings at coronations and other solemn occasions. 'It is in the public interest that crimes should not remain unpunished' is how the lettered ones put it, drawing on yet another Latin maxim.[48] The newly

[45] I sometimes feel that American football crowds would define a 'level playing field' very differently from, say, an English one at a cricket test match. They would expect a perpetual home field advantage in which the officials blow for penalties in the proportion of about two to one against the visitors, and crowd noise prevents the opposing players from hearing their quarterback calling the signals on crucial plays!

[46] See Lawrence M. Friedman, *Crime and Punishment in American History* (New York, 1993), and consider the common modern rhetoric of wars against drugs, crusades against organised crime etc. For the logic behind the other metaphor commonly used for repression in the name of law enforcement, therapy, a favourite in medieval moral writings, see Herbert Morris, 'Persons and Punishment', *The Monist*, 52 (1968), pp. 475–99, esp. 480–7.

[47] *La Summa de Legibus Normannie in curia laicali*, ed. E.-J. Tardif (Rouen and Paris, 1896), VI (I. 1. i. 4): *stipendium meritorum, secundum quod dicitur quod latro suspensus bene habuerit jus suum.*

[48] Richard Fraher, 'The Theoretical Justification for the New Criminal Law of the High Middle Ages: *Rei publicae interest ne crimina remaneant impunita*', *Illinois Law Review* (1984), pp. 577–95.

emerged 'persecuting society'[49] of the thirteenth century provided the political context for the successful efforts to shift the odds in favour of prosecution by legal innovations in the opposite direction from due process. Some had already been set in train in the twelfth century. Richard Fraher views as pivotal the turn of the century papacy of Innocent III (1198–1216)[50] whom he persuasively suggests to have crafted 'a concerted program . . . to impose hierarchical control over criminal procedure and to enhance the efficiency of criminal prosecution'.[51] He establishes his position from three Innocentian enactments to be read, he contends, as a group reflecting the will of the pope and his policy-making advisers. Though two of these come from the Fourth Lateran Council, all three ideas had been tried out by the pope in individual decretals before 1215. The first is inquisitorial process (IV Lateran, c. 8), the replacement of private accusers by judicial examination of the accused and others on oath. Next comes the prohibition of clerical participation in methods of trial of which the pope and his legal advisers disapproved (IV Lateran, c. 18), encompassing both judgements of blood (long forbidden by canon law) and trial by ordeal and duel.[52] And thirdly, Innocent modified the rules of the *ordo iudiciarius*, to admit the evidence of witnesses usually inadmissible in a broad category of exempt cases such as heresy, treason and simony.[53]

The ancient model for the prosecution of serious offences and dangerous sin, *crimina*, favoured two methods, *accusatio* and *denunciatio*. Neither was especially effective. The first depended on the willingness of an accuser to come forward. The second was geared more to secure penitence than as prosecution for punishment. Yet conviction could only be achieved either by the confession of the offender (patently the better option) or after proof by at least two witnesses. This had been foreshadowed, it will be recalled, by Stephen of Tournai in the previous generation. One could not

49 R. I. Moore, *The Formation of a Persecuting Society: Power and Deviance in Western Europe, 950–1259*, (Oxford, 1987).

50 The basic case is well argued by Richard Fraher in a series of articles. See in addition to the one noted above, n. 43, 'Preventing Crime in the High Middle Ages: The Lawyers' Search for Deterrence', in J. R. Sweeney and S. Chodorow, eds., *Popes, Teachers and Canon Law in the Middle Ages* (Ithaca, NY, 1989), pp. 212–33; and 'IV Lateran's Revolution in Criminal Procedure: The Birth of *Inquisitio*, the End of Ordeals, and Innocent III's Vision of Ecclesiastical Politics', in Rosalio Iosepho Card. Castillo Lara, ed., *Studia in Honorem Eminentissimi Cardinalis Alphonsi M. Stickler* (Rome, 1992), pp. 97–110.

51 Fraher, 'IV Lateran's Revolution in Criminal Procedure', p. 98. His argument is infused with an efficiency test for the repression of crime that is noteworthy as very foreign from American traditions of liberty descended from those canvassed earlier in this paper.

52 I may be permitted to point out once again that the prohibition actually covered only select unilateral ordeals (doubtless intended to be representative of all such) and the duel, and that duels nevertheless thrived strongly in the succeeding century.

53 I omit from consideration here as peripheral IV Lateran, c. 38 requiring written records to facilitate judicial review of judgements, which Fraher also adduced.

even place the burden of proof on a suspect, compelling him to clear himself by an exculpatory oath, unless a *prima facie* case were first established, a standard often hard or impossible to meet when the deed was done in secret. The facts had to be 'as clear as the light of day' (*luce clarior*).[54] All the smart villain needed was the courage to deny the deed and his guilt and keep on doing so.[55] The system's bias against default judgements converted flight into an even more effective defence in an age when jails were still relatively few and often insecure and there was no police force to trace and pursue a fugitive.

For right-thinking people, then, the case for some kind of aid to the prosecution in cases where the burden of proof 'ought' to be placed on the accused was simply the other side of the due process coin. Secular rulers turned in the course of the thirteenth century to physical coercion in order to secure convictions, sometimes extracurial violence but often institutionalised. The torture route must be discussed in a moment. Another was the *peine forte et dure,* the device used from the end of the century to induce English suspects to assist court proceedings by pleading not guilty and submitting their fate to a jury verdict.[56] The Church created two sophisticated alternatives of its own, first summary process and, second, the inquisition.

Summary process circumvented the full requirements of the *ordo iudiciarius*. It was promoted to deal with precisely the kinds of notorious or manifest offenders[57] who had no good claim to shelter behind the *ordo iudiciarius*. A Christian's first duty in such cases was to confess (*in foro interno*) and to purge himself of the wrong. His neighbours ought to do their best to encourage such obvious sinners to carry out their duty for the good of everyone's soul. The end effect of this perniciously plausible logic was to squeeze out protections for the accused. Respectable canonists like the redoutable Hostiensis had gone so far at

[54] Fraher, 'Conviction According to Conscience', p. 24.

[55] Richard Firth Green has noticed this strategy in *Placita Corone*, ed. J. M. Kaye (Selden Society suppl. vol. 4, London, 1966) and deduced from it (in the annual panel on 'Law as Culture in the Middle Ages', which Richard Kaeuper and I put on for the American Society for Legal History at Kalamazoo) that villains could have used the work as a guide to beating the rap. The flat denial strategy survived a long time; see, for instance, Miguel de Cervantes, *The Adventures of Don Quixote*, tr. J. M. Cohen (Harmondsworth, 1950), p. 173.

[56] H. Summerson, 'The Early Development of Peine Forte et Dure', in E. W. Ives and A. H. Manchester, eds., *Law, Litigants and the Legal Profession: Papers Presented to the Fourth British Legal History Conference at the University of Birmingham, 10–13 July 1979* (Royal Historical Society, London, 1983), pp. 116–25.

[57] Brundage, *Medieval Canon Law*, ch. 6 is a readable outline guide to canonical procedure with good indications of the relevant literature. I ignore here the important differences between *notoria* and *manifesta*. Richard Kay, 'Roman Law in Dante's *Monarchia*', in Edward B. King and Susan Ridyard, eds., *Law in Medieval Life and Thought* (Sewanee, TN, 1990), pp. 259–68 at 262–3 explicates the origins of the maxim *manifesta probatione non indigent*.

one stage as to claim that one might in cases of scandal, involving dangers to the salvation of other believers, or danger to the state, licitly omit even the formal summons.[58] How far the streamlining would go was in doubt into the fourteenth century when minimum limits were set at a less unreasonable level, along the lines set out by Johannes Monachus and outlined above.

The inquisition is one of the very few institutions of the *ius commune* that can count on modern media appeal.[59] The word *inquisitio* itself means no more than investigation, questioning. The inquisition process had two main components. It was first an extension of office prosecution by an ecclesiastical judge, that is, a prosecution made on the judge's own initiative, *ex officio*, as part of his duties and overall responsibility for his flock. Office prosecutions were even in the twelfth century a rapidly growing phenomenon already reaching a new scale of operations that was beginning seriously to affect lay practices.[60] The key novelty was the questioning of sworn witnesses, separately and in secret. This power of the judge extended to similar interrogation of the accused himself, perhaps to see if he could be lured into incriminating himself. This kind of 'fishing expedition', as modern lawyers call it – precisely the reason why the US has its privilege against self-incrimination – was, strictly speaking, an abuse. For many inquisitors it nevertheless became established custom.

The whole procedure seems in direct opposition to the painstaking efforts of the twelfth-century schools to construct the *ordo iudiciarius*. Some justification was needed. As always, the challenge was to make the new appear traditional, by basing it on good authority. The best Innocent and his advisers could devise was apparently the story of Susanna in which the accusations of the prurient elders were exposed by their separate examination followed by a comparison of their stories.[61] Nothing in the biblical anecdote, however, justifies the inquisition's standard practice of keeping each witness in ignorance of the others. This was allegedly done so wit-

[58] Fraher, 'IV Lateran's Revolution', p. 104.

[59] I refer here to the papal inquisition not the more notorious Spanish and Roman inquisitions of the fifteenth century. B. Hamilton, *The Medieval Inquisition* (London, 1981) is a very readable introduction with some account of legal procedure in chs. 4–5. Edward Peters, *The Inquisition* (London, 1988) deals with the medieval inquisition with comparable brevity and shows more interest in the law, esp. in ch. 2 and pp. 11–17.

[60] R. C. Van Caenegem, 'Public Prosecution of Crime in Twelfth-Century England', in C. N. L. Brooke *et al.*, eds., *Church and Government in the Middle Ages . . . Essays Presented to C. R. Cheney* (Cambridge, 1976), pp. 41–76.

[61] R. M. Helmholz, 'The Bible in the Service of Canon Law', *Chicago-Kent Law Review*, 70 (1995), pp. 1557–81 at 1573; Heermann and Speer, 'Facing the Accuser', pp. 515–22. The story was extracted from the book of Daniel (which is where it is found in the medieval Vulgate) and made literally apocryphal after the Reformation. For an early twelfth-century reference that draws the obvious moral *against* false prosecutions, see the story of Bricstan in *Liber Eliensis*, ed. Blake, p. 267 and also in Orderic Vitalis.

nesses would not be scared to tell the truth but must more often have had the opposite effect.

The inquisition undoubtedly raised conviction rates, especially for *occulta*, the kinds of secret or unwitnessed crimes where human certainty was unavailable.[62] Progressive secular governments all over continental Europe adopted the new and improved method of public prosecution.[63] The papal inquisition was probably not in the middle ages quite as repressive as legend has it.[64] Before the sixteenth century it mostly took the form of somewhat *ad hoc* commissions, without permanent institutional form. The accused were accorded the normal presumption of innocence. They had the rights to consult lawyers, to benefit from the usual trial procedure and to appeal conviction in much the normal fashion. Such was at least the position in law and principle.

What transpired in actual practice may have differed. The Church felt itself under threat and therefore justified in licensing activist judges to hector and harass, to do what it took to achieve the desired confession. Some jurists so over-rode their due process sentiment that they freed judges from the old rule that had prohibited the use of private information and restricted courts to the consideration of facts introduced publicly by the pleadings.[65] To encourage judges to use their initiative to seek out guilty men and women without too much worry concerning the means used endangers the whole community of believers. The end result is all too likely to resemble Judge Jeffries.

The old ordeals had once enlisted God's omniscience to deal with the threatening, hard cases. The Lateran Council removed this option for churchmen in 1215. Among the possible substitutes human ingenuity suggested was torture. It was not the sole response to the challenge presented by the Church's vehement expression of its disapproval of ordeals in 1215.[66]

[62] God's omniscience had come in handy in such cases. See Stephan Kuttner, 'Ecclesia de Occultis non iudicat', in *Actus Congressus Iuridici Internationalis, Romae . . . 1934*, vol. III (Rome, 1936), pp. 227–46.

[63] England is again the odd man out here, which may help to explain its low conviction rates in the later middle ages. But other good reasons have been proffered for these, and no study that I know of has compared conviction rates in the rest of Europe. R. H. Helmholz, 'The Early History of the Grand Jury and Canon Law', *The University of Chicago Law Review*, 50 (1983), pp. 613–27 treats the debt owed to canon law by England's version of public prosecution with characteristic economy and insight.

[64] Kelly, 'Inquisition and the Prosecution of Heresy', pp. 444–6.

[65] Fraher, 'Conviction according to Conscience', pp. 38–9, 53 and n. 243 shows that this started from the emergency powers accorded to temporary magistrates by Italian cities.

[66] Nor does the chronology of recourse to torture necessarily support the obvious view (as Hyams, 'Trial by Ordeal: The Key to Proof in the Early Common Law', in M. S. Arnold, T. A. Green, S. A. Scully and S. D. White, eds., *On the Laws and Customs of England: Essays in Honor of S. E. Thorne* (Chapel Hill, NC, 1981), p. 126) that torture entered respectable court practice as a substitute for the ordeals. Pennington, *The Prince and the Law*, pp. 157–60

The jurists could and did develop more flexible rules of proof, often involving the use of *fama*, a device that enabled them to use public reputation as an indication of likely guilt. In the course of the thirteenth century, they carefully reinterpreted this *fama* to fill the role of the 'undoubted *indicia*' required by Roman law and thereby justify the practice of the Italian city states amongst which they lived and worked. In doing so they had to step delicately around the imputation that *fama* was just another word for hearsay evidence, which Roman law banned.[67]

These procedures for summary and inquisitorial process against crime seem to lead inexorably towards judicial torture. Yet, according to Richard Fraher, 'every jurist knew that torture represented a dangerous investigative device, one that produced confessions regardless.'[68] They reserved its use to extreme cases, a last resort much as the ordeals had once been, licit only where 'vehement presumptions' of guilt already existed. They scrupulously analysed the degree of evidence, *indicia*, required to establish a presumption of guilt. The paradigm case conveys their ambivalence and discomfort well. It was a room with only one exit, a door from which witnesses saw a man leaving brandishing a bloody sword. When they entered, they found a man dying or dead from sword wounds. If the swordsman refused to confess, he could not under the older rules be convicted, for nobody had witnessed the act. In such a case, said jurists like Thomas de Piperata (*fl.* 1265/1282), torture was licit and appropriate. Italian colleagues adopted his viewpoint while repressing its author's name as that of a 'jurisprudential pariah'. Most justified torture in terms of the public interest and the deterrence of others tempted to offend, but some at least recognised that they were arguing as much for *in terrorem* coercion or even punishment as for an investigative tool. Just how widespread a fact torture was in later medieval Europe and from when remains uncertain in the present state of research. England is again the exception that 'proves' the rule. Though later medieval Englishmen doubtless shared all the worst personal characteris-

footnote 66 (*cont.*)
takes a sceptical attitude towards the evidence for early routine use of torture before the very late thirteenth century. Pennington very properly regards the whole phenomenon as an 'unfortunate' consequence of the revival of Roman law but his arguments as to timing fail as yet to convince me. Though it is true that the evidence for early court use is scarce, he himself cites (42–4) an Italian critique from the 1220s of those city podestàs who already use torture in cases where it is in breach of *mandata legis . . . secularis*. The demand for full textual proofs would cast doubt on many other contentions in this field, pending fuller investigation of all the archives for descriptive materials. Pennington seems uneasy with the thought that torture might share a single birth period with due process. I have argued above that this can make very good sense to respectable folk who see torture as being for the villains and due process reserved for themselves.

[67] Fraher, 'Conviction according to Conscience', pp. 28–30, 32f.

[68] Ibid., pp. 28–9. The rest of this paragraph largely follows ibid., pp. 32–48.

tics of their continental neighbours, and were certainly as capable as they of violent oppressions including judicial executions for political ends, their courts did not in the medieval period incorporate torture into the routine of criminal justice.[69]

V. ENQUETES A POURSUIVRE

This essay has focused on one of the central dilemmas that faces the citizens of any democratic society – the tension between the twin desires for personal liberty and personal security. From this undoubted tension we want our legislators and judges to strive for a settled and just balance. At least our cherished western values impel them to try, even if the attempt never succeeds in getting the balance quite right. That the main lines of our solution should have been laid at a time of such restricted democracy is striking enough.[70] But there are other more subtle lessons for the historian to take away from studying the medieval stage of the process. Due process is the legacy as much of the self-interest of respectable people from the ruling classes of medieval Europe as of any pure doctrines of freedom. Yet the thrust towards conviction of society's undoubted villains abundantly supports, I fear, the maxim that 'hard cases make bad law'.[71] But why, when civil law aims in principle to establish truth wherever the quest may lead, does criminal law seem designed more to reassure prosecutors and society in general that the villains they are going to put away really deserve what they get?[72]

There is rich material here for further study. I end with three suggestions among many. Consider first the legal maxims with which my text is studded. These were not merely random adornments but served as a major route for the influence of the *ius commune* into medieval secular law and on into the law of the modern West. To explain the diverse uses made of these maxims in the legal discourses of the various European systems would certainly

69 The convention by which the *peine forte et dure* (above at n. 56) is not interpreted as torture seems questionable. Can we really distinguish defensibly between coercion to make the 'free' choice to place one's life, liberty and inheritance on a jury from the judicial torture practised in wild lands across the Channel? One also wonders what to make of references to torture like that in Chaucer's *Man of Law's Tale*, ll. 885–9 (*The Riverside Chaucer*, ed Larry D. Benson, new edn, Oxford, 1988, pp. 99–100).

70 Pennington frequently remarks on this in *The Prince and the Law*.

71 This much-used maxim is to be found, for example, in *Black's Law Dictionary* (revd. 4th edn., St. Paul, MN, 1968), p. 847, s.v. 'hard cases', but the citations are to American cases only. I have traced this much-used maxim back only as far as Lord Tenterden, C.J. (*ob.* 1832). It may well be an example of a native English coinage *iuxta exempla Romanorum*. David Seipp suggests an analogy in the maxim *summa ius, summa iniuria* from Cicero, *De officiis* 1.33, which circulated among the glossators.

72 Cf. Fraher, 'Conviction according to Conscience', p. 52: 'criminal proof, in its essence is the fact-finder's certainty, and not an objective calculus'.

advance scholarship well beyond the restricted field of legal history. It will surely help to delineate, for example, the extent and the boundaries of the law's autonomous domain within western culture, and contribute also to our understanding of what is and is not unique about the West. I say a little more of this in the appendix.

Then there are the lawyers themselves. The emergence of a new breed of schools-trained lawyers may claim to be one of the most important consequences of the medieval legal revolution. We know most about the law-school professors themselves, the jurists whose glosses and treatises inform us about the intellectual advances in legal analysis and conceptualisation. But every advance widened the gap between legal discourse and everyday speech, to feed a demand for learned 'translators' which the schools avidly sought to satisfy.[73] Unfortunately, historians of the *ius commune* have lacked the materials for the study of case law, and perhaps also the interest to illuminate imperfect practice as opposed to the beauties of scientific jurisprudence. Information on practitioners of the two laws is consequently hard to come by.[74] We know a great deal about their schools training, far less about their professional organisation and accessibility to potential clients, and very little so far of the profit they drew in advising clients and argument in court.

On the occasions when we are unfortunate enough to come into court under the shadow of a traffic offence let alone a real criminal charge, we expect something more from our advocates. They should not only make the case for our defence; they should also have the necessary skills for dismantling that of the prosecution. The most crucial of these may well be cross-examination: 'the greatest legal engine ever invented for the discovery of the truth' as a modern common-law jurist has called it.[75] It is certainly a staple in the common-law system with its adversarial process. It is, I presume, much less so in continental systems of more inquisitorial bent. Why, one wants to know, was an adversarial process in criminal causes so slow to develop even in England and a non-starter elsewhere in Europe? In its absence, the skill of oral sparring never became routine in medieval courts,

[73] I take this image from Jack Goody, as indicated in my 'The Charter as a Source from the Early Common Law', *Journal of Legal History*, 12 (1991), pp. 173–89, esp. p. 184.

[74] I know no equivalent in English to Paul Brand, *The Origins of the English Legal Profession* (Oxford, 1992), ch. 9 of which is a model study on English canonists and has a good deal to say about practice. J. A. Brundage, 'The Rise of Professional Canonists and the Development of the Ius Commune', *Zeitschrift der Savigny-Stiftung für Rechtsgeschichte: Kanonistische Abteilung*, 81 (1995), pp. 26–63 signposts the way forward, and makes the claim that canon lawyers may have been the first group *c.* 1250 to create a profession in something like the modern sense; see also his *Medieval Canon Law* (London and New York, 1995), pp. 59–69, 135–8.

[75] This is from Wigmore's treatise of *Evidence*, cited by Heermann and Speer, 'Facing the Accuser', p. 544.

or at any rate is never routinely recorded. And yet the notion was neither difficult nor unfamiliar in the schools. Abelard's famous remark in his introduction to his seminal collection of conflicting opinions from the Fathers, *Sic et Non*, has been said virtually to have launched early scholasticism. 'Assiduous and frequent questioning', he said, 'is indeed the first key to wisdom . . . for by doubting we come to investigation (*inquisicio*!) and through investigation we grasp the truth.'[76] This kind of amazing faith in the powers of human reasoning featured prominently in the early stages of the twelfth-century renaissance. Lawyers were as over-confident as any other group. Much of the foregoing essay shows this, not least the way in which thirteenth-century jurists and legislators set to work to think out human substitutes for God's judgement after the effective demise of the ordeals in 1215. At much the same time, church leaders were deploying naked human reason against the parallel problem of forged documents with somewhat mixed results.[77] Popes and canonists led the way to set up procedures to test familiar kinds of document, while mouthing a cynical quip that seems to have been traditional at the papal court: since documents were simply the skins of dead animals, why trust them above the word of a living man?[78] The same brainpower could have been used orally in the courtroom against witnesses on oath, to establish in the open before others, as with a modern jury, the inconsistencies and outright impossibilities that can demolish otherwise damning testimony. One would expect that cross-examination would appeal to men who shared the kinds of bias towards private initiative that lay behind the confrontation rule. Pierre Ayrault, reading in sixteenth-century France the same civilian juristic sources available throughout the middle ages, found precedents enough and the incentive to make something of them.[79] But the thrust of thirteenth-century advances lay as we have seen in other directions and towards greater control in the name of the public. Canonical judges did examine witnesses but not

[76] Beryl Smalley, *Studies in Medieval Thought and Learning* (London, 1981), ch. 1, '"Prima Clavis Sapientiae": Augustine and Abelard' shows how Abelard improved upon a remark of St Augustine in this passage.

[77] See Brundage, *Medieval Canon Law*, p. 133; M. T. Clanchy, *From Memory to Written Record*, 2nd edn (Oxford, 1993), pp. 323–7.

[78] Brundage, *Medieval Canon Law*, p. 133 cites this from Innocent IV's Apparatus to the Decretals of 1234. Compare with this the account of Eadmer, *Historia Novorum*, ed. M. Rule (Rolls Series: London, 1884), p. 138 (= Geoffrey Bosanquet, tr., *Eadmer's History of Recent Events in England* (London, 1964), p. 146) of an early twelfth-century hearing at the Roman Curia, at which Canterbury's opponents are said to have argued in favour of oral testimony on the grounds that the (forged) bull on which they chiefly relied was only 'a sheepskin marked with black ink and weighted with a little lump of lead'. W. L. Wakefield and A. P. Evans, *Heresies of the High Middle Ages* (New York, 1969), p. 81 reports a heretic's complaint in 1022 against 'the fictions of carnal men scribbled on animal skins'.

[79] Heermann and Speer, 'Facing the Accuser', pp. 485–9, 540–3.

generally in public before other judges of fact. The examination of witnesses existed in the earlier years of the English common law but had almost disappeared by the age of the Year Books.[80] Perhaps also the scholastically trained jurists remained less confident of their students' ability to deal with villains in open court amidst the real world than to make critical readings of texts in the shelter of the study. If so we may sympathise but at the same time deplore the long-term consequences of their academic reticence.

APPENDIX ON MAXIMS

The emergence of the legal maxims[81] of western Europe is an essential premise behind the developments sketched in this paper and played a very significant role in the overall growth of a distinctively western law. The impulse to collect and use maxims reached European vernacular laws through the schools of the two learned laws. Professors in the medieval law schools selected texts from the body of ancient sources of the two laws that reached them. It was often they who gave to the selected tags and fragments something like the more easily memorable form in which they were absorbed into legal discourse. Wherever courts cited maxims, they did so in Latin, irrespective of the local languages of pleading and everyday life. They were the means by which the law schools offered a treasury of learning in easily digestible soundbite form, as if to cater for the practising lawyer's every need. This is why they appear so frequently at each stage of the story sketched above. The phenomenon deserves a book-length study of its own. It may help to set out here the bare bones of the story as well as it can be understood now.

Experts tell us that it was in the late classical period that Roman jurists began to apply the word *regula* to a new kind of proposition. It now denoted 'maxims so abstract that no relation with a concrete situation is discernible . . . a catch-phrase for use in legal argument, it indicates a broad general principle which pervades various branches of the law.'[82] In English law, rules survive only until a judgement against them. Once a court has

80 Pollock and Maitland, *History of English Law*, II, pp. 609–10; also Henry Summerson, 'Criminal Law in the Age of Bracton', in Hudson, *Centenary Essays on Pollock and Maitland*, pp. 133–4.

81 The word 'maxim' reached English in the fifteenth century from French where it is found from about 1330. It derives from the Latin phrase *maxima propositio* by which medieval philosophers referred to a fundamental axiom.

82 Peter Stein, *Regulae Iuris: From Legal Rules to Legal Maxims* (Edinburgh, 1966), p. 105. Stein gives to the evolution of some extremely subtle jurisprudential distinctions and processes over a very long period the most disarming appearance of comprehensibility. Pennington, 'Maxims, Legal', in Joseph R. Strayer, ed., *Dictionary of the Middle Ages* (New York, 1982–9), VIII. pp. 231–2 adds references to more recent literature.

found against a rule, it is thereafter as if it had never existed, or certainly never represented good law. Yet these *regulae* of the *ius commune* bear more than a superficial resemblance to legal principles, like those derived from the US Constitution, which no adverse judgement can destroy. Such principles wax and wane in their force and power with each success and failure against other, often contradictory principles.[83] This makes maxims worth learning by heart, and particularly useful in case argument, not least to disguise the weakness of a client's case. Medieval legal maxims most characteristically took this second form. Their ability to change shape and meaning through time gave them great staying power.

In late antiquity, the importance of all this lay largely in the future. A legal system staffed by able, well-educated practitioners had no need of short-cuts and simplifications. The first requirement for the growth of maxims was an impoverishment of legal culture such as followed the demise of Roman government in the West. Even then a number of conditions had to be met before maxims became prominent. First, there had to be a body of maxims worthy of citation. The sixth-century emperor Justinian invited his commissioners, towards the end of their great work of codification, to collect *regulae* for a final title with which to end his systematic *Digest* of juristic opinion. In this title (*Dig.*, 50. 17), they gathered 211 fragments of which only a minority are to be found elsewhere in the *Digest*. Most are so phrased as to suggest universal application; many start with *omnis* or *nemo*. They carry an explanatory air about them. They most often address questions of interpretation and procedure. And, though nobody now can say with confidence what exactly they were intended to do at the time, very many of them are the answer to an advocate's prayer, just the kind of thing with which to deck out an otherwise bald and unconvincing plea.[84] There they remained ripe for future development at the very end of a *Corpus Iuris Civilis* that was almost unknown in the West until its rediscovery in eleventh-century Italy.

Their time came in the twelfth century, when law teachers in the revived schools turned once more to the work of generalisation and analysis, and were once more concerned and able to relate the different parts of the system to each other in ways that made possible a workable legal education. Twelfth-century schoolmen early turned to the characteristic scholastic

[83] R. Dworkin, *Taking Rights Seriously* (London, 1977). The American legal scholar, keen at the time to make progressive, activist use of constitutional amendments, constructed this system of legal principles as a counter to H. L. A. Hart, *The Concept of Law* (London and Oxford, 1961), whose English author viewed law as of a body of rules, not totally unlike those manipulated by the judges of the English common-law courts. Thus even these two pre-eminent legal scholars, arguing from philosophical principle, seem in the end to follow the custom of their own legal systems.

[84] Stein, *Regulae Iuris*, pp. 114–23.

method permanently associated with them. They looked to pit contrary principles against each other around some knotty hypothetical situation or problem, and then to present in turn the arguments from reason and authority for each, in quest of a convincing solution. The lawyers' version of this exercise in disputation revolved around statements of a kind sometimes called a *brocarda*, but also known by the more indicative title of a *generale*. Views of the essential nature and significance of these differed. One area of disagreement concerned the significance of exceptions to the general rule. Must an exception inevitably defeat a rule or could a rule that covered enough cases to be of value survive the discovery of a few anomalies? The better view came to be that *Exceptio probat regulam in non exceptis*, the source for that perplexing and absurd nursery tag that 'the exception proves the rule'.[85] This maxim explains the status of maxims in general; they are generalisations that can stand exceptions.

Medieval law schools accepted that their rules derived from underlying principles quite frequently themselves represented by maxims. This was a highly significant concession, since they went on to hold that where new situations shared their *equitas* with one that was already settled, the old rule made, as it were, new law. The maxim *Ubi est eadem ratio, ibi est idem ius* and the principle behind it were in this way recognised as a norm.[86] Patently, this kind of meta-principle was a boon to jurists intent on assembling their scattered materials into a scientific system.[87] It established the possibility of consistent principle and predictability of judgement in much the way we attribute today to the modern doctrine of precedent.

The doctors of the early *ius commune* apparently found maxims so attractive that some wondered whether the deeper purpose of the *Digest* title containing the *regulae iuris* (*Dig*., 50. 17) was not to summarise the essential truths of the whole collection. Learn these and you had it all! This amazing notion, for which there is some very slight warrant in the text itself, gradually hardened into a students' commonplace.[88] Meanwhile Pope

[85] The formulation that won lasting approval and is quoted in the text is that of Bartolus in the fourteenth century. The basic idea was already present in the twelfth century and was probably given currency by Accursius' gl. ad '*regula est*', *Digest*, 50. 17. 1 in his Ordinary Gloss (standard commentary) of 1229/34. All this comes from Stein, *Regulae Iuris*, pp. 139, 143, 152. Once upon a time, I wanted to translate *exceptio* as objection and read the tag as saying that '(legal) objections test rules'. I am grateful to Nicholas Goodhue from UCLA and the 'Net' for setting me right on that.

[86] Stein, *Regulae Iuris*, pp. 146, 155.

[87] I use the word advisedly. Stein named his chapter II, on the classical age of the third century, 'Jurist Law and the Scientific Revolution'. It is similarly time that the contribution of the 'Twelfth Century Renaissance' to the scientific method of the West was placed beside the better publicised 'Scientific Revolution' of the early modern period. Certainly, the reshaping of legal thought during the period covered by this essay has a certain claim to be called at least an effort at scientific jurisprudence; Bellomo, *Common Legal Past*, pp. 163–6 takes the case as proven.

[88] Stein, *Regulae Iuris*, pp. 122–3, 141, 148, 150–1.

Gregory IX included a slim title of select maxims in his authoritative decretal collection of 1234, the *Liber Extra*. Perhaps the decisive breakthrough into the *ius commune* came at the end of the century when another pope, Boniface VIII, inserted no less than 88 maxims into a final title of his supplementary decretal collection, known as the *Sext*.[89]

Impressive sounding Latin maxims were, then, widely available in the law schools and courtrooms of later medieval Europe. They must indeed have constituted a major means by which the teachings of the *ius commune* dispersed into the common legal culture.[90] Once the maxim form was established as authoritative, it was not hard to coin new maxims, by rewriting texts of the two laws into some sufficiently pithy form. It was also possible to coin maxims without actual textual authority that sounded just right.[91]

Some genuine maxims took off to enjoy a life of their own outside the law, as one can see from their appearance in literary and other texts.[92] As a first approximation, I guess that men and women manipulated their use in something of the same way that they drew on the vast stock of proverbs, learned as well as popular in origin.[93] Maxims were in many ways the lawyer's own brand of proverb. Like proverbs, legal maxims enjoyed the freedom of arriving without context, ready for *bricolage* at the user's free will. Equally like proverbs, many maxims were for the most part pretty bland, while others contradicted each other in pairs and clusters. This nest of calming truisms almost invited cuckoo's eggs. One imagines that it might on occasion enable an enterprising advocate able to coin a plausible pseudo-maxim with the opportunity to pass something quite heterodox off on a gullible court.

This is a promising field for research. One might well start such a project back in the courtroom. Latin maxims stud the French language English Year Book law reports of the later middle ages. Pleaders and judges cite at

89 These were X, 5. 41 and VI, 5. 17. Particularly worthy of note in the present context is VI, 5. 17. 22 (*scienti et conscienti non fit iniuria neque dolus*) adapted from *Digest*, 50. 17. 145 and in due course reformulated as the tag *Volenti non fit injuria*, familiar and powerful far beyond the narrow circles of common lawyers.

90 Stein, *Regulae Iuris*, p. 148: 'By the second half of the thirteenth century, the term *regulae iuris* had become part of the common cultural patrimony of Europe.'

91 Kay, 'Roman Law in Dante's *Monarchia*', pp. 265–8 both gives two maxims apparently coined by Dante and also shows how careful one must be before any conclusion that a maxim is new. Dante happily referred to the *ius commune* as *la ragione scritta*, ibid., p. 261.

92 Chaucer has his reeve refer to the ubiquitous *vim vi repellere*, but also makes the students, probably law students, cite as another law the tag *qui in uno gravatum, in alio debet relevari*. In both cases manuscripts cite the original Latin in the margins. Here are two separate routes by which maxims joined the wider culture, manuscript translations and law students out to impress reeves and the like. My colleague, Andrew Galloway, kindly pointed me to these lines, ll. 3912m, 4180–2, *The Riverside Chaucer*, ed. Benson, pp. 78, 82.

93 Grace Morgan Armstrong, 'Proverbs and *Sententiae*', *Dictionary of the Middle Ages*, X, pp. 189–92 would be a fair place to commence a comparative study.

each other maxims that must occasionally have been their own original creations.[94] Their practice, though abundantly documented, has been little studied to date in its immediate context of the lawyers' discourse and argumentation.[95] And what can be seen of England must, I imagine, hold also among the lawyers of France and Italy and other parts of continental Europe. It would be a pity, though, just to end the research at the courtroom door. Some maxims at least circulated widely and were put to a diversity of tasks in the outside world. Those that reached a general public must have contributed in ways of which we currently know very little to inform ordinary folk (those whom the lawyers call laymen) what law was about. Their sense of law has been very little studied, apart from the conventional hostility to lawyers as a group.[96] These impressive-sounding tags lent authority to the *halbgelehrten*. They helped to bridge the gulf between the vernacular discourse of every day and the sonorous technicalities and mysteries of the law. That they also informed people about the actual content of the law in any useful way seems unlikely, given the gnomic phrasing of so many maxims. Still, it is enough for some of us just to quote a maxim to cover our discourse with the satisfying if spurious air that we know something about the law.

[94] Research into this must start with a collection of instances where maxims were first cited. My friend David Seipp has compiled a preliminary handlist of this kind from the English Year Books. I do not know whether similar lists of continental citations exist. I have hopes that Prof. Seipp might publish his list (he has been kind enough to show me a TS draft) in some form to stimulate contributions by other scholars.

[95] Stein, *Regulae Iuris*, p. 154, n. 2 gives references to some older studies. David J. Seipp, 'Roman Legal Categories in the Early Common Law', in Thomas G. Watkin, ed., *Legal Record and Historical Reality: Proceedings of the Eighth British Legal History Conference, Cardiff 1987* (London and Ronceverte, W.VA, 1989), pp. 30–33 cites a number of good examples concerning real property conceptualisation. To these may be added *The Earliest English Law Reports*, ed. P. A. Brand (Selden Society, vol. 112 for 1995), ii. 1286. 7 where Brompton, J. deploys 'melior est condicio possidentis' (cf. 'Possession is nine points of the law') against a pleader. Bellomo, *Common Legal Past*, ch. 7 contains many hints worth testing outside Italy and has clearly investigated the nature of legal discourse in something of the way I am suggesting in, for example, the article of his cited in ibid., p. 181, n. 53.

[96] I tried to make my own first approximation on this subject in my 'What Did Edwardian Villagers Understand by Law?', in Zvi Razi and Richard Smith, eds., *Medieval Society and the Manor Court* (Oxford, 1996), ch. 2, esp. pp. 92–9; the suggestions there are not limited to villagers.

6. *Inside the courtroom: lawyers, litigants and justices in England in the later middle ages*

PAUL BRAND

During the later middle ages civil justice in England (to use an anachronistic but serviceable term) was provided by a variety of different courts, from local manorial courts up through hundred and county courts to national royal courts. This essay concentrates on the latter, and more particularly on the Common Bench, the royal court which specialised in the hearing of civil cases. The Common Bench had emerged during the later twelfth century out of the Exchequer and (apart from periods when it moved to Shrewsbury and York) sat for the remainder of the middle ages hearing civil litigation just outside London, in Westminster Hall. The court played a major role in formal dispute resolution in later medieval England. Although it was a national court it heard not only disputes between members of the aristocracy and gentry and disputes between the aristocracy and gentry and their tenants and lesser neighbours, but also some disputes between litigants who were no more than members of the peasantry, of no importance outside their own small locality. One example is a case brought in Michaelmas term 1302 by William son of Roger Sedeman and his brother John against their elder brother Roger to assert their claim to equal shares with Roger in the inheritance of their father, another Roger. At stake was a holding consisting of no more than a messuage, twelve acres of arable and one acre of marshland in the Norfolk villages of Eccles by Happisburgh and Horsey.[1] This was obviously a peasant holding and there is no reason to suppose that either the claimants or the tenant were anything other than free peasants, quarrelling over whether the family holding was partible between males under local custom or subject to the normal common-law rule of primogeniture. The dispute could have gone to the court of Robert of Tattershall, the lord of whom both parties agreed the lands were held. The claimants, however, preferred to bring it to the

[1] The plea-roll enrolment of this case is in the Public Record Office (henceforth PRO) CP 40/144, m. 245d.

Common Bench and were allowed to do so. Nor was there anything particularly strange or unusual about their doing so.

An additional reason for studying this court is the wealth of the surviving documentation that it generated. The earliest surviving official records of the court's proceedings (its plea rolls) come from the mid-1190s and from the last quarter of the thirteenth century onwards the plea rolls of the court survive in an almost complete series. There is also from about 1270 onwards the complementary information provided by unofficial law reports, which seem largely, though perhaps not exclusively, to have been produced by the law students (apprentices) who attended the court.[2] These generally record what was said in court in the form of dialogue in direct speech (as opposed to the indirect, reported speech of the plea rolls) and when we compare them with the corresponding plea-roll enrolments it becomes clear that the enrolments omit much of the argument that went on in court, particularly when it seemed to be irrelevant to the final outcome of the case. At first law reports only survive (and were probably only compiled) in relatively small numbers. Less than one hundred and fifty cases heard in the Common Bench are recorded in surviving reports dating from the first two decades of the English law report (from the period prior to 1290) and for no individual term is it possible to find reports of more than seven cases.[3] From 1291 onwards many more reports survive, often in association with reports of other cases heard during the same law term in what are clearly termly collections. The first such collection comes from Michaelmas term 1291 and contains reports of no less than eighty-four cases heard during that term. Several other such collections survive from the 1290s and an almost continuous series of such termly report collections from Michaelmas term 1299 onwards. For the whole period between 1291 and 1307 reports survive of as many as 3000 different cases. Nor is it uncommon for there to survive several independent collections of reports for any given term. For Michaelmas term 1302, for example, there are as many as seven different collections though these collections are not wholly independent of each other. Four of the seven report the Norfolk peasant inheritance dispute already mentioned, although two of the four MSS reproduce what are closely related versions of the same report, leaving us with just three independent reports of the case.[4] As will be seen, such reports are in fact the

2 Paul Brand, 'The Beginnings of English Law Reporting' in Chantal Stebbings, ed., *Law Reporting in England* (London, 1995), pp. 1–14.

3 These are edited in Paul Brand, ed., *The Earliest English Law Reports, vol. I and vol. II* (Selden Society, vols. 111 and 112 (1996)).

4 One version is printed in *Year Book 30 and 31 Edward I*, pp. 57–61 but is also found in Lincoln's Inn (henceforth LI) MS. Miscellaneous 738, f. 33v; the second version is found in British Library (henceforth BL) MS. Stowe 386, f. 165r; the third in Cambridge University Library (henceforth CUL) MS. Ee.6.18, ff. 75v–76r.

single most important source of information about what really went on inside the courtroom when litigation was being heard in the Common Bench during the later Middle Ages.

I. PARTICIPATION IN LITIGATION IN THE COMMON BENCH

i. Serjeants

The official records of the king's courts (the plea rolls) almost invariably appear to show that it was either the litigants in person or those whom they had formally appointed to act as their representatives for the purpose of litigation (their attorneys) who did all the speaking in the royal courts. The plea-roll enrolment of our 1302 case, for example, mentions (though without naming them) the attorney who had been appointed by the claimants and the attorney who had been appointed by the tenant and gives the impression that the actual argument in court was one conducted between these two representatives: 'William son of Roger Sedeman and John the brother of the said William *through their attorney* claim against Roger son of Roger Sedeman . . . Roger son of Roger appears *through his attorney* and denies and will deny their right whenever. . .'

A moment's glance at almost any surviving report of litigation heard in the Common Bench from the 1290s onwards dispels what is evidently a false impression created by the official record. The reports make it plain that almost all the speaking and argument which went on in court was the work not of litigants speaking in person nor even of their attorneys but of members of a quite distinct group, men who can be identified as professional serjeants. Each litigant had a serjeant, often a group of serjeants, to speak for him in court.[5] In our 1302 Norfolk case, for example, all three reports agree that it was in reality the professional serjeant Richard of Ashby who argued the case for the claimants and two other professional serjeants (Simon East and Edmund of Pashley) who argued the case for the tenant.[6] Ashby had begun practice as a professional serjeant in the Common Bench in 1291 and remained active there until his death in the summer of 1304. Simon East (who himself came from Norfolk) had

[5] Paul Brand, *The Origins of the English Legal Profession* (Oxford, 1992), p. 96. Professor David Seipp has suggested to me that litigants may not have engaged more than one or two serjeants in advance and that the other serjeants mentioned in reports only joined in during the course of pleadings, hoping to be rewarded at the end of proceedings. I am not convinced by this hypothesis. There were obvious advantages for the wealthy litigant in hiring as many serjeants as he could. One was that this ensured that they were not available to the litigant's opponent.

[6] One of the three reports (that in CUL MS. Ee.6.18) mentions only Pashley and not East as acting for the tenant.

become a regular serjeant of the Common Bench by 1292 and remained in practice there till 1308. Edmund of Pashley had only become a serjeant of the Common Bench in the autumn of 1299 and remained in active practice in the court down to 1318. These three were members of a relatively small group. During the last decade of the thirteenth century and the first decade of the fourteenth century no more than thirty-five professional serjeants were in practice in the Common Bench at any one time.[7] Later in the fourteenth century this elite group of professional serjeants became even smaller, with no more than about a dozen serjeants practising in the court at any one time.[8]

It seems clear that there was no legal requirement, neither a customary rule nor a rule imposed by statute, which forced litigants to use the services of members of this group. It would have been perfectly possible in theory for litigants to speak for themselves or for their attorneys to do so. Very occasionally, the reports do indeed show litigants themselves speaking in court, though generally not as an alternative to using the services of a serjeant or serjeants, but rather in addition to it. A report of a novel disseisin case heard in the 1293 Staffordshire eyre, for example, indicates that after the serjeant Henry Spigurnel had answered on behalf of the earl of Warwick and another serjeant, Hugh of Lowther, had responded to him, it was the earl himself who asked for judgement on the grounds that the plaintiff had failed to disclose an adequate title to the easements he was claiming.[9] One of four reports of a 1302 dower case shows John son of William de la Hay doing some, though not all, of his own pleading in this case.[10] John was again no ordinary litigant. He was a prominent professional attorney with a busy practice in the court, a man almost as expert in the law and practice of the court as one of the serjeants. Reports also show members of another group with a special legal expertise (former royal justices) speaking in person in court when involved in litigation.[11] There are also a few reports which show attorneys participating in pleading in court

[7] Brand, *Origins of the English Legal Profession*, pp. 106–10.

[8] J. H. Baker, *The Order of Serjeants at Law* (Selden Society supplementary series 5 (1984)).

[9] *Year Book 20 and 21 Edward I*, pp. 425–9 (at p. 427).

[10] BL MS. Additional 31826, ff. 178r–v: *Johannes de la Hay (in propria persona) . . . Jon de la Haye . . . Jon de la Haye*. This is not noted in the reports of the same case in *Year Book 30 and 31 Edward I*, pp. 53–7, BL MS. Additional 37657, ff. 191v–192r or BL MS. Stowe 386, f. 164r.

[11] The former royal justice John de Lovetot appeared and spoke in person in court in a case of 1293 (*Year Book 21 and 22 Edward I*, pp. 45–7) and in another case of 1295 a different royal justice, master Thomas of Siddington, appeared and spoke in court (BL MS. Additional 37657, f. 106v). Both were themselves parties to the litigation concerned. For a 1296 case where the former and future royal justice Ralph of Hengham, who was only incidentally involved in litigation, appeared and spoke in person see BL MSS. Additional 31826, f. 96v and Egerton 2811, ff. 157r–v.

on behalf of their clients, though again this seems normally to be in addition to the use of serjeants rather than as a replacement for them.[12]

There were several good reasons why litigants would normally wish to employ professional serjeants to speak on their behalf and thus why it should have become the almost universal practice by 1300. The serjeants, as we see them in the reports, were specialists in the art of presenting claims and complaints and making defences and engaging in the extemporary legal argument which was an essential part of litigation. A litigant who was foolish enough to try to present his own case or make his own defence (unless he was a former royal justice or very expert attorney) was an amateur up against a professional or rather a group of professionals. Few litigants were willing to put themselves at such a disadvantage. The serjeants also enjoyed a structural institutional advantage, and one whose origins lie in the earlier history of the English legal system. Although serjeants did speak in court on behalf of a particular litigant (and often spoke as though they *were* that litigant) they were not seen by the court as their fully empowered agents. If they made a mistake, whether of omission or commission, in what they said it was generally possible, provided this was done without too much delay, for them to be disavowed by the litigant or his attorney and the mistake corrected. Any such mistake, if made by the litigant or by an attorney, might well be fatal to the litigant's chances of success.[13] The general rule was that once said or unsaid by either litigant or attorney such an error could not be corrected. There may also have been other, less immediately obvious advantages. The serjeants were all members of a professional elite whose members enjoyed a rough equality. For a man of lower social standing engaged in litigation with a man of higher social standing, it may have been valuable to have someone speaking for him whose very appearance and way of speaking was not a constant reminder to the court of the relative positions of the two sides in the case. It may also have been an advantage that the serjeants knew only what they had been told by the litigant or his intermediaries. This meant that they could with a clear conscience deny the truth of matters which the litigant present in person would have known to be true, and could not be closely questioned by the court about matters of which they were in truth themselves quite ignorant.

The legal system itself probably also derived advantages from the fact

[12] For examples see BL MS. Additional 31826, f. 140r (1302); *Year Book 33–35 Edward I*, p. 419 (1307); LI MS. Hale 188, f. 20v (undated); PRO KB 27/155, m. 2 (T1298). For cases where an attorney seems to be acting on his own (perhaps because the matter is a relatively simply procedural one) but where the report shows the attorney getting into difficulties see BL MS. Additional 31826, f. 119r and LI MS. Hale 174, f. 101r.

[13] Brand, *Origins of the English Legal Profession*, pp. 48, 98–100.

that the many interpersonal conflicts which were channelled into litigation could be fought out by proxies, rather than in person, in the courtroom. The reports give us an occasional whiff of bad temper on the part of one or more of the serjeants towards some of their colleagues.[14] This was not the same as the real hatred which might lie not far below the surface of any piece of civil litigation. The serjeants were clinically detached from the raw emotions which might be motivating their clients. They did not bring these emotions with them into the courtroom.

It is not entirely clear for how long professional serjeants had dominated the process of pleading civil litigation in the main royal courts. At first sight, the reports seem to suggest that their dominance was a fairly recent phenomenon in 1300. The earliest reports commonly, though not invariably, attribute what was said in court to the party for whom it was spoken or give no attribution for it at all. The attribution of speeches or arguments to particular serjeants becomes increasingly common during the 1280s but is is only after 1290 that it becomes relatively rare for speeches to be anonymous or for them to be attributed only to the parties for whom they were made.[15] However, this change seems not to mirror any change in actual courtroom practice, merely to be a change in the conventions of the fledgling tradition of law reporting. There was a comparable change during much the same period in these same reports from the practice of attributing many judicial interventions and even judgements to anonymous individual justices (*la Justice*) to ascribing them to specific and named royal justices. Other evidence indicates that there were already professionals acting as serjeants at the very beginning of the thirteenth century[16] and suggests that by the middle of the thirteenth century it had become the normal expectation that a litigant in the Common Bench at Westminster, though not necessarily in other royal courts, would have a serjeant speaking on his or her behalf and (though less clearly) that this serjeant would be a member of the group of professional serjeants of the Common Bench who seem also to have served litigants with business in other royal courts.[17]

ii. Justices and clerks

The plea rolls are almost equally unhelpful in shedding light on those who heard litigation in the Common Bench or in other royal courts. It is quite exceptional for them to show the justices of the court playing any active role in the pleading process and they normally cover even the giving of judge-

[14] E.g. Higham's response to an argument of Mutford in a case of Michaelmas term 1299: *Lessez vostre treffle* . . .: BL MS. Additional 31826, f. 109r.

[15] Brand, *The Earliest English Law Reports*, vol. I, pp. cxvii–cxxi.

[16] Brand, *Origins of the English Legal Profession*, pp. 52–4.

[17] Ibid., pp. 54–65.

ments of the court with a veil of collective anonymity: judgements are given by an impersonal court, not by any particular justice or group of justices. The impression they give, if only by default, is that all the justices of each court sat together impassively hearing all of the court's business and that the court's judgements were then likewise agreed by all of the justices collectively.

The first thing which the reports make plain is that the individual justices of the court and, as will be seen, others associated in the work of the court, did play an active role in helping to guide the pleading process. In our 1302 Norfolk inheritance dispute, for example, the plea roll simply records as the first substantive response to the complainants' claim a request by the tenant that the complainants should provide some evidence that the tenements were (contrary to the normal common-law rules of inheritance) partible between male coheirs, by showing between which of their ancestors the tenements had been divided in the past, and the complainants simply complying with this request. It is only one of the three reports which shows that in fact they only did so after receiving what amounted to an instruction from chief justice Hengham to do so. The complainants then showed that the tenements had indeed been divided between brothers on two occasions in the reigns of Kings Richard and John. This was not denied by the tenant's serjeants but his response was to cite a much more recent occasion (when their father had inherited the lands concerned from his grandfather) when the tenements could have been divided but had not been. This was not denied by the claimant's serjeant either. Both sides did, however, then produce explanations for the inconvenient facts produced by their opponents: the earlier divisions had been voluntary and not the consequence of any customary obligation to divide the tenement; the later failure to divide the tenement had been (according to one report) the result of the negligence of their two uncles or (according to another) simply because they had not in fact survived their father and neither of these could prejudice the divisibility of the tenement. It is only the reports which record these arguments and only the reports which show that it was the justices of the court (Bereford and Hengham) who pushed the parties into a satisfactory way of resolving their dispute; by a jury verdict which looked at the wider issue of whether these and other lands belonging to the same (Arundel) fee in these villages were rightfully partible and had been divided. One report specifically notes that Ashby was 'chased' by the court to take this issue. Where formal judgements are reported in the law reports they regularly tell us which of the justices gave them and sometimes even tell us which of their colleagues they had consulted beforehand.[18]

[18] *Year Book 33–35 Edward I*, pp. 77, 381.

Even the official records provide some hints to suggest that by the later thirteenth century the justices of royal courts may have been dividing the business of the court between them and that most cases were therefore being heard by far fewer than the full complement of justices assigned to any particular royal court. It has indeed long been suspected from such evidence that it had become normal by the reign of Edward I for the justices of the General Eyre to divide the business of the court between themselves and that 'the full commission did not sit for each section of the eyre's business'.[19] This evidence, which is indeed confirmed by the reports, indicates that some business was heard by only a single justice[20] though it was more commonly heard by groups of two[21] or three justices.[22] Only rarely did *all*

[19] D. W. Sutherland, *Quo Warranto Proceedings in the Reign of Edward I, 1278–1294* (Oxford, 1963), pp. 33–5. G. O. Sayles states more specifically (though with scarcely enough evidence to support so firm a conclusion) that 'We know that at this time it was customary for the court of the justices in eyre to be held in three divisions': G. O. Sayles, ed., *Select Cases in the Court of King's Bench, vol. II* (Selden Society, lvii (1938)), p. lxxx.

[20] For evidence of single justices hearing civil pleas see PRO JUST 1/365, m. 71d (Ralph de Hengham in the1271 Kent eyre); JUST 1/876, m. 33 (William of Northborough in the 1279 Kent eyre); JUST 1/1065, m. 12 (Roger Loveday perhaps hearing Yorkshire civil pleas on his own at the beginning of Michaelmas term 1279 during the 1279–81 Yorkshire eyre before he was joined by William of Saham); JUST 1/1068, m. 18d (John of Mettingham hearing foreign pleas in Easter term 1280 during the 1279–81 Yorkshire eyre); KB 27/98, m. 26d (Alan of Walkingham giving judgement alone in the 1281 Devon eyre). For evidence of a single justice hearing *quo waranto* pleas see *Placita de Quo Warranto*, p. 391 (John of Mettingham in the 1281–4 Lincolnshire eyre). For evidence of a single justice hearing crown pleas see PRO CP 40/58, m. 38 (Richard Boyland in the 1280 Dorset eyre); SC 1/20, no. 194 (Roger Loveday in the 1281–4 Lincolnshire eyre); JUST 1/710, m. 58 (Roger Loveday in the 1285 Oxfordshire eyre); *State Trials of the Reign of Edward I, 1289–1293,* ed. T. F. Tout and H. Johnstone (Camden Soc., 3rd ser., 1906), p. 14 (Richard Boyland in the 1286 Norfolk eyre).

[21] For evidence of pairs of justices hearing civil pleas see: PRO JUST 1/1065, m. 12 (William of Saham joins Roger Loveday to hear Yorkshire pleas in Michaelmas term 1279 during the 1279–81 Yorkshire eyre); *Chronicle of St. Mary's Abbey, York*, ed. H. H. E. Craster and M. E. Thornton (Surtees Society, 148 (1933)), p. 20 (grand assize heard in mid-December 1280 during the 1279–81 Yorkshire eyre before John of Mettingham and master Thomas of Siddington); JUST 1/501, m. 6d (John of Mettingham and master Thomas of Siddington sitting to hear foreign pleas in a house opposite the hall where other justices were hearing Lincolnshire civil pleas in Trinity term 1281 during the 1281–4 Lincolnshire eyre); *Chronica Johannis de Oxenedes*, ed. H. Ellis (Rolls Series, 1859), p. 266 (Solomon of Rochester and Robert 'de Redinges' (Fulks) hearing petty assizes and writs of right (civil pleas) in the 1286 Norfolk eyre). For evidence of pairs of justices hearing crown pleas see BL MS. Harley 662, f. 16r (Richard of Boyland and Walter of Stirchesley in the 1285 Essex eyre); *Chronica Johannis de Oxenedes*, p. 266 (Richard of Boyland and Walter of Stirchesley in the 1286 Norfolk eyre) – but BL Additional Rolls 14987 says that Boyland and Walter of Hopton heard crown pleas in this same eyre. For evidence of pairs of justices hearing *quo waranto* pleas see *Chronica Johannis de Oxenedes*, p. 266 (Hopton and master Thomas of Siddington in the 1286 Norfolk eyre); *Placita de Quo Warranto*, p. 292 (Mettingham sitting with an associate, Thomas of Belhouse, in the 1286 Huntingdonshire eyre); *Placita de Quo Warranto*, p. 1 and *Annales Monastici*, III, 329 (Mettingham sitting with an associate, Thomas de Bray, in the 1287 Bedfordshire eyre).

[22] For evidence of a group of three justices hearing a civil plea see PRO JUST 1/408, m. 42d

the justices commissioned to hold an eyre meet together to discuss particularly difficult cases.[23]

It has also long been known that the appointment of six justices to the Common Bench early in the reign of Edward II (in 1309) was justified on the grounds that the quantity of litigation made it necessary for the court to sit in two divisions,[24] and G. O. Sayles has drawn attention to evidence from the years just prior to 1309 which suggests that this arrangement was not entirely novel.[25] The strongest evidence he cited, the heading from a plea-roll membrane for Easter term 1307 referring to a 'second Bench'[26] (evidently a second division of the court), can in fact be paralleled by similar references to 'the second Bench' in several other terms in 1307, 1306 and 1305. Earlier, there are no explicit references to a 'second Bench' but there is evidence to show that Ellis of Beckingham had been running a separate division of the court either on his own or with a single associate since early in 1290. Before becoming a justice Ellis of Beckingham had been the chief clerk of the court, its keeper of rolls and writs. His predecessor in that post, Roger of Leicester, may have been running a similar second division of the court prior to 1290.[27]

This also fits with the evidence of the reports. These indicate that many Common Bench cases were heard before a single justice and that the vast majority were heard before no more than three justices.[28] In our 1302 Norfolk case, for example, the reports record interventions in the pleading on the part of only two justices, the chief justice Ralph of Hengham, and his colleague, William of Bereford. Although the number of justices

(Hugh of Cressingham, master John Lovel and William de Mortimer in the 1292 Lancashire eyre). For evidence of a group of three justices sitting to hear a trespass plea see JUST 1/541B, m. 30 (Richard of Boyland, Walter of Hopton and Walter of Stirchesley in the 1287 Hertfordshire eyre). For evidence of a group of three justices sitting to hear crown pleas see JUST 1/710, m. 58 (Roger Loveday, Richard of Boyland and Geoffrey Pichford in the 1285 Oxfordshire eyre).

23 The only direct evidence of this comes from a complaint made to the *auditores querelarum* in 1289–93 and relates to litigation heard in the 1287 Hertfordshire eyre: PRO JUST 1/541B, m. 30. For evidence from another complaint to the same group indicating that a grand assize taken in the 1286–7 Suffolk eyre was in fact heard by all the justices of the eyre see *State Trials*, pp. 67–70.

24 *Cal. Close Rolls, 1307–1313*, p. 231. In practice only five of the six justices appointed ever acted.

25 Sayles, *Select Cases in the Court of King's Bench, vol. II*, p. lxxx and note 7. But note that neither of his two references to Year Book cases of the reign of Edward I proves this point.

26 PRO CP 40/163, m. 286.

27 P. Brand, *The Making of the Common Law* (London, 1992), pp. 122–3.

28 Reports that show as many as four justices participating in the hearing of a case are comparatively rare. All seem to come from periods when there were at least six justices assigned to the court. For examples see BL MS. Additional 31826, f. 148r (Michaelmas 1301); BL MS. Additional 31826, f. 148v (Hilary 1303); *Year Book 32 and 33 Edward I*, pp. 389–405 (Hilary 1305).

assigned to sit in the Common Bench during the reign of Edward I varied between a low of four and a high of seven with an average of five or six justices there is not a single reported case in which more than four justices participated. Just occasionally (as in the Eyre) all the justices of the court do seem to have met together to take a joint decision. In Trinity term 1298 all the justices (*omnes socios justiciarios de Banco*) are recorded as agreeing to overrule a judgement which had been given by one of their number (Ellis of Beckingham) and ordering the resummons of the litigants for a further hearing of their case;[29] and during the course of proceedings brought against a disappointed litigant who had abused chief justice Hengham for a judgement he had given in Trinity term 1303 we are told that the judgement had been reached unanimously (*unanimo assensu*) and Hengham had merely pronounced it as one of the court's justices.[30] In another case heard the same term the record was said to have been emended in court 'by the common assent of the justices' (*communi assensu justiciariorum*).[31] But the strong emphasis given to the collective action of the justices in these cases (and the total absence of any reported cases recording such collective action) may indicate just how rare it was in the normal day-to-day practice of the court.[32]

It was not, however, necessarily only the justices appointed to a particular royal court who sat to hear litigation brought before the court or helped to determine the court's judgements. In his response to one of the complaints made against him during the so-called 'State Trials' of 1289–93, for example, Ralph of Hengham, the former chief justice of King's Bench, denied responsibility for a judgement made in the Common Bench. He did admit that he had sometimes come to sit in the court at the request of its justices when they had difficult cases to decide in order to give them 'counsel and assistance' (*contingit tamen aliquando quod dictus Radulphus ad rogatum ipsorum justiciariorum quando habent difficiles casus terminandos venit sedere cum eis in banco ad ipsorum consilium et auxilium*).[33] The presence of Hengham and his King's Bench colleague Saham as well as of other unspecified royal justices for the giving of a potentially contentious judgement in Michaelmas term 1287 is specifically mentioned in the enrolment of the case[34] and surviving reports record Hengham's presence in the Common Bench for other cases of 1279, 1285, 1286 and 1287.[35] From pro-

[29] PRO CP 40/115, m. 70. [30] PRO CP 40/148, m. 29d. [31] PRO CP 40/148, m. 13d.

[32] For the special status attached to a decision of *all* the justices see also the speech of Stanton in a case of 1300: 'Le(s) Justice(s) avant ses houres en semblable cas ne unt pas soffert la vewe estre graunte au tenant e par commun assent le unt agarde entre eaux en cas semblebles. E coe qe est une foys par commun assent entre eaux ordine ne deyt pas estre contre lute': BL MS. Additional 37657, f. 18r. [33] PRO KB 138/4, no. 81.

[34] PRO CP 40/57, m. 15d.

[35] Brand, *The Earliest English Law Reports, vol. I*, pp. cxxi–cxxii.

ceedings on another complaint made to the *auditores querelarum* we learn that one of the justices in eyre (John of Mettingham) had sat in court with the Common Bench justice Brompton for the jury stage of a case, not apparently at Brompton's own prompting but as a well-wisher (*benivolens*) to one of the litigants involved (the prior of Sempringham) and possibly at the prior's own request.[36] The practice of outside justices sitting in on Common Bench cases clearly continued after 1290 and is attested by the evidence of both plea rolls and reports.

Although there is nothing in the plea rolls to show this, the reports also make plain that senior clerks regularly participated in the hearing of cases. During the last decade of the thirteenth century and first decade of the fourteenth century they show two successive chief clerks of the chief justice of the Common Bench (Anger of Ripon and later Henry of Hales) doing so, as also the keeper of rolls and writs (John Bacun) as well as the future justice Hervey of Stanton; and some reports even seem to show clerks hearing cases by themselves. Reports also show the participation in the hearing of Eyre cases of the clerks John of Fressingfield and Henry of Guildford.[37]

iii. Attorneys

Although attorneys played little or no role in the process of pleading cases they did provide a service of considerable value and utility for the litigants who employed them. Once a plaintiff had appointed an attorney he could avoid the need for further journeys to court and use the attorney to sue the often protracted mesne process against his opponent which was necessary before the opponent was compelled to appear and the case could be heard. Although some litigants may have wished to be in court to see their cases being pleaded, others, perhaps a majority, did not. The courts required the physical attendance or appearance before them of both litigants before they would hear their litigation even if it was then the serjeants of both litigants who did all or almost all of the talking, but they were willing to accept the attendance of duly authorised attorneys in their place. Thus the appointment of an attorney was an essential step for the litigant who wanted his litigation heard but did not wish to attend court in person. The attorneys had then to be present in court whenever the case was pleaded and they were supposed to come up close to the bar of the court where the serjeants stood (and behind which the clerks and justices of the court sat) when their client's serjeants were pleading so that they could hear what was said. They might then be asked whether or not they avowed what the serjeants had said.[38]

[36] PRO JUST 1/541B, m. 36d. [37] Brand, *Making of the Common Law*, pp. 176–82.
[38] Brand, *Origins of the English Legal Profession*, pp. 87, 196.

In practice, attorneys may often have played an even more essential role in litigation as the link between the litigant and his serjeants. There is some evidence to suggest that it may often have been the attorney who was responsible for engaging the services of the serjeants for his client and for paying them on the client's behalf. It was also apparently the attorney who supplied the serjeants with the requisite background information they needed for pleading and with any relevant deeds belonging to the client that needed to be produced in court.[39] We glimpse something of the essential intermediary role of the attorney in a reported case of 1294 in which the court suspected that it was being deceived by a litigant and that he was trying to have an allegation of unjust distraint which had already been made and determined in previous litigation reheard by the simple expedient of changing his form of action and altering the date on which he alleged that a distraint had been made. The plaintiff's serjeant vouched the attorneys of his client as his source of information for the day of the supposed distraint. They in turn were warned by Chief Justice Mettingham of the punishment that awaited them if they had knowingly assisted their client in deceiving the court. They answered that they were merely repeating information given them by their client. They were then told by the court (evidently to pass on to their client) that if there really had been only a single distraint he would be heavily amerced.[40] In other cases we also see the courts treating attorneys as intermediaries for communication between the court and the litigant. In a 1300 case Chief Justice Mettingham told the attorney to tell his client (a bishop) that the court had been impressed by a deed in the client's name produced by his opponent and that it advised him to settle the case.[41] In a 1299 case Justice Bereford gave a judgement dismissing a debt claim and went on to tell the attorney to inform his client that in the court's view his client was no better than a usurer.[42]

[39] Ibid., p. 88. For evidence showing an attorney prompting his serjeant with additional information in court see CUL MS. Ee.6.18, f. 28v and Harvard MS. 206, f. 135v (reports of a case of Michaelmas 1299), and for a case where we can overhear an attorney asking a serjeant to take certain action for his client and the serjeant refusing to do so (and stating his reasons for his refusal) see *Year Book 21 and 22 Edward I*, p. 211 (1293).

[40] BL MS. Lansdowne 467, f. 115r (1294): '*Sottone*. Sire, il nunt ren change for le jour e co est lor malise pur nus grever . . . e prium qe votre malise seit ateint. *Metingam*. Simon, parnet garde qe co ne seit mie votre fet pur le peril. *Simon*. Veet si les aturnes que le me diunt. *Metingam*. Gardet vos qe este atourneye qe co ne seit mie votre malise. E il diceunt qe co fut le maundement lor seignur. E dit *le justice* qe co il passe encontre li qe il serra grevement amercie.'

[41] BL MS. Additional 37657, f. 18v (1300): '*Metig*'. Vous atorne, acertet le evesqe de soen fet demene a queu fet nous donum fey e avum graunt regard. E parlet de pes entre cy e la seint Johan.'

[42] BL MS. Additional 31826, f. 102v (1299): '*Ber*'. Tut ust sun cunte este acordant a sa renable demunstrance il nust point eu avantage pur ceo qe sun escrist soune en usure. Par quey agarde fut qe rien ne prent par sun bref mes fut en la merci e qe il se purchasont en curt crestiene sil veit etc. e les autres sant jor. Et dictum fuit attornato rei quod diceret domino suo quod erat usurarius.'

It was evidently still possible in 1300 for litigants even in the central royal courts to employ the services of relatives and friends to act as their attorneys and perfectly possible for men or women to appoint persons of either gender to act on their behalf.[43] But the general trend seems to have been increasingly in favour of the exclusively male professional attorney, and in 1300 over two hundred professional attorneys were practising in the Common Bench and between them accounting for around two-thirds of all attorney appointments in the court.[44]

II. SOME CHARACTERISTICS OF THE LITIGATION PROCESS

The plea rolls generally give the impression that all the pleading in individual cases took place in the course of a single, uninterrupted session held on a single day with each argument in the case following smoothly on from the next and leading inexorably up to the joinder of issue for jury trial, or the giving of judgement, or less commonly to the adjournment of the case for judgement in a subsequent term.[45] This may sometimes have been the reality. The reports, however, suggest that quite commonly it was not.[46] More difficult cases were evidently normally heard over the course of two or more days. Sometimes a hearing was simply continued on the following day. At other times it was simply continued 'on another day'. In at least two instances the reports tell us of pleadings continuing over no less than four different days within a single term.[47] When proceedings resumed it was often, perhaps always, the practice for someone to give a resumé of what had been said at the previous hearing for there would be no formal record of this. Both serjeants[48] and justices[49] performed this task. It was all the

[43] Brand, *Origins of the English Legal Profession*, pp. 73, 77. [44] Ibid., pp. 73–5, 77–8.

[45] But for an example of an enrolment where we are told not just of the original pleading during Easter term 1283 but also of pleading on three successive days during the following Michaelmas term see PRO CP 40/49, m. 32 (*Philip of Eye v. abbot of Reading*).

[46] One of our MSS. (BL MS. Additional 31826) is particularly good at noting the different days on which pleadings took place but this is also found occasionally in other MSS. as well.

[47] BL MS. Additional 31826, ff. 73v, 74r, 72v, 75v; *Year Book 33–35 Edward I*, pp. 339–49.

[48] BL MS. Additional 31826, f. 125r: 'Postea ad alium diem *Willu* reherca coment il aveint respondu qe ceus biens furent lur biens en comun e il tenderunt de averer qe checun de eus sout la severalte de ceu biens cum de ses biens propres, quel response de pleintifs fut recorde de justices . . .' (Michaelmas 1301); BL MS. Additional 31826, f. 182r: 'alia die *Warr'*. Bien vus membre coment le prior de C. se est pleint . . .' (Michaelmas 1302); BL MS. Additional 5925, f. 75r: 'Ad alium diem *Pass'* rehersa brevement tut le plee e en la fin idem dixit . . .' (Michaelmas 1302); Bodleian Library MS. Holkham Misc. 30, f. 93v: 'Et sic pendebat. E puis vint *Ass'* e reherca tut le proces . . .'; *Year Book 33–35 Edward I*, pp. 297–9: 'Ad alium diem *Bereford, Howard* existentibus in Banco, *Herle* rehersa ces proces et in fine . . .' (Michaelmas 1306); *Year Book 33–35 Edward I*, p. 351: 'Ad alium diem *Passeley* breviter rehersa ceo qe avant fust dit, e in fine . . .' (Michaelmas 1306).

[49] *Year Book 33–35 Edward I*, p. 343: 'Altera die processu predicto reiterato par *Howard*. . . .' (Michaelmas 1306); *Year Book 33–35 Edward I*, p. 429: 'Alio die *Howard* breviter repetiit et dit qe . . .' (Hilary term 1307).

more necessary because the group of justices hearing a case on the second or subsequent days might well not be the same as that which had previously heard it.[50]

There could be, and perhaps often were, interruptions even within the course of a single day's hearing. Only the reports tell us of serjeants requesting permission from the court to 'imparl', that is, to interrupt proceedings in order to consult with their fellow-serjeants and the client or his attorney(s). This was regularly requested and allowed where a litigant or his attorney had been asked whether he 'avowed' something said by the serjeant. It was also regularly requested and conceded when a deed was produced in litigation and the party had either to acknowledge it as genuine or impugn its validity. A serjeant might also request permission to imparl at other times. It is not clear how long the court allowed for imparling or under what circumstances, if any, permission to imparl might be refused. Nor is it clear whether the court got on with other business while imparling went on.

Potentially even more disruptive was the way the justices of the court themselves simply came into court during the course of a hearing. On the first day of what turned out to be a three-day hearing of a *quare impedit* case about the right to present a rector to a vacant church in 1302 the only justice initially present in court seems to have been Chief Justice Hengham. The reporter notes that at a particular point in proceedings his fellow-justice Howard came into court. Proceedings had to be interrupted while Hengham explained what was going on to him.[51] Something similar seems to have happened in a case of 1305 where the initial pleading took place before Justice Mallore and the senior clerk Henry of Hales. Pashley got a chance to repeat an argument he had already made once before in the presence of Chief Justice Hengham, evidently when Hengham came into court.[52] It may also explain why when the first stage of a debt case was being heard by Justice Mallore in 1307 his fellow-justice Howard is noted as intervening under the wholly mistaken belief that it was a plea of replevin and not a plea of debt that was being heard.[53]

50 We may often suppose this to be the case where the report mentions different justices on the second occasion but for clear proof see *Year Book 21 and 22 Edward I*, pp. 241–5 (Trinity 1293) where the initial pleading was before Mallore and on a subsequent day pleading was before Mettingham and Hartforth. Here we are specifically told (p. 245) that on the second day of pleading 'sire Peres Maloure ne fust pas en banc' and there was no other justice present able to 'record' what had been said at the previous day's pleading.

51 BL MS. Additional 31826, f. 134r: 'E adonke vint *Hou'* e quaunt sire R. ly out mustre le cas si demanda il . . .'

52 BL MS. Additional 31826, f. 337r: 'Postea presente R. de Hengh' *Passe* reherca coment . . .'

53 *Year Book 33–35 Edward I*, p. 503: '*Howard* putans illud placitum esse de capcione averiorum et quod *Wileby* dixerat advocando . . .' For a case of Michaelmas 1306 where the first stage of the case was evidently heard by Stanton alone who was subsequently joined by

What we can see of the medieval courtroom both in the plea rolls and in the reports tends to give the impression that it was primarily, indeed almost exclusively, a place where people spoke and other people listened, not a place where people acted or gestured. This is likely, however, to be a trick of the evidence. It probably reflects the difficulty, and may even indicate what was felt to be the inappropriateness, of transcribing or representing in written form other, non-verbal forms of communication. But there are exceptions. In a plea-roll enrolment of 1262 the defendant/tenant, who was probably appearing in person, is recorded as 'sighing' when he asked for judgement of a writ and as being 'in tears' when asking for a view of the land claimed against him.[54] It is not entirely clear whether we should be seeing a smiling or a laughing justice or justices or just hearing a particular tone of voice when we read reports which record that a particular justice or the court were perceived as 'laughing at' or 'mocking' a serjeant for an argument he had made.[55] It is fairly certain that there was a smile as well as a gesture in a 1303 replevin case. The serjeant acting for the abbot of Leiston in Suffolk had justified a distraint as made to enforce the performance of the homage and other services which he claimed were owed him. Serjeant Ashby in reply asserted that the homage was owed both for the tenement his client held and for other tenements now in the abbot's own hands. He asked for the court's judgement as to whether the abbot could still justify his distraint as made to enforce performance of all of the services he had mentioned. Chief Justice Hengham raised one of his hands and asked Ashby whether he could do one-handed homage.[56] The implication of his remark was that homage was not a service that could be divided any more than homage itself could be done with one hand rather than two: so this part of what he had said was clearly wrong. An action with a real 'prop' (an object that had been brought into the courtroom) is mentioned in the reports of a 1301 trespass case which concerned the seizure of some fishing nets. Serjeant Tothby produced in court the gauge which had been used by

Bereford see BL MS. Hargrave 375, ff. 165r–v: '*Berr*' (*a Frisk*'). Sire Hervi nostre compaynun nous recorde qe vous avez conu . . . Coment volez vous avenir al averement encontre vostre conisaunce demene . . .'

54 Brand, *Making of the Common Law*, p. 9.

55 BL MS. Stowe 386, f. 144r: '*Howard* dit (deridendo). Pur ceo quil ne voleyt fere la deliveraunce vus feytes wythernam sur ly (quasi diceret qe home ne le pout nient fere sanz agard)' (Hilary 1300); BL MS. Additional 31826, f. 122v: '*Heng*' (ipsum deridendo) supponebat illud esse illusorie' (Michaelmas 1301); BL MS. Additional 31826, ff. 120r–v: '*Ber*'. Jeo pos qe labbe deit qe cely ky vus vodriez fere prive qe il fust bastarde. Prierez vus rien bref a levesque? (ipsum deridendo)'; BL MS. Additional 31826, f. 130v: 'E fu moke de *Hou*'' (Easter 1302); *Year Book 33–35 Edward I*, p. 327: 'Et Laufare propter ultimam responsionem derisus a curia . . .' (Michaelmas 1306).

56 BL MS. Additional 31826, f. 274v: '*Hengham* (*levata manu*) demanda sil freit homage de la une meyn . . .'

the bailiffs of the earl of Cornwall to measure the size of the mesh of certain nets which had been used for fishing in the lake at Whittlesmere in Huntingdonshire and been confiscated. Those nets whose mesh was too small were, he claimed, liable to confiscation.[57] Objects were regularly produced and specific customary gestures and actions made on those relatively rare occasions when champions offered trial by battle in court. Each in turn had to offer a glove as 'gage' (or surety) for the battle they were to fight for their clients and the presiding justice would take them and twist them together to signify the joining of battle.[58] We also know that in at least one county court the offer of wager of law was accompanied by the litigant concerned stretching out his hand towards his opponent for that opponent to accept it, presumably by grasping or shaking it.[59] This may also have been the practice elsewhere. Some sort of symbolic gesture seems also to have accompanied a final judgement in an action of naifty holding that the defendant was an unfree villein. After a man had acknowledged that he was a villein in the 1302 eyre of Cornwall, Brompton said to the lord (according to Horwood's transcription) '*Prenez par le coupe . . . com vostre neyf*'. He translated this as 'take him by the neck, as your vilein'[60]. It has recently been suggested that this is a mistranslation and that what he was really being told to do was to 'take him by the elbow'.[61] However, a similar phrase also occurs (but this time in Latin) in a plea-roll enrolment of a naifty case of 1305 and here the entry seems to read '*et liberatur eidem priori hic in curia per tupam*'.[62] This suggests that Horwood may have misread 'toupe' as

57 BL MS. Additional 31826, f. 390r: 'si nul pechor fut trove pechant illoke ov reys hors de assise, sestasaver qe fusent de plus estreyt mak' qe estre ne dusent (issint qe un bilet qele il bota avant a la curt porreit entrer parmy les mayles) qe teles reyes fusent forfez'; also in BL MS. Additional 5925, f. 89v: 'si nul home peschour soit trove en lewe avantdite de pescher od reies qe sunt hors de forme qe sert a tele chose (et qe fust moustre a la court) ne puet passer parmy les malys del reis qe eles seient forfez'. The plea-roll enrolment also mentions the 'gage' and notes that it was produced in court: 'nullus piscare debet in eadem aqua cum aliqua rete nisi de certa et consueta assisa, scilicet quod maske hujusmodi recium adeo sint large quod quoddam bilettum ferreum quo uti consuevit super hujusmodi retibus assaiandis transire possit per foramina maskiorum recium predictorum . . . et profert quoddam bilettum ferreum vetus per quod hujusmodi recia assaiari consueverunt ut dicit etc.' (PRO CP 40/138, m.135d).

58 See LI MS. Miscellaneous 738, f. 111v. The account of wager of battle in the 1286 Norfolk eyre in BL MS. Stowe 386, ff. 94r–95r suggests that the defendant's champion offered his 'gage' on his knees; the demandant's champion while standing. The very detailed account of trial by battle in a teacher's lectures of the 1270s in BL MS. Lansdowne 467 at ff. 146r–v mentions that there had to be a penny in each of the five fingers of each glove and that after battle had been formally joined the justice threw the gloves back to the champions.

59 See the record of a case heard in the Staffordshire county court cited in R. C. Palmer, 'County Year Books Reports: the Professional Lawyer in the Medieval County Court', *Eng. Hist. Rev.*, 91 (1971), pp. 776–801 at p. 801.

60 *Year Book 30 and 31 Edward I*, p. 201.

61 J. H. Baker, *Manual of Law French* (2nd edn, 1990), p. 80. s.v 'coupe'.

62 PRO CP 40/154, m. 62d.

'coupe'. There is an Old French word 'toup' which means a tuft of hair, especially over the forehead. It seems to mean that the villein was taken by the forelock when he was handed over to his lord.

The surviving sources tell us much more about what was said in court. Not that it was always easy to hear what was being said. There was sometimes so much extraneous noise that it was impossible even for the court's justices to hear what counsel had said.[63] An attorney could plausibly claim in a case of 1300 that, although he had been in court, he had simply been too far away from the bar of the court when pleading took place to hear what his client's serjeant had said. He asked for the count to be repeated before he avowed it on his client's behalf. This gave the serjeant a chance to amend his previous count which had been defective.[64]

III. THE LANGUAGE OF PLEADING

The plea rolls provide a formal record in Latin of what was said (or some of what was said) in court: but they do not tell us (in general) in what language it was spoken. What the reports seem to demonstrate is that it was spoken almost entirely in Anglo-Norman French. They are almost all in French and they read and sound like reasonably faithful transcripts of what was actually said there. Anyone reading the reports of this period will find it difficult to believe that they could possibly be a translation of something

[63] For examples see BL MS. Additional 5925, f. 47r (1296): '*Spig' (pur le garante)*. Qei avez du lees? (mes il ne fut pas oy de la court) . . .'; IT MS. Misc. 1, ff. 3r–v (1296): '*Spigurnel*. Nus ne diums pas qe ele est nostre mes vus diums qe vus devez fere teu service en cele chapele qe est commune a tote gent pur oyer lur service. *Warr'*. E nus parnoums byen record qe vus le deytes. *Ber'*. Nus ne le recordum mye kant vus pledez taunt cum la noyse e nus ne poums escuter. E pur ceo dient coment il avowent la prise.'; BL MS. Hargrave 375, ff. 68r–v (1299): '*Tiltone*. Nus voloms demorer en record qe nus deymes qe les avers qe furent en la seisine R. sur qy nus avoms avowe etc. *Houw'* Tot deyssez vous cel, uncore ne contrepledastes mye la proprete des avers. E pur ceo qe la avowerie ne fut pas entendue de la court fut comande par *Met'* qe il avowaste de novel.'; BL MS. Stowe 386, f. 162v (1302): '*War'* De ceo vochom bien record qe nus deymes en avouant . . . *Les Justices* ne voleyent recorder le quel il le deseyent en avouant ou noun pur ceo qe eus ne lur puroeyent oyer'. On other occasions, however, something had to be repeated by counsel because the justices had not been paying full attention: LI MS. Misc. 738, f. 121v (1294): '*Heyham*. Sire, vous avez oy le count. En vos agarz seyt. *Metingham*. Nous devoms rendre les jugemenz en perille de nos almes e nous nentendoms nent le counte pur ceo qe nous ne donames mye garde ne entente. E pur ceo nous agardom qil countent autrefez.'

[64] BL MS. Additional 31826, f. 322r (1300): '*Ber'* comanda qe latorne J. Fresel venist a la barre. E il vint. *Ber'*. Avoeus entendu ceo qe vostre serjant ad cunte pur vus? *Attornatus*. Sire, quaunt il cunta si fu jeo loins de la barre e ne poey mie bien entendre ceo qe il dit e jeo ne ly voil point avoer si la que jeo ay entendu sun cunte. E pria a les justices qe il porreit recunter. E *lattorne le prior* demande jugement de la variance qe fut pur bref abatre. E pus les Justices soffrerent qe il reconta . . .'

which was actually spoken in English.[65] Direct evidence for proceedings being conducted in French comes from a report of a case of 1300. A defendant was challenging a writ used to commence the litigation for its defective latinity in claiming 'tria milia librarum *quas* ei debet' where it should have said '*que*' (to agree with *milia*). Chief Justice Mettingham in commenting on the challenge noted that prior to its being made the defendant's serjeant had requested and obtained a reading of the writ and the writ had been read out to him 'in French' ('*Le bref vous fut leu en fraunceys*'). This practice would scarcely make sense unless the proceedings themselves were being conducted in French.[66] There is also direct evidence from enrolments of two cases heard in King's Bench and the Common Bench during the final decade of the thirteenth century. In a 1291 King's Bench plea Roger of Somerton asserted a claim to the Norfolk manor of West Somerton on the king's behalf. The manor had been given by Ranulph de Glanvill to a leper hospital at West Somerton controlled by Butley priory. Towards the end of the pleadings the plaintiff challenged the form of words the prior of Butley had used in placing himself on the verdict of the grand assize. These had implied that the manor was the right of his church (the priory of Butley) rather than the right of the leper hospital. The prior said he had not avowed what his serjeants had said earlier in the proceedings about the manor having been given to the lepers rather than directly to the priory on behalf of the lepers and so had not been inconsistent. The king's representative said that he had implicitly avowed them because his attorney 'who understood French' ('*romanum intelligens*') had sat listening to the altercation for two days without specifically disavowing them. The clear implication is that the whole of the pleadings had indeed been conducted in French.[67] In a 1295 case of *quare non admisit* the prior of Lewes sued Richard of Gravesend bishop of London in the Common Bench for refusing to admit the prior's candidate to the church of Little Canfield in Essex after the prior had succeeded in establishing his right to present to the church in an assize of darrein presentment. The bishop's defence (which the plea-roll enrolment notes was given by the serjeant Henry Spigurnel) was that on receiving the prior's letters of presentation he had followed the proper procedure. He had instructed the rural dean to make the appropriate local enquiry and the dean had reported back that

[65] For the suggestion that although the formal initial pleadings were in French the language of the subsequent forensic dialogue may have been English see Michael T. Clanchy, *From Memory to Written Record*, 2nd. edn (Oxford, 1993), p. 209. But if the actual language of most legal discussion was English it is not clear why anyone should have bothered to translate this into French for the purposes of unofficial law reporting nor why (if most of what was said was translated) the reporter should have left the occasional phrase (mainly of a proverbial nature) in the original language and untranslated.

[66] BL MS. Additional 37657, ff. 21v–22r.

[67] PRO, KB 27/127, m. 9.

the prior's candidate was not a suitable candidate to receive a benefice. The justices had then asked Henry Spigurnel to be more specific about the grounds for his rejection but he had refused. The justices then recited his answer to the bishop's attorney in English 'because he said that he did not understand French' and asked him to avow this answer on his client's behalf.[68] The clear implication here too is that whatever had been said in the course of pleading had been said in French (here *gallicum*). Occasionally serjeants and justices used brief tags in Latin, most commonly from Roman or canon law,[69] though sometimes also from scripture[70] or other sources. They also used some proverbial or similar phrases in English.[71] But almost everything else that was said in court was clearly said in French.

Although French seems still to have been fairly widely spoken among the gentry and the aristocracy and among those who came into regular contact with them *c.* 1300, the 1295 case suggests that even the attorney of a fairly prominent bishop might at least claim (and be believed when he did claim) that he did not understand French. Also significant is an episode which took place in Michaelmas term 1298 and is recorded on the Common Bench plea roll of that term.[72] Robert son of Alan of Godesfeld of Sutton and his wife Margaret and Theobald of Halstead asked the court's permission to levy a final concord relating to Theobald's Lincolnshire manor of Stixwould. This was challenged on behalf of the earl of Lincoln, of whom Theobald held the manor. Theobald was told to come up from the bar of the court to the bench where the justices were sitting. They evidently doubted whether Theobald was fully *compos mentis* and understood the agreement he was making. After the court refused on other grounds to accept the concord the parties went away to change the terms. The court again hesitated before accepting them, as they were now even less favourable to Theobald and provided further reason for doubting that he was capable of understanding and making the agreement. To make absolutely certain that he did the justices repeated its terms to him (so the enrolment tells us) several times 'both in French and in English' to ensure that he did. Theobald was at the least a member of the gentry. By 1300 it was no longer

[68] PRO, CP 40/110, m. 239.

[69] E.g. CUL MS. Dd.7.14, f. 240v (Trinity term 1290): '*Mutford.* Qui nullum diem inponit incontinenti tenetur . . .'; BL MS. Additional 31826, f. 218r (1293): '*Hertford.* Celi que est bastard est nuli fiz juxta illud "cui pater est populus non habet ille patrem"'; LI MS. Misc. 87, ff. 28r–v (1293 Staffs. eyre): '*How*' . . . et sic fallit "ita quod ille qui habet honus despensionis habet emolumentum accionis"'.

[70] *Year Book 21 and 22 Edward I*, pp. 433–7 and BL MS. Additional 31826, ff. 64v–65r (1291E): '*Mutford.* Beatus venter qui te portavit . . .'

[71] CUL MS. Dd.7.14, f. 401r (1286); BL MS. Additional 31826, f. 321v; BL MS. Additional 31826, ff. 141v–142r (1302).

[72] PRO CP 40/125, m. 278'.

certain that even such a man would automatically understand French. Thus here we find yet another reason for litigants to employ serjeants to speak for them in court. They needed interpreters, someone who was literally able to speak the language of the court. What was also coming to be true by 1300 was that even a French speaker would not necessarily have understood much of what was going on in court. There was already coming to be a technical, specialised vocabulary of English law: words only used in a legal context and words which had come to bear a specialist meaning in their legal context which they did not bear in other contexts, e.g. *revertir, remaindre*, *descendre*, *tailler*.

More than half a century ago George Woodbine suggested that English had been the language of the English royal courts up until the middle of the thirteenth century; and that it was only at the very end of the reign of Henry III that their proceedings began to be conducted in French.[73] The only real evidence he cited was the English technical vocabulary used in 'Bracton' and the use of phrases in English on the plea rolls of the reign of Henry III. Although the direct evidence either way is slight there is, I think, just enough to indicate that Woodbine was wrong.[74] The number of English words found on the plea rolls of the reign of Henry III is not that striking and a re-examination of the English terms found in *Bracton* reveals that they are either everyday, non-technical terms or technical terms that are confined to one specific area of English law, the criminal law (and particularly the tithing system). Since the lower levels of the system of criminal justice were the one area of substantial continuity from the Anglo-Saxon legal past it is hardly surprising that some of the technical legal vocabulary of Anglo-Saxon survived here. There is also strong negative evidence: the absence of any technical terms derived from English in other areas of English law. This by itself would suggest how unlikely it is that proceedings were conducted in the major royal courts in English up to the middle of the thirteenth century since by that time the legal system had developed the need for a relatively sophisticated technical vocabulary. It seems much more likely that French had been the language of the royal courts from the reign of Henry II onwards and that French was their language because in that period it had been the first language of the men appointed as royal justices and of many, perhaps most, litigants. French remained the language of the courts in part because of cultural conservatism, the absence of any really compelling reason for changing accepted practice; in part because there were advantages to the professional elite

[73] George E. Woodbine, 'The Language of English Law', *Speculum*, 18 (1943), pp. 395–436.

[74] I discuss the matter in greater detail in 'The Languages of the Law in Later Medieval England', an unpublished paper given to the 1997 Aberystwyth conference on Multilingualism in Later Medieval Britain,

who dominated legal practice in using a language which needed to be learned and mastered by outsiders and which enhanced their mystique; in part because the courts had developed a technical French vocabulary that was not easily translatable into English.

IV. CHARACTERISTICS OF PROCEEDINGS

This essay has attempted to create a more general picture of the overall context of litigation as conducted in the royal courtrooms of late thirteenth- and early fourteenth-century England: who the participants were and what roles they played and of how justices, serjeants and others (but mainly justices and serjeants) interacted with each other within the courtroom, both verbally and non-verbally.

The conduct of litigation within the Edwardian courtroom in certain respects resembled a dramatic performance. The serjeants often spoke as though they themselves embodied the person of their clients and as though they were acting their part ('Sir, *we* acknowledge that *we* hold of R. but R. prior to this acknowledgment granted *our* services to one A., by which grant we attorned . . .'). They also often spoke as though the opposing serjeant embodied the person of his client and was acting his part ('*You yourself* had the wardship of all and then *you* leased it over to one W. de N. for so much and *you* will render account of what *you yourself* leased . . .'). This practice may not, however, have been wholly consistent and the serjeants (at least in the reports) also sometimes talked both of their client and of their client's opponent by name in the third person. We also read of entrances and exits and the names of the main characters involved in the dialogue are picked out for us in most reports by underlining, just like the characters in a play-script. There were humorous interludes too, even in the most serious of plays, though this seems to have been a speciality of the justices of the court. In a report of a case of 1296, for example, where one of the parties was trying to escape the consequences of having accepted the homage of one of the other parties Chief Justice Mettingham came up with what must have been intended to be a humorous simile. 'You resemble the young lady who took money to be fucked (*fotu*) and then repented and went back to the young man who had fucked her. "Dear, sweet young man, please take your money back and unfuck me (*si me defoutez*) because I have repented". The same here. Because you acted foolishly in taking the homage of master Richard you want now to repent . . .'[75]

[75] BL MS. Additional 35116, f. 186v: '*Met'*. Vous resemblez a la damoiselle qe prist del argent pur estre fotu et pus se repenti et dit al vallet qe laveit fotu "Beau duz vallet, parnez vostre argent arrere, si me defoutez car jeo me repenk". Auxi pardecea de pus qe vous avez fet folie en preignant homage mestre Richard repenter. Responez a la partie . . .'

There was also another way of looking at litigation: to view it as an instructional process. There were 'apprentices' (learners) in the court from at least 1290 onwards and soon after this they were assigned a special place in the court to observe and record proceedings there. Some of the early law reports are their record of what they had learned in court from the serjeants and the justices. The serjeants too talked on occasion not of the particular cases they had 'seen' or 'heard' but of the more general rules that they had 'learned' (*apris*).[76] It is possible that this refers to what they had been taught in formal instruction outside the court. If so, it is difficult to see why this should have been thought to have been particularly persuasive. It seems more likely that it refers to rules they had 'learned' from observing and even from participating in litigation in the court.[77] In at least one instance a serjeant talked of a demurrer on a point of a law as 'demurring there for instruction (*pur la aprise*) from your judgement'.[78] It was, after all, in the very nature of the common law as a constantly evolving system of customary law that it was not just beginners but also advanced practitioners who could learn, indeed had to learn, on a daily basis from the judgements given in and by the courts what the law was. The courtroom was a classroom for practising lawyers as well as law students. Even the justices must have learnt some of their law both from the lawyers practising before them as well as from their colleagues on the bench.

[76] E.g. *Year Book 20 and 21 Edward I*, p. 451: '*Howard.* Sire, a ceo ke nous avom apris, james en nuly counte de mounde ne deyt houme dire al fyn del counte 'e ke icel seyt sun dreyt yl en ad sute bone' fors a bref de dreyt ke serra termine par bataille . . .'; BL MS. Additional 31826, f. 260v (1293–4 Yorkshire eyre): '*Inge.* Sire, jeo nay mie apris a defendre les damages nostre neyve'; LI MS. Misc. 738, f. 121v (1294): '*Warr'.* Nous avom aprise qe en checun cas ou homme puet alegger nontenure qe homme puet demander par bref a recoverir en demene . . .'; BL MS. Additional 31826, f. 88r (1300): '*Tou'.* Sire, jeo ay apris qe la ou persone e vikere unt certeines porcions de terres e lun oste lautre de sa porcion qe celi qe est ouste ne peut point user la novele disseisine ver cely qe ly ousta dunt il me semble . . .'

[77] For a more specific reference to what a particular serjeant had learnt from Beckingham (either as a justice or as a clerk) during the time Weyland was chief justice of the court see *Year Book 21 and 22 Edward I*, p. 169. More puzzling is the reference to what a serjeant had learnt 'from himself and his ancestors' in a case of 1297: BL MS. Egerton 2811, f. 100r: '*Warr'.* Sire, nous avoms apris de nous e de nos auncestres qe clerk se put metter en enqueste sauf sa clergie. *Berr'.* Vous avez malement entendu qar vostre reson se lye endreit de la suyt le roy e nient endreit de la suyte la partie . . .'

[78] BL MS. Hargrave 375, ff. 42v–43v (1297): '*Ing'.* Nus demurrums la pur la aprise en vos juggemens . . .' cf. *Year Book 30 and 31 Edward I*, p. 449; BL MS. Harley 25, f. 69r: '*Herle.* Sire, nus vus fessunz un protestacion qe nous ne conissum mye estre seisi de xx souz estre lez xx souz de rente service, mes pur aprise vus dioms qe il conust qe sun pere fut seisi de cele rente charge e il poet aver venuz a cel rente par veye de destresce e demandonz jugement etc.' (1303).

7. *'Nemo mortalis cognitus vivit in evo': moral and legal conflicts in a Florentine inheritance case of 1442*

THOMAS KUEHN

Death was a morally and legally perilous moment in early Renaissance Florence. In that era of high mortality death threw into relief the fate of one's soul and that of one's property. Both ostensibly fell into the hands of one's kin. They would distribute charitable bequests, see to the saying of masses for the soul, take care of the distribution of assets to legatees and creditors, and come into possession of the rest of the property, including identity-defining elements like a city dwelling or a rural estate. If it is true that 'rules of inheritance are in the nature of ideology and are not guidelines for actions', then every inheritance potentially carries problematic elements.[1] Impartible inheritance seeks to maintain estates intact; partible leans to providing for all children. Neither can be fully realised, as ecological constraints expose contradictions. 'Thus, while the inheritance ideology provides a cognitive framework within which the *de facto* process must operate, both the mechanics of the process and its results are in the last instance determined by the forces of environment and market, and in spite of ideologies.'[2]

Such an anthropological perspective is more concerned with ambiguous processes and the arbitrariness of meaning than with discrete incidents. It recognises that rules may have achieved such a tangible hegemony that they do not appear to be ideology at all but merely part of a 'natural' order.[3] Still the historian must attempt to account for events, and while not wanting to fall prey to modern notions of agency that seek social causes in individual action, the historian needs to come to grips with specific and not generic forms of moral and legal dilemma. Actions of discrete agents are oriented to crystallising distinct outcomes (even if not always achieved or only

[1] John W. Cole and Eric R. Wolf, *The Hidden Frontier: Ecology and Ethnicity in an Alpine Valley* (New York, 1974), p. 264.

[2] Ibid., p. 203.

[3] John and Jean Comaroff, *Ethnography and the Historical Imagination* (Boulder and London, 1992), pp. 11, 29, 37.

gained in combination with others). These outcomes are best recovered and understood in the context of case studies. What follows is a study of one case from Renaissance Florence.

The inheritance ideology of Florence – the same as for most of the communes of northern and central Italy in the late middle ages – was partible agnatic succession. As captured in statutes enacted over the centuries, the basic rules limited female inheritance to dowry. Daughters were disadvantaged in favour of sons, grandsons, brothers, nephews and cousins; sisters were disadvantaged to the same agnates, as were mothers; and wives were quite thoroughly restricted as well.[4] These were the rules of intestacy. Jurists backed their agnatic bias and incorporated them into the terms of learned law (based on Roman and canon law). This was the blueprint for inheritance where the deceased, purposely or not, failed to leave alternative instructions in the form of other legal instruments – testaments, codicils, gifts in contemplation of death.

These rules left much out. Where there were multiple heirs, how was property to be divided? What, if anything, was to be done about charitable bequests? How were debts to be settled and credits collected? What might be left to more distant kin, friends, or others who had no claims on intestacy? It seemed good advice – certainly heeded by countless Florentines, as seen in the surviving notarial records – to leave a proper will in which such problems might be addressed. Paolo da Certaldo, a fourteenth-century moralist, put it succinctly when he advised those who fell ill, 'immediately arrange your affairs, take confession and communion and make your testament, if you did not do so when healthy'.[5] But he went on to give very pointed advice not to leave one's children's affairs in the hands of a wife, who would either attach herself to someone else by remarriage or simply be too weak to manage affairs successfully. This ideology of female weakness just reinforced that of agnatic privilege in inheritance, while providing another cautionary note in favour of using wills.

In point of fact, as I have argued elsewhere, dying intestate was also a choice, viable on its own terms, that eliminated legatees and other claims.[6]

[4] In general, see Franco Niccolai, *La formazione del diritto successorio negli statuti comunali del territorio lombardo-tosco* (Milan, 1940); Thomas Kuehn, *Law, Family, and Women: Toward a Legal Anthropology of Renaissance Italy* (Chicago, 1991), ch. 10, and '*Memoria* and Family in Law', in Giovanni Ciappelli, ed., *Art, Memory and Family in Early Renaissance Florence* (London, 1997), and 'Person and Gender in the Laws', in Judith Brown and Robert C. Davis, eds., *Gender and Society in Renaissance Italy* (New York and London, 1997); David Herlihy and Christiane Klapisch-Zuber, *Les toscans et leurs familles* (Paris, 1978), pp. 532–3.

[5] Paolo da Certaldo, 'Libro di buoni costumi', in Vittore Branca, ed., *Mercanti scrittori* (Milan, 1986), pp. 47, 90–1.

[6] See Thomas Kuehn, 'Law, Death, and Heirs in the Renaissance: Repudiation of Inheritance in Florence', *Renaissance Quarterly*, 45 (1992), pp. 484–516.

Wills, by modifying or circumventing the 'natural' order of agnatic succession, could excite controversy among survivors. In the case we will consider it was the will of Lodovico di ser Viviano that sparked litigation, rather than preventing it. All three different wills in this case worked some addition or readjustment to the intestate situation. All three raised problems and conflicts, even as they tried to foresee or preclude them.

The resolutive arbitration in the case bears the motto 'no known mortal has lived for ever'. It seems the notary who placed it there intended it not only as a salutary warning of death fully in keeping with the temper of the age.[7] It also conveyed a sense that only by living for ever could one prevent inheritance disputes and the passage of property into unwanted hands.

I. THE CASE

The property in question began as the possession of one of Florence's wealthier citizens of the early fifteenth century, ser Viviano di Neri Viviani, and it ended up with the most impressive new charitable institution of the city, the foundling hospital of the Innocenti. Ser Viviano served as chief notary for Florence's legislative councils, *notaio delle riformagioni*, for a long term spanning 1378 to 1414 – a post overshadowed only by that of chancellor held for most of those same years by the humanist Coluccio Salutati (at whose funeral ser Viviano spoke). From such an influential position ser Viviano was able to amass a sizeable fortune and valuable social contacts. Lauro Martines estimated that he was among the top 2 per cent of wealth in the 1403 *estimo*; and Gene Brucker has termed him influential and 'the most powerful figure in the permanent bureaucracy after Salutati's death in 1406'.[8] His wealth and connections were transmitted to his sons. Neri, for example, became son-in-law of the wealthy Antonio Macci, and Francesco (1379–1430) obtained a doctorate in law in 1407 and some political prominence in Florence in the 1420s.[9]

In all ser Viviano had eight sons – seven by two wives, and messer Francesco whose maternity was not ascribed in our sources (which, coupled with his exclusion from inheritance beyond a nice legacy, leads to suspicion that he was born illegitimate). It was the passage of property

[7] As elegantly captured by Alberto Tenenti, *Il senso della morte e l'amore della vita nel Rinascimento* (Turin, 1957; repr. 1977).

[8] Lauro Martines, *The Social World of the Florentine Humanists, 1390–1460* (Princeton, 1963), pp. 106 n. 58, 211, 360; Gene Brucker, *The Civic World of Early Renaissance Florence* (Princeton, 1977), pp. 265–6.

[9] On Neri: Ronald F. E. Weissman, *Ritual Brotherhood in Renaissance Florence* (New York, 1982), p. 13; on Francesco: Brucker, *Civic World of Early Renaissance Florence*, pp. 472, 484, 496, and Lauro Martines, *Lawyers and Statecraft in Renaissance Florence* (Princeton, 1968), p. 492.

among the four sons of the first marriage – Andrea, Neri, Lodovico, and Giovanni – that would give rise to legal problems, because they were substituted for each other as heirs. A separate division and substitution was set up in ser Viviano's will of 1414 for the three younger sons – Salvestro, Franco, and Lionardo.[10] There was also a daughter, Camilla, who received a legacy but otherwise does not figure in our case.

As death approached ser Viviano sought to arrange his affairs in keeping with Florentine sensibilities as expressed by Paolo da Certaldo. First, on 26 July 1414 he appointed his sons Neri, Lodovico, Giovanni and Salvestro (the latter as sole representative of the interests of the second set of siblings) as his legal agents (*procuratores*) to seek from the commune of Florence any sums owed him as salary.[11] On 5 August he drew up his testament and, beyond various *legata,* assigned to the four older boys the family dwelling in Santi Apostoli and another house purchased from the sons of a maestro Filippo. Messer Francesco, termed *primogenitus*, was not allowed to live there. Messer Andrea, papal protonotary in nearby Prato, was allowed to live there, but accompanied only by one servant, and only in case of need, because otherwise 'clergy do not live well with laymen'.[12] Another house went only to Neri, Lodovico and Giovanni, to all of whom also, along with Salvestro, went control over all *monte* shares and interest payments from Florence's funded public debt *(monte comune*). The seven sons were all named *heredes universales* in equal portions, with, as remarked, Andrea, Neri, Lodovico and Giovanni substituted for each other. Ser Viviano provided a division of *bona immobilia* between the two sets of sons, assigning to the older set all his holdings in San Jacopo di Sanbuco, in San Martino and San Gaudenzio and Santa Maria in Peretola, San Biaggio in Petriuolo, San Cristofano of Nuovoli, and Santa Maria in Cintoio. Messer Andrea, handsomely provided for by his ecclesiastical benefice, was asked to remain content with his full brothers splitting the fruits of his portion of the lands, as long as he was not in dire need.[13]

Ser Viviano's death soon followed, and his sons accepted the inheritance as he had worked out, with Neri, Lodovico and Giovanni moving quickly to a division of properties among themselves on 30 August. Neri took his

[10] Most of the information comes from the lengthy arbitration text of 1442: Archivio di Stato, Firenze, Notarile antecosimiano 19069, fols. 53r–54r, 61v, 71r–v, 116r–v, 193r–v, 305v–308r, 377r–394v (hereafter Arbitration); corroborated against the *punctus* of the *consilia* for the hospital: Biblioteca Nazionale, Firenze, Fondo magliabechiano xxix, 167, fols. 109r–120r (hereafter Consilium).

[11] Arbitration, fols. 377r–379r. The sons' occupations were given as notary (Andrea), merchant (Neri), silk merchant (Lodovico), student (Salvestro), and silk merchant again (Franco). No occupation was ascribed to Giovanni.

[12] Ibid., fol. 379r: 'non stant bene clericis cum laycis'.

[13] Ibid., fols. 379r–380r.

one-seventh of ser Viviano's and one-fifth of their mother's (Felice) estate, while Lodovico and Giovanni kept their shares of both estates in common. There was no specific share carved out for messer Andrea.[14]

Relations among these four brothers deteriorated thanks to the problem of sharing and dividing the inheritance. The following month the sons made a seven-part division of their father's *monte* credits, which amounted to 7239 florins in Florence and 1008 in Pisa, putting four shares in the name of three sons.[15] Even though messer Andrea was still alive in 1418 he was again left out of the division of a sum of 856 florins in the *monte* among his three brothers only.[16] In fact Andrea had tried in January 1415 to enter into his holdings by judicial decree (*missus in tenutam*), but his brothers resisted. Andrea obtained *tenuta* and on 18 June 1415 sought division of the properties, again countered by his brothers, successfully it seems, on the grounds that ser Viviano's will forbade it. Andrea was also able in November 1415 to get assigned to himself 71 florins in *monte* credits that had belonged to his father.[17] Meanwhile, on 6 June, Lodovico and Giovanni had separated some of their holdings in common (two farms in Sanbuco) by splitting thirty lots into twelve for Lodovico and eighteen for Giovanni. Lodovico's split, however, was still deemed better, so he also had to pay his brother 25 florins. Neri, Lodovico and Giovanni had also held in common a large *podere* at Peretola with its conjoined pieces of land, which they divided at that time.

That brothers fell out over the division of property was not uncommon. What happened with ser Viviano's sons hardly made them unique.[18] In late medieval Italy shared fraternal experiences under the same roof were no guarantee of avoiding tensions and rivalries, which were regularly ignited by the division of common inheritance. The escalation of fraternal quarrels has rarely led to the most extreme form of rivalry captured in the familiar example of Cain and Abel.[19] Fratricide was a rare crime, not only because it was too horrible to contemplate but because others, including kin, could and did step in and mechanisms like arbitration existed to defuse tensions. Moral literature abounded with the expression of concern about relations between brothers. In reality brothers could and did maintain personal and economic ties with each other.[20] Just as evident, however, are the

[14] Ibid., fols. 380r–381r. The *consilium* is pointedly explicit that *nullam mentionem fecerunt de suprascripto domino Andrea nec de eius parte bonorum* (Consilium, fol. 110v).

[15] Arbitration, fol. 381r–v.

[16] Ibid., fols. 381v–382r. The younger three sons got 235 florins and the rest went to two monasteries.

[17] Ibid., fols. 382r–385r.

[18] See Kuehn, *Law, Family, and Women*, ch. 1.

[19] Cf. Julius Kirshner, 'Citizen Cain of Florence', in *Mélanges Charles de la Roncière*, Université de Corse (1997).

[20] Francis William Kent, *Household and Lineage in Renaissance Florence: The Family Life of the Capponi, Ginori, and Rucellai* (Princeton, 1977), pp. 64–5.

numerous surviving arbitrations among brothers to divide inheritances and the expression of disdain toward a sibling, who was a natural rival for a share of the patrimony. In the case before us, ser Viviano's testamentary provisions for division of the inheritance, both between and within the two sets of brothers, were intended to preclude fraternal quarrels. The brothers themselves, through the careful movement of divisions of real properties and *monte* shares, seem to have proceeded with caution and to have preserved working relations among themselves (with the exception of the priest Andrea). But too much was at stake, the situations and interests of the brothers diverged too sharply, so that the underlying tensions could emerge. They would resolve these tensions legally, peaceably, without resort to violence; but they would succumb to them – and thus leave us a useful historical example of fraternal disputes.

In 1418 Lodovico precipitated the division of the family house in Florence. Neri and Giovanni at that point wrote to Andrea, who wrote to Lodovico to protect his interest. Lodovico protested that he had no intention of diminishing Andrea's share but that the others had asked for the *compromesso* and that he would pursue it, '*o per forza o per amore*'. With Andrea, he said, he had always been '*d'acordo*'. His ire was directed at Neri and Giovanni:

> And it can always be said that neither you nor the others will ever find yourselves deceived by me, because I never deceived anyone, but I have been deceived and robbed, not by you but by my other brothers, who have always done me great harm and do and will do whatever is possible and similar shameful things. But I believe God will pay them yet as will I if I can, and I am of this intent until they will have rendered account of the houses and other things.[21]

This all may have been subterfuge in view of later events, but it was posed as a plausible state of affairs. It impelled them by July of that year to make another division of the house in Florence, the house in Peretola, and more. Lodovico came away with these houses (except for a room in Peretola reserved to Neri), although he had to lend Neri 50 florins for two years. In August a letter from Giovanni to Lodovico revealed that Andrea was unhappy and would cause problems. But Andrea would not come to Florence, said Giovanni, 'I believe he does not want to abandon his nun whore.'[22] So for all that Giovanni had been

[21] Ibid., fols. 385v–386r: 'E questo vi sia detto per sempre che da me non introverrete mai ingannato, né voi né altri, però che io non ingannai mai persona ma io sono bene stato ingannato io, e rubato, non da voi ma dagli altri miei, i quali m'anno fatto sempre gran danno e fanno e farebbono in quello è loro possibile e simile vergogna. Ma idio credo ne gli pagherà ancora e io se potessi, e di questo animo sarò per insino a tanto non m'aranno facto ragione e delle case e dell'altre cose.'

[22] Arbitration, fols. 386v–387r: 'credo non voglia abandonare la puctana monica'.

depicted as an antagonist by Lodovico in 1418, in 1419 he emerged as a sympathetic brother put off by Andrea's sexual adventures. In 1420 the three brothers sold a house, pocketing the proceeds (none for Andrea).

In July 1423 Andrea came to draw up his own testament, and he named only his brother Giovanni as his heir. Giovanni quickly took title and possession of Andrea's estate. As in civil law brothers were not necessary heirs, the way sons were, Andrea did not need to provide for each. Had he died intestate, however, his three brothers would have been entitled each to an equal share. The peculiar feature of the devolution of that part of ser Viviano's estate was that these brothers had divided Andrea's property, so that in each share there was a portion of Andrea's fourth, even though he never possessed any real part of his father's property.[23]

The *catasto* of 1427 fortuitously allows us to chart the brothers' holdings. Messer Francesco had managed to acquire holdings valued at 1224 florins, including a house in Santi Apostoli he shared with Neri, part of an *albergo* at Sanbuco shared with Lodovico and Giovanni, and various other pieces.[24] His brothers, however, were considerably better off. Lodovico, younger by five years, had 2820 florins worth of property (placing him ninety-eighth in his quarter of the city), including the family house, a house and lands at Peretola, and the *poderi* in San Gaudenzio. He shared ownership of a house Giovanni lived in and had a quarter of two *case* and a *casolare* of which Giovanni had the remaining three quarters. Lodovico also reported several obligations arising from his father's will for charitable purposes, including those to the hospitals of Santa Maria Nuova, la Scala, and la Palla.[25] Neri, a year older than Lodovico, reported to officials a worth of 2214 florins, although he had more debts and four children. He too had a house in Florence, a house and land in Peretola, and holdings in Sanbuco. The house he owned half of with Francesco, he declared to be of no value, because it was also obligated for the *tornata* of a widow and Francesco lived there so Neri had never realised from it '*utile veruno*'.[26] For his part, Giovanni, the youngest (still thirty-eight), had 1661 florins. His estate had been supplemented by Andrea's *hereditas*, although that was not all to the good. He had a yearly obligation to his dead brother's church in Prato, and a bequest to deliver to a monna Santa, Andrea's *balia*. 'And of his brother Lodovico's property for the inheritance left by his brother, he has not done anything, but by arbitration he will inform you when it is clarified.' There was a further 200 florins owed him by Lodovico beyond '*quello di messer Andrea*'.

23 Consilium, fol. 110bis v.

24 ASF, Catasto 74, fols. 30r–31v. Only Francesco had holdings at Careggi and Monterappoli, indicating his acquisitions, it seems.

25 Ibid., fols. 54r–56v; Martines, *Social World*, p. 374.

26 ASF, Catasto 74, fols. 67v–69v.

Giovanni, however, had more debts than any other brother and five young children, as well as 'a son of the priest who was called a brother by the name of Ipolito', who was five.[27]

These brothers were comfortably established, not lavishly rich. But their father's estate had had to be divided seven ways, plus *legata*. The brothers also continued to hold some properties in common. Through it all their less-than-celibate brother (who perhaps indeed would have tried the patience of his lay brothers had he lived with them) was conspicuous by his absence. Only Giovanni was still bound to Andrea in any active sense by 1427.

Whereas Andrea had never married but left a bastard son, Lodovico died childless in 1435 but left a wife. His death set in motion the machinery of litigation and arbitration. The core of the problem was that in his testament Lodovico left his property not to his brothers – to whom it would have gone on intestacy – but to the hospital of the Innocenti with bequests to the benefit of his widow (mainly usufruct for life) and none for the brothers. Not only was the Innocenti not an agnatic heir but as an institutional heir it did not call for a substitution in case of death. Lodovico's attachment to the hospital began practically from the institution's inception. He served as *operaio* in 1424 and was its treasurer in 1431, as well as serving as consul of the oversight guild of Por Santa Maria in 1424, 1429 and 1435.[28] The Innocenti itself owed its existence to the handsome estate of the wealthy merchant Francesco Datini, who died leaving only an illegitimate daughter. So Lodovico di ser Viviano's involvement with the hospital was consistent with its founding and the charitable urges that continued to nourish it.

Included in the property he left it was his share of what had been, strictly speaking, Andrea's portion of the paternal estate. Yet Lodovico had reported it all as his to *catasto* officials, paid the fiscal obligations on it, and was acknowledged in the books of the *monte* as owner of Andrea's credits. Giovanni had reported this sum to the same officials as a debt owed him. In any case the hospital was able quickly to take possession of the estate and from that position of strength fought the lawsuit brought by Giovanni. Laudable and important as the Innocenti was, it was not family. Even the most remote of relatives could hope to gain by a suit; in our case the relative was about as close as possible – a brother. Hence the Innocenti was no stranger to lawsuits.[29]

[27] Ibid., fols. 49v–50v: 'E d'avere dal Lodovicho suo fratello per la redità lasciata di messer Andrea suo fratello, non à fato chome chollei è, però nel lodo per debitore quando serà chiarita s'achomunerà' and 'un figluolo del proposto che fu dignato uno fratello a nome Ipolito'.

[28] Philip Gavitt, *Charity and Children in Renaissance Florence: The Ospedale degli Innocenti, 1410–1536* (Ann Arbor, 1990), pp. 111–12.

[29] Ibid., p. 121.

II. LEGAL ARGUMENTS

Giovanni employed legal professionals to advance a case for him. Unfortunately the *consilia* drafted in his behalf have not emerged from an archival search. We know only a distillation of the arguments on which his case rested as derived from the opposing *consilia* and from the decisive arbitration. Initially at least, the plaintiff had two different attacks. The first and broadest was to argue that the substitution of the brothers for each other, as set out in ser Viviano's will, took precedence on the property inherited from him and thus redirected Lodovico's property to Giovanni and Neri. The second prong of attack was more modest – namely, that part of the property was Andrea's inheritance and belonged by the terms of his will to Giovanni. Giovanni sought not just the property but compensation for the revenue and for the *monte* credits alienated since Andrea's death.[30]

As a preliminary rejoinder for the defendant, it was argued that the substitution was 'direct', in which case it expired on the acceptance of the estate by the heirs. Also, in the formal divisions of property, which had included Andrea's share, all the brothers had bound themselves to observe the terms, so it was argued Giovanni could not seek to overturn the division. These arguments were bolstered by Florentine jurists. The sealed original text of their opinions has survived and its arguments and methods bear examination to see how the law in its technical richness and complexity gave shape to the moral and legal claims of these brothers.

In all, five jurists were retained by the Innocenti and Lodovico's widow Tita.[31] The lead opinion was that of Benedetto Barzi, a Perugian active in Florence for a period in the 1430s and 1440s – a man whose doctrinal writings would gain him some professional respect. He was joined by Filippo Balducci (*c.* 1398–1458), Guglielmo Tanagli (1391–1460), Salustio Buonguglielmi (1373–1461), and Piero Ambrosini da Iesi (1403–72). None of these men was a native Florentine, except Tanagli, who added only a corroboratory signature. He was a presence but not an active voice.[32] Their texts were composed at an uncertain date between 1435 and 1440, more likely toward the end of that five-year period, as Barzi's matriculation into the Florentine guild did not occur until 1440.

As so much of the case revolved around the technicalities of types of substitution, it is necessary to consider briefly the relevant law.[33] According to the civil law there were several different types of substitution. The

[30] Consilium, fol. 111r.

[31] Consilium, fol. 109r, makes plain that the *consilium* was '*in favorem domine Tite legatarie*'.

[32] On all these, see Martines, *Lawyers*, pp. 484, 501–3.

[33] What follows relies heavily on Andrea Padovani, *Studi storici sulla dottrina delle sostituzioni* (Milan, 1983), but see also Romualdo Trifone, *Il fedecommesso: Storia dell'istituto in Italia* (Naples, 1914), Luigi Tria, *Il fedecommesso nella legislazione e nella dottrina dal secolo*

Roman *substitutio vulgaris* generally provided a substitute in case the designated heir (*heres institutus*) refused the *hereditas*. The *substitutio pupillaris* provided a mechanism by which a *paterfamilias* could designate a substitute for his underage son (*impuberis*) should the boy die before reaching the age of majority. Thus the substitute succeeded not to the father but to the son, but by this means it was possible to prevent the flow of property to unwanted persons (presumably outside the family). The *fideicommissum* allowed someone to name even an *extraneus* as heir and a successor to him – that is, to ask him to deliver the *hereditas* to another at his death. This latter form experienced considerable doctrinal elaboration in the medieval schools and frequent and diverse practical application in the course of the fourteenth and fifteenth centuries. It made possible an extension of pupillary substitution to a son who had in fact reached the age of majority, as well as to heirs not subject to the testator's *potestas*.

As far back as the early thirteenth-century jurist Azo, there was precedent for seeing a clause substituting one heir for another '*si sine filiis decesseri*' as a fideicommissary substitution.[34] While the language in ser Viviano's will did not directly employ that clause (instead it simply '*ad invicem substituit*'), in the climate of early fifteenth-century Florence it is not hard to see that condition as tacitly behind the substitution. Why else establish it? Further, in jurisprudence there was a line of argument that use by the testator, whose wishes were to be implemented as much as possible, of jurisprudentially defined *verba communia*, of which one was the verb *substituere* (the only verb attributed to ser Viviano's will), was to be reckoned a form of substitution known as *compendiosa*, which was said to be an equivalent to or contain within it the *fideicommissum*.[35]

The exact language chosen, however, was more likely to be the result of formulae employed by a notary, and there was considerable variance in the practical needs of language in redacting documents and the use of technical and abstract language in jurisprudence. Notarial formularies ultimately sought a way past ambiguities by employing all apposite terms at once – '*vulgariter et pupillariter et per fideicommissum*'. This language was used in ser Viviano's will, but only on the second substitution of the younger set of brothers. Ser Viviano had not constituted his *immobilia* as indivisible and inalienable, bound to the family in an order of succession in primogeniture as would be common in later wills of elite Florentines.[36] Thus it was that

footnote 33 (*cont.*)
xvi ai nostri giorni (Milan, 1945), Andrea Romano, *Le sostituzioni ereditarie nell' inedita 'Repetitio de substitutionibus' di Raniero Arsendi* (Catania, 1977).

34 Padovani, *Studi storici*, p. 91.

35 Ibid., pp. 160–1, 255.

36 Cf. R. Burr Litchfield, *Emergence of a Bureaucracy: The Florentine Patricians, 1530–1790* (Princeton, 1986), pp. 220–8; Tria, *Fedecommesso*, pp. 11–12.

Lodovico was free to alienate his holdings by his will outside his family to the Innocenti, with usufruct to his widow. His moral sense of the family, in other words, went no deeper than his father's had. Ser Viviano had not looked past his sons. Each of them (except the priest Andrea) was, or would be, head of his own family in turn, and so each was left something (and by prevailing standards, something fairly substantial) to begin with or carry on. Having no children, Lodovico provided for his widow and left his property instead to the benefit of the children who would soon crowd into the Innocenti.

Because family property was not corporately owned, divisions and alienations occurred. Kin used lawsuits to press claims to such family property, but, according to William Kent, 'the principal means . . . to keep property and goods within the wider family was a careful attention to inheritance in wills'.[37] Were the Viviani lacking in an abiding sense of family such as Kent found in the three clans he studied? Was the lack of a *fideicommissum* making property inalienable within a wider family indicative of a lack of 'instinctive family piety' in these relative newcomers to power and wealth in Florence?[38] Do the wills of ser Viviano and Lodovico instead lend support to the notion of 'private wealth' in Florentine families of the Renaissance – marked by a 'lack of cohesion and continuity' such that beyond the household, 'where economic ties were loosened or altogether severed, relationships are more likely than not to be of genealogical interest only'?[39]

Kent noted that the last member of a branch of a Florentine lineage did not always leave his estate to the wider family. Daughters and charitable institutions figured as heirs even though markedly counter to the interests of other kin.[40] Had they not done so, the Innocenti would have had a hopeless time getting established. Concerns of piety could compete with family loyalties. It is perhaps symptomatic that there was no quiet letting go of Lodovico's property. The brother(s) saw it as theirs. And the same was true of many other estates left to the Innocenti.[41] Further, as we have seen, while Lodovico may not have left much mention of his brothers in his will, contrary to many Florentines, his *catasto* statements allow recovery of numerous economic ties, as presumably would any account books.[42]

The legal issues in the case, however, were not posed in terms of 'family property' or 'private wealth'. The legal conflict was over the nature of the

[37] Kent, *Household and Lineage*, pp. 127, 135. [38] Ibid., pp. 141–4.
[39] Richard Goldthwaite, *Private Wealth in Renaissance Florence* (Princeton, 1968), p. 155.
[40] Kent, *Household and Lineage,* pp. 146–8.
[41] Gavitt, *Charity and Children,* pp. 121–6.
[42] Cf. Kent, 'La famiglia patrizia fiorentina nel Quattrocento: Nuovi orientamenti nella storiografia recente', in *Palazzo Strozzi: Metà Millennio, 1489–1989* (Rome, 1991), pp. 70–91.

substitution in ser Viviano's will. The Innocenti's lead advocate, Benedetto Barzi, cultivated a certain expertise in his career about substitutions.[43] Such expertise begged to be heard first. Barzi began his *consilium* by making it clear that if the substitution in ser Viviano's will was fideicommissary, then all that Lodovico had acquired from his father would pass to his brothers. His *heres* would not have available an action for a trebellianic portion, as ser Viviano's will forbade such, and no *legitim* could be claimed because Lodovico had in his life alienated the equivalent sum. Clear support for the prohibition of a trebellianic portion lay in the commentaries of Bartolo da Sassoferrato (d. 1357), who had rejected the old rule of Roman civil law that a testator could not forbid such a portion. 'Lords, certainly,' he had declared, 'our moral laws are different from the variety of mores over time, as the *lex Quod de bonis* was made at a time when they were pagans and there was no hope in another life but they thought otherwise and did not consider the merits of the soul.'[44] The moral variation worked by the hope of salvation sent the case spinning away from moral obligations to leave something to one's kin/heir and crashing to earth on the hard ground of substitution. Was it *fideicommissaria*?

One line of argument was that the substitution applied to persons past the age of puberty, so its application was 'oblique' and not direct. The substitution of the second set of brothers had been explicitly '*vulgariter pupillariter et per fideicommissum*', and this coverage of all modes of substitution was meant to apply to the first one as well. Both the coupling expression '*nec non*' leading to the second substitution and the presumption of paternal desire for equality among sons militated for such a reading.[45] Barzi, however, overturned these arguments, mainly on the fact that ser Viviano's testament had not used the same covering terms for the substitution of the first, older set of brothers as it had for the second. Resting his argument on the commentaries of Bartolo, Barzi declared that a simple substitution such as that before him, having no temporal references (e.g., if one should die without children, which would point to the uncertain but specific future moment of death), could only be taken as *vulgaris.* In fact, in one commentary Barzi listed, Bartolo had addressed the situation of substitutions of pairs of half-brothers and decided that only the full

43 Padovani, *Studi storici,* pp. 344–5.

44 Bartolo to *C. 6.50.7, *Opera omnia*, 10 vols. (Venice, 1615), vol. VIII, fols. 48vb–49rb: 'Domini, pro certo ista nostra iura moralia variantur ex tempore secundum morum varietatem l. Quod de bonis [' i C. ad legem falcidiam] fuit facta tempore quo erant pagani, nec vita in alio seculo sperabatur sed aliud cogitabant nec aspiciebant merita animae . . .'

45 Consilium, fol. 113r: 'Ad hoc ut copula illa nec non equaliter terminet precedentia et sequentia et hoc etiam corroboratur quia cum omnes essent pariter filii testatoris non est verisimile quod plenius voluerit providere inter filios secundi matrimonii quam inter filios primi sed quod voluerit inter ipsos filios equalitatem servare . . .'

brother succeeded.[46] But Barzi did not dwell on the parallels to his case, needing instead to confront the meaning of the '*nec non*' that linked the substitutions in ser Viviano's will. Barzi claimed that both Bartolo and Baldo degli Ubaldi (1323–1400), but especially the former in his commentary on the *lex Centurio* (D. 28.6.15), said that if the persons substituted to each other were *impuberes in potestate* then there were two types of substitution (*vulgaris* and *pupillaris*), and if there was also added the temporal adverb *quandocunque*, then there were also *substitutiones fideicommissarie* – 'for there is then a mixed reciprocal substitution in the compendious one by virtue of which a fideicommissary substitution results'.[47] Crucial in the case before him was the fact that there was no such adverb in ser Viviano's will, so 'it is very certain that a fideicommissary substitution could not take place and that having taken the inheritance the force of the substitution to Lodovico totally expired'.[48] Barzi's argument was bolstered again by citation of Bartolo and Baldo, who, in discussing *legata*, had declared that terms laid out in a testament could not apply where there was not an *identitas personarum*.[49] Barzi dismissed the extension of the language of the second substitution to the first by posing that the two *dictiones* were *diverse*, the '*nec non*' did not couple the two substitutions; it only set out the '*ordinem verborum*'. Here the commentary of Baldo to the *lex Si fortidianum* (C. 6.37.7) provided crucial support. Baldo there worked a much finer distinction between adversative and conjunctive expressions and considered not the term '*nec non*' but the familiar '*item*' as linking two completed separate *capitula*.[50]

When Barzi's colleagues approached this issue they each managed to put

[46] Bartolo to D. 28.6.45, *In primam infortiati commentaria* (Lyon, 1544), fol. 145rb.

[47] Consilium, fol. 113r: 'est enim tunc mista reciproca in compendiosa cuius virtute resultat fideicommissaria'. Regarding Bartolo on this, see Padovani, *Studi storici*, pp. 270–4. In fact Bartolo placed greater emphasis on the matter of temporal distinction in the language of the substitution: 'Sol. intelligas sic, si quidem substitutio compendiosa est facta per adiectionem temporis importati per distributivum, quandocunque: tunc sine dubio continet fideicommissariam post aditam haereditatem et pupillarem, ut supra dixi. idem si non est apposita dictio quandocunque sed alia quae de natura sui temporis tractum significat, ut si decesserit sine liberis, licet non dicat quandocunque: quia tunc requiritur tractus temporis, ut appareat utrum decedat sine liberis, et tunc continet fideicommissariam d. l. Haeredes mei et d. c. i de test. li. 6. facit l. precib. Sed si dixerit testator, filio meo talem substituo, nullo adiecto quod requirat tractum temporis tunc illa substitutio non esset compendiosa sed vulgaris tantum vel pupillaris, si esset facta filio impuberi l. Gallus 'i secundum unam casus positionem de lib. et posth. approbatur in l. Iam hoc iure' i supra eod' *Opera omnia*, vol. III, fol. 127rb).

[48] Consilium, fol. 113v: 'certius est quod fideicommissaria locum habere non potuit et quod adita hereditate per Lodovicum virtus illius substitutionis totaliter expiravit'.

[49] Bartolo to D. 32.[1].63, *Opera omnia*, vol. IV, fols. 56vb–57ra; Baldo to C. 6.40.3, *Opera omnia*, 9 vols. (Venice, 1577), vol. VII, fol. 138ra.

[50] Baldo, *Opera omnia*, vol. VII, fol. 128vb: 'principaliter fuit intentio testatoris prospicere propter imbecillitatem etatis'.

a slightly different spin on it. In this way they made a stronger case. Filippo Balducci expressly noted that beyond Barzi's points, there was the argument of Baldo, Angelo, and '*moderni*' that any simple statement *amplius* without a pronoun to link it to another was not to be seen as a repetition. If the statement was 'I leave Seius 10 and more I leave Titius 100', it just meant the second legacy was larger. More to the point, the testator had been capable of making the first substitution fideicommissary, but he had not. In fact the distinction between the two substitutions made sense for with the second 'it was mainly the intent of the testator to provide for the weakness of age'. The older sons did not require such treatment.[51] Salustio Buonguglielmi brought forth the consideration that first statements have more influence on interpreting subsequent ones than the reverse.[52] From this point he moved to stress again the disparity between the two sets of sons. Finally he pointed out a matter of word order. The crucial clause read '*nec non Silvestrum Franchum et Leonardum vulgariter pupillariter et per fideicommissum substituit*'. Had the verb preceded the adverbs, then a case might be made that they were intended to apply to both sets of sons, but as they instead came framed within the clause by the verb they applied only to the three youngest.[53] Ambrosini took the discussion in yet another direction. Invoking a literature of treatises by Dino del Mugello (d. 1303), Ranieri Arsendi da Forlì (d. 1358), and Niccolò Alessandri of Perugia, Ambrosini set out that in the face of so many authoritative doctors there was no doubt that there was no fideicommissary substitution contained in the language in ser Viviano's will. Though he did not doubt that other *consultores* could work hard to argue the contrary, he also believed it firmly established that the first substitution was complete in itself. It did not depend on or even refer to the second. Indeed, the testator seemed to have kept the two substitutions separate not only because they concerned sons from different marriages but because they were different in form. In that way one could go with the plain and simple meaning of the words ('*prout adverba sonant et volunt*').[54]

The second difficulty was Andrea's portion. Undoubtedly if Andrea were alive he could seek his property, so could Giovanni as his heir 'as by legal fiction an heir is the same person with the deceased' ('*cum fictione iuris heres sit eadem persona cum defuncto*'). The *beneficium evictionis* that would seem to protect Lodovico from claims arising after the division did not hold, it was argued, because he knowingly accepted the property of another.

[51] Ibid., fols. 116v–117r.

[52] Here he notably cited Bartolo to D. 32.[1].95, *Opera omnia*, vol. IV, fol. 62rb, where he declared 'quod praecedens clausula est maioris efficacie ad determinationem sequentium quam sequentes ad determinationem precedentium'.

[53] Ibid., fol. 118r.

[54] Ibid., fols. 118v–119v.

Against these arguments Barzi conceded that Lodovico or his heirs could not simply resist Giovanni on the grounds that Andrea's rights had been remitted. But he did allow that the quickest measure available to Lodovico's heirs was the contractual obligation of Giovanni and all the brothers not to act against the terms of the division. This contractual obligation seemed to hold according to texts of Bartolo and others.[55] Barzi also argued that the brothers' knowledge of Andrea's portion did not matter; they had also freely obligated themselves to abide by the division.[56] This was resting a lot on a contractual waiver of right in a situation that was not at all straightforward.

Balducci weighed in with the thought that Giovanni was asserting not his right but that of Andrea, a third party, and he was obligated to defend the division against third parties. And he had to defend the entire division, not just part of it. Even if the *evictio* did not apply, said Balducci, Giovanni was bound by the nature of the contract of division alone.[57] Only Ambrosini returned to this matter, duplicating as he did so the language of the notarial text of the *divisio*. It was the overt nature of the commitment to hold to the terms that mattered to him. To the observation that Giovanni acted against the division with a different right (namely, as Andrea's heir) than he pretended to at the time of the division (when Andrea was still alive), Ambrosini replied that he could not act against his legal deed. Ambrosini also coupled Cino da Pistoia's assertion that where a third party evicted someone from a property, the evicted party could act against his partners or brothers, with Baldo's argument that an eviction affecting only one party's position of a divided holding allowed the evicted one an action against the other party to the division, to make the (reverse) argument that thus Lodovico could move against Giovanni for moving against him in the guise of being Andrea's heir.[58] That many other texts cited dealt with outright sales was glossed over with the assertion that division was a form of alienation comparable to a sale, even if the fact that the property belonged to another was known.[59] Lodovico's heirs had the right to 'repel' Giovanni's attempts to evict them from Andrea's property.

What all these arguments have in common is a resolute dodging of the basic issue that the property was Andrea's, taken without his consent. Had Andrea, in his will, taken the course Lodovico did – leaving his property to an *heres extraneus* – then both Giovanni and Lodovico would have had an interest in these arguments to keep this outside heir away from family

55 Especially Bartolo to D. 45.1.122,6, *Opera omnia*, vol. VI, fol. 44vb.

56 Ibid., fols. 114r–116r.

57 Ibid., fol. 117r–v.

58 Cino da Pistoia to C. 3.38.7, *In codicem et aliquot titulos primi pandectorum commentaria* (Frankfurt, 1578; repr. Turin, 1964), fol. 184va; Baldo to C. 3.36.14, *Opera omnia*, vol. V, fol. 338rb.

59 Ibid., fols. 119v–120r.

property. Instead, Lodovico's heir was an outsider and employed these jurists to frame these arguments to keep family property away from Giovanni. The clauses regarding *evictio* were indeed contractual and arguably should be enforced. But the rights in question came from one who was not a party to the agreement. No one, not Barzi himself, had adequately addressed the simple fact that Andrea himself could have challenged the division (and that as his heir so could Giovanni), while Barzi had made it clear that Andrea's right had not been lost by the agreement between his brothers.

III. ARBITRATION

The exchange of legal arguments had one notable effect on subsequent events. Giovanni appears to have backed off the larger claims that rested on defining the substitution in ser Viviano's will as fideicommissary. The legal arguments posed by Barzi and backed and expanded by his colleagues won the day. But Giovanni did not back off his claims to be Andrea's heir. To resolve that issue, he entered into an arbitration agreement (*compromissum*) with the Innocenti, whose rector, messer Tommaso da Perugia, was represented by Boccaccio di Niccolò Boccacci as *procurator,* and with Tita, represented by her brother, Lorenzo di Francesco di Giovanni di ser Segna. The arbitrators chosen were Pietro di Goro del Benino and Niccolò di Giovanni Carducci. Del Benino himself was another testamentary benefactor of the Innocenti. Like Lodovico di ser Viviano, a man without legitimate progeny, he left his estate to the hospital with provisions for an annuity of 18 florins to his illegitimate son.[60]

However, the process of arbitration with these people was not quick. First arranged on 20 July 1440 to be in effect by the end of the following month, it was renewed on 16 September, 15 November, 1 July 1441, 28 September, 30 November, 15 December, and 12 and 24 January 1442, when the arbitrator finally pronounced a finding. In the course of events a third arbitrator, Castello di Piero Quaratesi, was added, and then del Benino was replaced by Bernardo di Bartolomeo Gherardi. In the meantime, Piero d'Andrea di Piero became rector of the Innocenti and the widow Tita passed away.[61] Quaratesi, in fact, was sole arbitrator at the end, and the only one of them not to serve as *operaio* of the hospital.[62]

The text of the arbitration asserts that the three arbitrators had seen extensive argumentation, numerous documents, and *consilia* of both sides. But as this was clearly a complex legal matter, the arbitrators were not pre-

[60] Gavitt, *Charity and Children*, pp. 64–5.

[61] These events emerge across Arbitration, fols. 53r–54r, 71r–v, 116r–v, 193r–v, 305v–308r.

[62] Gavitt, *Charity and Children*, p. 122.

pared to pronounce sentence on their own. Just as the contending parties had sought resolution in outside arbitrators, these in turn sought guidance and resolution from outside jurists. So the relevant documents and arguments were transmitted to the college of jurists of Genoa, and the arbitrators simply accepted and enacted their determinations. Why Genoa? There seems no particular reason, at least none recoverable from the text itself. The parties simply must have found this a mutually agreeable measure, especially as they may have already involved all Florence's available jurists.

The Genoese jurists had to take a position on the argument that Giovanni was owed Andrea's portion and interest because the property divisions among the brothers had all ultimately been regulated by the terms of ser Viviano's will. They also faced the counter-argument that Giovanni could not act against the property divisions to which he had been a party and which he had known to cover Andrea's portion as well. Alienation of *monte* shares had also occurred in accord with the will, it was alleged, so Giovanni as *procurator* on that transaction similarly could not turn on it now. Any *fructus* realised had also been used by Lodovico to meet *onera*, so there was nothing to claim on that account. Lodovico's letter to Andrea recognising his rights was dismissed as telling evidence on the grounds that the property had already been divided three, not four, ways; and the letter from Giovanni to Lodovico showed that Giovanni 'did not have regard with Andrea'.[63]

The entire *collegium* of Genoa's fourteen *doctores* signed the brief *consilium*.[64] True to form for truly decisory opinions, in contrast to partisan opinions such as that of Barzi *et al.*, the determinations were simply stated; they were not 'motivated'.[65] It is nonetheless unusual to encounter so formal a text containing not a single citation to a text of the *Corpus Iuris Civilis* or a commentary or gloss of some sort. The finding was that the *immobilia* that belonged to Andrea and came into Lodovico's hands belonged to Giovanni. The Innocenti was ordered to return all such property to Giovanni along with all *fructus* derived from the time of Andrea's death, less expenses of obtaining them. The *monte* credits were also to be returned as well as Andrea's share of whatever credits from ser Viviano's estate had been realised. Lodovico's *catasto* expenses for this property were to be deducted.[66]

[63] Arbitration, fols. 387v–389v: 'non habebat gratiam cum dicto domino Andrea'.

[64] These were, in order: Niccolò de Nigro, Evangelista Salurigii, Prosper de' Roveli, Stefano da Catania, Damiano Pallavicini, Andrea Bartolomeo, Benedetto Ravescherio, Marco de' Franchi, Andrea da Benegassio, Demetrio Vivaldi, Giovanni Cioer, Gandunfo da Fossato, Cristoforo da Rutidiario, and Lodovico da Montaldo.

[65] Cf. Julius Kirshner, '*Consilia* as Authority in Late Medieval Italy: The Case of Florence', in Mario Ascheri, Ingrid Baumgärtner, and Julius Kirshner, eds., *Consilia in the Middle Ages and Early Modern Europe: Introduction to an Historical Source* (Berkeley, 1997).

[66] Arbitration, fols. 392r–394v.

The case ended here. The *operai* of the Innocenti quickly agreed to abide by the decision, seeking only reimbursement of expenses.[67] That does not seem to have raised any problems. In his *catasto* declaration of 1446, Giovanni listed five properties formerly belonging to Lodovico, four in the countryside and a '*casa per mia habitatione*' in Peretola.[68] The parties and their arguments were at least spent, if not satisfied. A few more pieces of ser Viviano's estate remained in the hands of one of his sons. But several others were in the hands of the Innocenti. Both the moral demands of family and those of an important charity had been met, but those of the latter had been curbed somewhat, despite the legal arguments advanced on behalf of the hospital by Barzi and the others.

IV. CONCLUSIONS: MORALITY, PROPERTY AND LAW

It is hard to see ser Viviano and his sons as ignorant of the law – most especially of local statutes, procedures, and courts. Nor was the Innocenti, quickly embroiled in inheritance disputes, allowed to remain innocent of the law. This case was another manifestation of endemic, systemic conflicts and tensions in the moral and legal life of Florence.

On the one hand was a range of tensions within a family.[69] Ser Viviano, like any good *paterfamilias*, attempted to establish and guide his sons, even from beyond the grave by means of his will. He anticipated an obvious conflict by separating the two sets of siblings, which also kept the younger set from being at a disadvantage. He also anticipated conflicts regarding an illegitimate son and a beneficed cleric. Tensions between brothers were hardly unique to this family.[70] Brothers were natural rivals for portions of the patrimony, in the divisions at earlier points and finally in the dispute over Lodovico's estate. Then there were tensions between the demands of family and those of one's soul. Property was leaving the *casa* for a hospital. The brothers did not press the matter of the substitution but gave in, thereby, to the legitimate values of salvation and to those of the charitable care of foundlings – demands they had also seen inscribed in their father's will and which they had had to carry out.

Law gave the means for expression of these tensions and the pursuit of valid, if conflicting, interests. Testaments and arbitrations of division figured prominently in our case. There was a certain dimension of risk assessment in these choices, most of it unrecoverable from our sources. But

[67] Gavitt, *Charity and Children*, p. 126.

[68] Catasto 667, fol. 131v. I thank Julius Kirshner for finding this source for me.

[69] Cf. also Thomas Kuehn, '*Il diritto di famiglia e l'uso del diritto nelle famiglie fiorentine nel Rinascimento*', in *Palazzo Strozzi: Metà Millennio*, pp. 108–25.

[70] Cf. Thomas Kuehn, 'Vicissitudini di un patrimonio fiorentino del xv secolo', *Quaderni storici,* 88 (April 1995), pp. 43–61.

we know something of the deliberations of the *operai* of the Innocenti in February 1442, following the arbitration, as they weighed the fact that they had already waited over six years for this estate against recovering expenses and meeting pious bequests also contained in Lodovico's will.[71] The resort to jurists, both in litigation and arbitration, involved some assessment of the risks regarding expenses and the chances of getting one's point across.

What the jurists brought to a dispute was certainly not a perception of conflict or of the interests at stake. They brought a professional expertise that could determine what rules to apply, a presumed impartiality even when retained by litigants, a type of charisma captured in their wax seals and textual citations, and a certainty of judgement. They were perhaps most free to do so in a case such as ours because it did not fall foul of local statutes or political interests.[72] The juristic product was a compromise that realised at least a minimal acceptable level of value such that parties would adhere to it as in some way approaching a community ideal of justice.[73] The jurists in this case were also outsiders – the Genoese, but even those in Florence were new arrivals – perhaps politically vulnerable to pressure but also not politically compromised. Against the particularities of names, times, and places, their boiled-down treatment could indeed seem to point to enduring principles even as they made these resolutive and effective momentarily.

But areas of law themselves, like the nature of property, also bore ambiguities. It was a juristic commonplace that the family was its *substantia*. That substance was both tangible or fungible objects and rights in them. That was property – *proprietas* or *dominium* in law. But this *dominium* was neither held collectively nor entirely individually. This much is clear from our case. When the brothers held property even together *pro indiviso*, their fractional shares were known; and those fractional shares could be assigned and alienated – a mark of ownership – as they were both in subsuming and extricating Andrea's share from Lodovico's. On the other hand, this was not individualistic, total, exclusive ownership as in modern property law. Lodovico's rights to exclude his brothers were at least conditional or contingent. He came to his property by virtue of being their brother. His rights in property were generated relationally, as were theirs. While they thus held distinct shares, even of common pieces, and thus could report separately to *catasto* officials and meet their fiscal obligations separately, they remained aware and even entwined with each other.[74] It is for this reason that William

[71] Gavitt, *Charity and Children*, p. 126. [72] Kirshner, '*Consilia* as Authority'.

[73] Cf. Adriano Cavanna, 'Il ruolo del giurista nell'età del diritto comune', *Studia et documenta historiae et iuris*, 44 (1978), pp. 95–138; Umberto Santarelli, *L'esperienza giuridica basso-medievale* (Turin, 1977).

[74] On property law, see the magisterial collection of Paolo Grossi, *Il dominio e le cose: Percezioni medievali e moderne dei diritti reali* (Milan, 1992), and for an anthropological view, see Nicholas Thomas, *Entangled Objects: Material Culture and Colonialism in the Pacific* (Cambridge, MA, 1991).

Kent can see family property where Richard Goldthwaite sees private wealth. All sorts of moral ambiguities were thus possible and exploitable in a situation of such legal ambiguity. Some branches of a lineage might prosper while others, not without some resentment, faced economic and biological extinction.[75] In our case that seems to have been true, to the point that the Innocenti stepped in and the interests diverged more sharply.

Another way of looking at the ambiguity of property in this case is by recourse to the anthropologist Annette Weiner's concept of an 'inalienable possession'.[76] These possessions, like the Viviani houses and farms at risk of falling to the Innocenti, are ineffably imbued with the identities of their owners. Ideally these are to be retained across the generations, for their loss would diminish the group. But time brings change, or a lack of direct heirs, and political and religious realities (and perhaps the influence of a widow) intervene. Careful effort, as in wills and divisions, is needed. Inalienable possessions are to be kept away, or retrieved, from the alternative, the play of reciprocal exchange (as here the bequeathing of property to the Innocenti could gain prayers and charitable credit toward the testator's salvation). By keeping them, the group (in our case Giovanni and Neri as brothers), 'creating a semblance of unity within a family, clan or dynasty that, in fact, is rife with rivalry', could assert their distinctiveness from others and superiority to most in Florentine society.[77]

Take the very situation of messer Andrea's share. In the name of equality and internal peace, the father enjoined him not to touch his share as long as he had a benefice; but he could not just take away his share. Andrea's will was actually a way to end this ambiguity by assigning it all to Giovanni. But as the share existed, it became caught up in the active owners' divisions, which ignored it as a legal factor, seeing as it was non-existent or at least contingent (as a moral factor?). That ambiguity, perhaps even without Andrea's will, could then be exploited by Giovanni against that perpetrated by Lodovico when he ignored agnation in the name of charity and salvation and put family property into circulation to others. These ambiguities in a relational framework of ownership thus arose particularly at and because of death. And just as each generation could take an estate and build on it or squander it, those heirs could also amplify or lessen such ambiguities.[78] A generation like that of ser Viviano's sons – so many of

[75] In addition to Kent, see Roberto Bizzocchi, 'La dissoluzione di un clan familiare: i Buondelmonti di Firenze nei secoli xv e xvi', *Archivio storico italiano*, 140 (1982), pp. 3–45.

[76] Annette B. Weiner, *Inalienable Possessions: The Paradox of Keeping-While-Giving* (Berkeley, 1992).

[77] Ibid., p. 103.

[78] Hence these were the ambiguities testators would try to overcome increasingly by employing elaborate clauses and even forms of primogeniture so as to render family property more fully that of one individual owner who would arise in a set order from among descendants or other kin, on which see Samuel Kline Cohn, Jr., *Death and Property in Siena, 1205–1800: Strategies for the Afterlife* (Baltimore, 1989), pp. 128–50.

them and in two sets – was perhaps fated to amplify the problems even as it fractioned the substance. Family property had its own moral imperatives that were not impervious to the operation of time, measured in generations, or of law.

8. *Law, litigants and the construction of 'honour': slander suits in early modern England*[1]

MARTIN INGRAM

In the Salisbury consistory court in 1673, the wife of a local householder told how the previous December she had seen a bailiff called John Mills follow a servant girl, Joan Browne, down the high street, 'calling her whore div[e]rs times, & at last the said Joane Browne turn'd back & said, "Goodman Mills, why do y[o]u call me whore? I am no more a whore th[a]n one of yo[u]r owne daught[e]rs."' This apparently modest attempt to claim moral respectability on a par with Mills's own female offspring only provoked further abuse:

> Whereupon . . . Jo[hn] Mills answered in a scandalous & revileing mann[e]r, 'My daught[e]rs, you whore! Do you compare yo[u]r selfe to my daught[e]rs, you shabby lousie bitch, you runagate whore!', & so continued following of her & revileing her in such obprobrious & scandalous terms untill she went into Widowe Tomlinson's house neare to the Close gate in High Street . . . & pr[e]sently aft[e]rwards came over to this dep[onen]t[es] ho[use] cryeing, & kept cryeing all th[a]t day, insomuch th[a]t this dep[onen]t & div[e]rs oth[e]rs could not perswade her to cease, & were very much afraid th[a]t she would have done her selfe a mischeife by it; & this dep[onen]t saith that she doth beleive in her conscience that that [*sic*] the said Joane Browne is a very vertuous & civill yonge maide as any in the towne; & saith that she hath often cryed about this business & doth still at certaine times fall a crying when she thinks how publiq[ue]ly in the open street she was abused by the said Jo[hn] Mills, insomuch that it often hind[e]rs [her] from following her work or ordinary employm[en]t.[2]

1 Part of the research on which this essay is based was carried out with the aid of a British Academy Personal Research Grant.

2 Wiltshire Record Office (henceforth Wilts. RO), D1/42/61, fo. 57. For other documents in the case, see ibid., fos. 55v–59v, D1/41/1/18 (unnumbered bundle), citation 6 December 1672; D1/41/3/13 (unnumbered bundle), libel and interrogatories; D1/39/1/58, fos. 209–228v *passim*. (In this and subsequent quotations from original sources, contemporary

Via a certain type of lawsuit, of which the quotation gives a flavour, this chapter explores some ways in which the moral world of the law – or rather, in this instance, several separate but interacting systems of law – was related to, was influenced by, and in its turn influenced early modern culture and society. From a historiographical perspective, it is necessary to focus on 'honour' as well as on law and litigants, since this term has been much used (not necessarily to advantage) in recent writing in this field. Substantively the discussion is concerned less with 'honour' than with slanders and the lawsuits to which they gave rise. In the sixteenth and seventeenth centuries the law of defamation was a labyrinth, in whose twisted passages many of the themes of this volume may be illustrated – not only the arcane legal rules that constrained would-be litigants, but also the streetwise strategies that enabled plaintiffs and defendants to exploit these rules to their own advantage; not only the ways in which law reflected the needs of society, but also how it helped to shape that society, including relations between the sexes.

Although concepts of honour are of central importance only to parts of the argument, it is necessary to start with this notoriously complex and protean phenomenon. 'But alas! Gentlemen,' lamented Fielding's Jonathan Wild, understandably concerned that honour should not be confused with honesty, decency or Christian morality, 'What pity is it, that a word of such sovereign use and virtue should have so uncertain and various an application, that scarce two people mean the same thing by it.'[3] Yet anthropologists have repeatedly essayed a definition. The most rigorous recent examination, by Frank Henderson Stewart, centres on the idea of honour as a right, specifically a 'right to respect'. Equally subtle in a different way is Pierre Bourdieu's exploration within the context of his ideas of practice, habitus, symbolic capital, and symbolic power. But still the best known and perhaps the most serviceable is Julian Pitt-Rivers's suggestion that 'Honour is the value of a person in his own eyes, but also in the eyes of his society. It is his estimation of his own worth, his *claim* to pride, but it is also the acknowledgement of that claim, his excellence recognized by society, his *right* to pride'; or, from another point of view, 'a nexus between the ideals of a society and their reproduction in the individual through his aspiration to personify them'. The advantage of such a definition lies in its flexibility, together with its recognition of both external and internalised aspects of honour; the various alternatives bring their own disadvantages.[4] But in the

spelling has been retained save that the use of u, v, i, j, ff and y [for 'th'] has been normalised according to current usage; punctuation has been modernised where necessary to convey the sense more easily.

[3] Henry Fielding, *The Life of Mr Jonathan Wild the Great* ([1743] Penguin edn, London, 1982), p.74.

[4] Frank Henderson Stewart, *Honour* (Chicago and London, 1994); Pierre Bourdieu, *Outline of a Theory of Practice*, tr. R. Nice (Cambridge, 1977), pp. 10–15 and *passim*; Julian

anthropological literature there has been heavy concentration on versions of honour, and its counterpart 'shame', that associate them closely with gender relations and with the family, and more specifically with an emphasis on male assertiveness and female chastity as indicators of social worth for individuals and their respective kin groups. These cultural traits have been taken to be characteristic of the Mediterranean, a proposition that seems to imply that the circum-Mediterranean lands may from this perspective be seen as a unity. While the problems inherent in these ideas are numerous and have been much debated, they have been influential among historians and indeed remain so.[5] A further feature of some of the honour and shame literature of the 1960s was that it gave so little attention to law and legal systems that unwary historians might infer that they were of little importance, and hence draw false conclusions about supposed contrasts between the honour and shame cultures of anthropologists and the societies they themselves were investigating. More recent anthropological work that is highly sensitive to the legal dimension is more easily related to the moral world of the law in early modern society.[6]

Whether informed by anthropology or not, 'honour' has been an important theme in the recent historiography of European society, though for the purposes of this essay only the most cursory survey of much of this work is necessary. Many historians have approached honour as an aspect of aristocratic or quasi-aristocratic culture.[7] But others have included, or even concentrated on, less exalted social groups, an approach that leads into very different territory including, for example, the values that bound gild members or groups of co-workers, and popular customs such as charivaris. Works in this vein include James Farr's study of artisans in Dijon, a number of pathbreaking works by Peter Burke and Natalie Davis, and Lyndal Roper's stimulating contributions that bring the issues of honour and gender into powerful juxtaposition.[8] Of more immediate concern for legal

footnote 4 (*cont.*)
Pitt-Rivers, 'Honour and Social Status', in J. G. Peristiany, ed., *Honour and Shame: the Values of Mediterranean Society* (London, 1965), pp. 21, 22.

5 David D. Gilmore, ed., *Honour and Shame and the Unity of the Mediterranean* (American Anthropological Association Special Publication, no. 22, Washington, D.C., 1987); David Cohen, *Law, Sexuality, and Society: the Enforcement of Morals in Classical Athens* (Cambridge, 1991), ch. 3. In the literature 'shame' is sometimes presented as the sense of personal humiliation that we normally associate with that word but is also employed, in a technical sense, as the female equivalent of 'honour'.

6 Pitt-Rivers, 'Honour and Social Status', pp. 30–1; cf. Stewart, *Honour*, esp. ch.7.

7 E.g., Frederick Robert Bryson, *The Point of Honor in Sixteenth-Century Italy: an Aspect of the Life of the Gentleman* (New York, 1935); Mervyn James, *English Politics and the Concept of Honour, 1485–1642* (*Past and Present* Supplement, no. 3, 1978); James S. Amelang, *Honoured Citizens of Barcelona: Patrician Culture and Class Relations, 1490–1714* (Princeton, NJ, 1986).

8 James R. Farr, *Hands of Honor: Artisans and their World in Dijon, 1550–1650* (Ithaca and London, 1988), esp. ch. 4; Peter Burke, *The Historical Anthropology of Early Modern Italy:*

historians, there has also been an important clutch of works centring on defamation and related issues in England. Beginning with the pioneering efforts of James Sharpe and others in the 1970s and 80s, they have continued recently with important and innovative contributions by a constellation of mostly younger scholars;[9] further contributions in this area are expected.[10] I shall draw on their findings in what follows (including, by the kindness of the authors, some material yet unpublished), integrating these approaches with the fruits of my own recent and not so recent researches on slander litigation in the period from the late fifteenth to the early eighteenth centuries. As I hope to show, this is a subject where a broad view and a long time span are necessary for a proper understanding of the phenomenon. Needless to say, the treatment here of this potentially vast and in some respects still under-researched subject can only be very cursory: many important issues are scarcely mentioned, far less fully explored.

Among the main stimuli for these recent studies has been a growing interest in gender and gender relations, strongly underpinned in the case of some authors by feminist theory and conviction. Another is the study of

Essays on Perception and Communication (Cambridge, 1987), esp. ch. 8; Natalie Zemon Davis, *Society and Culture in Early Modern France* (London, 1975), chs. 4–5, and *Fiction in the Archives: Pardon Tales and their Tellers in Sixteenth-Century France* (Stanford, CA, 1987), pp. 38–40, 96–8 and *passim*; Lyndal Roper, *The Holy Household: Women and Morals in Reformation Augsburg* (Oxford, 1989), and *Oedipus and the Devil: Witchcraft, Sexuality and Religion in Early Modern Europe* (London, 1994), esp. ch. 3.

9 Christopher Haigh, 'Slander and the Church Courts in the Sixteenth Century', *Transactions of the Lancashire and Cheshire Antiquarian Society*, 78 (1975), pp. 1–13; J. A. Sharpe, *Defamation and Sexual Slander in Early Modern England: the Church Courts at York* (Borthwick Papers, no. 58, York, [1980]); Martin Ingram, *Church Courts, Sex and Marriage in England, 1570–1640* (Cambridge, 1987), pp. 163–6 and ch.10; Susan Dwyer Amussen, *An Ordered Society: Gender and Class in Early Modern England* (Oxford, 1988), esp. pp. 95–104, 129–31, 152–5; Tim Meldrum, 'A Women's Court in London: Defamation at the Bishop of London's Consistory Court, 1700–1745', *London Journal*, 19 (1994), pp. 1–20; Laura Gowing, *Domestic Dangers: Women, Words and Sex in Early Modern London* (Oxford, 1996), esp. chs. 2–3, cf. Laura Gowing, 'Gender and the Language of Insult in Early Modern London', *History Workshop Journal*, no.35 (1993), pp. 1–21; Laura Gowing, 'Language, Power and the Law: Women's Slander Litigation in Early Modern London', in Jenny Kermode and Garthine Walker, eds., *Women, Crime and the Courts in Early Modern England* (London, 1994), pp. 26–47; L. R. Poos, 'Sex, Lies, and the Church Courts of Pre-Reformation England', *Journal of Interdisciplinary History*, 25 (1994–5), pp. 585–607; Elizabeth Ann Foyster, *Manhood in Early Modern England: Honour, Sex and Marriage* (London, 1999). Studies relating to colonial North America include Clara Ann Bowler, 'Carted Whores and White Shrouded Apologies: Slander in the County Courts of Seventeenth-Century Virginia', *Virginia Magazine of History and Biography*, 85 (1977), pp. 411–26; Mary Beth Norton, 'Gender and Defamation in Seventeenth-Century Maryland', *William and Mary Quarterly*, 3rd ser., 44 (1987), pp. 3–39.

10 For example, Dinah Winch is currently completing an Oxford doctoral thesis entitled 'Sexual Slander in England 1660–1700', while David Turner's work on representations of adultery in the late seventeenth and early eighteenth centuries is also of relevance: for some preliminary findings, see David Turner, '"Nothing Is So Secret But Shall Be Revealed": the Scandalous Life of Robert Foulkes', in Tim Hitchcock and Michele Cohen, eds., *English Masculinities, 1660 –1800* (London, 1999), pp. 169–92.

community. Yet another, more directly informing my own approach, is the exploration of the public regulation of morality by legal and extra-legal means – a subject in which slander litigation has a definite, albeit ambiguous, place.[11] A variety of sources has been exploited, including sermons and conduct books, social commentary, contemporary drama, and other forms of imaginative literature (including ballads, chapbooks, and similar popular genres). The work of Anthony Fletcher who, taking his cue from Thomas Laqueur, draws on contemporary medical treatises for his concept of the 'one-sex body', is particularly notable for its eclecticism.[12] However, much the most intense and rigorous work has been grounded in legal records, and in particular on actual suits for defamation; and it is on a review of this material that I shall concentrate hereafter.

As I have already hinted, it is doubtful whether 'honour' is the most helpful term with which to approach these sources, though the usage is now so current that it may be impossible to stem the tide. Admittedly this term is found in some (but by no means all) of the prescriptive literature, particularly that of the later seventeenth and eighteenth centuries;[13] and, in a very general way, the matters of reputation that feature in defamation cases have obvious links with the themes defined by anthropologists as honour and shame. The usage may also make sense in an early modern continental context, since in many regions notions relating closely to the English term 'honour' most certainly did apply to a wide spectrum of social groups.[14] However, in English usage 'honour' did not merely have very strong aristocratic associations but was sometimes claimed to be a virtual monopoly of gentlefolk; its use with reference to the rest of the society is at best dubious, and positively misleading if it obscures the fact that the attributions of honour were often denied to the lower ranks.[15] Further, many of the criteria by which honour might be measured were external and often highly

[11] Examples of these approaches are Gowing, *Domestic Dangers*, chs. 3–4; J. A. Sharpe, '"Such Disagreement betwyx Neighbours": Litigation and Human Relations in Early Modern England', in John Bossy, ed., *Disputes and Settlements: Law and Human Relations in the West* (Cambridge, 1983), pp. 167–87; and Ingram, *Church Courts*, pp. 164–6 and ch.10.

[12] Anthony Fletcher, *Gender, Sex and Subordination in England, 1500–1800* (New Haven and London, 1995), pt 1 and *passim*; cf. Thomas Laqueur, *Making Sex: Body and Gender from the Greeks to Freud* (Cambridge, MA, and London, 1992).

[13] E.g. Richard Allestree, *The Ladies Calling*, 2 parts (Oxford, 1673), pt 1, pp. 16, 19, 26, 28, 74, 75, 77 (*bis*), pt 2, pp. 27, 35. But other works rarely use the term, e.g. Stephen Ford, *The Evil Tongue Tryed and Found Guilty* (London, 1672); Richard Allestree, *The Government of the Tongue* (Oxford, 1674).

[14] Roper, *Holy Household*, *passim*; more generally, see Klaus Schreiner and Gerd Schwerhoff, eds., *Verletzte Ehre: Ehrkonflikte in Gesellschaften des Mittelalters und der Frühen Neuzeit* (Cologne, Weimar and Vienna, 1995).

[15] Keith Thomas, 'The Social Origins of Hobbes's Political Thought', in K. C. Brown, ed., *Hobbes Studies* (Oxford, 1965), pp. 191, 194; cf. Robert Ashley, *Of Honour*, ed. Virgil B. Heltzel (San Marino, CA, 1947), pp. 51, 69–70.

visible – title, whether a peerage or merely a claim to gentility; social rank; lineage; wealth, preferably of the landed sort; 'generosity', expressed in munificent almsgiving and conspicuous consumption; education; manners and gesture; and so on. Many of these features were remote from, or at least tangential to, the substance of slander suits. Thus the term 'honour' rarely appears in this context; when it does, it is usually because gentlefolk were involved.[16] The cognate terms 'honesty' and 'honest' do appear, but not as an all-embracing category like 'honour'. Rather, they emerge as one set of terms among many that were expressive (with subtle variations of usage and meaning) of moral status, social position, or an amalgam of the two: 'worth', 'standing', 'credit', 'fame', 'reputation'. Instead of 'dishonour', whether as a noun or a verb, we find words like 'defamed', 'discredited', 'disgraced', 'scandalised', or (perhaps implying a less comprehensive loss of standing) 'blotched', 'spotted', and so forth.[17]

In order to get deeper into the moral world of slander litigation, we must consider briefly the relationship between assault, abuse, slander and the law. There are both important linkages and significant distinctions to make here, the neglect of which can blind us to some vital issues; not all have been adequately recognised, though Garthine Walker's introduction of the concept of 'affront' into the debate offers a suggestive clue.[18] The key point is that opprobrious words do not necessarily attack reputation, at least not in ways that depend to any great extent on the subtleties of their intrinsic meanings. Frequently they serve simply as terms of abuse and are used as a substitute for, or concomitant of, physical assault or threatening gestures. Alternatively, rude or contemptuous words and actions, which cannot in any strict sense be seen as defamatory, may nonetheless offer extraordinarily powerful means of ridiculing, disgracing or humiliating their target. Scatological humour, along with imputations of deformity, mental and physical incapacity, or loathsome disease, have in all ages offered a particularly lethal weapon, capable of wounding virtually anyone but, above all, exquisitely adapted to puncturing inflated pretensions by appealing to the great primal joke that even the great are in thrall to base bodies.[19] But gestures and inarticulate utterances – grimacing, grinning, pointing,

[16] Gowing, *Domestic Dangers*, p.113; Foyster, *Manhood*, p. 8; cf. Metropolitan Archives [formerly Greater London RO], WJ/SR (NS) 42, no. 55.

[17] Faramerz Dabhoiwala, 'The Construction of Honour, Reputation and Status in Late Seventeenth- and Early Eighteenth-Century England', *Transactions of the Royal Historical Society*, 6th ser., 6 (1996), p. 201.

[18] Garthine Walker, 'Expanding the Boundaries of Female Honour in Early Modern England', *Transactions of the Royal Historical Society*, 6th ser., 6 (1996), pp. 236, 239; unfortunately Walker does not explore the significance of the term, but cf. T. V. Cohen, 'The Lay Liturgy of Affront in Sixteenth-Century Italy', *Journal of Social History*, 25 (1991–2), pp. 857–77.

[19] Sir Keith Thomas, 'The Place of Laughter in Tudor and Stuart England', *Times Literary Supplement*, 21 January 1977, p. 79.

'hemming' and humming were seventeenth-century favourites – may be almost as good and require a minimum of wit to make them effective. At issue here are not so much slanders as verbal or non-verbal acts of debasement or humiliation. On the other hand, genuine slanders, that is accusations of specific forms of criminal or immoral behaviour, may amongst other things constitute a kind of assault, especially when uttered in the context of a public confrontation; and both in this and in the violent responses they may well provoke, they at least threaten a breach of the peace.

English law therefore took cognisance of slander and other opprobrious words in a variety of ways. It offered some special remedies for nobles and gentry, clergy, or office holders – that is, people whose right to respect was reckoned to be fundamental to the maintenance of the social hierarchy. For example, a series of statutes from 1275 onwards had created a specific offence of *scandalum magnatum* to punish the publication of discreditable matter about important people; the post-Reformation church courts offered special disciplinary procedures for uttering opprobrious words against a clergyman; and the High Court of Chivalry in the seventeenth century entertained suits brought by gentlemen for 'scandalous words provocative of a duel'. All such words might well be demeaning rather than strictly defamatory.[20] For ordinary folk, verbal abuse could be prosecuted in the secular courts as criminal breaches of the peace, and again the precise words uttered were from a legal point of view of only tangential significance and were not necessarily confined to the strictly defamatory. The usual means of proceeding was by recognisance to keep the peace or issue of a warrant of good behaviour, though culprits could be indicted for assault if their words were accompanied by or likely to provoke physical force. Cases of these kinds occurred regularly in most jurisdictions in the Tudor and Stuart years; but Robert Shoemaker has shown that they were very numerous in London and adjacent areas by the late seventeenth century, while examination of the extant sessions files for Middlesex, Westminster and the City suggests that this pattern was already taking shape before the civil war. Examples from the Westminster Sessions in 1635 included the linked recognisances of Anne Manby 'for assaulting and beating' Alice Stephenson 'and calling her a pocki faced bitch and a murtherer', and of Alice Stephenson 'for asaulting and beating of Anne Manbi

[20] John C. Lassiter, 'Defamation of Peers: the Rise and Decline of the Action for *Scandalum Magnatum*, 1497–1773', *American Journal of Legal History*, 22 (1978), pp. 216–36; Ingram, *Church Courts*, pp. 110, 294; G. D. Squibb, *The High Court of Chivalry: a Study of the Civil Law in England* (Oxford, 1959), pp. 57–61, 101–2; cf. Jane Kamensky, 'Talk Like a Man: Speech, Power and Masculinity in Early New England', *Gender and History*, 8 (1996), pp. 32–5. Examples of demeaning words are given below.

the wife of John Manbi tayler and calling her a burst belli gut[es]'. At the same sessions Joan Crosse was bound over 'for laying of scandalous imputations upon Joys the wife of Richard Merrick, and saying that shee had three bastard[es] in Fleetstreet, and on[e] bastard more in a garett by on[e] Wa[l]ter Farmer, and calling her a bastard bearing whore'; on her appearance she was indicted for assault.[21]

Written defamations, or libels, came to be considered an even more serious criminal matter in this period, characteristically but not exclusively punished in Star Chamber before 1641 and later in King's Bench. Adam Fox and Laura Gowing, building on earlier work, have recently brought to light some of the more colourful cases in the form of scurrilous popular rhymes, which were sometimes extremely elaborate and given the widest possible publicity by their authors.[22] Words could be a criminal matter in other ways too. In the church courts, defamers could be prosecuted under 'office' or disciplinary jurisdiction – the ecclesiastical equivalent of criminal procedure – for 'breaking the bond of charity', in other words causing dissension and strife within the Christian community; there were also special disciplinary procedures for dealing with brawling in church or churchyard, which might well involve opprobrious words. People who repeatedly reviled their neighbours, or spread scandalous stories and rumours, could be prosecuted by the church or secular authorities as talebearers, makebates and common scolds; the last category, characteristically women, became increasingly subject to punishment by the cucking-stool in the sixteenth and seventeenth centuries.[23] With the partial exception of scolding and mocking rhymes, few of these various forms of criminal or quasi-criminal prosecution have been properly studied; and indeed there are barriers to doing so, since the actual words of abuse are often not specified in the records. One result is that the linkage between verbal abuse and

21 Robert Shoemaker, *Prosecution and Punishment: Petty Crime and the Law in London and Rural Middlesex, c.1660–1725* (Cambridge, 1991), p. 98; Metropolitan Archives, WJ/SR (NS) 41, nos. 110–11, 117, 197.

22 Adam Fox, 'Ballads, Libels and Popular Ridicule in Jacobean England', *Past and Present*, no. 145 (Nov. 1994), pp. 47–83; Laura Gowing, 'Women, Status and the Popular Culture of Dishonour', *Transactions of the Royal Historical Society*, 6th ser., 6 (1996), pp. 225–34; see also Martin Ingram, 'Ridings, Rough Music and Mocking Rhymes in Early Modern England', in Barry Reay, ed., *Popular Culture in Seventeenth-Century England* (London, 1985), pp. 166–97.

23 Ingram, *Church Courts*, pp. 110, 293–4; Martin Ingram, '"Scolding Women Cucked or Washed": a Crisis of Gender Relations in Early Modern England?', in Kermode and Walker, eds., *Women, Crime and the Courts*, pp. 116–36; cf. David Underdown, 'The Taming of the Scold: the Enforcement of Patriarchal Authority in Early Modern England', in Anthony Fletcher and John Stevenson, eds., *Order and Disorder in Early Modern England* (Cambridge, 1985), pp. 116–36. On scolding in the late medieval period, see Marjorie McIntosh, *Controlling Misbehaviour in England, 1370–1600* (Cambridge, 1998), pp. 56–65 and *passim*.

physical violence has probably been underestimated, which may in turn have contributed to a relative neglect of slanders involving males.

Whatever the importance of these modes of procedure, it is true that many, perhaps in the early seventeenth century most, complaints of opprobrious words were dealt with as defamation suits between parties. In the late middle ages – or at least from the late fourteenth century, after the virtual disappearance of defamation cases from manorial and borough courts – the Church had exercised more or less sole jurisdiction in this area. But from the reign of Henry VII the royal courts imposed restrictions on the scope of the church courts' slander business, and from the early sixteenth century gradually developed a law of defamation of their own.[24]

The precise extent of the spiritual and temporal jurisdiction in this area will be reviewed shortly; first some more general points must be made. One is to stress diversity. Within the church court jurisdiction, the rules by which the law was administered varied to some extent according to local custom and practice; so much is evident from detailed analysis of the business of different diocesan courts.[25] In the secular courts, there were some differences between practice in the two main common-law courts of King's Bench and Common Pleas, not to mention the complication of Star Chamber jurisdiction and the idiosyncrasies of some city and borough courts – certain of the latter seem to have worked within very flexible limits in the sixteenth century, though greater uniformity is evident by the seventeenth.[26] (Amongst other complexities in London was the involvement of the city Livery Companies, which in 1579 were specifically directed by the Court of Aldermen to handle complaints of defamation 'to avoid . . . suits in law for words which are but wind'.)[27] By the reign of Elizabeth, therefore, matters of slander were fragmented among a number of different jurisdictions whose moral worlds were, as we shall see, far from identical. To view the matter another way, the lines of legal demarcation cut across the realities of argy- bargy on the streets, in the fields, and wherever else that people quarrelled and fought. Party-and-party suits for words, whether in the spiritual or temporal courts, were an artificial category. In many cases slanderous abuse might just as easily have furnished matter for a criminal

[24] R. H. Helmholz, *Select Cases on Defamation to 1600* (Selden Soc., ci, London, 1985), Introduction.

[25] Cf. Sharpe, *Defamation and Sexual Slander*, pp. 10–15; Ingram, *Church Courts*, pp. 300–2; Gowing, *Domestic Dangers*, pp. 62–7.

[26] Helmholz, *Select Cases*, pp. lxxxvi–vii; J. H. Baker, *An Introduction to English Legal History*, 3rd edn (London, 1990), p. 507; the comments on borough and city courts are based on a survey of a variety of jurisdictions which I hope to discuss on another occasion.

[27] Steve Rappaport, *Worlds within Worlds: Structures of Life in Sixteenth-Century London* (Cambridge, 1989), pp. 212–13, cf. pp. 204–5, 209; for other complexities of slander jurisdiction in London, see below.

recognisance, or even been subsumed into some greater charge such as an indictment for assault.

To an extent these matters were within the control of litigants; and this brings us to another issue of great importance, the context and purpose of defamation suits. Characteristically the background was complex, and cases can rarely be understood solely in terms of reputation. This point has recently been reiterated by Laura Gowing with reference to London church court suits in the late sixteenth and early seventeenth centuries: indeed, she goes so far as to say that in that context 'the words of slander, ostensibly about sex, turn out to be about almost everything else'.[28] However, a less paradoxical and less extreme version of this position is well established in the literature. In favoured locations, where church court records may be matched against those of manor or borough courts, quarter sessions, and the central Westminster courts, enabling the connections and antecedents of the litigants to be explored in some detail, it has proved possible to recover many aspects of these latent dimensions. It is not surprising to find that abusive exchanges often arose from immediate quarrels over money, property, personal jealousies (whether sexual or otherwise), minor trespasses, boundary disputes and the like.[29] Just how altercations shifted from these matters to apparently unrelated issues of reputation varied according to circumstances. Sometimes what was at issue were generalised words of abuse – 'whore' is the most obvious example – that could also carry a more specific meaning of immorality or other reprehensible behaviour. Such words, which came easily to the lips in any quarrel, had the effect of swiftly propelling a slanging match into the arena of moral worth. But the shift was not always as automatic as this: some defamers deliberately chose to displace the quarrel into the sphere of reputation, either because they felt their own original ground to be shaky or with an unerring eye for the vulnerabilities of their opponents. Or quarrels simply escalated rapidly on to a plane where one or both sides felt they could do most hurt.

What damage could slanders do? In sixteenth- and seventeenth-century England, the existence of a system whereby crimes and lapses in personal morality were reported for punishment by the authorities gave defamation a particular potency. The church courts prosecuted individuals for offences such as adultery and fornication on the the basis of 'common fame' or well-substantiated rumour, and similar hearsay evidence had an important part in proceedings in the secular courts too. The corollary was that evaluative discourse of the kind that would nowadays be called 'gossip' was constantly circulating among both men and women, and defamers both drew on and

[28] Gowing, *Domestic Dangers*, p.118.

[29] Ingram, *Church Courts*, pp. 314–16; cf. Sharpe, *Defamation and Sexual Slander*, pp. 22–3; Gowing, *Domestic Dangers*, pp. 116–19.

contributed to these currents of information in framing their utterances. Depending on the nature of the slander and the circumstances in which it was uttered, there was a more or less serious possibility that defamatory accusations would get the victims into trouble with the courts. Of course, vague terms of abuse like 'whore' were in themselves far less dangerous from this point of view than circumstantial charges, but there was always a chance that they would trigger more serious investigations.[30] Other hazards included material or social effects: apart from the disruption of business dealings (which was a standard claim at common law and also featured in some church court suits), those most commonly mentioned included a threat to marriage prospects and disruption of relations between husband and wife.[31]

But such social consequences were not the whole story. Whatever the tangible impacts might or might not be, many of the words of abuse at issue in slander suits clearly had the power to wound deeply – so deeply that they seemed at times to go to the very heart, to the individual's sense of self. The case of Joan Browne which prefaces this chapter offers a vivid illustration of one variant of this psychological impact, to which historians have given too little attention. The fact that the defamer was a bailiff and his use of the word 'runagate' (meaning fugitive or runaway, with connotations of vagabondage) suggest that poverty and debt were in the background. Whatever the circumstances, Joan Browne plainly felt shamed, humiliated, publicly exposed; her psychic integrity shattered, she broke down into convulsive weeping. An alternative, more robust response to such an assault on the self – perhaps more common, to judge by the evidence of lawsuits – was furious indignation which, if it did not trigger immediate verbal or physical retaliation, might be vented in litigation. In either case, there are indications that these public affronts – miniature social dramas that were often deliberately staged before an eager audience, 'publiq[ue]ly in the open street' as Joan Browne bit-

[30] Ingram, *Church Courts*, pp. 44–6, 239–45, 306–7, 328–9 and *passim*; but cf. Sharpe, *Defamation and Sexual Slander*, pp. 25–6. The issues relating to 'gossip' are complex, and have been more discussed in the anthropological and sociological literature than among historians: see e.g. Max Gluckman, 'Gossip and Scandal', *Current Anthropology*, 6 (1963), pp. 307–15; Robert Paine, 'What is Gossip About? An Alternative Hypothesis', *Man*, new ser., 2 (1967), pp. 278–85; Sally Engle Merry, 'Rethinking Gossip and Scandal', in Donald Black, ed., *Towards a General Theory of Social Control*, 2 vols. (Orlando, FL, 1984), I, 271–302; cf. Steve Hindle, 'The Shaming of Margaret Knowsley: Gossip, Gender and the Experience of Authority in Early Modern England', *Continuity and Change*, 9 (1994), pp. 391–419; Bernard Capp, 'Separate Domains? Women and Authority in Early Modern England', in Paul Griffiths, Adam Fox and Steve Hindle, eds., *The Experience of Authority in Early Modern England* (Basingstoke and London, 1996), pp. 129–32; Dagmar Freist, *Governed by Opinion: Politics, Religion and the Dynamics of Communication in Stuart London, 1637–1645* (London and New York, 1997), *passim*; Turner, '"Nothing Is So Secret"', pp. 171, 176–7.

[31] Helmholz, *Select Cases*; pp. lxxix–lxxxii; Ingram, *Church Courts*, pp. 308–11. Gowing, *Domestic Dangers*, pp. 125–33.

terly complained – could not be ignored with impunity. Victims who failed to respond tacitly acknowledged either the justice of the aspersion or their inability to defend themselves, and on both grounds were liable to lose face.[32]

Beyond the social dynamics and the personal psychology of particular episodes of abuse or altercation, suits are frequently found to be related to wider or pre-existing quarrels and tensions, which had sometimes given rise, or were to give rise in the future, to other kinds of litigation in the same or other courts. Such disputes could extend over years and implicate not merely individuals but whole families or groups of families. Occasionally the circumstances are found to be akin to a feud. Thus to look at any given defamation suit is often to pick up just one element in a tangled skein of conflicts. It is impossible in retrospect, and must have been difficult even for contemporaries, to evaluate how important the specific matter of reputation ostensibly at issue actually was. Yet in a sense such questions were often irrelevant, since the specific point in controversy encapsulated much broader issues of reputation and standing. Some gentry and sub-gentry families were for years locked into conflict and rivalry with their neighbours, constantly jockeying for the power and precedence that conferred local influence and prestige. Certain slander suits emerge on investigation of the context as symptoms of such continuing status struggles, mutual demands for and denials of social recognition.[33]

These complications in turn raise issues about the sincerity of plaintiffs in commencing slander suits. At one extreme opprobrious words were sometimes seized upon deliberately to give specious grounds for action, a possibility that contemporaries were aware of and described as vexatious or malicious suits. More usually the circumstances were less clear cut. It is probable that many plaintiffs, especially when scurrilous abuse rather than specific slanders was at issue, were more exercised about the affront they had suffered, their hurt feelings or damaged dignity, than concerned about real damage to their reputation. In any case the degree to which slurs were resented was bound to depend in part on the nature of the relationship and state of feeling between the alleged defamer and victim. As a corollary, the motives of litigants were varied and often complex, and these subtleties in turn affected the outcome of cases and how they were viewed by contemporaries. In simple terms, defamation suits offered a means of peaceful action to seek redress for injury: the secular courts offered cash damages assessed by a jury, while the church courts awarded penances which simultaneously punished the defamer and gave the victim the satisfaction of a public or semi-public apology. Many cases in either jurisdiction – including Joan Browne's suit which began this

[32] Ingram, *Church Courts*, pp. 311–13; Gowing, *Domestic Dangers*, pp. 119–24.
[33] Ingram, *Church Courts*, pp. 315–16.

chapter – were not pressed so far, but abandoned, compromised, or otherwise settled informally at some stage in the proceedings. But plaintiffs could be enterprising and devious. Rather than to obtain just redress or seek the resolution of conflict, their aim might well be to exploit the law in prosecuting and prolonging quarrels; there was, in Tim Meldrum's apt phrase, 'a "tit-for-tat" vindictiveness' about much slander litigation.[34] The picture is further clouded by the fact that litigants, predictably enough, were not always clear-sighted or honest with themselves about their motives for action. There has thus been a perennial debate among historians, echoing the concerns of contemporary commentators, about whether these and other kinds of lawsuit were a means of promoting peace or a form of proxy violence, constructive or disruptive, functional or dysfunctional. Claims to have solved this particular conundrum should be viewed with caution. In truth no resolution is possible, not simply because as historians we generally lack sufficient evidence to make a judgement, but more basically because the role of litigation in this society was inherently ambiguous.[35]

There is, moreover, another area of moral ambiguity, which has attracted less attention from historians recently but was clearly important to contemporaries. This was the role of lawyers, who were dependent on the fees of litigants. It was a basic principle of ecclesiastical law that litigants should be encouraged to achieve a reconciliation and out-of-court settlement, to restore peace within the Christian community as swiftly as possible; many of the procedures of the church courts were indeed adapted to this end. In the secular courts, also, it was a commonplace that 'a good judge is concerned to make an end of suits' (*boni judicis lites dirimere*). But naturally such principles could not be taken too far. As we shall see, in the royal courts definite steps were taken to limit the numbers of defamation suits, but not necessarily for high-minded reasons. Church court lawyers, on the other hand, whose jurisdiction was gradually being whittled down by the royal courts, had a positive incentive to maintain and if possible expand their slander business. And both common-law and ecclesiastical lawyers were fertile in devices to further the not always legitimate interests of their clients, if necessary by bending the legal rules.[36]

[34] Meldrum, 'Women's Court in London', p. 13.

[35] Gowing, *Domestic Dangers*, pp. 136–7; cf. Sharpe, '"Such Disagreement Betwyx Neighbours"', *passim*, C. W. Brooks, *Pettyfoggers and Vipers of the Commonwealth: the 'Lower Branch' of the Legal Profession in Early Modern England* (Cambridge, 1986), ch. 4; Ingram, *Church Courts*, pp. 33–4, 314–19; Craig Muldrew, 'The Culture of Reconciliation: Community and the Settlement of Economic Disputes in Early Modern England', *Historical Journal*, 39 (1996), pp. 915–42.

[36] Ingram, *Church Courts*, pp. 50, 318; Baker, *Introduction to English Legal History*, pp. 501–3; R. H. Helmholz, *Roman Canon Law in Reformation England* (Cambridge, 1990), pp. 59–60; *Sources of English Legal History: Private Law to 1750*, ed. J. H. Baker and S. F. C. Milsom (London, 1986), pp. 640–2.

How far such manipulation was possible, either by litigants or individual lawyers, was within limits which were gradually established in the development of the law of defamation in the sixteenth and seventeenth centuries. Much of the story, particularly up to the early seventeenth century, has been skilfully elucidated by Richard Helmholz and other legal historians.[37] First of all it needs to be reiterated that defamation suits were in themselves never the occasion for the demonstration or vindication of honour, credit, or reputation, if these are accepted to be the multifaceted phenomena that I described earlier. Their scope was much narrower. They simply provided a means of redress or at least partial aid in situations where credit or reputation had been brought into question in particular ways, and so put the victim into jeopardy. Indeed what was at issue was really the threat of infamy, disgrace or ignominy in circumstances recognised by the law. The range of such situations countenanced by the courts was gradually extended over time. But the core principle, inherited from the middle ages and never wholly lost to view in the sixteenth and seventeenth centuries, was that it had to be shown that the reputations of slander victims had been impugned in ways that made them liable to some form of criminal prosecution.

This basic principle was applied in different ways by the two main jurisdictions, creating divergent moral worlds that litigants had to negotiate. As noted earlier, before about 1500 the church courts had dealt with all matters of defamation, including imputations of both spiritual and temporal crimes. The former were those within the Church's own jurisdiction, such as adultery, fornication and heresy; the latter were crimes cognisable in the royal courts, such as theft or murder. It was these temporal matters that the royal courts stopped the church courts handling from the early sixteenth century. On the other hand, at about the same time the church courts did extend the scope of their jurisdiction to include 'words of reproach' that did not strictly impute a crime, such as 'brabbler and lying knave'; and this area of activity was re-emphasised amid the Reformation conflicts over religious divisions, in particular by the insistence of the Royal Injunctions of 1559 on the 'knot of charity' which reproachful speeches threatened to break. These developments brought the English church courts closer in line with the Roman law of *injuria*.[38] If they had really taken off, the scope of the church courts' action for words could have expanded indefinitely. In reality,

[37] Helmholz, *Select Cases*; see also S. F. C. Milsom, *Historical Foundations of the Common Law*, 2nd edn (London, 1981), pp. 379–91; Baker, *Introduction to English Legal History*, ch. 24. W. S. Holdsworth, 'Defamation in the Sixteenth and Seventeenth Centuries', *Law Quarterly Review*, 40 (1924), pp. 302–15, 397–412, 41 (1925), pp. 13–31, though superseded on many points, is still worth attention.

[38] Helmholz, *Select Cases*, pp. xiv–xlvii, and *Roman Canon Law*, pp. 56–60; *Tudor Royal Proclamations*, ed. Paul L. Hughes and James F. Larkin, 3 vols. (New Haven and London, 1964–9), II, p. 128.

pressure from the common-law courts kept 'reproachful words' within very strict bounds during the sixteenth and early seventeenth centuries. 'Words of reproach' may have been better established in the practice of the courts of the northern province than in Canterbury's area of jurisdiction, while in England as a whole in the period after the Restoration there may have been something of a reassertion of the courts' right to hear such words – to the bemusement of some historians, who have assumed that their presence indicates that the courts were indifferent to the niceties of law, when in fact the opposite is the case.[39] Still, however, these words of reproach did not constitute a very high proportion of the courts' business. The real growth area in the sixteenth and seventeenth centuries was in a different direction, namely the proliferation of cases centring on accusations of being a 'whore'. The importance of this will be discussed shortly, but the point to make here is that the church courts' jurisdiction was flexible and potentially very wide, most of the restrictions being imposed externally by the royal courts.

Meanwhile the jurisdiction of those courts had gradually taken shape during the sixteenth century. They offered a remedy for accusations of venereal disease, of bankruptcy in the case of traders and merchants, and of malfeasance or professional incompetence in the case of officials, lawyers, physicians and surgeons. But the heart of the remedy was for accusations of crimes triable before a secular judge – treason, murder, infanticide, robbery, burglary and larceny. In practice accusations of theft heavily predominated in the courts. Because the common law in general laid such stress on fact and precision, it applied similar criteria in deciding what words were actionable. Thus there was a bias towards cases where clear, ascertainable damage could be demonstrated, while action was denied for vague, unspecific accusations of theft or other crimes, and in cases where the alleged words could bear a non-criminal interpretation (this was the famous rule of taking words *in mitior sensu* or 'in the milder sense').[40]

How far the secular courts had cognisance of sexual slanders is more complex than is often supposed. Venereal disease cases could obviously veer very close to accusations of sexual immorality. Thus in a suit in 1724, Helen Macartyriagh claimed that Thomas Welton had called her 'a pocky bitch . . . & you . . . had so many stones [i.e. testicles] at your asse . . . that it . . . is rotten and worn out . . . you . . . must go to Rumford for a new bottom'.[41] It had been established by the 1590s that a woman who had been defamed of having a bastard, or even simply of fornication, whereby she lost the chance of a particular marriage, could sue either in the spiri-

[39] The points made here are based on my own current researches and those of Dinah Winch, but see also Amussen, *Ordered Society*, pp. 102–4; cf. Sharpe, *Defamation and Sexual Slander*, pp. 11–15. [40] Helmholz, *Select Cases*, pp. lxvi–cvi.

[41] P[ublic] RO, KB 122/109, rot. 426r.

tual courts for her reputation or in the secular courts for the damage she had sustained; in theory the same principle applied to a man also. Imputations of sexual immorality could also be actionable if they otherwise resulted in some particular loss, technically known as 'special' damage; and it was claimed that to say of a woman that she had had a bastard was actionable since bastard-bearing was punishable by the justices of the peace. There are indications also that the peculiar circumstances of the Interregnum, when the church courts were in abeyance and the famous act of 1650 brought sexual offences within the scope of the secular courts, made the common-law judges slightly more sympathetic towards sexual slander.[42] These developments explain cases like that in King's Bench in 1664, when a widow called Emma Chapman sued Anne Simpkins with her husband Thomas for saying that 'shee . . . was Anthony Hungerfords whore . . . and her son Mathewe Chapman . . . was his bastard . . . you may looke on the haire of his head . . .'[43] Moreover there were special provisions for London: on the grounds that by the custom of the City 'whores' were punished by being carted through the streets, the royal judges explicitly recognised that imputations of whoredom were actionable.[44] Thus in 1694 Agatha Collins complained that Henry Lewis had said in the parish of St Mary le Bow in Cheap Ward that 'shee . . . is a whore for John Wise . . . lay with her . . . and Nicholas Lucas . . . gave her . . . halfe a crowne to lye with her . . .'[45] This case occurred in King's Bench, but the usual locations for such actions were the City's own tribunals, the Sheriffs' Court and the Mayor's Court, which together handled an immense body of litigation of which defamation was a significant part. Typical cases of sexual slander in these courts were little different from many church court suits: 'Thou . . . arte a comon hore & a comon hackney hore' (1574); 'thou . . . art a whore and the salt man's whore' (1607); 'thou . . . art a whore, you . . . are a com[m]on strumpett, you . . . are as very a whore as ever pissed and I . . . will prove you . . . a whore' (1665); or, more circumstantially, 'Goodwife Sawll . . . was w[i]th child by her m[aste]r in Burchenlane . . . before shee . . . was maried to this man . . . and hee . . .

[42] John March, *Actions for Slaunder* (London, 1647), pp. 57, 94–6; William Sheppard, *Action upon the Case for Slander* (London, 1662), pp. 68–9; Keith Thomas, 'The Puritans and Adultery: the Act of 1650 Reconsidered', in Donald Pennington and Keith Thomas, eds., *Puritans and Revolutionaries: Essays in Seventeenth-Century History Presented to Christopher Hill* (Oxford, 1978), pp. 257–82.

[43] PRO, KB 27/1859, rot. 109v.

[44] William Style, *Narrationes Modernae, or Modern Reports* (London, 1658), pp. 69–70, 100, 229, 245; but cf. *The Reports of Sir Edward Coke*, ed. George Wilson, 13 parts separately paginated in 7 vols. (London, 1776–7), pt 4, p.18. By the early years of the eighteenth century it was recognised that the custom justifying these special provisions 'was obsolete, and never put into practice': Robert, Lord Raymond, *Reports of Cases Argued and Adjudged in the Courts of King's Bench and Common Pleas*, 2 vols. (London, 1743), I, 771.

[45] PRO, KB 27/2101, rot. 572r.

was fayne to give a peece of money to her husband . . . to marry her . . . and soe to put her of' (1603).[46]

The various differences of jurisdiction were crucial to the possibilities open to litigants, and they are equally important for historians trying to understand the relationship between honour or reputation and slander litigation. It is obvious that an examination of one jurisdiction alone will provide only a partial view of reputation and possible threats to it. However, most of the detailed work on slander cases has centred on the church courts: social historians, unlike legal historians, have proved very reluctant to get to grips with the much more intractable and basically less informative records of King's Bench and Common Pleas, while idiosyncratic jurisdictions like those of the City of London courts have received even less attention. Yet even a synoptic view across jurisdictions does not give a full picture of issues relating to reputation. The spiritual and temporal courts were separated by lines of demarcation, but they were not truly complementary. Moreover many elements that may well have had a place in the social definition of reputation – including not only matters of social and economic standing and personal attributes such as strength, dexterity and skill in one's trade, but also moral or quasi-moral issues touching on generosity, hospitality and so forth, and even veracity when it did not relate to perjury – were outside the scope of legal remedy. Some – but still only partial – light is shed on these hidden dimensions of reputation by the criminal and quasi-criminal prosecutions for opprobrious words mentioned earlier. They reveal such choice epithets as 'beggarly servingman' (spoken to a minister), 'a base stinkinge and a pispott doctor' (addressed to a physician), and 'goe on, go shite, I care not a turde for yee . . . what art thou? thou art but John Hawkins & I am Tho[ma]s Carter', this last being said 'in a brawling & brutish man[ne]r' to an esquire.[47] Such disparaging invective, characteristically directed at social superiors or those whom the speaker regarded as 'upstarts', must have been common but did not ordinarily provide the grounds for a defamation suit either in the church courts or at common law. This in turn may help to explain the

[46] Corporation of London Record Office (henceforth CLRO), MC1/6, no.38; MC1/160, no.268; MC1/115, no.182; MC1/17, no.132. Levels of business are hard to establish, since the surviving records of the Mayor's Court are patchy and those of the Sheriffs' Court vestigial; but on their importance and procedures in the fifteenth century, see Penny Tucker, 'London's Courts of Law in the Fifteenth Century: the Litigants' Perspective', in Christopher W. Brooks and Michael Lobban, eds., *Communities and Courts in Britain, 1150–1900* (London, 1997), pp. 25–41.

[47] Ingram, *Church Courts*, p.110; Squibb, *High Court of Chivalry*, p. 58; Wilts RO, D1/42/61, fos. 29r, 30v. Despite such insights, a full understanding of reputation 'in the round' demands recourse to sources independent of prosecutions relating to defamation. A valuable starting point is Richard Gough, *Antiquities and Memoirs of the Parish of Myddle, County of Salop . . . A.D. 1700* (Shrewsbury, 1875 edn), *passim*.

fact, noted in numerous studies, that party-and-party slander suits characteristically involved people of roughly comparable status rather than social unequals.[48]

In other respects too these points have an important bearing on how we interpret the evidence. A feature of the post-Reformation church courts is the relatively high and in some areas growing proportion of *women* among litigants in defamation cases, especially as plaintiffs; and study of the slanders they complained of at first sight suggests that sexual morality was virtually the sole determinant of female reputation. 'Women's worth depended on sexual probity', it has been said, and 'honesty, for women, was interpreted as sexual honesty'; an apparent affinity with the supposed 'Mediterranean' model of honour and shame has probably tended to reinforce such judgements. It is indeed universally accepted that sexual reputation was of much more central importance to women than to men. Male 'credit' was important, but it depended on a much broader range of criteria among which trustworthiness in business, social dealings and public affairs, something like 'honesty' in its modern sense, seems to have been most prominent.[49] But that female worth did not rest entirely on sex can be demonstrated in several ways. Examination of defamation suits at common law shows that women, although a small minority among plaintiffs, did regularly complain about accusations of theft or other crimes. The same point emerges, as Dinah Winch has nicely shown, from 'articles of exception' in the church courts, when the characters of opposing witnesses were subjected to detailed scrutiny: on these occasions the characters of women were not by any means evaluated solely on the basis of sexual reputation. Garthine Walker makes a similar point on the basis of different materials – including non-legal sources such as Richard Gough's *History of Myddle*, which shows, for example, that skill and prudence in housekeeping contributed to women's credit. And Faramerz Dabhoiwala uses a wide range of evidence to argue more generally that female honour was by no means necessarily expunged by accusations of sexual laxity; indeed, quite the converse could be true. The paradox, as the moralist publisher John Dunton put it at the end of the seventeenth century, was that 'temptations of honour' often drove women to whoredom.[50]

[48] Sharpe, *Defamation and Sexual Slander*, p. 17; Ingram, *Church Courts*, p. 304; Gowing, *Domestic Dangers*, p. 61.

[49] Gowing, *Domestic Dangers*, p. 52; cf. Ingram, *Church Courts*, pp. 302–3; Amussen, *Ordered Society*, pp. 102–4.

[50] Walker, 'Expanding the Boundaries of Female Honour', pp. 235–45 (though she appears to confuse 'housewife' in the literal sense with 'housewife' or 'hussy' as an epithet meaning 'immoral woman'); cf. Gough, *Myddle*, pp. 18–19, 64, 66, 115 and *passim*; Dabhoiwala, 'Construction of Honour, Reputation and Status', pp. 201–13, quoting Dunton at p.211; see also Fletcher, *Gender, Sex and Subordination*, p. 226.

What bearing did sex have on men's reputations? This is an issue on which more research is needed. Perhaps the greatest opprobrium attached to cuckoldry, especially when the husband was aware of his wife's infidelity but unable or afraid to do anything about it – a situation that qualified him for the particularly opprobrious term 'wittol' – and/or when his own sexual inadequacy was the root cause of the disaster. Here again is an apparent link with the Mediterranean culture of honour and shame as it has been represented in numerous anthropological studies. Cuckoldry represented the utmost loss of a man's control over household discipline in general and his wife's sexuality in particular; but there was also some atavistic association, symbolised in the cuckold's imagined horns, with inhuman beastliness – it is necessary to recognise this dark current to understand fully the bitter contempt with which the cuckold was derided.[51] Accusations of cuckoldry could be sued as defamations in the church courts since they were construed as implying a charge of adultery against the wife. But they were less common than one might suppose in most jurisdictions – perhaps because they were at one remove from direct imputations of crime, perhaps because the charge was too shameful to air in public.[52] A safer mode of proceeding was for a man to persuade his wife to defend herself in court against charges of whoredom, and it is indeed significant that a high proportion of women who sued for their sexual reputation were married. It follows that not all women's suits should be interpreted, as they often have been, as examples of female agency: the women concerned may in effect have been doing men's business, or engaged in a joint endeavour to clear the name of both partners in the marriage.[53] In the London city courts, it should be noted, suits alleging slanders of whoredom required the involvement of both husband and wife as joint plaintiffs; and incidental references to married women's slander actions, whether in the church or the secular courts, imply that they were regarded as being as much their husbands' concern as their own.[54]

What of the actual sexual behaviour of men? Laura Gowing has emphasised the powerful elements of misogyny in mocking rhymes and other libels; but, as Adam Fox has recently confirmed, such sources indicate that imagery and innuendo implying sexual immorality were also potent means

51 Cf. Anton Blok, 'Rams and Billy-Goats: a Key to the Mediterranean Concept of Honour', *Man*, new ser., 16 (1981), pp. 427–40; Elizabeth Foyster, 'A Laughing Matter? Marital Discord and Gender Control in Seventeenth-Century England', *Rural History*, 4 (1993), esp. pp. 7–11.

52 Ingram, *Church Courts*, pp. 300–2 and the references there cited; cf. Gowing, *Domestic Dangers*, pp. 62–4.

53 Cf. Anne Tarver, *Church Court Records: an Introduction for Family and Local Historians* (Chichester, 1995), p.114; Foyster, *Manhood*, pp. 162–3.

54 Cf. Foyster, *Manhood*, pp. 58–62, which reaches rather similar conclusions on the basis of different evidence.

of attacking men, and they could be particularly useful to deflate the pretensions of figures in authority or those, like puritan ministers or laymen, who laid special claim to moral rectitude.[55] Whether or not men's reputation was thought to be tainted by the act of illicit sex itself, its wider implications could certainly expose them to obloquy. Sexual promiscuity or excess provoked charges of 'debauchery'. The seduction and abandonment of an otherwise respectable woman, especially when a promise of marriage had been made or implied, even more readily invited moral criticism: indeed it made sexual behaviour a matter of 'honesty' in the sense of trustworthiness, the concept at the heart of constructions of male reputation. By the same token men who betrayed their wives were at best looked on askance, not least because maintaining a mistress or spending heavily on prostitutes threatened to shipwreck their household economy, while men risked infecting both themselves and their wives with sexually transmitted diseases by 'running after whores'. The dubious standing of such men is nicely caught in a Wiltshire case of 1697: a Froxfield man was slandered as 'a knave . . . [who was] with two whores in Charnam Street', and it was said that 'by reason of the scandalls laid on the plaintiffe by the defendant, the plaintiffes wife is soe concerned, that she thinks it some shame for her to goe abroad in her husband['s] company'.[56] In any case males could be, and often were, prosecuted in the church courts for adultery or fornication, or pursued by local officers and justices of the peace on paternity charges. Accusations of these crimes were subject to the slander jurisdiction of the church courts and a significant proportion of cases heard there centred on such matters and were brought by men who were clearly desperate to clear their reputations.[57]

All this suggests that the double standard was only a matter of degree; yet Laura Gowing's London evidence leads her to reject such a view and to claim that, on the contrary, the reputations of the two sexes were utterly incommensurable. Men, she insists, were rarely made culpable for their sexual misbehaviour and never defined by it; thus 'women were at the pivotal centre of the circulation of blame and dishonour for sex: responsibility was channelled entirely through them'.[58] One index of this, she suggests, was that men were prepared to boast of their sexual exploits, flouting any suggestion of personal culpability for fornication or adultery by slandering women as *their* whores. This certainly indicates important

[55] Fox, 'Ballads, Libels and Popular Ridicule', p. 56 and *passim*; Ingram, 'Ridings, Rough Music and Mocking Rhymes', pp. 183–5; see also Richard Cust, 'Honour and Politics in Early Stuart England: the Case of Beaumont *v.* Hastings', *Past and Present*, no. 149 (November 1995), p. 92; Turner, '"Nothing Is So Secret"', *passim*.

[56] Wilts RO, D1/41/3/23, nos. 201, 207, 207a, 208.

[57] Sharpe, *Defamation and Sexual Slander*, pp. 10, 16; Ingram, *Church Courts*, pp. 302, 304–6; Amussen, *Ordered Society*, pp. 102–4; Gowing, *Domestic Dangers*, p. 64.

[58] Gowing, *Domestic Dangers*, p. 109 and chs. 3–4 *passim*.

differences in the way men and women experienced and thought about sex in relation to themselves, but does not necessarily imply that promiscuous males escaped social stigma. If I have understood the statistics aright, cases of sexual boasting were not common in Gowing's material, and elsewhere they seem to have been very unusual, at least before 1640.[59] In any case it would be a mistake to assume that sexual braggarts invariably got off scot free. In 1609 John Croshawe, present in the London Bridewell court to give evidence against a certain Mistress Kelsey and Anne Broughton, was brought into question himself on the grounds that 'he to the face of the said Broughton, called her whore, and affirmed that he had lien w[i]th her att the Bell at Putney and there had the use of her body twice'. He denied the charge, except that 'it may be he had in coller affirmed so much', but refused to swear on oath. Efforts were made on his behalf by the Lord Mayor, 'because it was supposed Croshawe was crased in his witt[es]' – 'albeit yt evidentlie appeareth he doeth counterfeite', noted the governors of Bridewell cannily – 'and therefore doubted po[nishment] would make him worse'. Nonetheless he was eventually whipped.[60]

Yet if Gowing overstates the case, there are at least some grounds for thinking that the burden of sexual culpability was tilting exceptionally far towards women in early seventeenth-century London, a fact suggested by the unusual preponderance of female plaintiffs in the metropolitan church courts. The probability is that London and its suburbs had expanded so rapidly that the church courts were by then slackening their grip on moral regulation far more than in most other areas. By the same token, the wardmote courts which had formerly exercised a parallel secular jurisdiction against whoredom and bawdry in the city parishes had by the early seventeenth century become haphazard in their operation. Even the impact of Bridewell on sexual offenders seems to have been declining by the 1630s. Hitherto these institutions had, to an extent, insisted on male culpability. Their desuetude, only partly offset by the increased involvement of justices of the peace in bastardy and paternity cases, may well have encouraged the development of a more extreme version of the double standard. As will be seen, what may have been true of London before the civil war applied to England as a whole a century later.[61]

59 Gowing, *Domestic Dangers*, pp. 64, 74–5; Meldrum, 'Women's Court', pp. 10–11; cf. Foyster, *Manhood*, pp. 42–4.

60 Guildhall Library, Bridewell Court Book [microfilm] 5, fos. 384r–385r, 386r (apart from his boasting there was some circumstantial evidence that he had had intercourse with Anne Broughton and allegedly 'did pysse in her privities'); for a man punished for (amongst other things) boasting of having had sex with his mistress, see Bridewell Court Book [microfilm] 8, fo. 109v.

61 These remarks are based on sampling of all the sources mentioned; I hope to substantiate them more fully on another occasion.

Terminology offers another approach to male and female sexual reputation; the matter is more complex than is often imagined, with legal as well as social and linguistic aspects. The word 'whore' denoted a sexually unchaste woman, though not necessarily a prostitute. It implied fornication or adultery, which could be punished in the church courts, and in that sense constituted a criminal accusation. On the other hand, for centuries the word had been used as a generalised term of abuse against females, with little specific meaning. On those grounds royal judges sometimes tried to prevent the church courts taking notice of the word (and its equivalents, such as 'jade' and 'quean') when they were not coupled with some more definite accusation of sexual immorality.[62] That this restrictive view failed to take hold was probably the result of several interacting factors. The terms 'whore' and 'whoredom' were not mere colloquialisms but had a status in official discourse, for example in the church's Homily on Whoredom and, crucially, in the English version of the ecclesiastical canons that defined what offences were to be reported to the church courts. Further, 'whore' and 'whoredom' had an important place in the Bible and hence in contemporary religious polemic concerning the true and false church; by a curious paradox, the effect was to dignify what was in other usages a vulgar term of abuse.[63] And, as Laura Gowing has brilliantly shown, these biblical resonances blended with popular traditions of invective to create an abusive stereotype with great power to shock and wound and well adapted to public, dramatised utterance – the ideal tool for the defamer.[64] Contrariwise, the fact that this term was among the most common words of abuse in daily use offered perennial opportunities to take an adversary to court. Hence the constant appearance of the term in church court slander proceedings in the early seventeenth century; a process that in itself constantly reinforced the importance of sexual reputation to women.

It is often said that there was no male equivalent to 'whore'. Setting aside the term 'cuckold' – the inverse counterpart of 'whore' according to the logic of the double standard, in that the term combined maleness with

[62] Style, *Narrationes Modernae*, p. 299; John Godolphin, *Repertorium Canonicum: or, an Abridgment of the Ecclesiastical Laws of this Realm*, 3rd edn (1687), pp. 520–1, 522–3; John Ayliffe, *Parergon Juris Canonici Anglicani* (London, 1726), pp. 438–9.

[63] *Sermons or Homilies Appointed to be Read in Churches in the Time of Queen Elizabeth* (Liverpool, 1799 edn), pp. 82–92; *Synodalia: A Collection of Articles of Religion, Canons, and Proceedings of Convocations in the Province of Canterbury, from the Year 1547 to the Year 1717*, ed. Edward Cardwell, 2 vols. consecutively paginated (Oxford, 1842), I, p. 308. Note also that for sexual slanders to be actionable at common law in London they had actually to include the word 'whore' or words tantamount to the same thing; to say of a woman, 'Do you hear the news? . . . Mrs Branch's thighs are bare, and Backhurst is between them; . . . [with] many words too obscene to be repeated', was simply not good enough: Raymond, *Reports*, I, pp. 103–4.

[64] Gowing, *Domestic Dangers*, pp. 79–87.

loss of sexual agency – this was strictly speaking true. But there were some words that approached it. 'Whoremaster' and 'whoremonger' cannot be discounted simply because they appear to denote concepts defined in relation to whores. The sense was not that of 'pimp' or manager of whores, but simply habitual fornicator or adulterer. The words were biting ones, like 'whore' carrying powerful biblical overtones enshrined in the Homily on Whoredom, and regularly cropped up in defamation suits. James Sharpe's data, for example, show that they were quite prominent in the York diocesan courts in the 1590s.[65] Other relevant words were 'rogue' and 'knave'. These were generalised terms of abuse applied to males, implying low condition, lack of principle, dishonesty, and (in the case of 'rogue') a vagrant disposition. However, they could also carry strong connotations of sexual immorality. Dinah Winch has shown this for the late seventeenth century, but it is clear that already in Elizabethan and early Stuart times 'knave' and 'rogue' had emerged as words which could serve as functional equivalents of 'whore'. This is revealed by the frequency with which the terms were linked. 'A knave and a whore', 'a rogue and a whore' – these couplets occur regularly in circumstances where it is crystal clear that the emphasis for both the man and the woman is on sexual immorality. Thus in 1611, Thomas Lowe, baker of St James's Clerkenwell, was bound over to the Middlesex sessions 'for keeping a notorious bawdy house and suffering whores and knaves to be locked up in a private room together'; while at Burton on Trent in 1618, a constable and his posse invaded a house 'to fynde a knave and a whore in bedd togeather', and dragged them from their house along the streets 'w[i]th greate noyse and w[i]th ringing of cow bells, basons, candlestick[es], frying-panns, and w[i]th the sounde of a drumme, crying alowd "A whore and a knave, a whore, a whore!"'.[66] There are also indications that 'knave' was contrasted with 'cuckold' – an adulterer as against a victim of adultery. In 1617 Alice Gough, in rejecting the sexual advances of a neighbour,

65 *Sermons or Homilies*, p. 82; Sharpe, *Defamation and Sexual Slander*, pp. 10, 16–17; cf. Gowing, *Domestic Dangers*, pp. 63, 64, 114.

66 *Middlesex County Records: Calendar of Sessions Rolls . . . [etc. 1609–12]*, 8 vols. (London, 1927–33), V, 191, cf. p. 190; cf. ibid., II, 70; PRO, STAC 8/104/20; cf. KB 122/110, rot. 142r. On the background of the Burton case, see Joan R. Kent, '"Folk Justice" and "Royal Justice" in Early Seventeenth-Century England: a "Charivari" in the Midlands', *Midland History*, 8 (1983), pp. 70–85; Martin Ingram, 'Juridical Folklore in England Illustrated by Rough Music', in Brooks and Lobban, eds., *Communities and Courts*, pp. 72–4. For other examples of the knave, etc./whore couplet, see *Episcopal Visitation Returns for Cambridgeshire: Matthew Wren, Bishop of Ely, 1638–1665*, ed. W. M. Palmer (Cambridge, 1930), p. 54; Ayliffe, *Parergon*, p. 42; Metropolitan Archives, WJ/SR (NS) 44, no. 88; CLRO, MC1/19, no. 74; Wilts RO, D1/41/3/20, nos. 75, 101, 105–6, D1/41/3/22, nos. 5, 21, D1/41/3/23, no. 153, 192, 207, 207a, 208, cf. no. 158. Gowing asserts that 'knave' and 'rogue' were 'non-sexual words', even though some of the evidence she herself cites indicates otherwise: see Gowing, *Domestic Dangers*, p. 63, cf. pp. 71, 72, 90, 98.

affirmed that she 'had rather say to her husband, "Goe, poore knave" then "poore cuckhold"'.[67]

In a different legal context the sexual resonances of these terms might have assumed greater social importance than they did. In the early decades of the common-law remedy such words as 'knave' and 'villain' featured quite prominently in slander suits. Depositions from the City of London in the 1540s – referring either to the Mayor's Court or Sheriffs' Court or to related arbitration proceedings – vividly reveal the importance of these and similar terms in male invective. Just as women slanged each other as 'whore' and used this as a touchstone to compare their 'honesties', so did men with the term 'knave' – with the difference that such altercations in the male context led more easily to the drawing of weapons and physical violence. In 1547, for example, when William Wood discovered that some barrels of wine on his lighter had been broached and the vessel was 'spewyd and arayed', he exclaimed:

> 'What knaveis brought upp this lyghter?' . . . 'Nay [replied a certain Ambrose Thurston] they are no knaveis more then thowe kepest any; but be as honest men as thowe kepest anye.' 'Mary then,' quod Wood, 'yf thowe saiest soo, & take their parte, thowe arte the mayntener of false knaves'; then quod Thurstone to the sayde Wood, 'thowe arte a false knave;' 'and so,' q[uo]d Wood, 'thowe art a false knave,' and with that they drew their weapons . . .

and fought till they were parted.[68] But in the later sixteenth century the secular courts decided that words like 'villain', 'knave' and 'rogue' were 'words of choler', 'of passion', 'mere wind', of uncertain meaning and hence not actionable. This restriction was supposed to apply to the church courts too; and though this was never absolutely so in practice, there could be no question of such words becoming, like the term 'whore', a staple of court business.[69] Pushed to the limits of legal consciousness, 'knave' and 'rogue' were confined to the sphere of vulgar abuse and the sexual connotations of the words remained half-latent and eventually faded. This was not, I think, the result of any positive desire to deny the culpability of men for sexual misdeeds; it was the arbitrary result of legal decisions made for other reasons, and serves as yet another example of the complex relationship between law and reputation.

In the concluding paragraphs, I will focus on much broader changes over time that give a further perspective on how moral worlds were defined by

67 Ingram, *Church Courts*, p. 252; Wilts RO, D1/42/32, fo.130.

68 CLRO, Journal 15, fol. 325/328v [dual foliation], cf. fol. 313/316r.

69 Helmholz, *Select Cases*, pp. xcix–c, 89, and *Roman Canon Law*, pp. 62–4; *Sources of English Legal History*, ed. Baker and Milsom, pp. 640–2; Sheppard, *Actions upon the Case for Slander*, p.74; Ayliffe, *Parergon*, p. 215.

law. Relative to the population, the numbers of defamation suits rose in the sixteenth century, peaked in the early seventeenth, and declined in the later part of that century and on into the eighteenth – a decline that is clearly evident in both the ecclesiastical and the secular courts. (The figures so far available are admittedly fragmentary, especially for the secular courts from the later seventeenth century onwards, but the general outline is clear enough.)[70] This story needs to be understood within a broader context of social and legal shift, which in effect transformed the nature of the moral world within which people lived. Early and mid sixteenth-century society displayed the features noted earlier: many forms of personal behaviour, including sexual morality, were closely regulated by courts of law whether ecclesiastical or secular. Adultery, fornication and similar matters were regularly denounced to the courts and punished by confession and penance. Recent work on London, in particular, reveals an exceptionally close mesh of moral control at that time, but essentially the same principles operated elsewhere in England. The working of the secular criminal law was also closely enmeshed with communities – including policing by unpaid local amateurs and a high level of participation in juries and similar bodies. This was the milieu in which church and secular court procedures for dealing with defamation were grounded and made most sense.[71]

In many respects the system of legal regulation was intensified in the late sixteenth and early to mid seventeenth centuries. Admittedly certain segments of it were, towards the end of this period, showing signs of strain – notably, as we have seen, in the rapidly expanding metropolis. However, in most areas this was the era when church court prosecutions for personal immorality were at their peak and where the activities of justices of the peace greatly expanded to include alehouse regulation and the punishment of bastard-bearing. Indictments for felony also increased markedly, as did the infliction of capital punishment. At the same time, the volume of party

[70] Sharpe, *Defamation and Sexual Slander*, p. 9; Ingram, *Church Courts*, pp. 299–300 and the references there cited; Helmholz, ed., *Select Cases*, pp. xlv–xlvi, lxxxvi–lxxxvii, and *Roman Canon Law*, p. 58; W. A. Champion, 'Recourse to Law and the Meaning of the Great Litigation Decline, 1650–1750: Some Clues from the Shrewsbury Local Courts', in Brooks and Lobban, eds., *Communities and Courts*, p. 180. But cf. C. W. Brooks, 'Interpersonal Conflict and Social Tension: Civil Litigation in England, 1640–1830', in A. L. Beier *et al.*, eds., *The First Modern Society: Essays in History in Honour of Lawrence Stone* (Cambridge, 1989), esp. pp. 390–3, which, while establishing the general context of a decline in litigation in the late seventeenth and eighteenth centuries, questions whether there was any significant drop in disputes over contentious words.

[71] Richard Wunderli, *London Church Courts and Society on the Eve of the Reformation* (Medieval Academy of America, Speculum Anniversary Monographs, no. 7, Cambridge, MA, 1981); Shannon MacSheffery, ed., *Love and Marriage in Late Medieval London* (Kalamazoo, MI, 1995); Martin Ingram, 'Reformation of Manners in Early Modern England', in Griffiths, Fox and Hindle, eds., *Experience of Authority*; McIntosh, *Controlling Misbehavior*, pp. 12, 24, 62, 80, 119–22 and *passim*.

and party litigation in all courts was reaching an unprecedentedly high level. In 1640, it has been said, there was probably more litigation per head of population going through the central courts at Westminster than at any time before or since. There was a variety of reasons for this last development, only partly overlapping with the causes of the increase in disciplinary prosecutions and the growing numbers of criminal trials. But all these changes together fostered a law-mindedness, and sensitivity both to the dangers posed and to the opportunities offered by the law, which formed a characteristic feature of English culture in this period. Inevitably it was at this time, in the days of Elizabeth and the early Stuarts, that the numbers of lawsuits for defamation were at their height, with an ambiguous relationship to the legal context. On the one hand, the danger that slanders would 'raise fames' of immorality or other wrongdoing, and so lead to delation to the church or secular courts, was at its most intense. On the other, the spirit of litigiousness was running high and the temptation to exploit and manipulate the forms of action at common law and in the church courts, to bring interpersonal and neighbourhood quarrels into the legal arena, was at its greatest. Defamation suits centring on terms like 'whore' were among the readiest means of doing so, a fact reflected vividly in the huge numbers of such lawsuits in early seventeenth-century London.[72]

As the later seventeenth century moved into the eighteenth, the relationship between courts and society shifted again. It is not possible here to discuss fully the far-reaching cultural changes that were transforming English society by 1750, but some key developments may be identified. Most strikingly, the mesh of legal regulation in the sphere of personal morality slowly unravelled. A crucial development was the collapse of the church courts in the 1640s and 50s, in the wake of the downfall of Charles I's personal rule. They were revived after the Restoration, but in most areas never attained their former vigour. Faramerz Dabhoiwala has shown that in London the disciplinary side of the church courts' work never really got going again after 1660; while in many areas of provincial England the restored ecclesiastical discipline, such as it was, all but collapsed as an unforeseen consequence of the Toleration Act of 1689.[73] The resultant gap

[72] There is a huge literature on these themes. Useful introductions are provided by Keith Wrightson, *English Society, 1580–1680* (London, 1982), esp. chs. 6–7; James Sharpe, 'The People and the Law', in Barry Reay, ed., *Popular Culture in Seventeenth-Century England* (London and Sidney, 1985), pp. 244–70; Ingram, *Church Courts*, ch. 4 and *passim*; and Brooks, *Pettyfoggers and Vipers of the Commonwealth*, p. 79 and chs. 4–5, *passim*. On London, see Gowing, *Domestic Dangers*.

[73] G. V. Bennett, *The Tory Crisis in Church and State, 1688–1730: the Career of Francis Atterbury, Bishop of Rochester* (Oxford, 1975), pp. 9, 14–15; Ingram, *Church Courts*, pp. 372–4; Faramerz Dabhoiwala, 'Prostitution and Police in London, *c*.1660–*c*.1760' (Oxford Univ. D.Phil. thesis, 1995), pp. 94–7; but cf. Mary Kinnear, 'The Correction Court in the Diocese of Carlisle, 1704–1756', *Church History*, 59 (1990), pp. 191–206.

was only very partly filled by the secular magistrates. Even in London, where the city authorities and suburban justices were quite active against 'vice' in the late seventeenth century, their zeal slackened thereafter. The activities of the Societies for the Reformation of Manners in the 1690s and 1700s may be seen as a kind of artificial respiration, an attempt to find an alternative means of sustaining a collapsed system of local, communal regulation.[74] These changes, it can be plausibly argued, liberated male sexuality more than female; the result was a reinforcement of the double standard, intensifying the differences between the constructions of male and female reputation.[75] There were other changes too, including (outside London) a marked decline by the end of the seventeenth century in the level of formal criminal prosecutions and in the incidence of capital punishment;[76] and, for complex reasons, a massive drop in the volume of party and party litigation in the central courts. Slander suits probably shared in this decline in King's Bench and Common Pleas, and they certainly fell in the church courts.[77] Socially reputation continued to be important, of course; but it is significant that *The Spectator*, that barometer of genteel opinion, discussed gossip and slander without reference to the legal context. Changed legal and social conditions gradually made it less necessary or less appropriate to defend aspects of reputation in the courts, less desirable and perhaps less respectable to bring interpersonal quarrels into the legal arena in the guise of slander suits.[78] It was a world, if not disenchanted, then at least in part deregulated, and one in which the construction of honour or reputation was less dependent on the moral world of the law.

[74] There now exists a large literature on the Societies for Reformation of Manners. Still the best introduction is Dudley W. R. Bahlman, *The Moral Revolution of 1688* (New Haven and London, 1957), but for some recent perspectives, see Robert B. Shoemaker, 'Reforming the City: the Reformation of Manners Campaign in London, 1690 –1738', in Lee Davison *et al.*, eds., *Stilling the Grumbling Hive: the Response to Social and Economic Problems in England, 1689–1750* (Stroud and New York, 1992), pp. 98–120; Dabhoiwala, 'Prostitution and Police', ch. 5; Tony Claydon, *William III and the Godly Revolution* (Cambridge, 1996). On the decline of communal regulation, see also Champion, 'Recourse to Law', pp. 195–7.

[75] Dabhoiwala, 'Construction of Honour', pp. 212–13.

[76] James Sharpe, *Crime in Early Modern England, 1550–1750* (London, 1984), ch. 3.

[77] Sharpe, *Defamation and Sexual Slander*, p. 9; Meldrum, 'Women's Court in London', p. 2; Champion, 'Recourse to Law', p.180; but cf. Brooks, 'Interpersonal Conflict', pp. 390–3.

[78] *The Spectator*, ed. Donald F. Bond, 5 vols. (Oxford, 1965), I, pp. 97–100, II, pp. 558–60, III, pp. 296–8, 463–6, IV, pp. 1–3, V, pp. 31–4, 87–90; but cf. ibid., IV, pp. 86–90; *The Tatler*, ed. Donald F. Bond, 3 vols. (Oxford, 1987), II, pp. 73–7; Lassiter, 'Defamation of Peers', pp. 232–5, and for later developments, Anna Clark, 'Whores and Gossips: Sexual Reputation in London, 1770–1825', in Arina Angerman *et al.*, *Current Issues in Women's History* (London, 1989), esp. pp. 239–40, 245.

9. *Story-telling and the social imagery of religious conflict in nineteenth-century French law courts*

CAROLINE FORD

In 1845, Jeanne-Françoise Le Monnier, who had been a nun in the Norman monastery of the Saint Sacrament in Bayeux, brought a case to civil court charging the superior of the order to which she belonged and four other women religious for incarcerating her first in a convent and then in the insane asylum of Bon Sauveur in the nearby city of Caen. Her lawyer, Léon Tillard, presented her case to the court in the form of a legal brief, a *mémoire judiciaire*, which narrated the facts of the affair from his client's point of view, and he concluded with a legal justification for her allegations.[1]

This article explores the problem of how the case of Jeanne Le Monnier was told as a story to the court by her lawyer in order to examine the elements comprising the social imagery that was employed in public debates surrounding conflicts between the Church and state in nineteenth-century France. In particular, I wish to assess how Tillard appealed to a set of moral categories and images that reveal some of the underlying bases of the fierce anticlericalism that shaped French politics and society in the nineteenth century. I will examine Le Monnier's *mémoire* from three perspectives in this regard. First, in terms of how changes in the law and legal procedure following the French Revolution contributed to the way in which Le Monnier's story was told to the court, and secondly, in terms of how courtroom narratives intersected with contemporary social commentary and novelistic literature during the first half of the nineteenth century. Finally, I wish to explore how such cases helped to redefine a new relationship between secular and canon law.

Story-telling is, of course, a part of any legal system and frequently

[1] *Affaire de Dame Jeanne-Françoise Le Monnier contre dame Marie Le Caplain, Dame Caroline de St.-Severin, Dame Reine Jourdain, et Dame Renée-Charlotte Le Chasseur* (Caen, 1845). The *mémoire*, as the case became more widely publicised, went through two editions. Publishers in Bayeux refused to print it. *Récits par elle-même, la procédure, les enquêtes, la preuve, orgueil et placement au B.S.* (Caen, 1846), p. 10.

reveals in a clear and compelling way prevalent social stereotypes that can range widely and reveal much about how individuals in specific historical settings fashion themselves and their motives to others. Natalie Davis has recently studied, for example, how ostensibly contrite wives or husbands tried to exonerate themselves in the wake of a violent act through strategies of self-presentation in order to justify their actions. Ruth Harris has shown how women accused of crimes of passion in late nineteenth-century France spoke directly on their own behalf in court and drew on the tropes of melodramatic literature and on moral assumptions about female honour to defend their behaviour. The extent to which they successfully avoided conviction often depended more on how effectively they told their stories and appealed to these categories than on rules of procedure and law.[2] The study of narrative in legal courts thus provides a window on to the social and moral categories of a given society as well as hidden and sometimes unspoken cultural codes and societal fears that might go otherwise undetected by the historian.[3] Indeed, these narratives reveal how these cultural codes were often created out of collective anxieties and why certain anxieties become particularly charged at given historical moments.

I have chosen the Le Monnier case to explore these issues for three reasons. First, cases of the kind brought by Jeanne Le Monnier proliferated following the French Revolution. Courts and the Ministry of Religious Affairs were deluged by such charges, which are entirely absent from the eighteenth- and twentieth-century legal record. This was a nineteenth-century case, *par excellence*. Secondly, I wish to explore why charges of claustration and confinement were so prevalent during this period and to place them within the context of the fascination with Gothic narratives and novels in this period. Thirdly, I will examine how such narratives structured broader discussions about the relationship between Church and state as well as religious and secular authority.

The Le Monnier case must first be placed within the context of the transformation of the French legal system following the French Revolution, a transformation that changed the relationship between secular and canon law. This is important because, in the words of Peter Brooks, 'the law at least implicitly recognizes the power of story-telling' and for this reason, in

[2] Natalie Davis, *Fiction in the Archives: Pardon Tales and their Tellers in Sixteenth-Century France* (Stanford, 1987) and Ruth Harris, *Murders and Madness: Medicine, Law, and Society in the Fin-de-Siècle* (Oxford, 1991), pp. 208–42.

[3] For a discussion of story-telling in forensic trials, see Lance Bennett, 'Story-Telling in Criminal Trial: A Model of Social Judgement', *Quarterly Journal of Speech*, 64 (1978), pp. 1–22, and 'Rhetorical Transformation of Evidence in Criminal Trials: Creating Grounds for Legal Judgment', *Quarterly Journal of Speech*, 65 (1979), pp. 311–12; and Lance Bennett and Martha Feldman, *Reconstructing Reality in the Courtroom: Justice and Judgment in American Culture* (New Brunswick, 1981), pp. 3–10.

different social contexts, 'it has been intent . . . to formalize the conditions of telling – to assure that narratives reach those charged with judging them in certain rule-governed forms'.[4] I will then explore the narrative strategies of Le Monnier's lawyer before concluding with a discussion of the theme of claustration and legal story-telling during this period.

I. CHANGES IN THE LAW

Secular law during the eighteenth and nineteenth centuries was based on an inquisitorial as opposed to an accusatorial model.[5] Most criminal trials during the eighteenth century were conducted entirely in private, and the first stage of a criminal investigation was carried out by judges. This amounted to questioning the principal witnesses as well as the plaintiff and defendant, out of which a dossier would be created that would complete the *instruction préparatoire*. In the second stage of the investigation, the *instruction définitive*, witnesses were required to repeat testimony, and plaintiffs and defendants sometimes confronted each other for the first time. All evidence and paperwork collected during these two stages of investigation became part of a general file which the judge consulted in deciding a case. Two distinct features characterised this system: the proceedings were conducted almost entirely in private and although plaintiff and defendants had recourse to lawyers, they often faced judges without their counsel present. So the role of the lawyer was, in essence, to advise and draw up legal documents setting out the facts of the case and then to argue legal points to the court.[6]

These legal briefs, or *mémoires judiciaires*, were initially hand-written documents intended for the eyes of the judges alone, and they were the principal means through which the facts of a case were presented to judges in a written form. *Mémoires judiciaires* were constructed in the form of a story. They could range from several to several hundred pages in length. With time they were printed and circulated among family members and other parties interested in a case. The *mémoire judiciaire* and later the newspaper became the principal channel between the courtroom and the street.[7] It soon became a form of popular pamphlet literature, especially when the *mémoire* centred on a *cause célèbre* or a particularly titillating legal case.

[4] Peter Brooks, 'The Law as Narrative and Rhetoric', in Peter Brooks and Paul Gewirtz, eds., *Law's Stories: Narrative and Rhetoric in the Law* (New Haven, 1996), p. 19.

[5] Katherine Fischer Taylor, *In the Theater of Criminal Justice: The Palais de Justice in the Second Empire* (Princeton, 1993), pp. 5–9.

[6] For a discussion of these procedures see Sarah Maza, *Private Lives and Public Affairs: The Causes Célèbres of PreRevolutionary France* (Berkeley, 1993), pp. 34–5. Also see David Bell, *Lawyers and Citizens: The Making of a Political Elite in Old Regime France* (Oxford, 1994), p. 31.

[7] Maza, *Private Lives and Public Affairs*, p. 36.

While the *mémoire judiciaire* presented the facts of cases and made legal arguments to the court, it increasingly, from the late eighteenth century onward, spoke in the name of and appealed to a new social entity known as the 'public'. It is for this reason that historians of eighteenth-century France have in recent years devoted considerable attention to these legal documents. They have argued that they played an important role in the creation of the very concept of 'public opinion', which increasingly came to represent a distinct secular authority in opposition to a morally and politically flawed monarchy. In doing so, the *mémoire judiciaire* contributed to the democratisation and secularisation of the political and corporate culture of the Old Regime. In some cases, *mémoires judiciaires* in the Old Regime became a form of opposition journalism which criticised political and social elites for their exclusivity and high-handedness and argued for more democratic legal norms. Ultimately, as Sarah Maza has shown in a recent book entitled *Private Lives and Public Affairs*, they played an important role in challenging the authority of the French monarchy, thus laying some of the ideological groundwork for the French Revolution.[8]

The legal system of the Old Regime and all the privileges attached to it were, of course, abolished during the French Revolution and replaced by institutions based on principles of ostensible equality before the law. However, with the Revolution and the writing of the Napoleonic code, certain rules and procedures were retained, including the use of the *mémoire judiciaire* in presenting the facts of a case. While the accusatorial model also survived the Revolution and judges continued to play an important role in the direct investigation of cases, important aspects of the system changed. The courts of the Old Regime were abolished as well as the privileges attached to them. The legal profession was opened, in principle, to all. One of the greatest changes in the nature of French criminal law was to render public what had been essentially private during the Old Regime: court proceedings and cases. It also gave more advantage to the accused through trial by jury. *Mémoires judiciaires* remained a significant part of post-Revolutionary legal culture, and historians have argued that they continued to foster a new secular and democratic morality in the nineteenth century.

But how did changes in the law affect the status of ecclesiastical cases during this period? It must be stated clearly that Le Monnier's case would never have been brought before a secular court during the Old Regime. All matters governing cloistered religious orders and their members fell under the jurisdiction of canon law. This was because an aspirant who wished to

[8] Sarah Maza, 'Le tribunal de la nation: Les mémoires judiciaires et l'opinion publique à la fin de l'ancien régime', *Annales, économies, sociétés, civilisations*, 42 (1987), pp. 73–90 and *Private Lives and Public Affairs.*

enter a religious order was required to take a solemn, lifelong vow as a result of which he or she died to the secular world or became *mort civilement*. Indeed, a nun's civic death was expressed through ritual. In taking her vows, the nun would lie prostrate before the grille, covered by a funeral pall, while the Office of the Dead was recited.[9] All disputes governing her property or person came under the jurisdiction of her order and canon law. She had no rights or protection under civil law as technically she did not exist as a legal being.

The Church had more power to adjudicate its own affairs in the eighteenth century, independent of secular legal authority, and religious authorities also had an extraordinary influence over the secular justice system. One need merely think of the terrible fate of Jean Calas, whose body was broken on a wheel for allegedly killing his son for converting to Catholicism. The public outcry that the case evoked, partly through the efforts of the vituperative philosophe Voltaire, revealed the extent of the Catholic Church's power in eighteenth-century France, despite signs of dechristianisation and the gradual desacralisation of the monarchy.[10]

Napoleonic law, which established the legal system for post-Revolutionary France, rationalised what were a confusing set of procedural practices based on customary law and royal ordinance. However, the Napoleonic civil and criminal codes were silent about the rights and status of the clergy in secular society, and the boundary between secular and canon law was exceedingly unclear. It is true that the Concordat of 1801 established the formal relationship between Church and state until their separation and the abrogation of the Concordat in 1905, providing general guidelines for governance, but it did not define how conflicts between members of the clergy could be resolved in case of deadlock. Indeed, a law governing the conditions under which female religious communities could be legally recognised and the status of their members was not passed until 1825.[11] No legislation was ever passed for male religious orders, many of which remained unauthorised, existing at the margins of the law (as did many unauthorised female orders) for most of the nineteenth century.

[9] Elizabeth Rapley, *The Dévotes: Women and the Church in Seventeenth-Century France* (Montreal: McGill-Queens University Press, 1990), p. 175.

[10] See Marc Chassaigne, *L'affaire Calas* (Paris, 1929); David Bien, *The Calas Affair: Persecution, Toleration and Heresy in Eighteenth-Century Toulouse* (Princeton, NJ, 1960), and Edna Dixon, *Voltaire and the Calas Case* (New York, 1961).

[11] For Revolutionary legislation governing religious congregations, see Alphonse Aulard, *La révolution française et les congrégations: exposé historique et documents* (Paris, 1903). For the legal status of religious congregations following the Revolution, see Paul Nourrisson, *Histoire légale des congrégations religieuses en France depuis 1789* (Paris, 1928); A.Vuillefroy, *Traité de l'administration du culte catholique: principes et règles d'administration* (Paris, 1842); Armand Ravelet, *Traité des congrégations religieuses: commentaire des lois et de la jurisprudence* (Paris, 1869).

Until the 1860s, governments tried to keep cases involving priests or nuns out of secular courts because in the increasingly public world of the courtroom they feared that religious scandals and conflicts might undermine morals and public order.[12] So prefects, subprefects, *procureurs* and the Ministry of Religious Affairs often stepped in to seek administrative solutions. But in cases of serious crime, like murder or rape, or when a conflict became intractable, the clergy found itself in court. Le Monnier's case fitted this pattern in that the subprefect of the arrondissement of Bayeux first intervened in order to try to adjudicate the conflict, but to no avail. In short, cases like that of Jeanne Le Monnier's increasingly found their way into secular court.

The cultural and social context in which cases were tried in the nineteenth century was quite different from that of the eighteenth. *Mémoires judiciaires* addressed the general public more directly and could assume a much broader readership. Cases would be reported in other ways, notably through the newspaper – and principally, in legal cases, in the *Gazette des Tribunaux*. Legal cases also provided plots for the theatre and the novel. One need only think of the famous murder trial of Antoine Berthet, accused of shooting his former mistress, which was recast in Stendhal's 1830 novel, *Le Rouge et le noir*. And all these printed materials reached a vastly expanded readership, which now included large numbers of people who had not had access to them before. This new readership was reflected in the success of the *cabinets de lecture*, which were in their heyday during the 1820s, 30s and 40s, and in the popularity of the serial novel, of which Eugène Sue's *Mystères de Paris* and *Le juif errant* were two of the most important examples.[13] Nineteenth-century *mémoires judiciaires* were now frequently filled with literary references that would have been absent from their eighteenth-century counterparts, even though those references might have been implied before the Revolution.

The effect of these legal and cultural changes are immediately apparent in Léon Tillard's statement of Jeanne Le Monnier's case. The *mémoire judiciaire* was, for example, printed for public consumption and soon went into a second edition. From the start Tillard addressed himself to the general public, although he dedicated the *mémoire* to the subprefect of Bayeux, and he invested the case with a larger political significance. He placed Le

[12] Jean Maurain, *La politique ecclésiastique du Second Empire* (Paris, 1930), pp. 77–9. This was one of the 'privileges' that the clergy enjoyed until the 1860s.

[13] Ernestine Dumont wrote to Eugène Sue in November of 1843, 'your work is everywhere – on the worker's bench, on the merchant's counter, on the little lady's divan, on the shop-girl's table, on the officeworker's and magistrate's desk. I am sure that of the entire people of Paris, only those who cannot read do not know your work.' Quoted in James Smith Allen, *In the Public Eye: A History of Reading in Modern France, 1800–1940* (Princeton, 1991), p. 55, and Françoise Parent-Lardeur, *Lire à Paris au temps de Balzac: Les cabinets de lecture à Paris, 1815–1830* (Paris, 1981).

Monnier's complaint squarely in the context of then current press debates concerning the need for new legislation to govern religious orders, and he suggested the case of Jeanne Le Monnier represented a kind of unresolved pre-Revolutionary atavism: 'No doubt,' he told his readers,

> we no longer have the lettre de cachet, those Bastilles . . . but every day reveals miserable feminine antipathies in the shadow of cloisters, supported by the inflexibility of hierarchical will . . . The victim perishes, not hierarchical absolutism . . . Is this the liberty and the equality of our national charters? . . . How these unhappy women murmur in the silence of monasteries without their voices being heard by public authority . . .[14]

By implication he suggested that until the voices of these women were heard the spectre of the Revolution would continue to haunt French society. The issues of the case thus became immediately inscribed in broader arguments regarding the necessity of asserting secular authority over religious authority – a concern that dominated French politics for much of the nineteenth century – and in the conflict between Gallicanism and Ultramontanism.

II. TELLING THE STORY

Tillard's *mémoire*, like the *mémoires* of the late eighteenth century, created a Manichean world and used the devices of theatrical melodrama. Tillard himself acknowledged at one point in his narrative that he knew that he might be accused of employing cheap theatrics in presenting the facts of the case.[15] The characteristics of this melodrama included 'extreme moral polarities, hyperbolic expressions and gestures, sketchy characterization, complicated plotting, and emphatic moral didacticism'.[16] The narrative strategies used by Léon Tillard consisted of first-person account by the nun in question, which lent immediacy and pathos to her story – a practice that was increasingly common in the eighteenth-century *mémoire* – direct literary references to two of the best-selling texts of the day, notably Eugène Sue's *Le juif errant* and Jules Michelet's hugely popular 1845 attack on the power that priests had in the confessional, *Le prêtre, la femme, et la famille*, and the use of plot lines and imagery drawn from claustral literature of the eighteenth and nineteenth centuries.[17]

[14] *Affaire de Dame Jeanne-Françoise Le Monnier*, p. 5.

[15] 'Ici, nous ne craignons point que l'on nous taxe d'une sensibilité théâtrale, factice, montée pour le besoin de la cause.' Ibid., p. 64.

[16] Maza, *Private Lives and Public Affairs*, p. 66.

[17] Michelet's work was reprinted at least eight times between 1845 and 1875. See Theodore Zeldin, 'The Conflict of Moralities: Confession, Sin and Pleasure in the Nineteenth Century', in *Conflicts in French Society: Anticlericalism, Education, and Morals in the Nineteenth Century* (London, 1970), pp. 13–50.

The relationship between the copious claustral literature produced between 1760 and the 1840s and courtroom story-telling during the early nineteenth century is a fascinating one, and has not received the consideration it deserves.[18] The literary critic Peter Brooks has argued that the theme of claustration was crucial to the development of melodrama in its earliest forms. It represented the 'ultimate (Gothic) nightmare of burial alive, loss of mobility and of identity'.[19] Between 1789 and 1799 twenty-six claustral plays, including one authored by Olympe de Gouges, the author of the *Declaration of the Rights of Woman and Citizen* (1791), were performed in Paris alone.[20] One of the most popular, Boutet de Monvel's *Les victimes cloîtrées* (1791), was performed eighty times between 1791 and the Restoration and was a great success. Indeed, *Les victimes cloîtrées* has been considered the first example of a new type of melodrama in France and concerns the incarceration of the novel's hero and heroine in separate religious houses by monks and nuns working for a nefarious aristocrat. Ultimately, both are liberated from their subterranean cells in a final scene by a republican mayor wearing the tricolor. In Brooks's words, 'the play suggests the connection of the claustral space of the Gothic on the one hand, to the Revolution on the other: the Revolution as the opening up of and liberation from the claustral, the victory of democracy as virtue and innocence'.[21]

Le couvent, ou les voeux forcés, by Olympe de Gouges, which was performed 89 times between 1790 and 1792, follows a similar plot line.[22] She

[18] Denis Diderot's tale of the victimisation of Suzanne in *La religieuse* (1760) is perhaps the best-known example of a genre of literature that explored the forced confinement and/or libertinage of women within religious institutions. Diderot's novel was followed by a plethora of literature on the subject. Jeanne Ponton, *La religieuse dans la littérature française* (Quebec, 1969), pp. 382–6. The subject of the nun and the convent were not confined to literature or to France during this period. See Susan P. Casteras, 'Virgin Vows: The Early Victorian Artists' Portrayal of Nuns and Novices', in Gail Malmgreen, ed., *Religion in the Lives of English Women, 1760–1930* (London, 1986), pp. 129–60.

[19] Peter Brooks, *The Melodramatic Imagination: Balzac, Henry James, Melodrama, and the Mode of Excess* (New Haven, 1976), p. 50.

[20] Louis-Caroogis Carmontelle, *Le couvent des religieuses, comédie en un acte*, 1789. Ms. B.N. f.f. 9326; Maurin de Pompigny, *La bonne soeur ou elle en avait besoin* (Ambigu-Comique, 17 December 1789); Anonymous, *Le couvent, drame* (Théâtre de la Nation, April 1790); Joseph Fiévée, *Les rigueurs du cloître* (Les Comédiens italiens ordinaires du Roi, 23 août 1790); Olympe de Gouges, *Le couvent, ou les voeux forcés* (Théâtre français, October 1790), and Pierre Laujon, *Le couvent, ou les fruits du caractère et de l'éducation* (Théâtre de la Nation, 16 April 1790); Anonyme, *La religieuse danoise, ou la communauté de Copenhague* (Théâtre de Montansier, 1791); Boutet de Monvel, *Les victimes cloîtrées* (Théâtre de la Nation, 29 March 1791); Carbon de Flins, *Le mari directeur, ou le déménagement du couvent* (Théâtre de la Nation, 25 February 1791); Pujoulx, *Amélie, ou le couvent* (Théâtre Feydeau, 28 February 1791); Jacques-Benoît Demautort, *Le petit sacristain* (Théâtre de la Vaudeville, 13 March 1792); Desprez et Rouget de Lisle, *Les deux couvents* (Opéra-Comique, 16 January 1792).

[21] Brooks, *The Melodramatic Imagination*, p. 50.

[22] The play was first performed at the Théâtre français. Olympe de Gouges, *Le couvent, ou les voeux forcés* (Paris, 1792).

tells the tale of a mother and infant daughter confined to a convent by a wicked brother/uncle. The latter, a violent man who had disapproved of his sister's marriage, had murdered her husband. When the daughter, Julie, reaches the age of sixteen, her uncle, the marquis of Leuville, and the mother superior in effect force the unwilling young girl to take her vows by threatening to withdraw her pension. The marquis does so to hide his infamy, while the mother superior looks forward to a fat dowry. However, the marquis's young son, who has fallen in love with Julie during visits to the convent with his father, is intent on liberating the heroine. The young chevalier gains access to the religious house by disguising himself as a Capuchin monk and declares, 'I will only leave here to bring Julie to the marriage altar.'[23] Ultimately, the young chevalier frees Julie, with the help of an honest priest and *commissaire*, and the Marquis de Leuville begs his family's forgiveness. The convent's servant, who acts as a kind of chorus, concludes, 'Undoubtedly God does not forbid living honestly and quietly in a convent; but I am of the opinion that he much prefers marriage.'[24]

In evoking a pre-Revolutionary social imagery regarding bondage and liberation drawn from claustral literature – the most famous of which was Diderot's *La religieuse* – Tillard conjures up a fascinating hybrid of conflicting social types and is provided with a wealth of plot lines and motives. He makes Le Monnier into a romantic heroine whose purity was assaulted by the evil machinations of a cabal of women. Tillard made an emotional appeal to the court and the public by presenting her as a feminine victim in need of protection, the damsel in distress, who is denied her natural vocation as wife and mother through incarceration in a convent. On another level, he must subvert this plot line and reassert her rights as an individual because Le Monnier actually wants a pension or to return to her order.

The bulk of the *mémoire* and the story of her ordeal is taken up with the story of her incarceration. To this extent, the social image of the incarcerated nun, which is central to the construction of Le Monnier's story, became a larger metaphor, in Tillard's telling of it, for the intolerance and hierarchical oppression of the Ultramontane Church in post-Revolutionary France. It allowed him to attempt to gloss over the conflicting images of the nun as victimised and as vain, disobedient, and self-regarding, both of which emerge in the text. How is this achieved?

Tillard's narrative covered a nineteen-year period, from Le Monnier's entry into the Benedictine convent in 1825 at the age of 27 to her departure in 1841, at the age of 43; from her transfer to the asylum of Bon Sauveur in Caen in 1841, to her departure in 1842; and from 1842, when she was forced to enter the secular world, to the beginning of the case in 1844.

[23] Brooks, *The Melodramatic Imagination*, p. 48. [24] Ibid., p. 83.

Le Monnier was born near Coutances in the Norman department of Manche in 1798. Her parents were shopkeepers. Her father was also a municipal councillor, who provided his daughter with an education. At seventeen she became a schoolteacher. She had long been drawn to the religious vocation, particularly to a cloistered order, despite the fact that she was offered a more than satisfactory position in secular life, according to her lawyer. This point is made for the purpose of indicating that she did not simply enter a religious order because she had no other options.

After taking her vows, for example, Le Monnier became the *de facto* bursar for the convent and ran its school for girls. Le Monnier's difficulties began in 1827, barely two years after she entered the convent. She was allegedly resented for her accomplishments and was the object of jealousy because of her intelligence. She suffered many small humiliations as a result. She was ordered, for example, to be the last nun to receive confession and frequently banned from the confessional and denied communion.

It is at this point that Tillard introduced Le Monnier's first-person account of her persecution. Le Monnier's story consisted of a detailed description of various punishments and her growing alienation from the other members of the convent. By 1840 she had ceased associating with the other nuns in the order, she was banned from recreation and the confessional, and the mother superior installed a lock and iron bar to her cell where she frequently found herself an unwilling prisoner. She was allegedly then placed in a kind of boarded-up prison which contained only a straw mattress and which received no light and little air. She was given a ration of bread, apples and a small measure of cider.

If Tillard drew on the most important literary texts of the day, he also used religious narratives in constructing his tale. Le Monnier, for example, allegedly stayed in her 'prison' for a biblical seven days, and during each of those seven days a nun came to ask her if she would consent to go to another religious house. She refused. She was taken to the Bon Sauveur de Caen, an insane asylum for women, along with a letter written by her superior, a priest and a doctor, attesting to her deranged mental state.[25] Tillard added in a note to Le Monnier's account that the place where she was incarcerated was no larger than the mattress, that her hands had been tied behind her back and that when she was taken to Bon Sauveur, one of the servants was required to carry her because of her weakness.

Part two of the *mémoire* is an account of her incarceration in the asylum of Bon Sauveur and begins with a commentary introducing Le Monnier's

[25] The asylum of Bon Sauveur in Caen was one of the most important clerical asylums serving in a public capacity in the 1840s. The nuns also ran asylums in Saint-Lo in the Manche and at Albi in the Tarn. See Jan Goldstein, *Console and Classify: The French Psychiatric Profession in the Nineteenth Century* (Cambridge, 1987), pp. 311–12.

resumed narrative: 'Here we have Sister Marie taken from her monastery and transported to a house of crazy women for alleged madness – does it not seem that the family of this nun should have been alerted of this event immediately?'[26] At this point we return to Le Monnier's personal narrative and her attempts to free herself from her frightful surroundings.

She wrote to the bishop and to her community. The bishop allegedly replied that even if she were not mad, she was still guilty and should remain where she was. The drama continued: 'Here I am detained pitilessly, in the midst of noisy din, cries, furies, agitation, swearing, blasphemy and the imprecations of the mad among whom are found fallen women [as well].'[27] She vowed to see the *procureur du roi*, a secular authority, and was refused.

Finally, one day the doctor came to inform her, at the instruction of the superior, that she had lived a long time as a nun and that she should now re-enter secular life, that she was to set her rosary aside to work each day sewing. She refused. As a result, she was cast out of the asylum to earn her living in the world. She therefore found herself, in her words, 'on the pavement, without any human aid, without money, without clothing or linens. It is thus that after having tasted the sweetness of celestial life in the cloister and not being able to force the doors to return to it, that I was in the world through force.'[28] Tillard wrote: 'one can now see: it is not at all scandal that we are after. We are asking for bread; we are asking for certain guarantees for the future . . . we understood that the time has come for social justice that has been refused us . . . We count on all that is generous . . . in all classes of society.'[29]

The persuasiveness of the story told by Tillard and Le Monnier was predicated on how Le Monnier's actions and motivations were perceived within the general context of social stereotypes regarding cloistered nuns and what one might call collective fantasies of claustration. We have seen the way in which Tillard used the claustral narrative to gain sympathy for his client and how he focused on her industry and zealous dedication to the rule of the order. The mother superior undoubtedly saw her as a pretentious trouble-maker, who refused to adhere to the order's rule of obedience, and it was this that accounted for her troubles and for the punishment that she received. Her doctors, while seeing her as entirely sane, nonetheless supported the views of her religious superiors regarding her personal qualities. M. Faucon, the medical doctor assigned to Bon Sauveur, wrote that she was 'perfectly regular in her behaviour. She has continued in her pious exercises and although ardently desiring to return to her community, she was never impatient. She appeared to us to have in her character a very pronounced tendency toward stubbornness, which explains her recalcitrance in not

[26] *Affaire*, pp. 19–20. [27] Ibid., p. 21. [28] Ibid., p. 26. [29] Ibid., p. 49.

recognising her wrongs toward her community.' Other than that, he concluded, she could certainly leave Bon Sauveur.[30] Tillard was not able to suppress entirely the 'troublesome' aspects of Le Monnier's personality, but at the same time he emphasised her religiosity and industry. Indeed, this is crucial to his case because the public would not necessarily view the plight of the nun sympathetically. Tillard faced two problems in this regard. First, the cloistered nun was a distinctly unpopular figure in eighteenth- and nineteenth-century France.

The social stereotype of the avaricious, lazy, and debauched monk and nun who lived off the honest toil of others was an inherent part of much of the Revolutionary caricatures and broadsides against the Catholic Church. This view of men and women religious pervaded debates over the banning of religious orders and dispersing their members in 1791. Although most of the anticlerical Revolutionary caricature centred on the figure of the corrupt priest or monk, where women religious appeared in such caricature, it was in the figure of the cloistered nun.[31] Stereotypes regarding the cloistered nun persisted after the Revolution and were perpetuated in novelistic literature. Women who assumed the religious vocation and who lived behind the grille were frequently regarded as the saddest women of all because they lacked a purpose and renounced their natural calling as women.[32] The cloistered nun, who lived isolated from the world and who had no identifiably useful role in society, in contrast to the *congréganistes* who taught or cared for the sick, was frequently an object of suspicion or scorn.[33]

Tillard countered the image of the debauched or idle nun with a counter image – that of the woman as the victim of sequestration. In so doing, he consciously tapped not only into the tradition of claustral literature, but also into one of the most popular literary works of the day, Eugène Sue's immensely successful *Le juif errant*, which tells the story of Adrienne de Cardoville, who is incarcerated in an asylum by relatives intent on stealing her inheritance. Tillard sprinkled his text with quotations from Sue's anticlerical novel, which was an explicit attack on the Jesuits. Tillard began his account of Le Monnier's incarceration with a passage from Sue describing Adrienne de Cardoville's imprisonment and, having concluded his narrative, he prefaced his critical examination of the facts with another quote

30 Ibid., p. 26.
31 Antoine de Baecque, *La caricature révolutionnaire* (Paris, 1988), pp. 89–143.
32 Caroline Ford, 'Private Lives and Public Order in Restoration France: The Seduction of Emily Loveday', *American Historical Review*, 99, no. 1 (February 1994), pp. 21–43.
33 While the figure of the *congréganiste*, the active nun who taught or cured the sick, was generally positive in the nineteenth century, the image of the contemplative nun continued to be very negative. See Ponton, *La religieuse dans la littérature française*.

from Sue regarding the doctor's diagnosis of Adrienne de Cardoville. Like Adrienne, Le Monnier was diagnosed as suffering from 'exalted ideas'.[34] Like Adrienne, she is unsuspecting when she is carried away by two sinister female attendants with evil intent, and like Adrienne, she suffered greatly amid the mad and the violent. And let us not forget that Sue ends *Le juif errant* with a plea for greater regulation of religious and medical institutions by public authorities.[35]

Tillard not only faced the problem of having to counteract a pervasive social stereotype in the figure of the cloistered nun by capitalising on the themes of claustral literature, he faced another problem. Unlike most of the female victims of claustral literature, Le Monnier wanted to return to the world of the cloister and to the order that expelled her. If, up to this point in the narrative, Le Monnier is presented as a victim of the cloister, as the woman in bondage, Tillard used a language of right and contract to make his final arguments. It is this language that links the two separate parts of her complaint: the charge that she has been a victim of incarceration against her will and the demand for monetary damages and that she be allowed to return to cloistered life. Her rights and individual liberties had been violated by being imprisoned against her will, and her order had unlawfully violated its contract with her without just cause.

But how did Tillard make the case for her return to her order and for a promise that it would continue to support Le Monnier financially? Tillard likened religious vows to marriage vows, the marriage contract to a kind of religious contract. He asserted that just as a husband is legally obligated to support and honour his association, so a religious order must do the same. Marriage and entering an order are forms of contract. Her expulsion was nothing more than an illegal breaking of an associational contract between Le Monnier and the community of Benedictines of Bayeux. (He glosses over the fact that under post-Revolutionary law lifelong religious vows, unlike marriage vows, were illegal. They had to be renewed every five years, and even then, they were not binding on the nun, who could leave when she wished.) While her order might claim that she was subject to expulsion because she was intractable, disobedient, and therefore violated the order's rule, Tillard argued that whether or not she was 'reasonable or mystical, obedient or rebellious, humble or vain', this could not justify – 'canonically, juridically and constitutionally, philosophically' – her incarceration in an insane asylum.[36] The act of incarceration constituted an attack on the civil liberties of the citizen. In short, the core of Tillard's argument is that Le Monnier was a nun, but she was a citizen in civil society first.

[34] *Affaire*, p. 51. [35] Eugène Sue, *Le juif errant*, vol. III (Paris: Marabout, n.d.), p. 531.
[36] *Affaire*, p. 77.

Set within an almost novelistic narrative of bondage and liberation, right, contract, and finally the last piece of the triad, social justice, were the basis of Tillard's arguments to the court. This is not simply the case of a recalcitrant nun, who for her sins found herself incarcerated among the insane against her will, but it is the case of a woman left without resources or a means of a living. It is here that the narrative of the incarceration of Eugène Sue's heroine, Adrienne de Cardoville, and the narrative of Le Monnier's ordeal intersect. Sue ends his novel with a plea for social justice:

> [W]e have said and we repeat that there are terrible and innumerable miseries; that the masses, more and more conscious of their rights, but still calm, patient, resigned, ask that those who govern finally concern themselves with the amelioration of their deplorable position . . . Permit us to resume in a few lines the questions raised in this work. We have tried to prove the insufficiency of women's wages and the horrible consequence of this insufficiency. We have asked for new guarantees against the facility with which someone can be put in an insane asylum.[37]

Tillard ends his *mémoire* with the following remarks:

> A poor nun, victim of an abuse of revolting power and who has been pitilessly refused daily bread and a few faithful guarantees for the future . . . but above all these are larger interests, more philosophical, social . . . that is the struggle of individualism against monastic despotism, the Gallican spirit against the Ultramontane spirit, of civil liberties against the oppressive allures of certain establishments forgetful of their philanthropic mission.[38]

And so ends the *mémoire* of Léon Tillard.

The case that he constructed, drawing on what I would call fantasies of claustration, revealed a myriad of cultural assumptions and social archetypes regarding women, the religious life and the cloistered nun. But how do we explain these fears and anxieties centring on the theme of claustration, which is a staple part of Gothic literature in this period? Why were there so many cases of this type and why did they abruptly disappear in the late nineteenth century? A simple answer might be that the law had changed. These cases could be brought, and they disappeared as courts asserted the primacy of secular law over canon law, as the state increasingly involved itself in the regulation of religious institutions. Their disappearance might then be seen as a reflection of the victory of secular republicanism during the early Third Republic, which was manifested in the widespread laicisation of educational and medical institutions.

It is no accident that the Le Monnier case appeared when it did, in the year of Michelet's attack on the confessional and on the power that the

[37] Sue, *Le juif errant*, vol. III, p. 581. [38] *Affaire*, p. 98.

priest exerted over women. In a little-known passage from *Le Prêtre, la femme, et la famille*, Michelet admitted to fearing the mother superior more than the priest/confessor, this 'great converted lady who thinks herself for government, among a troop of trembling women' like a female Bonaparte.[39] He admitted fearing the Jesuitess more than the confessor and siding with him in the face of such a creature. These social stereotypes form the stuff out of which a culture's *imaginaires sociaux* are created.[40] The constituent elements of this imagery were many and varied, revealing anxiety about the porous boundaries between Church and state as well as secular and canon law. As legal trials no longer took place in a climate of secrecy, they increasingly galvanised the public and spawned debates over the need to regulate religious institutions. Much of this public discussion came to a head during the Second Empire, in the early 1860s, a period in which the groundwork was laid for the anticlerical legislation governing religious congregations in the early 1880s. Pamphlets such as *Crimes, délits, scandales au sein du clergé pendant les derniers jours* (Paris, 1861) documented numerous cases of abduction, incarceration and coercion exercised by religious communities, and debate focused on some of the most lurid cases of sequestration, the most prominent of which was the Bluth case of 1861, which involved the conversion and imprisonment of several young Jewish girls, who were sisters, in different convents over a number of years. In sum, cases involving the alleged incarceration of religious women became a larger metaphor for the tyranny of the hierarchical Catholic Church and dramatised the symbolic stakes inherent in the conflict between Gallicanism and Ultramontanism. Women religious were at the centre of this conflict, just as the adolescent girl wearing the Muslim veil in French classrooms has come to symbolise the backwardness of Islam and to justify the need to reassert the primacy of secular republican values in French society in the 1990s.

III. THE SOCIAL IMAGERY OF RELIGIOUS CONFLICT

Léon Tillard's story-telling played an important part in settling the case in Le Monnier's favour. But what does his legal story-telling reveal about the *imaginaire social* of nineteenth-century France? Although this is a case

[39] J. Michelet, *Le Prêtre, la femme, et la famille*, 7th edn (Paris, 1861), p. 242–3.

[40] I borrow this term from Bronislaw Baczko, who defines the concept in terms of 'representations of social reality and not simple reflections of it. Invented and elaborated by material taken from a symbolic store, they have a specific reality which resides in their very existence, in their variable impact on mentalities and collective behaviours, in the multiple functions they exercize in social life.' Baczko, *Les imaginaires sociaux: mémoires et espoirs collectifs* (Paris, 1984), p. 8.

based on the real distress experienced by a woman expelled from a religious order, it is a story constructed and presented by a republican anticlerical man. While we know little of Tillard, we do know he ultimately became a *quarante-huitard* who supported the new republic in 1848.[41] His *mémoire* must be read on several levels. He devoted two years of his life to the trial and his zeal came from political conviction. His tale of bondage and liberation was one that allowed him to make his case in powerful and unequivocal terms. It was the principal metaphor through which critiques of royal despotism and ecclesiastical intolerance were made during the eighteenth century. It became a central republican trope for expressing political emancipation. It had a particular resonance in the 1840s. Following the law of 1838, which established France's first system of public asylum, there was huge concern about possible abuses of this system, as Eugène Sue's remarks suggest – a fundamental ambivalence, even among the bourgeoisie, about what Michel Foucault has called the great confinement. In short, the case was a way of talking about and expressing a variety of social and political anxieties.

It may also have tapped into a new sensibility and deeper societal concerns. Karen Haltunnen has recently argued that narratives of captivity as expressed in the Gothic novel and other forms of popular literature in this period abounded in Anglo-American culture and expressed a kind of 'pornography of pain'.[42] The fear and titillation they inspired dovetailed, in her view, with profound changes in views toward pain and the human body at the end of the eighteenth century and to the emergence of a new humanitarian sensibility. To this extent the appearance of the same themes reflected the appearance of new attitudes toward violence and bodily suffering, which has recently been documented in France by Alain Corbin.[43] To this extent, one might argue that the issues raised by the case of the recalcitrant nun may well reflect broader cultural transformations that occurred in France during the eighteenth and nineteenth centuries.

Social anxieties and fears regarding the stunning rise in the number of women entering religious life contributed to the indignation that the case provoked. The phenomenon of the 'feminisation of religion', with all the implications that this might have for a growing cultural divide between men

[41] Léon Tillard was born in Bayeux on 14 June 1813. He was the author of *Février révolutionnaire et la situation actuelle, mai 1849* (Bayeux, 1849). Tillard also authored a short work entitled *Réflexions sur les prisons des ordres religieux* (Caen, 1845) and an overview of the case, *Récits par elle-même, la procédure, les enquêtes, la preuve, orgueil et placement au B.S.* (Caen, 1846).

[42] Karen Haltunnen, 'Humanitarianism and the Pornography of Pain in Anglo-American Culture', *American Historical Review*, 100, no. 2 (April 1995), pp. 303–34.

[43] Corbin, *A Village of Cannibals: Rage and Murder in France, 1870*, trans. Arthur Goldhammer (Cambridge, MA, 1992).

and women, the principle of paternal authority, the integrity of the family, and the disposition of property under the Napoleonic code shaped the way in which Tillard presented his evidence. The existence of these fears, which were expressed in collective fantasies of various kinds, are worthy of consideration. Jacqueline Oulette, for example, has very recently discussed the pervasive late nineteenth-century French fantasy of nuns who habitually and sadistically forced their young charges to sit on red hot stoves – satirically called *les rôtisseries congréganistes*.[44] The extent to which these events happened is one question, how and why they became constituent elements of an *imaginaire social* at a particular moment in time, is another. In short, the case of Jeanne-Françoise Le Monnier raises larger questions for the historian about why cases are brought at some historical moments and not at others; about how legal story-telling is constrained by the social and political context in which it is told; about the ways in which it appeals to unwritten moral categories, and about how the types of legal cases that are brought before courts are themselves markers of social, political, or moral preoccupations that in turn shape the way in which stories are told to the court.

[44] Jacqueline Oulette, *La Libre Pensée en France 1848–1940* (Paris, 1997), p. 241.

10. *'Their idea of justice is so peculiar': Southern Rhodesia 1890–1910*[1]

DIANA JEATER

On the afternoon of 26 June 1900, a wedding took place in the courthouse of the District Magistrate of Melsetter, an isolated town in the mountains of Southern Rhodesia, near the border with Portuguese East Africa. The bride was the ward of a local paramount, Chief Mutambara, and the District Magistrate, William Longden, presided as Marriage Officer. There was nothing unusual about this event – except for the fact that, minutes earlier, Longden had been, not a Marriage Officer, but a Magistrate hearing a case of criminal abduction against a 'colonial native' (now transformed into the groom), and Mutambara had been the chief witness for the prosecution.[2] A criminal trial had been converted into a civil marriage ceremony; and the only people to whom this seemed a little unusual were the white administrators who claimed to dispense justice in the district.

The Mutambara 'abduction' case highlights the frustration faced by officials of the British South Africa Company (BSACo) in attempting to administer the law in Southern Rhodesia. Categories that ought to have been fixed and straightforward kept shifting and changing. Even basic ideas like 'criminal', 'father' and 'abduction' seemed very hard to pin down. The universal criminal code of the territory, imposed a few years earlier on all inhabitants regardless of hue or provenance, was Roman-Dutch law. In abduction cases, the parents of an abducted minor needed to give evidence that they had not consented to the removal of their child. 'Parents', it seemed clear to the administrators' legal minds, meant biological parents, or guardians where biological parents were dead.[3] Mutambara, it turned out, was not the girl's parent, who was alive and well and working in

[1] I would like to thank the Scouloudi Foundation for partial funding. All references are to the National Archives of Zimbabwe.

[2] R vs Willem Bezuidenhout @ Msorowenzowo, Preliminary Examination (PE) 64/1900, 29 June 1900. D3/3/1.

[3] This was made explicit in the Acting Public Prosecutor's comments on this case, communicated in a letter to Longden from the Law Department, 18 July 1900. DM 2/4/1.

Umtali, a town to the north of Melsetter, unaware of the court case involving the alleged abduction of his daughter. Mutambara defined himself as the girl's father, because he was the man to whom bridewealth had to be paid on the marriage of the girl.[4] The reasons why he claimed the bridewealth seemed perfectly clear to local Africans, but both complicated and illegitimate to the legal minds of the BSACo. Moreover, even if he *were* the legitimate claimant on bridewealth paid for her, that did not make him the girl's 'father'; or, at least, so it seemed to William Longden.

Faced with a 'father' who was not really a 'father', and an 'abduction' which was not really an abduction but a failure to discuss bridewealth payments, Longden felt he had no option but to abandon the criminal proceedings. Instead, he attempted to regularise the situation by recording an agreement about bridewealth between Mutambara and the erstwhile defendant, and registering the marriage. The Africans involved were not particularly interested in the niceties of a shift from a criminal to a civil court. There were matters to be settled, a man had behaved in a way he should not have done, and some accommodation had to be reached. In effect, Longden had presided over a negotiation regarding bridewealth which had been instigated by an elopement – a common, indeed commonplace, method of arranging marriages in the district.

Although Africans were required to obey the universal criminal code, they were not expected to conform to European law in civil matters. The ambiguity in this case about what constituted a 'father' was compounded by an ambiguity about the difference between a criminal and a civil offence. It was genuinely not clear whether the man was guilty of an offence under the universal criminal code,[5] in which case the state had a duty of interest in the matter, or simply involved in a perfectly legitimate transaction in what the Legal Department saw as 'civil matters', in which case Longden's involvement was contingent and peripheral.

In his report on the case to the Native Department, the local Native Commissioner (NC), Llewellyn Meredith, urged that a written civil code for Africans be instituted. The code should recognise that 'the Native law . . . could not be made to agree with our law' on guardianship and similar matters, and should establish a set of clear and universal rules about African kinship and its attendant legal implications.[6] He was not the first

[4] In its simplest form, bridewealth is due from a woman's husband's family to her father's family at marriage. (It is therefore the opposite of a dowry payment.) It should be agreed at the time of the marriage, although actual payment may be spread over years, and even over generations.

[5] This was the opinion of the Acting Public Prosecutor, who roundly censured Longden for his failure to take evidence from the girl's mother and to continue the prosecution. Secretary, Law Dept to Magistrate, Melsetter, 18 July 1900. DM 2/4/1.

[6] NC Melsetter, Quarterly Report (QR), 3 July 1900. NUE 2/1/3.

to make this suggestion and he was certainly not to be the last. However, the Administration consistently declined to impose a written civil code for Africans.

There were two factors influencing the policy not to establish a system of 'customary law'. The first was the pragmatic issue of how best to exercise power in the occupied territory. As a chartered company, the BSACo was not obliged to follow British government guidelines on the pacification and control of natives.[7] Instead, the BSACo was trying to find its own way. The issue of whether to rule local populations directly, or whether to rule indirectly, utilising the co-operation of African authorities such as chiefs, was far from settled. On the whole, the Administration felt that most chiefs were unlikely to be reliable allies, and that any codification of local civil law which might reinforce their influence was not to be encouraged.

Linked to the BSACo's pragmatic mistrust of chiefly power was the bigger question of the entire moral universe which local laws and chiefly power represented. There was widespread bafflement and concern at African legal practices. As one missionary put it, when asked whether Africans dispensed justice fairly, 'It is difficult to say, as their idea of justice is so peculiar.'[8] Africans and their laws were not 'civilised'. What exactly this meant was much debated, but in general it was understood to mean that African legal systems were, by definition, a Bad Thing, and white legal systems were, by definition, a Better Thing. It was both the duty of and the justification for white occupation of the territory to ensure that African 'barbarism' gave way to white 'civilisation'. The Administration's fear was that a codification of existing African civil law would ossify barbaric practices, and stand in the way of the progress of civilisation. As the Resident Commissioner testified in 1904:

> I think that experience has shown us that while the codifying of criminal law is a distinct advantage, the codifying of civil law is stereotyping a state of law and custom which is naturally in a state of transition, and I think it would be very unwise to do so.[9]

Whatever the merits of this argument, its outcome was to leave in place a grassroots system of civil law[10] which was based on a fundamentally different model of jurisprudence from that of the administrators. This civil law, which did not distinguish between crime and dispute, constantly spilled over into the sphere of criminal law.

[7] These were increasingly coming under the influence of Lord Lugard's policies of indirect rule in Nigeria.

[8] Evidence of Rev. C. D. Helm to the Southern African Native Affairs Commission, 9 September 1904. S36,311.

[9] Evidence to the Southern African Native Affairs Commission, 31 August 1904. S34,980.

[10] Or rather, systems, as there was considerable regional diversity.

The criminal and civil cases heard in the courthouse and NC's office in Melsetter district in the period 1890–1910 were occasions when the gulf between white and African ideas about society, justice and authority had to be confronted. Africans were required to appear in the magistrate's court for criminal hearings, but they could also choose to bring cases to the NC for civil arbitration. In Melsetter District, the NC's clerk kept a record of these informal arbitrations, while the town clerk kept a record of the hearings before the Resident Magistrate.[11] In these records, the 'anthropologist in the archives' can find statements and actions revealing fundamental beliefs about right, wrong and the role of the individual within the community. Both when defending themselves and when presenting a case against another, African and white participants had a strong vested interest in making a powerful assertion of what they perceived to be justice. Their views of justice were informed by their entire sense of what constituted a well-ordered society. Even when sharing in a joint venture to prosecute or defend, there remained an antagonistic tension about these matters between the Africans and whites in the court.

In settling matters according to their own principles of justice, whether before a chief or the NC, Africans were living out and reaffirming a world-view which was profoundly at odds with that of the white intruders. The vibrancy of African jurisprudence in the African communities provided a barometer of how far local people were prepared to make an accommodation with the moral universe of the intruders. The 'civilising' of 'native law and custom' under white influence was not much in evidence. That is not to say that the occupation by the BSACo, and the spread of a capitalist economy, was not affecting the *content* of both criminal and civil cases. For at least a generation, however, it did not greatly affect the fundamental principles of jurisprudence on which local law operated. NCs who attempted to rule on civil matters could report that 'the Natives are not sufficiently educated to appreciate our customs . . . by forcing our modern laws on them they are placed in a dilemma and cannot comprehend'.[12] However, NCs likewise lacked both education and comprehension when it came to administering African civil law. Being required to make rulings on African civil matters, the administrators were forced to engage with and attempt to understand a world very different from the one they called 'civilisation'.

[11] The 'native civil disputes' are in two large red notebooks catalogued as S1069 and S1069/2. The criminal cases are in the D3/3 series. Civil cases heard by the Resident Magistrate (mostly divorce cases) are in the S666 series. The Melsetter District provides a good case study not only because of its excellent records, but also because of the difficulties faced by William Longden in understanding African jurisprudence. It must be noted, in fairness, that not all officials in Southern Rhodesia before 1916 were as mentally inflexible as Longden, and Meredith's understanding was much better than Longden's.

[12] NC Melsetter, QR, 3 July 1900. NUE 2/1/3.

The most significant difference between the two ideas of justice, from which much else followed, was that African law was basically restorative, while European law was retributive (criminal) or contractual (civil). In an African court, the aim was to agree compensation. In a white *criminal* court, the aim was to establish guilt and agree punishment. In a white *civil* court the aim was to ensure that what was due, according to a previous agreement, was paid. These were three distinct aims, and the attempt to equate African restorative justice with European contract law led to abundant confusions and difficulties.

As we have seen, the African system of restorative justice did not need to make a distinction between criminal and civil law. Crimes, as well as disputes over rights or property, were supposed to be settled by the payment of appropriate compensation. Consequently, criminal offences were treated like any other offence, and brought to the NC or his deputy for arbitration. Surprisingly, in many cases the white officials heard the cases as requested. Even crimes of theft were heard as civil disputes in the NC's court, including a claim about harvested crops that had already been heard as a criminal case before the Resident Magistrate.[13] We cannot know whether this compliance was because the officials could not be bothered to make a criminal matter out of cases where white power or property was not threatened, or because they simply did not recognise a criminal offence when presented in radically different terms. However, given both the respect for the rule of law, and the intellectual mediocrity of the bulk of Native Department officials, one is tempted to suspect the latter.

Africans took time to recognise the importance of the civil/criminal distinction for the whites; whites took time to recognise the absence of the distinction among Africans. A case of rape might be taken to a civil court, or to a criminal court. In either case, the perpetrator was likely to offer to pay compensation, in accordance with the principle that a man should make reparations to the father or husband if he had sexual contact with a woman for whom he had not agreed to pay bridewealth. This offence was translated into English as 'seduction', to be punished by a 'fine'. The Native Department saw this as an example of Africans making an offence out of a matter which was not criminal under Roman-Dutch law, and which could therefore be dealt with as a 'native civil dispute'.

If he was lucky, the rapist would find his case being heard by a Native Commissioner who would rule that compensation should be paid, in accor-

[13] Moyowakafa vs Makadza, 18 June 1912. S1069 p. 357. In another instance, the case was brought by a white employer, who clearly preferred to get compensation for the theft of money and eggs than to see his employee tried in the criminal court: Mr Pritchard vs Pangeyi, 14 May 1912, S1069 p. 342. Other cases of theft being heard by the NC as 'native civil disputes' include S1069 pp. 333, 346–7, 350.

dance with 'native law and custom'. For example, in July 1910 a man turned up at the NC's office in Melsetter demanding payment of compensation for what the clerk recorded as the 'seduction' of his wife. She had been thrown to the ground and raped while walking home. She cried out for help and the man was caught in the act. He offered goats in compensation, but failed to pay up, so, some months later, the case was taken to the NC to enforce payment. The NC ruled that he should pay £10, and no move was made to institute criminal proceedings.[14] The criminal offence had spilled over seamlessly into the civil forum.

However, if he were unlucky, the rapist would be subject to criminal proceedings. In the latter case, the family of the rape victim also lost out, since no compensation would be paid to them. In 1905, a man whose wife had been raped refused the proffered compensation of seven goats, a hoe, 2/6d cash, plus a roll of tobacco and two shillings for the wife. He took the case to court, demanding the much larger compensation of '£25 or a girl'. He ended up with nothing. The rapist ('I was drunk at the time, & did not know what I was doing') ended up with twenty lashes and five years' imprisonment with hard labour.[15] It seems to have been simply a matter of chance as to which court heard such cases. However, the restorative principle of African justice, which straddled the criminal/civil distinction of European justice, and which was based on lineage rights, was not properly recognised or understood by the white officials in either forum.

European criminal law could not accommodate the principle of compensation because it was based upon the principle of retribution. It was not the task of the Resident Magistrate to make peace between criminals and those they injured, but to punish criminals on behalf of the wider community. This idea belonged to a society with a retributive God who exacted punishment for sin. Supernatural beings in African cosmologies, for all their huge variety, did not have this obsession with individual wrongdoing and punishment. African cosmologies dealt much more with the well being of wider communities – families, lineages, even polities. Supernatural beings did not 'punish' so much as 'hassle'. Their concern was to maintain good relationships within communities, and they would make life difficult for those who threatened those good relationships, until they acted to mend their rifts and make amends for harm caused.

Restorative justice worked on similar principles. It had no place for punishment as an act in itself, but rather insisted upon recompense and

[14] Maguya vs Sipangwe, 27 July 1910, S1069 p. 175. Similar cases may be found in S1069 pp. 184, 228, 327–8, 332, 335.

[15] Rex v Hlaya, PE 50/1905, 23 October 1905. D3/3/2. Similar cases where an offer of compensation is ignored by the crown prosecution include PE 53/1900 in D3/3/1; PE 5/1905, PE 45/1905 in D3/3/2; PE 64/1907, PE 141/1909 in D3/3/3; PE 139/1912 in D3/3/4.

reparation. This is not to suggest that people were never harmed for upsetting others, but to emphasise that the justice system did not normally harm people on behalf of the community. Women, for example, would often be beaten by fathers or husbands, in private retribution. But if a man beat a woman without socially sanctioned justification, she could bring a case against him, even if the man was her husband or father. The broader society would not take it upon itself to punish him for causing her harm, but arbitrators would require him to make amends to her by paying her compensation. Irredeemable reprobates such as witches could be exiled from communities entirely, depriving them of vital social support as well as their social identity; but their families would still be required to compensate their victims. The exile was a practical measure; the compensation was justice.[16]

Retributive justice, of the sort practised by the white intruders, requires that the state have a monopoly on justice. Only those with appropriate authority may be permitted to cause hurt on behalf of the community. This is fundamental to 'the rule of law', which was part of the 'civilisation' the BSACo was claiming to bring to the territory. However, white settlers outside the administration quickly realised that African jurisprudence allowed for a wide range of arbiters, and that arbitration was good business. African cases could be settled by face-to-face negotiation between families, or by resort to a diviner (who would assess by supernatural means whether there was human agency behind a misfortune), or by appeal to the arbitration of a 'big man'. 'Big men' were those whose wealth enabled them to act as patrons. Chiefs were often asked to rule on compensation claims, provided that at least some of the people involved were under their authority. For this service, they expected to receive payment and some part of the compensation. Other 'big men' would also hear cases, and they were often cheaper than chiefs. White settlers were keen to offer their services, using the opportunity to take a 'cut' from the compensation. The pioneering settler Dunbar Moodie, for example, toured Melsetter District in 1893, hearing cases and taking payment, so that within ten days he had amassed a holding of thirty-two goats.[17] Two years later, the Native Commissioner complained about local white farmers claiming to be Justices of the Peace and obstructing his work, by hearing cases and forcing Africans to work on their land. The Administration confirmed that Moodie really had been appointed as a

16 There was, however, an important exception to the principle of restoration: violation of sacred sites or sacred people was a capital offence. It offended the very foundation of life, and could not be absorbed by recompense because it was wholly outside the life-system of internal balance and reconciliation which compensation was designed to maintain.

17 Dunbar Moodie's Diary, 5–14 July 1893. MO 11/2/5.

local JP (he was too powerful in the District to exclude), but several other farmers making the claim had not.[18]

The problem was not confined to Melsetter District, but was found throughout Southern Rhodesia – white settlers claiming judicial authority for themselves and hearing cases from Africans.[19] It took some years for the Legal Department of the BSACo Administration to enforce its monopoly over criminal jurisdiction, and it continued to struggle over the issue of civil jurisdiction. One of the aims of the reorganisation of the Native Department in the late 1890s was to establish NCs as the only whites with authority to hear 'native civil disputes'. Not only was this supposed to enhance their ability to 'manage' the Africans, by setting them up as 'big men',[20] but it also reinforced the principle that the state should have a monopoly over justice. State control over the white farmers was thereby reinforced; but Africans continued to take their cases to a wide range of arbiters, as before.

Because white magistrates thought that crime had to be met with retribution, they had real difficulties understanding what compensation was all about. When faced with a defence statement such as 'I have nothing to say; I am prepared to pay' or 'I wish to say that I am willing to pay for the damage done',[21] magistrates confused this with the altogether different issue of fines. Compensation is paid to the injured party to make reparation; fines are paid to the state as punishment. Generally, a fine is seen as a 'light' punishment, as it does not act directly on the body of the accused, unlike flogging or imprisonment. The magistrates thought that offers to pay compensation indicated that the crime was not viewed as serious, but only punishable by a 'fine'. Regarding a rape case in 1897, the Magistrate told the prisoner:

> The charge against you is a very serious one according to the white man's law altho' I know that it is not considered so serious by Native Custom; & is usually settled by a fine.[22]

Similarly, in 1900, after the defendant in an arson case stated, 'I burnt the huts because I was heartsore about my wife & I am willing to pay damages for the burning', the Magistrate remarked:

> I know that by Native Law a matter of this nature would have been settled by the infliction of a Fine, & therefore is not looked upon in so serious a light as it is in our Law.[23]

[18] NC Melsetter to the Administrator, 1895, NUE 1/1/1.
[19] T. O. Ranger, *Revolt in Southern Rhodesia 1896–7* (London, 1967), pp. 62f.
[20] Chief Native Commissioner to Resident Magistrate, Melsetter, 1 August 1895. DM 2/9/1.
[21] Rex vs Mangwende and Matipedzi, PE 64/1907, 18 June 1907; Rex vs Gwendere, PE 86/1912, 17 May 1912. D3/3/3 and D3/3/4.
[22] Rex vs ByandBye, PE 59/1897, 26 October 1897. D3/3/1.
[23] Rex vs Munotyani, 24 January 1901. D3/3/2.

The defendant in this case was sentenced to nine months' imprisonment with hard labour, which, no doubt, inflicted an appropriately 'serious' degree of harm on him, but did nothing to mend the rift between the arsonist and his victim.

However futile and unpleasant the principle of retribution must have seemed to local Africans, the idea of compensation for crime appeared actively abhorrent to white administrators. They came from societies with significant disparities in wealth, where people could move away from land or kin fairly easily. The principle of compensation without punishment could have given almost unlimited licence for the wealthy to commit crime. The idea that even murderers could simply pay for their crime and go on their way could not be countenanced. Murder was the ultimate frontier, allowing for no cosy blurring between local and Roman-Dutch law. As far as the administrators were concerned, the Africans had a system of 'blood money', *maropa*, which had to be stopped, at once. Some commentators believed that *maropa* ('thing to do with blood') was paid entirely to the Chief, as a form of fine.[24] However, others noted that a significant portion went to the family of the person killed.[25] In either case, the NC Marondella expressed a general view when he reported:

> I informed all the chiefs . . . that they were to discontinue the custom, and report all cases of assault and murder, and arrest the offenders; who would be dealt with by a Magistrate.
>
> My reason for discouraging the custom is the murders would never be reported, and the offenders would get off with a fine.[26]

Paying for murder seemed to imply a lack of remorse, to the whites' minds. 'Even deliberate murder could be paid for,' noted the NC in Melsetter.[27] As late as 1928, when the amateur ethnographer and Native Commissioner, Charles Bullock, tried to explain the indigenous system to the authorities, the Minister of Native Affairs airily dismissed his account:

> I do not agree with the conclusion that the object of punishment (*sic*) under the old tribal system was to rehabilitate the criminal or offender and to return to him his place in society and his self-respect. My idea would be that the 'offender' never lost his self-respect or social status by the commission of crime and therefore no rehabilitation was required.[28]

It seemed to the BSACo Administration that, without punitive suffering, there could be no real understanding of wrongdoing.

[24] NC Marondella (*sic*) to Acting CNC, 17 August 1904. ED 6/2/1/1.

[25] Notes on Mashona Law and Custom, prob. written by W. E. Edwards, n.d. ED 6/5/1/1; Special Report on Natives, NC Melsetter to CNC, 16 July 1900 NUE 2/1/3 p. 366.

[26] NC Marondella (*sic*) to Acting CNC, 17 August 1904. ED 6/2/1/1.

[27] Report on Native Laws and Customs, NC Melsetter, AR, 31/3/1900. N9/1/6.

[28] Minister of Native Affairs to CNC, 1 March 1928. S138/26.

The insistence upon punishment missed the point about compensation for murder. It was not 'guilt money', a gesture towards saying 'sorry', but a practical means of redressing the loss of a family member. The bulk of the *maropa* went to the victim's family – enough to ensure that they had the bridewealth to obtain a fertile woman, who would replace the person lost, with interest (her progeny). Indeed, in many cases, it was actually a young woman who constituted the compensation, as the NC, Melsetter observed in 1900:

> Murder was (*sic*) generally punished by fine, the delinquent being made to pay two girls, one to the chief as blood money and the other to the relatives of the murdered as compensation.[29]

The compensatory principle meant that there was no idea of the 'blood feud'. If a family felt angry at the murder of one of their members, they gained nothing by causing the death of the murderer or his family. They wanted a woman – or even two – to enable the family to recover from its loss.

The disposal of fertile women underpinned and gave coherence to the social, economic and judicial systems of the local African societies. Claims to fertile women were not confined to murder, but lay at the heart of most compensation claims. Women represented both assets and investments; the bridewealth system ensured that families which controlled many women were wealthier than those who did not. The overwhelming proportion of 'native civil disputes' were about control over women, described by the NC's clerk in terms such as 'seduction' or 'adultery', which made sense to the white legal mind. Even cases which were not directly about control over women, such as theft or assault, usually involved claims for goods which could form part of a bridewealth agreement. Restorative justice in Southern Rhodesia cannot be understood in isolation from an understanding of bridewealth, the family and gender relationships in the African communities.

Whites did not appreciate the centrality of gender to restorative justice; nor did they understand that it was not primarily about punishment. Their understanding of justice failed to accommodate a non-retributive approach to what they saw as 'crime'. They overlooked the significance of bridewealth and the control over women in the claims for compensation. It was not only in the criminal sphere that this oversight caused confusion. To view compensation as 'fines' was to impose inappropriate ideas of justice on to the local system; but equally inappropriate was to impose the idea of 'property contract' on to the bridewealth system. If local systems of justice did not map easily on to the whites' ideas of criminal law, they fitted no better on to the whites' ideas of civil law.

[29] Special Report on Natives, NC Melsetter to CNC, 16 July 1900. NUE 2/1/3 p. 366.

Civil law for Africans was defined as 'native law and custom'. In 'native civil disputes', the NCs were supposed to act as 'big men' arbiters. The majority of cases they heard were bridewealth disputes, which they attempted to deal with as claims in civil law.[30] In this they were guided by their understanding of agreements about property and damages. The entire African bridewealth system was viewed through contract and tort-tinted spectacles.

The white administration could only understand the bridewealth transaction as a form of sale or transfer, in which items of equivalent market value were exchanged. Women were being 'bought' and 'sold':

> The woman's consent is not regarded as part of the contract. The husband acquires a marital right over the wife which is absolute and she is regarded as an article paid for, except that the husband cannot dispose of her to anyone else.[31]

> The Native laws do not allow women to have any right of property as they are themselves considered property.[32]

Civil disputes, in this view, arose when one party failed to deliver the goods, such as failing to provide a wife who didn't run away and did bear children. In such circumstances, the other party had a claim in law for a refund; or for the restoration of his wife.

In fact, the bridewealth relationship was not a 'property sale', in the sense described by the white commentators. Bridewealth is better understood as a means of compensating a lineage for the loss of one of its women. Marriage, in bridewealth systems, was not an event, but a process. The steady provision of bridewealth goods by the husband to his wife's family represented the gradual consolidation of the marriage over a number of years, or even across generations. In its classical formulation, the bridewealth relationship involved the exchange of cattle for women, but there was no fixed 'market price'. The exact details of what would be paid depended in part upon the success of the marriage and the number of children produced. An agreement about cattle might be agreed in principle at the start of the marriage, but this would be open to renegotiation. The

30 Bridewealth was called 'lobola' by the Native Department, although this was not the indigenous term in Melsetter District.

31 Response to questions from the Southern Africa Native Affairs Commission, NC Melsetter, 14 January 1904. NUE 2/1/4.

32 Report on 'Native Law and Customs', NC Melsetter, AR, 31 March 1900. N9/1/6. The examples are taken from Melsetter, but this understanding was found throughout the Native Department. All NCs were asked to report on 'native laws and customs' in the ARs for the year ending 31 March 1900, and similar statements may be found in many of those reports.

transfer of bridewealth goods would take place over many years, as the couple became 'more married'. Moreover, there was no fixed currency of exchange. If asked by a white enquirer, local Africans would say that 'according to custom', women were exchanged for cattle; but this would not necessarily reflect the *actual* goods that were exchanged. In practice, bridewealth goods could consist of cattle, hoes, cloth, goats, cash or a mixture of these. Moreover, the exchange did not need to involve the transfer of property at all. In poorer areas, service marriages were common, where the husband joined the wife's family and became part of their workforce, without controlling land in his own right. In Melsetter District, it was very common to omit the intermediary item altogether, and simply to exchange women.

Moreover, rights to bridewealth could be transferred away from a girl's own lineage, to the lineage of someone else. In times of hardship, girls were often pledged 'in marriage' to 'big men', in exchange for the 'big men' taking responsibility for meeting her family's immediate needs, particularly grain. The 'big men' might take the girls as wives, but were equally likely to arrange for these girls to be married to someone else (to fulfil or to create an obligation) when they reached maturity. The point about pledging was not to marry off young girls to old men (although this happened), but to transfer rights to their bridewealth, in exchange for food and protection. Bridewealth agreements and transactions were not 'sales', but long-term patronage relationships which governed the control and circulation of fertile women, cattle and productive tools.

However, this point was lost on the whites, who failed to grasp the nature and flexibility of bridewealth exchanges. The emphasis in the minds of the NCs hearing bridewealth disputes was not on the relationships between the families involved, but on the *value of the goods exchanged*. They saw their job as ensuring that the terms of the original contract were met, or that suitable refunds, of comparable value, were made. Ideally, those refunds would be in cash – the most 'civilised' form of exchange.

The records of the 'native civil disputes' in Melsetter District are full of pound sterling symbols and the language of property law. For example, a case heard in 1910 was recorded as follows:

> Plaintiff claims girl *the property of* his deceased father, he inherited the girl and mother. His father died when he was away in Port[uguese] Territory and on his return he found that the mother had died and the girl was *in the possession of* the Defendant.
>
> Defendant does not deny being *in possession of* the girl but says he paid lobola for her to people with whom she was then staying.

> J[udgement] – girl to return to her *rightful owner* Plaintiff – Defendant has redress in action for recovery of lobola paid against people who *sold her to him*.[33]

The obsession with purchase even led to the alteration of records to spell it out more clearly. In recording a case from 1912, the clerk initially wrote:

> Chinoza took a girl whom I was given & from the stock which came from her I was to get a wife.[34]

The 'get' was then amended to read 'I was to *buy* a wife', and the language of purchase – 'buy' and 'bought' – was used throughout the rest of the record. Clearly these are not verbatim accounts of the cases as presented by the Africans, but interpretations, based on property law, which made sense to the NC and clerks. They were trying to cram the system of restorative justice and mutual obligation into the mould of European property law. They could not understand the cases in any other way.

However, European property law is not well designed to deal with the sale of items which resist the terms of the contract. Sold goods in Europe normally acquiesced quietly in the agreement. Women, however, were not unproblematically disposable goods. Not only might they die soon after marriage, or fail to produce children; they could be kidnapped, seduced or simply run away. Trying to fix the bridewealth exchange as a pre-agreed contract was not a good idea, and not something which Africans normally attempted. For them, fixed contracts were hostages to fortune, which only a fool would contemplate. For whites, on the other hand, it seemed not just foolhardy, but childishly irresponsible, *not* to agree fixed contracts. Coming from market-dominated economies, they could not understand how anyone could overlook the need to secure their property rights by clear agreement at the time of the bridewealth exchange (or the 'moment of marriage', as the whites understood it). The 'sale' analogy entailed the assumption that a fixed contract about price must have been agreed, notwithstanding any delays in the actual handover of goods.

Records of civil disputes heard by NCs reveal that the whites could not make sense of what they were hearing unless they imposed on the accounts the model of a contract agreement based on a pre-agreed price. This 'price' – the fixed market price of wives – was deemed to be £20 or four head of cattle. The figure was derived from the provisions of the 1901 Natives Marriages Ordinance, which had been passed by the Southern Rhodesian Legislative Council in an attempt to stamp out the pledging of young girls (perceived by the whites as some kind of paedophiliac practice).[35] Section

[33] Chako vs Matimaurine, 27 April 1910. S1069 p. 158. My emphasis.

[34] Nyama vs Chioza, 9 May 1912. S1069 p. 336.

[35] Diana Jeater, *Marriage, Perversion and Power: the construction of moral discourse in Southern Rhodesia 1894–1930* (Oxford, 1993), pp. 74ff.

4 had placed an upper limit of four head of cattle, or equivalent, on bridewealth payments, in the belief that this would prevent older men 'outbidding' younger men, and 'buying' young girls against their will. The entire legislation, which was almost entirely ignored by Africans, was based on the misconception that bridewealth involved an individual purchase.

In June 1909, Longden became NC in Melsetter as well as Resident Magistrate. He was not minded to ignore the territory's Ordinances. He imposed the NMO's 'valuation' of wives rigidly in his rulings about repayment of bridewealth. In almost every dispute, his judgements deal primarily with the 'value' of the woman in contention, and that 'value' is fixed at twenty pounds.[36] In many of these cases, no specific claim was recorded from the plaintiff, and one may reasonably doubt whether they actually *wanted* twenty pounds, or whether they were likely to get it. For example, in one case, the defendant claimed that, over the years, he and his father had actually handed over thirty goats for his wife. He was lying; but it seems clear that goats had been agreed as the medium of payment. Even so, Longden ordered the man to pay twenty pounds cash, not goats, for his wife.[37] In another case, a man had already paid some cloth, ten shillings cash and a hoe, and his wife had borne two children. These things ought to have been taken into account when her family came asking for more, but the fixed 'price' – twenty pounds – was imposed regardless.[38] This mechanistic assumption that agreement about 'sale' entailed agreement about 'price' was a long way from the local conception of what was owing in bridewealth disputes. It put cash values rather than human relationships at their heart.[39]

The perception of the bridewealth relationship as simply an exchange of goods, divorced from larger human relationships, could lead to all kinds of absurdity. A striking example occurred in 1911. There had been an exchange of wives (in lieu of bridewealth). One woman's family considered that they had had a raw deal, because the wife they received had died young;

[36] These are his judgements on bridewealth claims heard during his first six months in office: 'judgement given against him for £20'; 'for Plaintiff in convention for the sum of £20 . . .'; 'if woman does not return to Plaintiff then Defendant to refund lobola viz £20'; 'D[efendant] to return girl or pay value £20'; 'for Plaintiff for £20'; '. . . D[efendant] to pay to P[laintiff] 4 head of cattle or £20'; 'ordered that . . . D[efendant] pay 4 head of cattle to P[laintiff]'; '2nd D[efendant] to pay 1st D[efendant] the sum of £20 and 1st D[efendant] to pay this sum over to P[laintiff]'; 'Woman to be returned to P[laintiff] or D[efendant] to pay £20 to P[laintiff]'; 'P[laintiff] to receive back wife and children on paying £20 . . .'; 'he has already given £12 on a/c and is willing to give the balance of £8'; 'D[efendant] ordered to hand over £5 to P[laintiff] and to pay balance of £15 within 6 mths'; 'for plaintiff £20'. S1069, 3 June–24 December 1909.

[37] Jongwe vs Manyadza, 30 August 1909. S1069.

[38] Dachengidzwa vs Musimbo, 21 October 1909. S1069.

[39] It even did some violence to the standard European idea of market exchange, not allowing for 'depreciation' or for part payment in kind.

so, when their kinswoman's husband died, they took her back. However, the NC ruled that she had been fairly exchanged, and now 'belonged to' her deceased husband's family. He seemed to find it difficult to conceptualise an exchange which did not entail the absolute transfer of ownership. However, feeling unhappy about the idea of 'widow inheritance', he allowed that the woman ought to have the right to return to her own family, but – and here we see just how unserviceable and inaccurate was his understanding of bridewealth – 'lobola must be paid on her behalf'.[40] He obviously intended that the husband's family should be compensated for losing a wife for which they had (in his view) already paid in full. In effect, however, he had asked a family to pay bridewealth for one of their own women! This was offensive nonsense. The error arose because he was thinking of 'lobola' as simply the word used for the price of a woman, and thinking of women as transferable commodities whose ownership passed absolutely to whoever paid the appropriate sum for them. The complex web of patronage and kinship which the bridewealth relationship encompassed was crudely misinterpreted as the open-ended transfer of disposable goods.

The perception of bridewealth exchange as a transfer of disposable goods raised real moral difficulties for the white administrators. Women, it was clear, were *not* always amenable to disposal. Consequently, the whites found the system, as they understood it, most uncomfortable to sustain. The collision between the moral worlds of the two communities emerges clearly in cases where women did not behave like marketable commodities, and the whites could not find it in themselves to insist that they should. On the one hand, the whites could not understand the bridewealth relationship except as a 'sale'; on the other, they felt uneasy about the moral responsibility of colluding in that 'sale' by hearing the disputes.

The presentation of women as objectified commodities occurs throughout the civil dispute records. For example, in one case the woman is treated as a missing exhibit:

> Evidence adduced goes to show that woman was seen living at D[efendant]'s kraal but has evidently been hidden & could not now be produced.[41]

However, the whites did not like to think of women in this way. Only very rarely would they award a woman in arbitration; the judgement was almost always for cash or cattle. This was despite the fact that in a large number of cases it was a woman who was claimed, and, in local terms, the claimant had a reasonable right to make this claim. This was not because NCs thought women should have greater autonomy: they required wives who

[40] Chigonya vs Seve, 22 July 1911. S1069 p. 278.
[41] Katsawora vs Mutimbanyoka, 15 October 1909. S1069.

had deserted to return to their husbands. However, they did not like 'awarding' women in settlement of a claim; it seemed to smack of the 'barbarism' they were hoping to eradicate.

There are only a handful of cases where the ruling includes the possibility that a woman might be handed over, rather than her 'value'. In all of these cases, the NC did not make the order, but simply acquiesced in an agreement reached by the parties. In one case, the record absolves the NC by noting explicitly that it was 'in accordance with native custom' that the defendant was to return the bridewealth or 'give another girl'.[42] In cases where a woman was claimed, the NC preferred to order that any bridewealth received for the woman in question should be paid over, or, failing that, twenty pounds.[43] This was made explicit in a 1911 case, where bridewealth had been paid but no woman delivered. The defendant admitted his fault and promised to hand over a woman. This agreement was duly noted, but conscience forced the clerk to add at a later date:

> Parties were informed that if the girl was willing to become the wife of Plaintiff she might do so, otherwise Plaintiff will only retain the right over her that when she marries he will be entitled to receive his lobola paid for her by her chosen husband.[44]

The discomfort about awarding women as part of a settlement seems to have arisen from a distaste for human beings being the bone of contention in a civil dispute. It was one thing to order women to return to their 'lawful husbands'; it was another to dispose of them as goods owing in a market exchange.

The white men's discomfort arose because they thought that the bridewealth relationship was simply an exchange of goods. To note that they were wrong about this is not to deny that bridewealth exchanges disposed of women without their consent. However, bridewealth exchanges were not disposing of women *as property*, in the way that whites thought that they were. They failed to grasp this, despite the dilemmas which their misunderstandings raised, because in most cases they could make rulings within the

[42] Maweni vs Masona, 3 August 1910. See also Kuwatawingwa vs Keta, 9 July 1909 and Chiteiwa vs Zaba, 26 April 1911. S1069.

[43] As in all these cases, where the claim was actually for a woman (or, failing that, compensation), but where the woman was not recognised as the claimant's wife: Zaramba alias Chizamkuri vs Chyokwe and Mutangi, 9 September 1909; Gumirepi vs Ndararana, 10 September 1909; Juba vs Jeye, 14 October 1909; Marwiro vs Mukunga and Madzeni, 15 October 1909; Tshabeni vs Mesimunguri, 3 November 1909; Kuwatawingwe vs Siyawacho, 11 February 1910; Kufandada vs Mawenu, 8 June 1910; Chikukwa vs Zwinera, 27 July 1910; Bongana vs Mapomba, 4 May 1911; Mapanga vs Mpanzi, 22 May 1911; Chitemba vs Chinovo, 26 May 1911; Muhlaba vs Chidembo, 19 June 1911; Kari vs Magava, 5 October 1911; Dzavamakani vs Sikiro, 13 July 1912; Zano vs Simoumi, 19 July 1912; Demba vs Garipi, 1 August 1912. The trend continues throughout the rest of the records. S1069.

[44] Chitemba vs Chinovo, 26 May 1911. S1069 p. 238.

property law framework, and were not forced to think outside that framework. They did not have to confront the fundamental differences between their idea of a civil dispute and the ideas of the litigants. Had they understood better, they might have felt less uncomfortable with the claims for women; but they would probably have felt much less complacent about the chances for the steady onmarch of 'civilisation'.

It is clear from this survey of the court records of Melsetter District across the first generation of white administration in Southern Rhodesia that local systems of justice were not seriously challenged by their interactions with 'civilised' European law. As long as the patronage-based bridewealth system continued, and there were strong vested interests in the African communities to ensure that it did, then the local system of justice continued to have meaning and relevance, and people continued to think of justice in terms of lineage, community, compensation and obligation. Property law and state retribution were at best irrelevant, and at worst actively damaging.

The gulf between the two systems was so wide that the same case could be understood in completely different ways by the white and African participants. Particularly in criminal prosecutions, the white administration failed to address the real judicial issues perceived by local people, so for many years there was little enthusiasm for taking criminal cases to the white authorities. In civil arbitration, the failure of the whites to understand what a case was about was less important than their power to summon people to come to a hearing to talk. There is little evidence to suggest that the details of the Native Commissioner's rulings were observed by the litigants, whatever he may have thought.

Over subsequent generations, it is true, ideas of contract and of retribution took a deeper hold. A hybrid law passed in 1916, taking elements of both Roman-Dutch and local views of justice, criminalised adultery by Africans.[45] By 1923, at least one cuckolded African husband agreed that legal retribution was the business of the state, and that the adultery law should be used to punish his two wives:

> 'I want them to be put in gaol', he said, 'and I want them to be put to real hard labour . . . I want them to feel the pain of prison.'[46]

The growing demands of a capitalist and cash-based economy also had its impact on bridewealth payments as well as on ideas about jurisprudence.[47]

[45] Jeater, *Marriage, Perversion and Power*, chs. 5 and 6, discusses why and how this hybrid came about.

[46] NC, Shabani to Attorney-General, 30 April 1923. N3/17/2.

[47] Randal Carson Smith, 'The struggle to control dispute proceedings in Southern Rhodesia 1930–1970, with special reference to the lower courts' (School of Oriental and African Studies, University of London PhD thesis, 1994).

However, by the 1930s it was clear that African systems of jurisprudence had not folded in the face of the superior justice of the white men. In 1937, chiefly courts presided over by recognised African arbiters and operating under local 'law and custom' were given formal recognition. For each community, the judicial systems of the other continued to seem very peculiar.

11. *Kenyatta's trials: breaking and making an African nationalist*[1]

JOHN LONSDALE

> ... the time might come when a decision had to be taken either to 'bust' or 'buy' Jomo Kenyatta. It would depend how the campaign went against the Mau Mau. Unless action was taken against Jomo the Africans might say that he was too important for the Kenya Government to tackle.
>
> *Note of meeting at the Colonial Office, 23 September 1952*[2]

I. COLONIAL RULE AND RULES OF LAW

In 1907 Winston Churchill visited the East Africa Protectorate, later annexed as Kenya colony. Liberal under-secretary of state for the colonies, he was inspecting the most troublesome territory in British tropical Africa. His comments were as acute as always. They were to be as pertinent, years later, to the criminal trial of a violent African nationalism he could not have imagined – held at Kapenguria, a district headquarters of which the world had never heard. Churchill pondered the relations of rule, racial inequality and the law, as too did Sir Evelyn Baring, Kenya's governor in its later crisis. Both thought legal due process, the subject's shield, to be vital to the lawful exercise of punitive instrument, the sword of state. Churchill assumed rela-

[1] This essay is preparatory to a work, co-authored with Bruce Berman, *The House of Custom: Jomo Kenyatta, Louis Leakey and the Making of the Modern Kikuyu*. David Anderson, Kenya's foremost legal historian, Richard Waller and Anthony Costa have advised; as have Achhroo Kapila and Ian Henderson, who played opposite each other in the Kenyatta trials. Seminars at the Australian National University's Humanities Research Centre, Oxford's St Anthony's College, and the *Past and Present* conference at Birmingham prompted much thought. Any errors are mine.

[2] W. L. Gorell Barnes, assistant under-secretary of state, in conference with Kenya's new governor, Sir Evelyn Baring; Public Record Office (PRO): CO 822/544/1.

tions between executive and judiciary would be smooth; Baring learned better. Neither gave thought to the deep politics of African society, stirred up by colonial conflicts of laws. Churchill did fear, however, that the law could do little to resolve racial conflict. How far Baring's experience bore him out is a question for this essay. All these issues appeared in the legal drama which was enacted upon and acted out by Jomo Kenyatta and five others, on trial at Kapenguria.

In 1952 Kenyatta was charged with managing Mau Mau, a secret society sworn to force British rule and white farm settlement out of Kenya. The first settlers had barely preceded Churchill. They brought energy, they spelt trouble. Their 'fierce self-interest', he thought, menaced the colonial claim to native trusteeship. Conflict between white capital, Indian trade and black labour created 'rhinoceros questions – awkward, thick-skinned, and horned, with a short sight, an evil temper, and a tendency to rush blindly upwind upon any alarm'. He feared future governors would face 'one of those apparently hopeless antagonisms of interest which baffle and dispirit all who are concerned in their adjustment'.

Legitimate government was difficult in any case. One evening Churchill reflected on the paradox that personal rule, such as the British practised in Africa, derived authority from obedience – its own subjection to an impersonal rule of law. His host, district commissioner (DC) of a newly conquered region, far beyond the white farms, had raised the issue by way of complaint. The high court, in its reviewing role, had told him to retry a criminal case over which he had presided. The legal ground seemed absurd: he had not noted in his trial report that the accused had questioned his witnesses. All those involved, he alone excepted, had been Africans, native subjects. Their loyalty, the British believed, was best inspired by their DC's personal mastery. Often the only white man in a population of thousands, recruited from the finest of his race, his prestige must surely be destroyed if his decisions were questioned from on high.

Churchill disagreed, for two reasons that go to the heart of all rule, the protection of civil rights and promotion of lawful authority. The law must be a shield; there was 'scarcely anything more important in the government of men than the exact – I will even say pedantic – observance of the regular forms' by which guilt or innocence was decided. And personal mastery alone was an unsteady sword. Without due process, justice was 'a rough-and-ready practice dependent entirely for its efficiency and fairness upon the character and intelligence of the individual responsible'. Prestige was thus reinforced, not weakened, by the rule of law. 'The tribesmen', or so he imagined, 'see that their ruler – to them all-powerful, the man of soldiers and police, of punishment and reward – is himself obedient to some remote external force, and they wonder what that mysterious force can be and marvel dimly at its greatness.'[3]

To be a marvel, rulers must hope, is to have won the moral battle of turning superior strength into hegemonic authority. All states attempt this political alchemy. Hegemony transmutes the dross of domination into the gold of symbolic sway. It sets a cultural seal on political necessity, especially the ruler's need to differentiate forms of violence; it honours some, restrains others and criminalises others still. In a colonial context, a hegemonic regime may give credit to past conquest for present progress. If itself subject to law, it may also justifiably outlaw insurgent violence. But how far is legal due process itself the political alchemist's stone, as Churchill believed, turning an instrument of partisan power into a shield of universal protection? The idea of hegemony was first used to explain an otherwise unexpected working-class constitutionalism in industrial democracies. But there, it appears, it is the cultural unities of nationhood, not forms of law, that have soothed the material divisions of class; habit has cooled passion. Colonies by contrast were pre-industrial; often their only 'national' history was that forged by alien rule. Even to consider the possibility of their political hegemony is therefore controversial.[4]

That many Africans consented in alien rule may be doubted; but some did and for their rulers they offered hope. The conditions for consent were particular, not general. Some Africans pursued self-interest in new fields of power protected or created by colonialism – as in some evangelistic, educational or medical fields, or in some arenas of litigation. For them alien rule dignified the commonplace; it became vulgarised within their normal social relations.[5] These intimations of hegemony sustained in white officials a hope that their power might rest more generally not on wary respect for superior force alone but on willing compliance with a domestic convenience, daily negotiated. Such ruling ambitions, perhaps vanities, can shape decision, especially during crisis.

However much colonial rulers claimed to have brought peace and no matter how much older Africans gave thanks,[6] a colonial state found it

[3] Winston S. Churchill, *My African Journey* (London, 1908), pp. 25–41.

[4] See discussions of Gramsci's concept in Dagmar Engels and Shula Marks, eds., *Contesting Colonial Hegemony: State and Society in Africa and India* (London, 1994).

[5] John Lonsdale, 'The Conquest State of Kenya, 1895–1905', ch. 2 in Bruce Berman and John Lonsdale, *Unhappy Valley: Conflict in Kenya and Africa* (London, 1992), pp. 36–9 for vulgarisation.

[6] D. A. Low, 'British East Africa: the Establishment of British Rule, 1895–1912', ch 1 in Vincent Harlow and E. M. Chilver, eds., *History of East Africa* (Oxford, 1965), vol. II, p. 34.

hard to convince its officers or the imperial parliament of its subjects' willing consent. It lacked the reassurances of either electoral approval or totalitarian self-delusion. It also had many publics to satisfy, lacking the sovereignty that cut them down to one. On the spot they were ethnically and racially divided; 'at home' they held left- and right-wing opinions. After 1945 they included America and, with many Asians in East Africa, India too, with its prickly new independence. It was especially difficult, and all the more necessary, to claim due authority when a colony turned to violence in its own defence – as when Kenya's police seized indigenous leaders at gunpoint and at dead of night, not fifty years after Churchill's visit, in 1952. Coincidentally, he was now the British prime minister.

The scholars' scepticism that due legal process could have lent colonial rule a quotidian authority echoes, if on different premises, the doubts of DCs. Historians question the plausibility of what would have been needed, the general vulgarisation of alien power in deep, familiar, cultural terms. Officials used to criticise, rather, the high politics of executive and judicial relations. They could be as angry as Churchill's host, one of their pioneers. The politician's verandah paradox was an office nightmare. There was twofold friction between the rulers and their law; both their structure and their culture were divided.

All states face tension between government by men and by law; their elites limit their powers, to protect their sway from the stigma of arbitrary action. Some, British colonies formerly among them, practise less institutional restraint than others; they trust in a ruling culture of self-control, a habit of command disciplined by the opinion of one's peers and the likely reaction of subject notables. In British Africa these private laws of anticipatory calculation outweighed any legal check on misrule. Field officers held the conjoint powers of the executive, as DCs; of the law, as magistrates; and of the 'tribal police', as commanders. They held to the self-critical doctrine that personal character best resolved these contradictions in role. As executives they must be firm, as judges fair. Such discretion needed reliance on their seniors' support. DCs also had ideology on their side; their persuasive command was a tool of progress. Trustees of their African wards, they were schoolmasters in modernity. Knowing their people, they could deliver substantial justice even if legally unqualified. Energetic enlightenment was their title to rule, not obedience to every pettifogging letter of the law. Their most consistent complaint was that any local 'bad hat' could make an ass of executive authority by getting its legal decisions overturned on a technical appeal. Judges, separate from the executive at the appellate level, had never been called on to quell a crowd with a look, unsupported by a library of books. Their legal niceties seemed made to belittle, not buttress, the dignity of the district office.[7]

More than one official culture, therefore, infused British rule. Most field officers served out their career in one colony; they judged reputation, white and black, by the self-regarding rules of a gentleman's club, at times best observed with a blind eye if a good man was not to fall. In Kenya they spent their early, formative, years in African districts. The colonial judiciary, by deliberate contrast, were global professionals. They circled the world on promotion within one legal service; their precedents were imperial. Unfamiliarity with local ruling culture was deemed to be a strength, a shield of impartial judgement that relied not on 'some one who knew the people and their ways' but on evidence proven in court.[8] But a desire to fit in with local culture could also create, as critics of the Kenyatta trials alleged, a nervous complaisance with local prejudice.

So Churchill was only partly right and wholly misleading. Even for its rulers, for whom a sense of lawful mastery was of more concern than for their subjects, Kenya's legal world was morally divided. In the African reserves power was fused together. The resolution of its contrary logics of action and arbitration required honour and caution. At the centre, executive and judicial power was separated; it also lost the prudential ballast of anticipated African reaction. Further, legislation was subject to settler consent. Whites were, in effect, enfranchised citizens from 1919. Their representatives could demand the curtailment of the few liberties Africans enjoyed, should the rhinoceros of race snort in alarm.

If Africans accepted the force of domination rather than welcoming its hegemonic beauty, they also endured new conflicts of law. These, one may assume, dimmed any impulse to marvel at British sway. Some turned to colonial courts to fix claims to land but not many went so far as to trust the law. No African entered the legal profession before 1952; none till then owned enough to habituate recourse to lawyers. Meanwhile, beneath judicial notice, Arican law grew in chaos. Markets in land and labour challenged patriarchal authority. Male workers married on the surety of their pay rather than their father's livestock. Women pitted the sale of produce

[7] Ronald Robinson, 'Non-European Foundations of European Imperialism', ch. 5 in Roger Owen and Bob Sutcliffe, eds., *Studies in the Theory of Imperialism* (London, 1972), pp. 117–40. T. H. R. Cashmore, 'Studies in District Administration in the East Africa Protectorate, 1895–1918' (Cambridge Ph.D. thesis, 1965); Bruce Berman, *Control and Crisis in Colonial Kenya: The Dialectic of Domination* (London, 1990); generally, Mahmood Mamdani, *Citizen and Subject: Contemporary Africa and the Legacy of Late Colonialism* (London, 1996).

[8] *Report of the Commission of Inquiry into the Administration of Justice in Kenya, Uganda and the Tanganyika Territory in Criminal Matters*, Cmd. 4623 (1934), p. 20.

against obedience to men. Christian converts followed 'a new law of liberty' as a missionary put it, quoting St Paul. Penny capitalism broke clannish ties. 'That plough is now his wife', a father explained as he disinherited his son.[9]

Any state would find it hard to make such rapid social change justiciable; Kenya's state twice compounded the problem. First, chiefs, British creatures, wielded unprecedented power. Second, 'customary' law, the main field in which the British sought to hitch local culture to ruling hegemony, rested on a legal delusion. DCs and senior African men together tried to limit the new liberties with allegedly 'customary' rules that were equally novel. Chiefly influence in the African courts made the position worse. Repeated efforts failed to separate 'custom' from the corruptions of office. The state could not disengage from the partiality of its African agents; these in turn were trapped between colonial coercion and moral community. As land values rose in the 1940s, with growing markets and population, so litigants discerned British connivance in chiefly graft. Nor did the higher courts resolve deep confusion. British judges mistrusted the way in which Africans constructed truth; it looked like lying. In an appeal case in 1920, chief Kinyanjui had been asked about his evidence in the lower court. He asked the judge to remind him on whose behalf he had appeared; 'what I said depends on whose witness I was'. For Kinyanjui (as for his DCs) truth was something negotiated with his peers; the judge thought his credit was ruined by his 'accommodating nature'.[10] Different legal worlds had no agreed standard of proof.

Kenya's post-war crisis, after 1945, sharpened these conflicts of law. Settlers pressed home their claims. Africans could not; and broke their legal bounds. The state responded with rigour. By 1952 its authority was on trial, on the brink of settler capture and African revolt. Government had no choice but to show its repression was justified by policy and in law, not dictated by prejudice; its officials had neither run before the rhinoceros of white panic nor avenged professional pride, hurt by not knowing their natives. It was not enough to detain the African leader, Kenyatta, without charge, however much emergency laws and precedent allowed. 'Kenyatta and his henchmen' must be convicted in the open court that held the ring between shield and sword. The charges were management of an unlawful society; and conspiracy to forcibly administer oaths, to excite disaffection,

[9] Harry Leakey, 'Report on the Work of the British East Africa Mission, 1917', Birmingham University Library, Church Missionary Society Archive: G 3/AL (1917–1934); P. K. Mugo to editor, *Muigwithania,* 1, 11 (Nairobi, April 1929), p. 3. Generally, John Lonsdale, 'The Moral Economy of Mau Mau' in Berman and Lonsdale, *Unhappy Valley*, pp. 315–504.

[10] Arthur Phillips, *Report on Native Tribunals* (Nairobi, 1945). Also, Martin Chanock, *Law, Custom and Social Order: the Colonial Experience in Malawi and Zambia* (Cambridge, 1985). Supreme court case 4358/20, in *Kenya Land Commission Evidence Vol I* (Nairobi, 1933), pp. 280–3.

and promote 'ill will and hostility between different classes'. Under cross-examination and before the world's press, the crown would prove Kenyatta guilty, not of holding lawful nationalist ambitions, of course, but of inciting Mau Mau's criminal terror in their pursuit.[11]

More history is needed to explain why Baring proclaimed a state of emergency on 20 October 1952. Knowledge of the past is also essential to an understanding of Kenyatta's trials; it certainly informed his own. The laws of evidence forbad the retelling of this history in court, but in vain. Inadmissible examination by the prosecution and leading questions from the defence allowed both Kenyatta and the crown to interpret the past. Recorded at length in the trial transcript, he was not understood by the court, fresh testimony to a white inability to fathom African grievance.

II. POST-WAR CRISIS AND HOUSEHOLD HISTORY

After the second world war, as after the first, the discordant strands of Kenya's history were tied into the knotty question of future control.[12] Was Kenya to become a minority white dominion, like South Africa; a multi-racial partnership, as mooted for Central Africa; or a black state? How long could colonial rule, on the wane around the world, keep the future unravelled? Settlers found it hard to believe that London could not grant minority rule. Yet they were only 40,000 strong, less than one fifth of them farmers, in a population of 100,000 Indians and five million Africans. Africans had come to demand nothing short of majority rule but had yet to imagine the nation that could hold a regime to account. As to Asians, while the British thought the Muslims moderate and Hindus extreme – which meant that they were betting on African nationalism – most believed that economic survival required political silence.

The colonial office, baffled but not dispirited, concluded that multi-racialism was the only answer; in the long run immigrant capital must be redefined as the privileged engine of African power. That did not make it a solution. How could settlers concede so much or Africans accept so little? Officials pursued two concealed lines of advance in widening black opportunity while keeping white confidence, in search of a multi-racial middle class as the 'the backbone of the country'.[13] Politically, Africans were permitted more local government powers and trade union rights – in the long

[11] For an eye-witness account, Charles Chenevix Trench, *Men Who Ruled Kenya* (London, 1993), p. 234; charge sheets in Kenya National Archives (KNA), RR 9/5. The conspiracy charges were later dropped.

[12] For the earlier crisis, R. M. Maxon, *Struggle for Kenya: the Loss and Reassertion of Imperial Initiative, 1912–1923* (London, 1993). For the later, David Throup, *Economic and Social Origins of Mau Mau* (London, 1987).

[13] Sir Charles Jeffries, minute, 17 February 1953, PRO: CO 822/440.

trek, and the longer the better, towards the undeclared aim of preponderant black power. Economically, government tried to defend the white highlands, a vital dollar-earner, by relieving African land hunger. To this end, Africans had to conserve their own eroded soils with an enforced labour that wrecked political gradualism. Agricultural officers were then freed, too late, from the bonds of white farm protectionism to promote, with tentative steps of hope – to which the emergency gave costly wings of resolution – the smallholder cash crops that might buy off African envy. Such official adjustment of racial conflict, as Churchill might have warned, would be but academic spindrift in any political gale.

The storm that broke in the 1950s was long brewing. African songs traced it back sixty years, when the first upcountry leader died in British hands.[14] Black anger nonetheless took whites unawares. The blinkers of race made it hard for officials to blame themselves; they hesitated to fan settler fury by blaming them. A few evil men, Kenyatta their leader, must have created Mau Mau; this had recruited by fear of witchcraft; half-educated peasants, mentally unhinged by the rush of modernity, were all too susceptible; African grievance, even when acknowledged, scarcely justified the movement's atrocities. Besides, it killed many more Africans than white landlords.[15] Colonial ignorance is not surprising. Scholars have only now begun to uncover the sources of black grievance, studying not so much what Africans addressed to the British as what they argued out between themselves.[16]

Land was the core issue. Property conferred identity. Possession confirmed white superiority; for Africans, loss undermined British hegemony. Whites also needed cheap labour. They called it a school for idle natives; the coercions to which labour was subject certainly mocked the liberty the missions preached.[17] Indian traders were men in the middle. Living more cheaply than whites, 'off the smell of an oily rag', they enabled Africans to sell produce rather than work for wages. Settler alarm at their economic subversions alerted nationalists in India. In 1923 the colonial secretary, the Duke of

14 John Lonsdale, 'The Prayers of Waiyaki', ch. 11 in David M. Anderson and Douglas Johnson, eds., *Revealing Prophets: Prophecy in Eastern African History* (London, 1995), pp. 240–91.

15 For reactions to Mau Mau at the time see, John Lonsdale, 'Mau Maus of the Mind', *Journal of African History*, 31, 3 (1990), pp. 393–421; Dane Kennedy, 'Constructing the Colonial Myth of Mau Mau', *International Journal of African Historical Studies*, 25, 2 (1992), pp. 241–60.

16 See especially Greet Kershaw, *Mau Mau from Below* (Oxford, 1997).

17 David M. Anderson, 'Policing, Prosecution and the Law in Colonial Kenya, c. 1905–39', ch. 11 in David M. Anderson, and David Killingray, eds., *Policing the Empire: Government, Authority and Control, 1830–1940* (Manchester, 1991), pp. 183–200; David M. Anderson, 'Policing the Settler State: Colonial Hegemony in Kenya, 1900–1952', ch. 11 in Engels and Marks, *Contesting Colonial Hegemony*, pp. 248–64.

Devonshire, calmed the imperial tension by declaring African interests paramount; and trumped both immigrant rivals by reserving their trusteeship to Britain alone. African land petitioners saw the Devonshire declaration as their Magna Carta.[18] But a hegemonic imperial trusteeship failed in practice, baulked by settler self-interest and lost in the African moral maze.

This history was in Kenyatta's mind as he stood in the dock; it had been his life. He was born around 1895, the year British rule arrived. The political, he knew, was supremely personal. No conflict was more central to the origins of Mau Mau than the struggle for mastery within African households; and this was engendered within particular ethnic crucibles of moral uncertainty. Some elaboration is needed to show how much in fact, and how little in practice, was on trial with Jomo Kenyatta.

African land loss had an ethnic geography which Kenyatta's trial reflected as if in a distorting mirror. The Rift Valley's pastoral plateaux, once managed by Maasai herdsmen, furnished most of the 11,000 square miles of 'white highlands'. Twice removed to make way for settlers but small in number and slow to take to school, Maasai did not so much protest as recover a pastoralist autonomy that risked as little colonial contact as possible.[19] No Maasai faced trial with Kenyatta. His colleagues were farmers or townsmen. An evasive autonomy was not open to them; they had to engage with the British. That some, in the end, did so by violence was due to a paradox. White settlers saw themselves as mixed farmers; yet only half their area was farmland; and this, as distinct from dry ranching country, was in turn only one fifth of Kenya's arable land. Most of the latter remained under African control. African farmers thus kept enough good land for their existing differentials of wealth to widen, embittering the quest for unity.

Kikuyu, the largest ethnic group, one fifth of Kenya's population, occupied its best land. Suffering famine shortly before the first settlers arrived, they withdrew from some of their territory – the southern tip, next to the future capital, Nairobi, and soon under plantation coffee. This area became the first of two cockpits of the land question. Out of necessity and in hope, Kikuyu took to lives of labour, clerical authority, trade – and politics. Of Kenyatta's five co-defendants three were Kikuyu and the other two, it always appeared, were charged in error. Kenyatta himself was among the first generation of Kikuyu Christians, baptised in the month that cut open the heart of the imperial world, August 1914.[20]

[18] Marius Karatu to Arthur Creech Jones, MP, 21 April 1937: Rhodes House, Oxford, Mss. Brit. Emp. S332, Box 21/1, folios 21 and 117.

[19] Thomas Spear and Richard Waller, eds., *Being Maasai: Ethnicity and Identity in East Africa* (London, 1993).

[20] John Overton, 'The Origins of the Kikuyu Land Problem', *African Studies Review,* 31 (1988), pp. 109–26; Jeremy Murray-Brown, *Kenyatta* (London, 1972), pp. 43–52.

Kenya's colonial history was a conflict between two moral worlds, peasant and capitalist; multiple rights in land faced fenced-in rights to private property. White settlement broke a basic African law of land and labour. To African farmers land was people and authority, land was labour and obedience. The equation was reversible. People were land, obedient labour deserved land from a patron. Land alienation and the growing produce market broke that moral couplet of community. The Mau Mau movement was only the latest to try to repair it, to restore indigenous authority. This section explains that point – half seen by police witness at Kapenguria but not grasped by the defence until too late.

Kenyatta's trial set legal against moral memory. The supreme court (as the high court became) ruled in 1921 that the Crown Lands Ordinance of 1915, with other legislation, had made Africans the crown's tenants-at-will. Kenyatta never forgot this, to his judge's bemusement. Colonial governments had shorter memories than their subjects. Rulers had legal memories and could change laws; subjects, not controlling the law, retained moral memories that endured. Legal history was also fixed in Kenyatta's mind because it divided Kikuyu opinion; land loss turned internal debate into external weakness. Always a mobile society, Kikuyu disagreed on the nature of landed community, whether formed mainly by descent or contract. Both parties now wanted British title deeds to protect their land, but deeds of very different social pith. Chiefs wanted registers to distinguish clan landowners by descent, a minority, from the majority, their tenants. Their opponents in the Kikuyu Central Association (KCA), with Kenyatta their secretary, called for individual titles for both owners and tenants, with managerial rights reserved to clan elders.[21]

This split over land widened into a gulf between dynastic and generational political theories.[22] The question was how to adapt land relations to new conditions. Defence needs had once made followers welcome; market competition now raised the profits of property, if freed from clients. Dynastic theory reserved authority to descent, to landed patrons who were beginning to shrink from those who leaned on them. The KCA looked to other past principles of solidarity, annual age-sets and cyclical generations, to shape more inclusive alliances between propertied heads of household. Dynastic theory, descent, was well dug into the soil but divisive, clan against clan, owners against tenants. Generational theory saw 'land' as a contractual alliance; it carried the germ of unity. The question was how to combine them in a common ethnic cause.

[21] Lonsdale, 'Moral Economy of Mau Mau', pp. 362–3, 375–9.

[22] For which see Lonsdale, 'Waiyaki'.

Kenyatta, in London to represent his people, reinforced their case with an academic monograph. But in his *Facing Mount Kenya* he failed to unite clan and generation in a theory of progressive politics.[23] A former enemy, Chief Koinange, worked out the practice. He tried to create, out of a congeries of language and culture, a self-aware tribe. Honouring the dynastic principle, he convened in 1938 a pan-Kikuyu alliance of clan elders but took care to assert no joint trusteeship over any one clan's land. He also founded an independent school, with his overseas-educated son as its head. Age-sets competed to raise funds; the old generational cycle of land-cleansing sacrifice inspired a new vision of self-help.

Koinange tried to federate an institutional mosaic. He was defeated by byzantine clan politics, beneath which lay the religious duty owed by elders to their own parcels of ancestral land.[24] Kikuyu were nonetheless discussing the nature of authority. This arena fostered a sense of moral or civic ethnicity – that critical grasp of the need to renovate the rights and duties that make us 'we'. But they were far from agreeing to the surrender of multiple land loyalties that would have permitted a united ethnic nationalism.[25] This distinction between a discursive moral ethnicity and decisive ethnic nationalism, between civic accountability and central command, each patriotic, fuelled Mau Mau's later violence.

When he returned in 1946, after sixteen years away, Kenyatta was coopted into the landed alliance. Six years later the crown charged him with managing its rivals. The weakness of this case had several sources, of which the foremost was the practical difficulty of 'managing' any Kikuyu project. Marrying one of Koinange's daughters, Kenyatta became son-in-law to the elders and spent much energy in proving himself his own master. He too wanted a unity to impress the British. Like Koinange, he too failed. But their use of legal culture in this attempt gave the crown a major source of evidence: the oath of unity. Past disunity had made Kikuyu a contractual, oath-swearing, fee-paying culture. There was more disunity now; fear of neighbours' sorcery was a cancer within rural capitalism. The oath protected political solidarity against that, but oaths were dangerous in themselves. Their symbols of life – goats' blood, earth and its fruits, symbolically linked to sexual power – could be handled safely only by men obliged to use

[23] Bruce Berman and John Lonsdale, 'The Labors of *Muigwithania*: Jomo Kenyatta as Author, 1928–45', *Research in African Literatures*, 29, 1 (1998), pp. 16–42.

[24] Kershaw, *Mau Mau from Below*, pp. 184–96.

[25] John Lonsdale, 'Moral Ethnicity, Ethnic Nationalism and Political Tribalism: the Case of the Kikuyu' in Peter Meyns, ed., *Staat und Gesellschaft in Afrika* (Hamburg, 1996), pp. 93–106.

them with care, the propertied elders nearest to ancestral judgement. Their alliance was bound to be cautious.[26]

The elders' leadership was first challenged in the other cockpit of conflict, the white farms, on which two generations of African 'squatter' labour had now lived. By 1950 one fifth of all Kikuyu were squatters. The legal theory that people are land gave them the right to share in their white patrons' inheritance. On this their traditions were adamant; they had emigrated by settler invitation; their resident labour had cleared the undug wilderness of Maasailand. In the 1940s the settlers – lured by new markets and fearful lest the law admit squatters' rights – cut back on their customary access to private cultivation and grazing. Settlers wanted to turn squatters into mere labourers, to whom responsibility was discharged with each monthly wage. Whites were as brutal as Kikuyu patrons in shedding clients. Squatters organised to resist this white 'hypocrisy'.[27]

The highland crisis came to focus on Olenguruone, a settlement for former squatters. Were its Kikuyu members state tenants or landowners, compensated at last with land they could call their own? Officials set land usage rules and demanded impartible inheritance. Ex-squatters refused thus to renounce their householders' rights and duties. 'We . . . were given land . . . for the compensation of our original land deprived from us by White Settlers, now detrimental laws are framed which compel us to divorce our wives and denounce fatherly rights to our sons.'[28] Fathers oathed their wives and children to resist. It was a scandalous extension of adult male responsibility, but sworn solidarity had to match the legal burdens which the settlement rules had laid on juniors. All were evicted, all the same. The state had inflamed the smouldering issue of how seniors and juniors should relate; Mau Mau proved how bitter it was.

The contour trench-digging labour of soil conservation brought this struggle into the Kikuyu reserve. It was all the sharper for being fought on unquestionably ancestral land, which was often land disputed between questionable ancestors. Could chiefs rightly conscript the labour

[26] Carl Rosberg and John Nottingham, *The Myth of 'Mau Mau': Nationalism in Kenya* (New York and London, 1966); John Spencer, *KAU: the Kenya African Union* (London, 1985); David Throup, 'Moderates, Militants and Mau Mau: African Politics in Kenya, 1944–1952' (MS, n. d).

[27] Rebmann Wambaa and Kenneth King, 'The Political Economy of the Rift Valley', in B. A. Ogot, ed, *Hadith*, 5 (Nairobi, 1975), pp. 195–218; Tabitha Kanogo, *Squatters and the Roots of Mau Mau* (London, 1987); Frank Furedi, *The Mau Mau War in Perspective* (London, 1989).

[28] Olenguruone petitioners to Arthur Creech Jones, 22 July 1946, PRO: CO 533/544/2 (by courtesy of Joanna Lewis); Throup, 'Moderates, Militants and Mau Mau', ch. 6.

of other men's wives – their husbands were generally working away – and what right did that confer, and to whom, over the soil conserved? Townsfolk had their own anxieties; a general strike, led by Kikuyu, was crushed between British force and the strike-breaking of other ethnic groups less committed to town. Unmarried and therefore landless, younger migrants were legal juniors, incapable of moral responsibility. They were also impatient; they needed land for marriage and insurance against the risks of town. Olenguruone's oath showed that juniors could share authority.

As Kenyatta warned London, 1950 saw elders lose control to the young.[29] The first had asked for help; the latter took their chance. Politics had had its day; direct action's time had come. Union leaders, defeated in town, agreed to help the rural movement, at a price. Its oath must be open to juniors, and to more militant ends. Elders conceded this vulgarisation of civic virtue with great reluctance, accepting it only as a lesser evil than the colonial pressures that had first broken household authority.[30] The oath of unity became a warrior or killing oath. Two leading urban militants, Fred Kubai and Bildad Kaggia, were among the 'Kapenguria six'.

Kenyatta did not resign. The militants shrank from deposing him; he was a tree under which many might shelter. Nor may he have wholly regretted the afforcement of his hitherto peaceful project, even by men whom an elder would despise. But moderates can beat militants only if an incumbent regime is prepared to split the opposition with concessions, as Kenya's was not. Freedom of African association was more subversive than any cavilling judge. Even the moderate Kenya African Union (KAU, pronounced 'cow'), founded in 1944, poached influence from chiefs.

Kenyatta had been elected president of the pan-ethnic KAU in 1947. From that moment it was divided. Outside Kikuyuland it was known as the teachers' party, of young men with liberal hopes and little experience, wordy in petition but wanting in action. In Kikuyuland, Kenyatta's old KCA – and it seems never to have relaxed the rule that members must have been circumcised before the mid-1920s – remained under a wartime ban. However, those members who were also clan seniors in the elders' unity movement ran KAU's Kikuyu branches. Kenyatta's attention to Kikuyu politics led him to neglect the wider KAU, and in 1951 he lost its executive to the young urban militants, whose supporters were often ex-squatters. They had already acquired the nickname 'Mau Mau' – which may or may not mean 'the greedy eaters', from their 62-shilling initiation fee. Under this name they had been banned in August 1950, for forcibly administering an

[29] Kenyatta to John Dugdale, 14 Aug. 1950, PRO: CO 533/566/7.
[30] Kershaw, *Mau Mau from Below*, pp. 317–19.

oath. Like Kenyatta's elders, however, they called themselves 'unity' or the 'council of Muumbi', the Kikuyu Eve. By 1951 therefore, KAU was divided in three parts: pan-ethnic moderates with little public support; Kikuyu elders who wanted to back constitutionalism with a controlled popular unity; and Kikuyu militants who used ethnic disciplinary symbols to authorise their own actions. Internal division, however, took second place to external opposition to alien rule.[31]

In 1952 Kenyatta embarked on what the prosecution was to call his 'stump campaign', round KAU branches in the Rift and Kikuyuland. But was it a counter-attack against the militants or a deception plan? Some thought it his last bid for peaceful change; in the dock at Kapenguria he claimed his main purpose had been 'to speak to the people to refrain from entering such evil organization [Mau Mau]'. But the safari was also a band-wagon; he could not shake off militant lieutenants (or rivals) who, when speeches were done and Kenyatta slept, oathed recruits after dark for darker deeds. At his trial he claimed he had risked death by denouncing violence; the militants have confirmed that in retrospect. That is not how government saw it at the time. Rather, the KAU tour was a master plan to spread Mau Mau mayhem under legal cover. It was the centrepiece of Baring's case for calling an emergency, of which the first act, soon after midnight, would be the arrest of the master mind, Kenyatta.[32]

III. PANIC, TERROR AND LAWFUL AUTHORITY

By 1951 Kenya faced constitutional impasse. In the legislature the eleven white elected members – who enjoyed numerical parity with non-whites – could defeat government if supported by members of other races. There was little chance of that. The few unofficials co-opted to ministerial rank were also white – a racially skewed taste of power. Further, the four African members were not directly elected but nominated from district council shortlists. It was an unworkable formula for multi-racialism; but to revise the representative equation would face whites with a future of political decline. James Griffiths, ex-coalminer and Labour secretary of state, visited Kenya. Baffled, he counselled delay, with a constitutional conference in two years' time. And that, more or less, was that.

[31] Spencer, *KAU*, pp. 222–5; Bildad Kaggia, *Roots of Freedom, 1921–1963* (Nairobi, 1975), pp. 78–82. Berman, *Control and Crisis*, pp. 322–38.

[32] Kenyatta under cross-examination, Kapenguria Trial Transcript vol. 5, p. 1063, 30 Jan. 1953, KNA: RR 9/9; Rosberg and Nottingham, *Myth of 'Mau Mau'*, pp. 274–5; Spencer, *KAU*, pp. 229–32; Throup, 'Moderates, Militants and Mau Mau', pp. 18–19. Bildad Kaggia, *Roots of Freedom*, p. 114; Fred Kubai, in Brian Lapping, *End of Empire* (London, 1985), p. 411; Baring to Lyttelton, 10 Oct. 1952, PRO: CO 822/443/1.

It was not just that Britain recoiled from unseating settlers; African politics had no friends in high places. The colonial office felt Africans had much civilisation still to learn before bearing high political office. The governor, Sir Philip Mitchell, scorned their nationalism as a device to give demagogues 'liberty to exploit and oppress the mass of the people'. DCs distrusted KAU. Official harangues were no match for the popularisation of politics. Record companies sold thousands of vernacular songs; not for years did they or government realise that many were inflammatory. Settlers had long tried to nail Kenyatta for conspiracy. Their leading moderate, Michael Blundell, felt betrayed by 'an element which although nurtured, fostered and brought forward by the advice and example of our western civilization, nevertheless intends to use that western freedom to disrupt the state'.[33] Nor did missionaries proffer a contrary view. Conservative in theology, their private faith did not rebuke structural sin.

African opinion was anyway divided. As Kikuyu militancy rose, other ethnic leaders withdrew from KAU. With few urban workers or farm 'squatters', most non-Kikuyu found local government satisfied their more equable energies. Kikuyu themselves became more at odds. Their conservatives hated the vulgarisation of politics; to their saved Christians the 'blood of the Lamb' transcended animal sacrifice. Both refused the oath. By early 1952 Mau Mau intimidation had provoked a 'resistance movement'. Battle lines were forming. To a London friend Kenyatta seemed trapped between them.[34]

By August the police commissioner thought Mau Mau beyond his power to contain. He had created a 'special bureau' to bring activists to trial, but witnesses either recanted or, increasingly, were murdered. To uncloak its enemy, the bureau turned to tracing links between the covert Mau Mau and overt KAU leaderships.[35] Settler leaders demanded of government that KAU be summarily 'dealt with', and its nationalism declared seditious. Statements to police should be taken as legal proofs; judges must adapt to the political situation. Otherwise whites 'might take matters into their own hands'. The attorney general (AG), John Whyatt, reported all this with

[33] Mitchell to Creech Jones, 30 May 1947, Annex, in Ronald Hyam, ed,. *The Labour Government and the End of Empire* (London: British Documents on the End of Empire, Series A, Volume 2, Part I), p. 137; *East African Standard*, [*EAS*] Nairobi, 19 Aug. 1955: 'Killing Urged on Banned Record Song'; *EAS*, 10 July 1953, reporting Blundell in legislative council.

[34] Bruce Berman and John Lonsdale, 'Louis Leakey's Mau Mau', *History and Anthropology*, 5, 2 (1991), p. 182; Peter Abrahams, 'The Blacks', in Langston Hughes, ed., *An African Treasury* (New York, 1960), pp. 50–62 (recording a visit to Kenyatta in 1952).

[35] M. S. O'Rorke, 'Kikuyu Political Activity', 14 Aug. 1952, KNA: GO 3/2/72; Ian Henderson, evidence, Jan. 1959, Macharia Trial Transcript vol. 1, pp. 128–30, 167, 170, KNA: RR 9/21. R. W. Heather, 'Counterinsurgency and Intelligence in Kenya, 1952–56' (Cambridge PhD thesis, 1993), ch. 1.

ironic alarm: 'the thought flashed through my mind, "This must be what it is like to be present at a coup d'etat."'[36]

The colonial office (CO) woke to the need to save Kenya from settler capture. Mitchell had retired in June 1952; Baring would not succeed him until late September. It was a bad time for decision. Kenya's law officers drew up 'repressive measures' – the CO's term – heeding private deputation to avoid dictation by white uproar. The new bills allowed affidavits to be proofs, to protect witnesses; imposed corporal punishment on oath administrators; licensed the press; and restricted motor-traffic after dark (it was the mix of atavism and modernity that made Mau Mau so sinister). The CO liked none of this – it looked like surrender – but with minor amendments let the legislation through. It saw Nairobi's need to soothe a white minority 'which was either tending to panic or out to make the best of what seemed to be a good opportunity, or a bit of both'. But repression on its own would lose the battle for African opinion. The CO sent Baring out with a checklist of racial inequalities, urged on him the need to get liberal white support for a 'second prong' of social reform, and wondered aloud about 'busting' or 'buying' Kenyatta.[37]

Baring could scarcely have bought Kenyatta. The latter had a mass following to satisfy; his caution had risked much from his militants. His price in land and representation would have been unthinkable to whites. Baring did however contemplate an interview.[38] Events intervened. He went on tour. Everybody he met, black and white, urged swift surgery on Mau Mau's cancer. A senior Kikuyu chief was murdered, white farms attacked. The iron was hot; Baring struck. He cabled Oliver Lyttelton, Conservative secretary of state, to get his approval for an emergency. The case seemed strong. Kenyatta and his KAU henchmen were the planners or movers of Mau Mau crime. If they were not taken out, Kikuyu chiefs would change sides to save their skins. Other tribes would defect. The crisis would break after the arrests, in the grace period before detention specified by one of the new laws or during the judicial enquiry required by an old deportation ordinance. Kikuyu would revolt, whites resist. An emergency would result. It were better to have it first. With the extra powers and troops already in place, he could smother the risk that by beheading Mau Mau he might ignite civil war.[39] Baring's instinct was that in a crisis legal due process was a hazard, not a resource.

36 Notes on Discussion at Government House, 8 August 1952; KNA, GO 3/2/72; Whyatt to Rogers, 2 Sept. 1952, PRO: CO 822/437/1.

37 Draft legislation in PRO files CO 822/437 and 822/544. Sir Thomas Lloyd to Henry Potter (acting governor), 23 Sept. 1952: CO 822/437/35.

38 Anthony Clayton, *Counter-insurgency in Kenya 1952–60* (Nairobi, 1976), p. 5 (Clayton's informant was Whyatt: personal communication).

39 Baring to Lyttelton, telegram 616, 10 Oct. 1952, PRO: CO 822/443/1.

British troops flew in to reinforce the local African battalions and balance the white police reservists. Kenyatta and over one hundred others, leaders of KAU and of Kikuyu independent schools, were arrested in the small hours of 21 October. The police seized Kenyatta's books and papers and loaded them – one and a half tons, it was said – into a pickup van for future study. The seven-year Mau Mau emergency had started.

Philip Rogers, wisest head at the CO's East Africa desk and a future permanent secretary at the ministry of health, summed up the danger to British policy. London had been urging Kenya's whites to let Africans rise as fast as they proved capable. That might prevent an inevitable black nationalism from setting its face against the racial co-operation on which the future depended. This middle road of gradualism was now ambushed on either flank. Mau Mau, one extreme, had to be destroyed, to give room to African moderates. Yet tough action unleashed tough settlers, the other extreme. That would alienate all shades of African opinion. The answer was to press liberal whites, many of them farmers, to ally with their black counterparts. The CO had put that to Baring before he left. It was more difficult now. Nor could London offer prizes for such courage. There could be no early self-government, long demanded by settlers in order to keep their lead in any African awakening. In the British view colonialism had yet to complete its task; more African development was the only sure basis for multi-racialism. Both white and black had to accept that social advance needed political compromise – a thesis for which Kenya's history offered small comfort. Rogers found it difficult to see the way forward.[40]

Margery Perham, Oxford's moral tutor to the empire, argued similarly in the London *Times* – that whites must ally with rather than thwart African ambition if colonial progress were not to collapse in racial conflict. Kenya's police commissioner despaired on reading her; moral revolution was unthinkable in the present bitterness. White police reservists had detained suspects with a brutality he thought 'crazy'. Many thought this 'black and tannery' was swelling Mau Mau's ranks. Yet whites denounced the minor reforms mooted under the 'second prong' as appeasement of terrorism.[41] Kingsley Martin, journalism's friend to south Asian nationalism, split them into 'the "bash 'em" and "bash 'em but what afterwards?" schools'. Public meetings demanded instant death for oath administrators caught in the act of inciting treason, a concentration camp on every farm, self-government 'under European leadership'.[42]

40 Philip Rogers, minute, 24 Oct. 1952, PRO: CO 822/440/195.

41 Margery Mumford to Ethel Rayne and Margery Perham, 27 Oct. and 23 Nov. 1952 (by courtesy of Mary Bull); Margery Perham, 'A changing continent', *The Times*, 28 Oct. 1952; Kingsley Martin, 'Kenya Report', *New Statesman and Nation* (15 Nov. 1952).

42 Martin, 'The Settlers' Case', *New Statesman and Nation* (29 Nov. 1952); *EAS*, 28 Nov. 1952 (several reports) and 1 Jan. 1953: 'Settlers Call for Vigorous Action.'

The British had little to offer the moderates on either side. The law's majesty was the least and the basis of all else. Only if defendants were seen to be shielded from political vengeance in open court, could the sword of state be said to cut cleanly. Due process offered the only hope that Kenyatta might be discredited as a criminal rather than followed as martyr. Only then might the voice of multi-racial moderation be heard once more. The legal forms would have to be unusually pedantic. The crown must prove itself anti-Mau Mau alone, neither pro-settler nor anti-African.[43]

IV. DISAPPEARING WITNESSES AND A PRESUMPTION OF GUILT

Once Mau Mau's alleged leaders were detained and the crisis, as he thought, past, Baring aimed to get 'a case if possible for prosecution'; if not, then deportations after judicial enquiry; and, only as a last resort, executive detention orders. Lyttelton flew out and told settlers not to shoot on sight; force must be subject to law. He also warned the governor that parliament would give trouble if Kenyatta were not soon brought to trial. Baring's own problems were different, the inherent lack of evidence for secretive activity and the lack of African witnesses ready to risk death by testifying against Mau Mau. In the past two months alone twenty-seven possible crown witnesses had been murdered.[44]

On 2 November Whyatt decided to prosecute. He had the evidence, if his witnesses spoke up. Police protection was normal in the circumstances; but his plan contained a double menace, thinkable only in respect of native subjects. If witnesses repeated in court what they had already sworn, their home community – doubtless penetrated by Mau Mau – would be charged with their care, 'under threat of collective fine'. If they retracted, their evidence would be treated as hostile; their approach to the police would be known; they would get no protection. The fate of the twenty-seven suggested that was a death warrant.[45] Four days later a new witness, Rawson Macharia, 'bush lawyer' and former KAU branch official, appeared with apparently key evidence of Kenyatta's part in a Mau Mau initiation. Whyatt's junior, Anthony Somerhough, deputy public prosecutor (DPP), decided to see him. This was irregular, witnesses should be handled by the police alone, but he wanted to see that Macharia was not a crank. The interview determined his approach to the trial.

[43] Lyttelton to Baring, 5 March 1953, PRO: CO 822/440/204.

[44] Baring to Gorell Barnes, 27 Oct. 1952, PRO: CO 822/450/1; David Percox, 'The British Campaign in Kenya, 1952–1956' (Lancaster MA thesis, 1996), pp. 39–40; Baring to Lennox-Boyd, 13 Dec. 1958: CO 822/1848/35.

[45] J. F. Marnan, 'Rawson Macaria [*sic*] and the Kapenguria Trials', 8 Dec. 1958, in Baring to Lennox-Boyd, 18 Dec. 1958, PRO: CO 822/1849/76.

Somerhough was impressed by Macharia and struck by two features of his account. First, many Kikuyu believed (wrongly) that Kenyatta had visited Germany in the war, to study Hitler; he had a parallel government, as the Nazis had before taking power. How far the DPP's Nuremberg experience as a war-crimes prosecutor made this latter allegation plausible one cannot tell, but he was to draw analogies between Mau Mau and the Nazi *führer prinzip* in court. Macharia also stated, with truth, that Kenyatta came from a line of witchdoctors; Africans looked on him with dread; none would dare face him in open court, however much they hated what he stood for. The DPP was left with the fear that the law could not deal with a man 'who commands awe on superstitious grounds as well as from the presence of an unlimited number of thugs'.[46] With a defendant compared to the empire's worst foe yet beyond the reach of the law, it is not unreasonable to suppose that the crown would take any procedural short cut suggested by the ingenuity of the legal mind.

A trial of uncertain outcome would gamble on white opinion; capitulation to white clamour for action took an equal risk with African compliance. But no Briton dreamed that Kenyatta could escape sentence; there was a universal presumption of his guilt. The police had eighteen files on him. Conviction after due process – if only witnesses kept their life and nerve – was clearly the safest way forward, and that seemed assured. Officials joked about it. During debate on the repressive laws introduced after the settler 'coup', the solicitor general rebutted a call that they be confined to Mau Mau offences alone with the thought that 'there is no magic in the name Mau Mau. By to-morrow it might be Jo Jo.'[47]

Belief in one man's guilt rested on white prejudice about Africans in general. Their 'tribal mind' was conformist, not free-thinking like the British; tribal politics was conspiratorial, not competitive; new ideas had to spring from an educated mind or external influence or religious error, or all three. Kenyatta was steeped in outside knowledge, anthropology and, it was (again wrongly) supposed, communism. The police circularised a digest of his book, accordingly. Rogers, the cool man at the CO, was certain Kenyatta was Mau Mau's 'brains'. Baring thought his private schools were its 'mainspring'; their equivalents had taught Afrikaner nationalism in South Africa. In Kenyatta, as the official history later put it, 'all the Kikuyu organizational strands eventually met'.[48] While historians now 'split'

[46] Note of conversation, 6 Nov. 1952, copy in PRO: CO 822/1848/27; Kapenguria Trial Transcript vol. 4, pp. 839–40, KNA: RR 9/8.

[47] Somerhough to Webber, 16 Dec. 1958, PRO: CO 822/1848/56; *EAS*, 26 Sept. 1952: 'Legislature Debates new "Unrest" Measures.'

[48] Mumford to Rayne, 27 Oct. and 1 Nov. 1952; Rogers, minute, 11 Oct.; Baring to Gorell Barnes, 27 Oct. 1952: CO 822/443 and 822/450/1; *Historical Survey of the Origins and Growth of Mau Mau*, Cmnd. 1030 (1960), p. 51.

African opposition politics, the government and white opinion then 'lumped' it together, moderate and militant, cautious elder and fiery upstart; Kenyatta's prosecution did so too, and it was a premise which his defence, possibly knowingly, accepted.

The presumption of guilt raised doubts about the trial from the start. Defence lawyers were critical, naturally. Their leading counsel thought the prosecution overconfident and careless. Another felt standards of proof were sure to slip, undermining the authority of any conviction. But it was not just the defence lawyers; a white observer thought some settlers uneasy and Africans mystified.[49] The majesty of the law did not beyond doubt cast out partisan white interest with pedantic procedure. Nor did Kenyatta's criminalisation allow more legal room for African politics than before, indeed the reverse.

V. CONTRADICTIONS OF IMPERIAL AND COLONIAL HEGEMONY

In setting up the trial Nairobi was besieged by contrasts between its own colonial and the wider imperial legal worlds. The legal cement of the empire-commonwealth was the common law, based on the universal validity of judicial precedent and respect for the liberties of individuals who are deemed to be equal. It was more of a tie than parliamentary democracy, the crown or even cricket. Kenya's racial order, however, rested on collective and unequal rights and disabilities, seen for instance in the contrast between the right of settlers to trial by jury and its denial, as if a privilege, to Africans. Other aspects of the trial, the defence counsel's provenance, the court's geography, the judge's reputation, the relations between judiciary, Nairobi government and Westminster – all raised the question whether imperial hegemony was compatible with colonial authority. If it were not then, from the dock, Kenyatta suggested a way out, not through law but by political will.[50]

49 D. N. Pritt, *The Defence Accuses* (London, 1966), pp. 71–80; Peter Evans, *Law and Disorder: Scenes from Kenya Life* (London, 1956), chs. 5, 19; Margery Mumford, 'O! Brother Man' (typescript, 1953), pp. 275, 506.

50 There are many accounts of the trial. D. H. Rawcliffe, *The Struggle for Kenya* (London, 1954), ch. 8, thought prosecution weak and defence evasive. Ione Leigh, *In the Shadow of Mau Mau* (London, 1954), Pt III, was hostile to Kenyatta but satisfied with the crown. Montagu Slater reproduced ten per cent of the transcript, of which Pritt's copy is at the London School of Economics, in *The Trial of Jomo Kenyatta* (London, 1955). He omitted most defence evidence, to show at length how weak the crown case was. Gaps in testimony, however, can hide problems for the defence. Evans, *Law and Disorder*, gave valuable legal insights. George Delf, *Jomo Kenyatta: Toward Truth about 'The Light of Kenya'* (London, 1961), ch. 10, offered little analysis. Chaman Lall, 'Wonderful Opportunity Lost', in A. H. Patel, ed., *Struggle for Release Jomo and Colleagues* (Nairobi, 1963), pp. 48–52, recalled an attempted out-of-court settlement that is denied by others present. Pritt, *The Defence*

The rump of KAU, led by its acting general secretary Joe Murumbi, recruited the defence.[51] No local white lawyer accepted the brief; either they dared not break racial ranks or KAU did not put them to that test – the evidence is contradictory. But it was an open bar; anyone qualified imperially could be briefed in Kenya; for whites that inclusiveness was hard to bear. The defence was led by Denis Pritt from Britain, former MP and communist by repute yet also Queen's Counsel, to rumoured African delight: fancy the Queen sending to help Kenyatta! His team included Chaman Lall, Balliol man and friend to Nehru; Dudley Thompson, black Jamaican, wartime Royal Air Force bomber crew and Rhodes scholar; Chief Davies, respected by the colonial government of Nigeria; and two Asian members of the local bar, Achhroo Kapila and Fitz de Souza. None could be more imperially professional; all had dined at London's Inns of Court; but only Pritt, red yet white, could enter any white-owned hotel in Kenya.

Baring was appalled by this multi-racial plague of lawyers; they would turn a criminal trial into a racial contest. Settlers were furious; African moderates would be ignored. He strove to stem the legal tide. Lyttelton could not help; defendants had a British right to choose their counsel; barristers, once briefed, were entitled to come. Nor would Baring's fellow governors in West Africa lend a hand; if Kenya banned their men they feared ructions in their own nationalist backyards. London was nervous of Nehru; post-imperial goodwill counted for more than a colonial governor's comfort. Baring got the worst of all worlds. He had to accept most of the KAU team. His refusal to take them all tested his credit, not least with the secretary of state, who had a hard time in the Commons. The makeup of the defence counsel proved the socially – and in Kenya's case racially – levelling potential of court hearings. But if here was an unwanted, niggardly but nonetheless real intimation of hegemony, all else about the trial's setting extinguished its glow.[52]

The political geography of the trial excited suspicion. It should have been held in Nairobi. Many of the alleged offences had been committed in or

footnote 50 (*cont.*)
Accuses, was robustly partisan. Guy Arnold, *Kenyatta and the Politics of Kenya* (London, 1974), ch. 8, and Murray-Brown, *Kenyatta*, ch. 20, depended on Slater. Dudley J. Thompson, *From Kingston to Kenya: the Making of a Pan-Africanist Lawyer* (Dover, MA, 1993), ch. 8, gave details not found elsewhere. None read the files. I refer to the 8–volume Kapenguria trial transcript, of 2,064 pages (KNA: RR 9/5–12) as KTT, with volume number. Correspondence on the Macharia trial and its 9–volume transcript (MTT), of 1,618 pages (KNA: RR 9/21–30) tells how the earlier case was assembled. Both transcripts were photocopied by kind permission of the Archives' director, Mr Musembi.

[51] Murumbi MS, ch. 7 (seen by courtesy of Mrs Sheila Murumbi).

[52] Communications between London, Nairobi, Accra, Lagos, Khartoum and New Delhi, 29 Nov. to 16 Dec. 1952, PRO: CO 822/452; House of Commons *Debates*, 508 (5th ser.), cc. 1764–70, 4 Dec. 1952.

near the city; the accused had been arrested there; most witnesses lived nearby. It is a legal maxim that truth is more likely told before a public with local knowledge; that is what 'open court' means. Yet Whyatt felt well justified in holding the trial 300 miles away. Nairobi was the centre of subversion and Mau Mau had added a clause to their oath, if need be to rescue Kenyatta; witnesses might refuse to testify in a hostile city; the police could not guarantee public order; Kapenguria, by contrast, was in a closed, outlying district, to which entry by all races was controlled. Finally, the charges were such as a magistrate could hear; and since a magistrate's court, unlike a judge's, required no committal hearing before a full trial, the witnesses' nerve would not be twice tested in court. To use a court in Nairobi would reduce that advantage; Kapenguria was as far as one could go while remaining in the cool green highlands.

Kapenguria had one snag in law. Its court lacked jurisdiction, authority to try the case. The remedy required ingenuity – in some legal opinion a trick. No offence had been committed nearby nor, another title to jurisdiction, had the accused been arrested there. They were already in custody. Somerhough saw a solution. The six were taken to Kapenguria and released, free men. Whereupon they were rearrested, charged, and remanded for trial. A week earlier around twenty crown witnesses had gone, in covered lorries, to the police training school, eighty miles from Nairobi. There they were protected, prepared for their court ordeal and – or so it was later said – rehearsed in their bought and perjured evidence. The witnesses certainly cost the crown over £10,000.[53]

If Kapenguria was suspect, its magistrate was more so. At least one magistrate refused the AG's invitation to preside, it was said because, sharing a judicial disdain for the ruse of jurisdiction, he thought so important a case should be heard by a judge, after committal.[54] A senior judge would admittedly carry weight; but he would have to sit as a mere magistrate to avoid the witnesses' double jeopardy. Another artful dodge lay to hand in the recent local retirement of judge Ransley Thacker, who was augmenting his annual pension of £474, one third of his former pay, by private legal practice in Nairobi.[55] Accepting appointment as special magistrate, he had all

[53] Mumford to Rayne, 27 Oct. 1952; Mumford, 'O! Brother Man', p. 196; crown brief, 12 June 1953, p. 12, PRO: CO 822/492, in item 61; Henderson in MTT 1, p. 143, 29 Jan. 1959; Whyatt to Vasey (Kenya Treasury) 10 Nov. 1952, in Baring to Lennox-Boyd, 18 Dec. 1958, PRO: 822/1848/76; judgement in the Macharia trial, 4 April 1959, in Rawson Macharia, *The Truth about the Trial of Jomo Kenyatta* (Nairobi, 1991), p. 286.

[54] Evidence is guarded; see Baring's letters and Somerhough's note, April–May 1953, PRO: CO 822/453/1 to 4; Somerhough to Whyatt, 21 July 1953, in Baring to Barnes, 11 Aug. 1953: CO 82/483/97; Pritt, *The Defence Accuses*, p. 78.

[55] Supreme court to tax commissioner, 21 Dec. 1953; establishments to accountant general, 22 Oct. 1952, KNA: Judicial 1/2105 and 1/2097.

the seniority one could wish: Fiji's attorney general in the 1930s, a supreme court judge in Kenya since 1938 and, more than once, acting chief justice. Settlers, however, thought him 'a sound chap', friendly to prosecutions, and at Kapenguria there would be no jury. Still more open to defence objection, he was now a settler himself.[56]

The chief justice backed the DPP's legal sleight of hand. Sir Hector Hearne, in his last post before retirement, rejected the defence application to change venue and judge. At the hearing, Pritt held that far Kapenguria could not be open court; for the state to 'seem to pick its judge' aroused suspicion. Also, while earlier acquitting one of the accused, Kubai, on a charge of attempted murder, Thacker had called him 'unworthy of belief'; an impartial trial was now impossible. Hearne was more persuaded by the need for security. Four days earlier, the black city councillor, former KAU secretary and convinced moderate Tom Mbotela, a possible crown witness, had been hacked to death within a mile of the courts.[57]

The trial opened on 3 December. Kapenguria seemed to be not open court but settler picnic party. There was no majesty in the converted schoolhouse and much force on show. Armoured cars stood outside, an armed policeman by the judge. The only Africans present were the defendants, witnesses, police, settlers' servants and Murumbi, Pritt's link with Nairobi. There was white laughter in court, at its most boorishly ignorant on greeting Kenyatta's complaint that the Crown Lands Ordinance of 1915, to which he attributed most African troubles, was passed when Africans were dying in their thousands in the imperial cause. Whites now found that comically incredible. The nearest town with hotels, shops and telephone was Kitale, thirty miles away, a centre of settler extremism. While denying any disrespect to imperial command its men volunteered as commandos; the police guarded Pritt against them. The colour-bar in bars and hotels split up the multi-racial defence team; Thacker stayed at the white club. British press reporters watched with incredulity.[58] The prosecution scarcely looked like the sword of blindfold justice.

The press, however, helped the defence to act as shield. Kapenguria was closed locally but its proceedings were wired to the world; even the Russians read Reuters. Pritt daily protested against his handicaps; questions were

[56] Evans, *Law and Disorder*, pp. 50–3; Pritt, *The Defence Accuses*, p. 78; Pritt's cross-examination of Somerhough in Macharia trial, MTT 1, pp. 42–4, 27 Jan. 1959.

[57] *The Times* (London), 2 Dec. 1952; Cmnd 1030, p. 89, for Thacker on Kubai.

[58] Kenyatta, in KTT 4, p. 928, 27 Jan. 1953. Commandos: Mumford to Rayne, 10 Jan. 1953; *EAS*, 6 and 13 Feb. 1953. Local conditions: Evans, *Law and Disorder*, pp. 53, 58–9; Leigh, *In the Shadow*, pp. 98, 102; Pritt, *The Defence Accuses*, pp. 82–7.

asked in the Commons. Lyttelton said Pritt was content; four Labour MPs cabled Kitale to ask; Pritt responded with his troubles. Kapenguria was half a day's drive from law libraries and witnesses, and closed to the African public, as Kenya had been closed to some duly briefed lawyers; in all it was 'a denial of justice', an incendiary phrase. Since the MPs would inform the British press, Pritt showed his telegram to the *East African Standard* so as not to penalise local readers. Thacker read the *Standard* and was hurt; Pritt was still complaining, 'not to any court but to the world', despite the supreme court's ruling that justice could be done at Kapenguria. Pritt tried to explain that it was government, not the court, that was obstructing justice. Thacker retorted, as if to blame the defendants, that the difficulties of distance were necessary to security. He refused to continue until Pritt's action was tried for contempt.[59]

The question of contempt turned, at bottom, on how far the trial was 'political'. Thacker blamed Pritt for that imputation, Pritt blamed the DPP; it was he who proposed to prove Mau Mau was KAU's militant arm. Lyttelton feared the domestic repercussions; the four MPs said he had misled the House; others thought Whyatt risked contempt of parliament if he charged Pritt with contempt of court. Quentin Hogg, MP, a future Conservative Lord Chancellor, offered to defend the communist Pritt.[60] He had no need; Kenya's judges agreed privately there was no case to answer; Pritt had rebuked government not Thacker. The latter threatened to resign if the matter were not brought to court. Whyatt then moved the case for contempt, perhaps because he hoped to get Pritt removed from the case; possibly to show settler critics that he could be firm. Pritt, he argued, had excited prejudice against Kapenguria with intent to throw doubt on any conviction. But the supreme court again agreed with Pritt and, adding financial insult to professional injury, awarded costs against Whyatt.[61]

Contempt was a lawyers' issue; all their precedents were English. To the defendants the case was a Christmas break. The contrast made a point. The 'mysterious force' that Churchill trusted to uphold colonial rule lay in Westminster, not in Kenya's courts; it always had, but rarely was that made so plain. The episode confirmed Kapenguria's political status; Labour MPs had served notice that Kenyatta was their concern; the secretary of state had listened. Here was a curb on 'rough-and ready' late-colonialism that Churchill could not have foreseen. In a world remade by imperial and

[59] KTT 1, pp. 305–38, 15–16 Dec. 1952; Pritt, *The Defence Accuses*, pp. 88–93.

[60] KTT 1, pp. 307, 310, 15 Dec. 1952; Baring, Lyttelton and Whyatt exchanges, 16–18 Dec. 1952, PRO: CO 822/452/59 *et seq.*; Roland Brown, former AG of Tanzania, to author, 27 Nov. 1996.

[61] Baring and Lyttelton exchanges, 19 Dec. 1952 to 13 Jan. 1953, PRO: CO 822/452/77 *et seq.*; Pritt, *The Defence Accuses*, pp. 95–7; Nairobi's file on Pritt (KNA: RR 9/19) is heavily weeded.

anti-imperial energies, African leaders now had a global audience. A governor's discretion, even the autonomy of a local rule of law, had become more difficult to square with parliament's sovereignty.

Baring no longer controlled external information but failed to grasp the implications for his rule. He intended to restore the contradiction – unsustainable now it was open to scrutiny – between the fusion of ground-level power and legal freedoms above. He hoped a conviction at Kapenguria would, by releasing a flow of evidence, permit him to lift the emergency; but at the same time insisted that power must remain with the executive.[62] Scandals over the unlawful use of force soon showed that lack of legal restraint was disastrous even in an emergency; but lawful hegemony can also lay traps for rulers. While concessions to imperial dominion could be privately negotiated with London, as over the entry of defence lawyers, legal due process was different. Its unscripted public theatre was unpredictable. Despite the weight of guilt presumed to lie upon Kenyatta, officials had enough respect for legal forms to fear an explosion were he found innocent. Press reporters, more cynically, thought the crown case so weak that some wanted to ask Thacker, 'When you find Jomo guilty what excuse are you going to make?'[63]

VI. THE TRIAL THAT NEVER WAS

There were seven Kenyatta trials in all. The Kapenguria trial opened on 3 December 1952. With fifty-eight days in court, counsel made their final speeches three months later, 'approximately as long as it took Napoleon to get from Elba to Waterloo' as Pritt put it with an eye to the fate of empires.[64] Thacker gave judgement on 8 April 1953, sentencing Kenyatta and the other five to the maximum term available, seven years' imprisonment with hard labour, with a recommendation for indefinite restriction thereafter. Judgement was given at the seventh and last trial almost exactly six years later on 4 April 1959. Why were there so many?

First, Kapenguria became a trial that never was, on the defence's appeal to the supreme court in July 1953. The government had assigned Thacker to the Northern province, when Kapenguria was in the Rift Valley! Somerhough had undone his own sleight of hand. He had created jurisdiction by the re-arrest of the defendants at Kapenguria; he removed it again by misplacing their magistrate in the official gazette. In the Commons,

[62] Baring to Lyttelton, 24 Nov. 1952, PRO: CO 822/450/10.

[63] Barnes to Lloyd, 19 Feb. 1953, PRO: CO 822/440/181; Mumford to Rayne, 8 Dec. 1952. Cf Richard Rathbone, 'Law, Lawyers and Politics in Ghana in the 1940s', ch. 10 in Engels and Marks, *Contesting Colonial Hegemony*.

[64] KTT 7, p. 1838, 2 Mar. 1953.

Geoffrey Bing summed up the ruling: 'this magistrate was completely incapable and incompetent of holding this trial and the whole proceedings were an entire nullity'. The court ordered a re-trial, as it had directed Churchill's host long before, and again on a technicality. But had not Churchill insisted that pedantry is the stuff of the defendant's shield? The crown counter-appealed to the appeal court for eastern Africa; this ruled for the crown, restored the convictions and remitted the case to the supreme court, to hear the defence appeal on its merits. Meanwhile Pritt had petitioned the privy council in London to back the supreme court view that Kapenguria lacked jurisdiction. The privy council dismissed him; the case reverted to Kenya's supreme court. This confirmed five of the six convictions but the man reprieved, Achieng Oneko, one of the two non-Kikuyu defendants, was detained nonetheless. Pritt again appealed to the privy council, in order to test points not only of law but also of fact. Their lordships rejected this second petition in July 1954. There matters rested until, in late 1958, Macharia swore an affidavit that the crown had 'procured and suborned' him and six others, to give false evidence in 1952. Pritt defended him as a means to refresh Kenyatta's cause, but Macharia was convicted of swearing a false affidavit. The court accepted that he had lied at Kapenguria, but for his own reasons, not because he had been bribed.[65] What was this legal procession all about?

It was a cavalcade of authority, the majesty of the law in pedantic array. All its cast – judges, counsel, defendants and witnesses – played the ambiguous game of hegemony by which power is said to strengthen its grasp by being brought within its subjects' reach. Kenyatta, who might have refused to accept the imperial law's legitimacy, as nationalists have done before and since, played the game and played it well. The crown, which could not evade the contest while upholding its own authority, played splendidly, badly, and at great cost. Due process was intended to produce forensic fact by shutting politics out. Politics kept breaking in; the court, despite every precaution, was a public arena, and the law a double-edged instrument. It seemed the crown had won; its sword of judgement beheaded Mau Mau; its various publics (Mau Mau fighters included) differed on the effectiveness of that dramatic stroke. To many it appeared that Kenyatta had used the law's shield to turn the blow, to convert hegemony from mask of empire to argument for nationhood.

To Kapenguria, then, process and judgement, before returning to the grand and contradictory parade. Trials should exclude much evidence, to protect fact from prejudice. Historians, for whom setting and sentiment are

[65] House of Commons *Debates*, 5th ser., vol. 517, c. 2066, 15 July 1953; process summarised in Eric Griffith-Jones to F. D. Webber, 8 April 1961, PRO: CO 822/2930/1; also, Macharia, *Trial of Jomo Kenyatta*, pp. 310–14, 274–99.

the stuff of life, are fortunate that Thacker's judicial control was not up to the task. He was often supine before Somerhough and Pritt's sharper skills, until gathering up what reads on the page like a pipsqueak dignity. The defence thought much of the prosecution evidence inadmissible, not accepting Thacker's ruling that the crown could enquire into the period before August 1950 when Mau Mau was banned. By hearing earlier evidence, he allowed the DPP to build a historical case for Kenyatta's maturing subversion. As if to balance the crown's peregrinations, however, Thacker also let the defence put what he silently deplored as 'classic examples' of leading questions on Kenyatta's political life; and that could just as well be seen as a history of British deafness to openly stated African distress.[66]

Kapenguria was poor theatre all the same. Its moments of drama, spurred on by Pritt's diabetic liability to afternoon tempers, turned on legal rather than material issues. Otherwise it moved at half speed, interpreted between English and Kikuyu for the benefit of one of the six. The handicaps put on the defence also meant that stories repeated themselves. With no committal hearing, the six could not tell what detailed case they had to answer; since ignorant cross-examination of witnesses is futile, Pritt often reserved that task, consulted his clients, and returned to it at a later date. Finally, the crown followed no clear narrative but piled up unrelated facts. Taken together, Somerhough argued, they proved a cumulative case; as he later recalled, 'it was a question of how many stones made a heap'.[67] Only in the trial's third month did he tie the string of incidents to a theory of political continuity. His strategy had three causes. He had scant evidence anyway; he had to drop a star witness; and presumption of guilt always had a prejudiced history to fall back on.

Somerhough turned the weakness of his evidence into a virtue, asking the press to grant his witnesses anonymity as protection against Mau Mau. Pritt thought that an encouragement to perjury. 'There was no question whatever of perjury', the DPP replied, 'but there was a question of their committing suicide.' Thacker was impressed: in his judgement he first denied but then affirmed that witnesses were more likely to risk their life for the truth than a lie.[68] The DPP congratulated himself on having any evidence at all. This focused on four aspects of presumed Mau Mau activity – oath initiations, propaganda, management, and the 1952 stump campaign. The first African witness he called was Rawson Macharia.

Macharia was among the witnesses to six supposed initiations. The

66 Magistrate's notes vol. 2, pp. 226, 228, 27 Jan. 1953, KNA: RR 9/2.

67 Under cross-examination by Pritt, 27 Jan. 1959: MTT 1, p. 88.

68 Somerhough, opening statement, 3 Dec. 1952, KTT 1, p. 13. For his changing view on the likelihood of perjury see Thacker's judgement, KNA: MAC/KEN 68/1, pp. 4, 16.

three which allegedly involved Kenyatta had all occurred in March 1950, five months before Mau Mau was proscribed and its management became illegal. Macharia's was one of them. Pritt objected; Thacker ruled that such earlier evidence was acceptable corroboration, provided there was also evidence for management in the period of Mau Mau's ban.[69] A latent presumption of the seamless continuity of Kenyatta's politics was thus present from the start. Many days also went in the interpretation of propaganda, as found in three booklets of *nyimbo* – songs frequently set to hymn tunes – printed in quantity in late 1952. The translations were made by Louis Leakey, white Kenya's only intellectual of renown, to the world a palaeontologist, to settlers a 'white Kikuyu', born on a mission station in 1903, fluent in Kikuyu and yet, as one of their own firstborn, living proof that Kenya was a white man's country. Valuable as sources of political imagery, with Kenyatta portrayed as Moses or Christ the liberator, the *nyimbo* proved only that politics was becoming popular religion.

The question of management focused on a letter and a committee meeting. The letter was one of only two relevant documents found in Kenyatta's house. It dated from 1948: the continuity was lengthening. The letter also dealt with KCA business. The KCA had been unlawful since 1940. Nonetheless, Kenyatta's invitation to a meeting was admissible in evidence only on the crown's premise that KCA and Mau Mau were the same body differently named. The KAU executive committee meeting, the only incident that brought all six defendants together, was in the post-proscription period, in April 1952, but its meaning was contested. The crown claimed that the executive tried to force a constitutionalist KAU branch at Limuru, in southern Kikuyuland, to join its militant neighbour, Chura. The defence saw only a politically neutral, purely managerial, response to government limitations on the number of public meetings.

In his opening address, Somerhough had laid stress on the stump campaign. While this had been an ostensibly KAU affair, he would prove Kenyatta had used it to manage Mau Mau. He had two self-contradictory episodes in mind. After a public meeting at the Rift Valley township of Ol Kalou, for instance, Kenyatta was alleged to have privately cautioned his closest associates against too much violence; but a 'wild outbreak' of Mau Mau activity had then followed a rally further north, at Thomson's Falls. To testify to the latter the DPP summoned the DC, Neil Loudon. Pritt protested; sequence in time could never be cause – or not without the eye-witness evidence that no DC could give. Somerhough gave way. It was a key

[69] Thacker's ruling, 3 Dec. 1952, KTT 1, p. 16A.

moment. The centrepiece of Baring's justification for calling an emergency had fallen to due process.[70]

The crown closed its case in late January; Pritt submitted that there was none to answer. The evidence since August 1950 was thin; it dealt in reputation as much as action; and yet, on the stump, Kenyatta had publicly denounced Mau Mau. Thacker ruled against him. This was the cue for political history to elbow recent incidents from centre stage. Kenyatta was the first defendant to testify. Led by Chaman Lall and cross-examined by the DPP, he was in the dock for over two weeks. He declared himself a constitutionalist; he had taken his people's troubles to the archbishop of Canterbury and the moderator of the Church of Scotland, to Sir Philip Mitchell and his DCs. He reminded the court – and press – of the history of land, the 1915 Crown Lands Ordinance (CLO) that had enfeoffed Africans to the crown, and the Devonshire declaration that had made their interests paramount. Thacker confronted this moral history with legal fact. Asking to study the CLO and being given the 1948 amendment, he could find in it no reference to an African tenantry. Nor had there been such in the 1915 original; only when combined with Kenya's annexation as a colony in 1920 had it had that effect on African status. Kenyatta was morally right; he could not prove it. His credibility was undermined on the record, not merely in the white imagination.

On Kenyatta's last day in the dock, Somerhough summed up – not what he had learned in court but with the conspiracy thesis that was white common knowledge. Thus, Kenyatta had imposed on the KCA, then Mau Mau – they were the same – oaths that bound recruits to force whites out; he had raised Mau Mau into a religious cult, with the *nyimbo* its hymns. These, by intent, had permeated KAU. His denials of Mau Mau, of which the defence had made much, had been impostures, using the evasive ellipsis for which the Kikuyu language was known. Pritt protested, point by point, that this thesis was entirely unproven in evidence. Kenyatta rebutted Somerhough in his final speech before sentence with a loftier thesis of his own. To oppose injustice was not to stir up strife; KAU was the only body working for racial harmony; his colleagues were human; they had families; they could never condone violence. Violence – he quoted a Kikuyu proverb – could not bring harmony. He stood for African rights, 'so that Africans may find a place among the nations'.[71]

In his judgement, Thacker accepted Somerhough's thesis; like other whites, he was a lumper. Under cover of KAU the educated had used the

[70] KTT 1, p. 11, 3 Dec., and pp. 154–8, 10 Dec. 1952. For what Loudon might have said, see his Laikipia district report 1952, KNA: DC/LKA 1/3.

[71] Pritt's submission in KTT 3, pp. 659–774, 19–21 Jan.; Kenyatta's evidence in KTT 4 and 5, pp. 875–1318, 26 Jan.–9 Feb.; exchanges on CLO, pp. 914–15, 928–31. Somerhough's summary history in KTT 5, pp. 1292–5, 9 Feb.; key part of Pritt's final speech in KTT 7, pp. 1847–57, 2 Mar.; Kenyatta's final speech, 8 April 1953, in KNA: MAC/KEN 68/1, pp. 94–6.

masses, inciting violence as a short cut to power. He knew this because he knew Africans; rarely had he met such truthful crown witnesses or such shifty ones for the defence; and there was too much common ground between them for the crown to have invented its stories. On one issue he agreed with Pritt. The *nyimbo* proved nothing; they sowed hatred, they idolised Kenyatta; that did not mean he had authorised them. Otherwise the prosecution had carried the day. Of the six oathings in which one or other defendant was said to have shared, he thought four proven. The two that involved Kenyatta were before the ban; one was seen (if it had been) by Macharia; the other was heard (if it was heard) as a night of song. As to management, Thacker accepted that Kenyatta had led the KCA in the 1940s, unlawful in itself and – in the crown's narrative – parent to Mau Mau. Within the banned period, he ruled that KAU's hostility to its moderate Limuru branch showed that the KAU executive was, in effect, 'the executive committee of Mau Mau'. He ended by doubting Kenyatta's castigations of violence; their evasions fatally damaged his credit. Thacker obviously knew Kikuyu idiom better than Kenyatta.[72]

It was a thin case. It would have been weaker still had the DPP dropped two of his criminatory incidents. One was the singsong in March 1950. This, he later admitted, had celebrated an innocent age-set meeting, not a Mau Mau initiation. The other was Kenyatta's alleged word of managerial caution to oath administrators, at Ol Kalou. The sole crown witness, young Tabitha, had wobbled; and Somerhough did not call a KAU official, by whom he seems to have been convinced, who denied Kenyatta had offered any advice.[73] What Thacker most relied on in his verdict was the demeanour of witnesses and defendants. Prosecution witnesses had looked comfortable, the defence had not. That was crucial; this opinion, based on direct scrutiny, was the one part of the trial that no higher court could challenge. He had no right to such confidence; when Oneko, KAU's general secretary (and the only defendant later reprieved) had denied approval of violence, Thacker twice noted privately, 'firm denial'. And his proof for Kenyatta's control of Mau Mau was nonsense. Dismissing Pritt's suggestion that this would have invited retribution, he complained that Kenyatta could have denounced violence more plainly. 'If he denied the policy of Mau Mau with the knowledge and consent of Mau Mau he would be in no danger whatever.' On that reasoning, equivocation was surely the best argument that Kenyatta was not Mau Mau's manager.[74]

72 Thacker's 91-page judgement, 8 April 1953, KNA: MAC/KEN 68/1.
73 Crown brief, 12 June 1953, for the first appeal case, PRO: CO 822/426/61, pp. 18, 46.
74 Oneko: Magistrate's notes vol. 3, pp. 261–2, 20 Feb., KNA: RR 9/3; Pritt's suggestion that Kenyatta's denunciations were risky, his final speech, KTT 7, p. 1860, 2 Mar.; Thacker's rebuttal, his judgement, 8 April 1953, KNA: MAC/KEN 68/1, p. 84.

One cannot now, as many did not then, trust Thacker's ability to stand above the adversarial evidence. Whose interest did the evidence serve, whose was it construed to serve? There are four possibilities, not mutually exclusive. Most simply, the constructions which Thacker put upon the evidence set a legal seal on the white presumption of Kenyatta's guilt. Had the crown witnesses been less random in origin, one could also suggest that the prosecution case represented moderate Kikuyu opinion. Six years later Macharia was to say the coincidence was no coincidence; it had been bought. But there is another case to consider. The outcome may well reflect a calculation by the defendants, especially Kenyatta. By obeying the law's rules, even with the dice loaded against him, he might hope to win the game of hegemony.

Kenyatta could hope to win in either of two ways; the game was therefore worth playing. First, the crown case was weak, as he must have known when he first saw his ill-assorted fellow defendants; he might be found not guilty. That was the view not only of British press reporters but of the white press in Kenya too. In early 1953 the editor of the farmers' weekly thought Mau Mau fighters were 'stimulated by the conviction that Jomo Kenyatta will be released and that he will lead the Kikuyu to victory over the white men'.[75] This seeming attempt to intimidate the judge showed the second possibility open to Kenyatta. He might win the politics of the trial whatever the verdict. The crown might win in court but lose in public opinion; there were so many publics. It had lost credibility with some before the trial began; the opposition at Westminster mattered; it included Kenyatta's long-standing Labour friends. How valid knowledge was constructed during the trial was therefore vital. To help the crown, tricky as some thought it to be, the case had to be incontestably proven. Any suspicion of reliance on 'common knowledge' could only help Kenyatta; it could so easily be called colonial prejudice.

Any trial should construct knowledge by its own processes alone. These protect defendants under three rules of procedure. Evidence must be proven. Prior knowledge, unproven, is not evidence. The judge must be an arbiter, above the arena, not a player.[76] Defence, prosecution and judge all failed one or other of these tests at Kapenguria. The twin impenetrabilities of imperial legal culture and Kikuyu political idiom nonetheless made the procedures appear to be bafflingly exact.

The following exchange between Kenyatta and the DPP exemplifies the

[75] *Kenya Weekly News*, 20 Feb. 1953; KTT 7, pp. 1711–12; this second contempt was expunged by written apology, not in court.

[76] On the first two rules, see the 1933 enquiry by the CO's legal adviser: Cmd. 4623, (see above, note 8); for the third, Patrick Devlin, *Easing the Passing: the Trial of Dr John Bodkin Adams* (London, 1985), pp. 74–5, a reference I owe, with other procedural advice, to Ivan Hare.

mutual puzzlement. We shall never know how or why Kenyatta wanted to qualify his view. All we can know is that the crown did not want to know. Somerhough was asking about a KAU meeting near Nyeri, in northern Kikuyu, in July of the previous year. He used as his prompt an account by Ian Henderson, of the police special bureau.[77] This had reported Kenyatta as criticising those who branded every petty criminal as Mau Mau. In court Kenyatta explained that he had advised against false accusation. The DPP asked him to confirm that.

> A. I said not to do it. That is not to indulge, because if you know what is going on in many parts that many trouble[s] are made because of these petty jealousies, you are –
> Q. I think you have given me my answer – whether you want to go on?
> A. Well, I wanted to qualify, I was giving my advice.
> Q. That really was not what I asked you.
> A. And when the people know, if only –
> Q. I have had my answer.
> A. Which was it? I thought –
> Q. I just wanted to ask you another question.
> A. You do not want me to say –
> Q. I do not want to know why you advised the people to say what you told me. I will ask you the next question . . . [78]

The evidence proved only that it was itself subject to African dispute. This suited neither counsel nor judge; the trial became what it should not, a white contest in 'knowing' their Africans. Each enlisted a partisan image of the colonial situation. Pritt evoked a manichean world, divided between upright nationalism and shameless police informers or snivelling fence-sitters, in which terror from Mau Mau scarcely appeared. The crown also, but to opposite effect, dismissed all idea of debate within militant politics, in arguing for a continuous conspiracy in subversion. The magistrate, needing a verdict, relied on what all whites knew, even if he did not know what he knew, at one point sighing, 'I cannot follow the African mind.' Yet Thacker was said to have been appointed for his long local experience. This reputation allowed him to appear to act like a DC, honestly able to dispense substantial justice because, knowing his people, he could see behind the evidence sworn – and often perjured – in an alien court. Yet Thacker was not a DC, even if he was no longer an imperial judge; he had just entered settler society. All settlers knew that Mau Mau was a darkness of the spirit, not a desperate protest. As Kenyatta was telling the history of land Thacker complained, 'Why am I having to listen to so much of the grievances? . . . I

[77] This report is reproduced in Cmnd. 1030 (see above, note 48), appendix F.
[78] KTT 5, p. 1183, cross-examination of Kenyatta, 3 Feb. 1953.

gather grievances have nothing whatever to do with Mau Mau, and Mau Mau has nothing whatever to do with grievances.' One could not ask for more prejudiced knowledge. Conversely, envy of real expertise looks to have driven the bitter crown accusation, echoed by Thacker, that Kenyatta 'knew [his] own people'.[79]

Claims to common knowledge cloaked an ignorance of African life, symbolised in the nicknames Pritt coined to aid white memory. All were English, the 'mugwump association' of fence-sitters, the 'season-ticket witness' who changed the identities of oath-takers, the 'three tailors of Tooley Street' who spoke for the people. Sympathy with nationalism did not exempt him from a crude evolutionism then common to whites; he thought the pastoralist people of Kapenguria 'too backward even to till the soil'. He was infuriated by slow African witnesses and their natural resort to hearsay. Somerhough knew his conspiracy theory; he was not above being amused by African grievance. Thacker thought it 'odd' that a Kikuyu witness should sell milk from white suppliers; in its surprise at inter-racial commerce, that 'odd' was the single most revealing, if unuttered, word in the trial.[80]

Defence and prosecution disputed technicality more fluently than evidence, raising points of African debate to the (uninterpreted) eminence of imperial, often Indian, precedent. Both would have hotly denied it, but shared racial ignorance and professional expertise made for a tacit collusion between them in shaping the case to be proved. Both accepted unquestioningly the reality of Mau Mau. Neither probed differences in African political opinion, central to the determination of innocence or guilt. Each was uneasy at expert evidence on Kikuyu oaths. In the production of evidence generally, both sides seemed reluctant to muddy the clarity of prior knowledge with the complexity of African thought.

The white use of the term 'Mau Mau' casts doubt on all the African evidence; coined by political opponents, it was not a self-description. It could be onomatopeia for 'greedy eaters'; or a white policeman's attempt to say *muma* or oath. True, it became a daily usage, but among Kikuyu always within the quotation marks that imply dissent from a term or its meaning. Somerhough was irritated with Kenyatta's replies that he had 'denied' Mau Mau whenever the former queried if he had denounced it. How, Kenyatta asked, could he condemn what he did not know? 'It is still a mysterious word to me, and I think to many people.' What then did he mean by denial?

[79] Thacker's despair, KTT 6, p. 1675, 23 Feb.; his expertise, in crown brief (see above, note 73), pp. 8, 13; for the final envy, Somerhough in KTT 5, p. 1292, 9 Feb., and Thacker's sentence, 8 April 1953, KNA: MAC/KEN 68/1, p. 97.

[80] Pritt, *The Defence Accuses*, p. 47; Mumford to Rayne, 10 Jan. 1953; Somerhough in KTT 5, p. 1223, 5 Feb. 1953; magistrate's notes vol. 3, p. 112, 10 Feb.

His phrase was *ndiui Mau Mau*, '"I do not know that particular thing, and I have no connection with it." In other words you are disassociating yourself . . . It is an emphatic way of denying connection with something, but not just a mere "I do not know."' Thacker could not tell if Kenyatta had rejected an outsider's definition of political choice or condemned a social reality, regardless of its name.[81] Nor can we. Contrary evidence does not exist; his ambiguity was useful to all concerned.

Here was the heart of the collusion. The state did not attempt to split the accused; they stuck together. Pritt expected the crown to set them against each other; it did not know enough to try. The police had little inkling of division between 'Kenyatta and his henchmen'. When in 1953 they found Mau Mau's central committee, *muhimu*, they thought it a second rank of leadership to replace the first, now on trial. But *muhimu* had existed a couple of years; by Kikuyu accounts, Kenyatta knew nothing of it until its leaders threatened him in late 1952. *Muhimu* excluded the top KAU leadership. If the crown knew nothing of this – it was the vital distinction between Mau Mau and KAU – the defendants saw to it that their counsel knew nothing either. They met daily. Kaggia and Kubai, both *muhimu* men, could have broken the crown's continuity thesis by telling Pritt that Mau Mau was in part a revolt against the KCA's caution. By admitting their warnings to Kenyatta, they could also have confirmed his political courage. Kenyatta could have fingered them in return; but he mentioned political risk once only, in passing, under pressure from the DPP over an issue of Kikuyu idiom, and nobody took any immediate notice. Pritt made little of it in his final speech. Merely to suggest any courtroom dissension among the defendants is to show its impossibility for either side, at a time when their people were at war. To the militants, Kenyatta was the only possible national figurehead. Had he denied them, he would have betrayed them; to a government he had no reason to trust; at the cost of the only consolation in his present predicament – the prospect of a martyr's crown.[82]

The most visible instance of tacit collusion was the reluctance of both counsel to probe the expertise of the Kenya-born, Kikuyu-speaking superintendent Henderson. Case officer for the trial, he had had charge of the African crown witnesses for some weeks. Somerhough asked him about Mau Mau oaths, wanting both expert support for his witnesses' accounts of initiations and to show that, steeped in custom, the oaths had power.

[81] Kenyatta's cross-examination, KTT 4, pp. 935–44, 951, 27 Jan. 1953.
[82] Baring to Lyttelton, 19 April 1953: CO 822/440/246; Lapping, *End of Empire*, p. 411; Eliud Mutonyi, 'Mau Mau Chairman', (MS, n.d., privately held); Kaggia, *Roots of Freedom*, pp. 108–13, 194; Kenyatta's disclosure of risk, KTT 5, p. 1204, 5 Feb.; Pritt in final speech, KTT 7, p. 1860, 2 March 1953.

Henderson gave him more than he asked. Yes, blood and earth, goats' meat and bones, banana and sugar cane arches were all part of, but not peculiar to, Mau Mau ceremony; they featured in litigation and in rites of passage. Somerhough tried to narrow Henderson's replies; Pritt, new to Kenya, failed entirely to grasp their import. He objected to all mention of Mau Mau practice; his clients had no proven connection with it. He declined to cross-examine; that must have been on Kenyatta's advice, since Pritt first asked to reserve the opportunity to do so.

Too late, Pritt came to regret that. When he later submitted there was no case to answer he argued that by Henderson's account an alleged Mau Mau oathing could be any other, entirely legal, occasion; how could a witness know the difference? And in his final speech he used Henderson again, to attack the continuity thesis for Kenyatta's guilt. The crown had accused him of 'imposing' oaths on the KCA and Mau Mau; yet they were old oaths, not new; adapted, not imposed.[83] Pritt knew he could not score in speeches points he had not proven in examining evidence. But if he had missed his chance to ruin the conspiracy theory, it never occurred to him – which means that if it occurred to Kenyatta he put it behind him – to chase what most mattered to Kikuyu. This was not the oaths' apparatus but their sociology, how their participants' authority related to the land on which they were sworn. But to pursue that would have exposed what the defendants wished to keep hidden, the gap between elderhood and impatience that had so divided Kikuyu in authorising political action.

Counsel found other evidence hard to handle. Neither side called Joseph Otiende, KAU secretary general until mid-1952, a known moderate and present at the executive committee meeting – the one incident at which all six defendants were present – which had disciplined the Limuru branch. One can only speculate on the reason; his non-Kikuyu, outsider's, disinterest may have been feared to sap the adversarial vigour of both crown and defence cases, persecution versus rationalisation. There was silence, too, over the protection of crown witnesses. Somerhough did not disclose its terms but nor did Pritt enquire, although he knew that they had for weeks been in police custody. Whyatt, AG, thought Pritt did not wish to know; an admitted need to protect fearful witnesses might tell against his clients.[84]

The loudest silence over production of evidence concerned the curse which Kenyatta said he had laid on Mau Mau at his last public meeting, at the Kikuyu township of Kiambu on 24 August 1952. This alleged curse, 'Let Mau Mau go to the roots of the *mikongoe* tree', caused confusion in

[83] Henderson's evidence, KTT 1, pp. 247–59, 12 Dec. 1952.

[84] Otiende, crown brief, 12 June 1953, (see above, note 73), pp. 46–7; non-disclosure of protection, Baring to Lennox-Boyd, 13 Dec. 1958; Whyatt to Webber, 10 Dec. 1958; PRO: CO 822/1848/35 and 37.

court. *Mikongoe* was an underworld tree. Kenyatta could not explain that; Thacker refused to understand. The curse would have banished Mau Mau for ever; helpfully, Thacker thought it was advice to go underground. Press reports mentioned a curse but not its terms. Kenyatta demanded that the sound recording, made by officials and later broadcast by radio, be heard in court. Silence then fell, masked by legal debate on whether a tape could be examined. Counsel and judge learned that the tapes had been doctored, to delete any equivocation by Kenyatta before being broadcast; but nor was there any audible curse. Crown and defence each had reason not to call the tapes: their man could not be heard to have played to either of their scripts. Neither explained in court.[85]

To conclude, in three ways the Kapenguria trial dramatised the decline of empire. One of its episodes showed colonial rule as Whitehall farce; another that liberal paternalism had lost its authority to speak for Africans; and all the while Mau Mau violence, however horrible, was reinforcing the case for Africans to be given a political voice of their own.

The farce of fused colonial power concerned Paul Ngei, with Oneko one of the six who was not Kikuyu. Although a KAU official, the reason for his inclusion among the defendants was that, in his cups, he had made outrageous jokes about Mau Mau and then, in prison, sung 'Bless Mau Mau', words composed by a white South African prisoner to George Formby's wartime favourite 'Bless 'em all'. He had been jailed for resisting arrest on a charge of drinking after hours. His district officer, Geoffrey Pedraza, had laid hands on him, not as a DO but as a policeman, and then, in his role as magistrate, had heard Ngei's statement. The combination of Ngei's foul-mouthed ex-Army slang, repeated in court, and Pedraza's abject confusion over what legal power he had exercised under which official hat was a comedy that nobody but Thacker could have taken seriously as evidence of Ngei's criminal guilt. It was better evidence, as Churchill might have put it, of the need for some mysterious force to curb such rough-and-ready ruling practice.[86]

Liberal paternalism fared no better. Louis Leakey, now fifty and verging on fame, was its epitome. He had long foretold the day when black peasants would dominate Kenya; he had spoken up for his Kikuyu between the wars; he had done so with Kenyatta. Unlike most whites he believed their life deserved the title of civilisation. With many elders (with indeed Kenyatta) he hated what Mau Mau had done to his people. The state turned

[85] Kenyatta, KTT 4, pp. 976–85, 28 Jan., and KTT 5, pp. 1187–1212, 1231, 3 and 5 Feb.; discussion between counsel, KTT 6, pp. 1456–88, 13 Feb. 1953. *EAS*, 25 Aug. 1952; crown brief, 12 June 1953 (see above, note 73), pp. 43–4; John Reiss, formerly director of Kenya's African information services, to Bodil Folke Fredriksen (by courtesy of the latter), 26 Feb. 1993.

[86] Pedraza's evidence in KTT 1, pp. 158–75, 265–79, 10 and 12 Dec. 1952.

to him for translation of Kikuyu documents that were put in evidence; he was court interpreter. But he had also published, soon after the start of the trial, a book, *Mau Mau and the Kikuyu*, which, while naming no names, had clearly blamed Kenyatta for Mau Mau. Pritt demanded he be replaced; author of a criminal libel against his clients, Leakey was also a partisan interpreter. The drama symbolised a moment of political transition. The white liberal was no longer a friendly advocate; Africans could speak for themselves; due process had given them the chance. Leakey left; his translations remained. As Somerhough read from one *nyimbo* the words, 'The love of Jomo Kenyatta is very great. He gave himself to be an agitator', Kenyatta protested, apparently to the DPP but surely to Leakey, the absent translator, 'You are after my blood, my friend. I am not an agitator. The word means a fighter with words or deeds.' Years before, in his book, Kenyatta had called himself a 'rabbit turned poacher'. Speaking for his own people, he no longer needed any 'pretenders to philanthropy', those white '"professional friends of the African"' – but only in court could he throw one of them out.[87]

Meanwhile, far from Kapenguria, the emergency piled horror on horror, as guerilla wars do. If any had doubted the existence of Mau Mau in October 1952, there was no doubting it by April 1953, when Thacker delivered judgement. After so much bloodshed it would have have been difficult for him to tell settlers that their government had got the wrong men. As the fighting continued, however, it was also clear that force was no lasting solution. Reform was needed to broaden the African political base of counter-insurgency war. The atrociousness of the war, on both sides, also affected the reception of Thacker's verdict.

VII. HEGEMONY AND NATIONALISM

Opinions of the trial were inseparable from perceptions of the emergency. There were three audiences for both, the British broadsheet reading public and Kenyans, white and black. When Thacker gave judgement, Mau Mau still held the military initiative. On the right of British opinion, London's *Times* and *Daily Telegraph* congratulated the Kenya government for its courage in proving the connection between KAU and Mau Mau in open court. Kenyatta had enjoyed 'all advantages of British justice' in 'a trial of scrupulous fairness'. The *Manchester Guardian* sorrowed only that Kenyatta had not been big enough to ally with the post-war liberalism of colonial rule and had

[87] Leakey's dismissal, KTT 2, pp. 509–11, 7 Jan. 1953; 'after my blood', KTT 5, p. 1235, 5 Feb. 1953; Kenyatta, *Facing Mount Kenya* (1938), p. xviii. Conversely, Leakey had indirect influence on the decision to imprison his intellectual rival Kenyatta: see, Berman and Lonsdale, *House of Custom*, forthcoming.

therefore to pass from the stage. But as fighting continued and more was heard of the brutalities of the security forces, white and black, so the British opinion which considered Africa at all feared that they were little better than Mau Mau. *Punch*, still a journal of influence, summed up the anxiety with a full-page cartoon early in 1955, called 'Pax Britannica: Kenya 1955'. The figure of Justice stood before a burning African village, both hands severed, her sword and scales of justice at her feet – barely distinguishable in the heap of Mau Mau's swords, spears and home-made guns.[88]

White opinion in Kenya, official and unofficial, was more robust. Lawful authority had not been disarmed; but there was a war on, and against a peculiarly barbaric enemy. Dreadful deeds were sometimes necessary. Iain Macleod, in 1959 the newly appointed secretary of state, was of opinion that during the emergency the Kenya government had 'thought little . . . of the letter of the law'. Perhaps so, but in the view of officials it was Kenyatta who was to blame for the short cuts forced upon them; and Kapenguria had proved that. As late as 1960, when Kenya was clearly embarked on the road to majority rule, the governor justified the decision to keep Kenyatta in restriction by the fact that this 'African leader to darkness and death' had been 'sentenced by due process of law' not only to prison but to restriction thereafter at the governor's discretion.[89]

Africans saw matters differently. For most Kikuyu, British power must have been discredited by its partisan force, a thesis supported by the feeling of some white officers that they had been pressed into somebody else's civil war. At the Macharia trial, in 1959, nearly three years after the army was withdrawn from the forest war, Kenyatta was asked if he seriously believed Africans were still terrorised by government. He replied, 'You as a European do not know what a terrible thing it is to be an African under the emergency.' But nor did Africans appreciate the legal theatre which, in the view of whites, had justified the emergency with a verdict reached by due process in open court. Africans had procedural grounds for doubt, as Kinyanjui did thirty years before, or any British appeal court in its unwillingness to overturn the verdict of a lower court of record. How did one prove knowledge and reputation other than face to face, before one's peers? Some Kikuyu witnesses felt that an unknown barrister from overseas, like Pritt, had no power to discern truth. As one of the Limuru branch officials, one of the three tailors of Tooley street, rebuked him: 'you were not there, so you do not know'. Later, one of his colleagues, when asked by Pritt if he, Pritt, might be Mau Mau, answered with perfect legal logic, 'I do not know – you come from Europe.'[90]

There is evidence that the British soon gave up trying to overawe Africans with the mysterious force of the law. Officials had so little faith in getting the crown witnesses to speak in court that it was suggested, and at government house, that they undergo the Kikuyu legal ordeal of swearing on the seven-holed *githathi* stone. Nor did any official think the law so

[88] *The Times*, *Daily Telegraph* and *Manchester Guardian*, editorials, 9 April 1953; *Punch*, 26 Jan. 1955, p. 134.

[89] Robert Shepherd, *Iain Macleod, a Biography* (London, 1994) p. 244; Sir Patrick Renison in *EAS*, 10 May 1960.

[90] Kenyatta, MTT 7, p. 1314, 4 March 1959; Johana Kairu and Ephraim Gichiriri, KTT 1, p. 59, 5 Dec. 1952, and KTT 2, p. 396, 5 Jan. 1953.

awesome that Kapenguria must be reported by the African press. Eliud Mathu, sole African member of the governor's emergency council, complained that DCs in Kikuyuland were publicly proclaiming Kenyatta's guilt weeks before the verdict; so much for respect for the law. Worse was to come. In August 1953 the appeals process had started to wend its uncertain way with an initial defeat for the crown. Kikuyuland's DCs agreed to suppress all news of Kenyatta's success; they would stress to their public that he would never be allowed to return home; but not when observed by the press, 'to avoid any suggestion of contempt of court'.[91]

Everybody could therefore make what they liked of the seventh and final 'Kenyatta' trial. In October 1958, Macharia swore an affidavit that the Kapenguria evidence had been fatally flawed. The crown had bribed him and others to give false evidence; his own evidence, the only account that put Kenyatta in a Mau Mau initiation,[92] had been perjury; witnesses had been coached in their false evidence, in a mock court at the police training school; while his reward had been a course in local administration at Exeter University College and a seat near Westminster Abbey at the Queen's coronation, the other witnesses had been resettled on land at the coast, far from Kikuyuland. After a hasty search through the attorney general and governor's files it was decided to charge Macharia with swearing a false affidavit. Pritt and Kapila defended him. Kapenguria was re-run in flashback. Henderson, by now the settler hero of the victory over Mau Mau, and Somerhough, now high court judge in Northern Rhodesia, were firm in their testimony. Africans had taken most of the initiative in volunteering evidence against Kenyatta. Most statements had been made before different magistrates before the witnesses had gone to the police school. The only coaching was in the truth as the witnesses had first told it, to ensure that they could stand up to questioning in court. Policeman and prosecutor had not conspired to concoct the cues whereby Somerhough could set the perjury flowing in court. Witness protection had been necessary. Their payments were not bribes but compensation for loss of livelihood. Their terror had required that Whyatt's protection plan be abandoned. To have returned them to the care of their neighbours would have been to put them in the 'jaws of Mau Mau'. One witness had tried to kill herself on being told what she had let herself in for; all were under guard, less to protect them than to stop them running away. These were nervous Africans, not hardened informers whose evidence was devalued by what it cost. In the verdict,

91 *Githathi*: J. F. Marnan, 'Rawson Macaria and the Kapenguria Trials', 8 Dec. 1958, in Baring to Lennox-Boyd, 18 Dec. 1958, PRO: CO 822/1849/76; Mathu: Emergency Council minutes, 20 March 1953, KNA: MAA 8/70; Meeting to Consider Ways and Means of Improving Propaganda within [Central] Province, 14 Aug. 1953, KNA: DC/NYK 3/1/2.

92 Given Somerhough's admission in the crown brief, 12 June 1953 (see above, note 73), that the second alleged oathing had been an age-set meeting.

Macharia was found to be the sole perjurer, and hard bargainer, among them. He had told lies against Kenyatta; Henderson was not to know they were lies. Macharia had demanded the overseas training course; it had not been suggested to him. One reason the judge gave for reaching this conclusion was that the original case had been too thin to be concocted; any conspiracy would have been to better effect.[93] The crown had won again. Many were not convinced. And if it had not bribed its way to Thacker's verdict, it had certainly been running scared. If that were so, an alternative source of authority over Africans was even now emerging.

By the time Macharia's remorse had overcome him, Africans had had their first direct elections; their leaders were welcome around the world. Kenyatta's arrest seven years earlier had had an electrifying effect; the challenge had converted the remaining KAU leaders from part-time amateurs into full-time politicians; mass politics became multi-ethnic. The police commissioner noticed at once that

> a spirit of nationalism has been born in Kenya and . . . it is the obvious intention of the intelligentsia to exploit this fully. The scene at Kapenguria, providing . . . clear evidence of the support which the Kenya African can expect from the West Coast, India and the Sudan, is having a far reaching effect on Africans who look upon it, not only as a trial of Kikuyu leaders, but also as a trial of strength between 'nationalism' and 'imperialism'. This insidious external influence is most dangerous and, as is obviously its intention, will encourage the belief that the Kikuyu are fighting for a righteous cause.[94]

As elsewhere, so in Kenya, nationalism had the power to enthral many diverse groups. Emergency and trial transformed KAU from Kikuyu cabal to international front. Its new non-Kikuyu officers used the Indian mission in Nairobi to get news of Kenyatta out and legal assistance in. Turning the legal tables on government, they refused to condemn Kenyatta for fear of contempt of court. His fate also transformed a trade unionist into nationalist politician, Tom Mboya, soon to be the man the British most feared and then trusted. Within divided Kikuyu opinion, some thought Kenyatta's arrest the final proof that peaceful protest was futile; others that if he really was Mau Mau's leader then the movement must be respectable after all. The courtroom was not the only theatre; with an international defence team, Nairobi airport was also a stage. As a crowd watched Pritt depart, a British official told the American journalist John Gunther, 'Now at last I am ready to concede that the Kikuyu may represent a national movement.'[95]

[93] Somerhough evidence, MTT 1, pp. 23–128; Henderson, MTT 1 and 2, pp. 128–211; judgement, 4 April 1959, in Macharia, *Trial of Jomo Kenyatta*, pp. 274–99.

[94] Police situation report, 10 Dec. 1952, PRO: CO 822/447/3.

[95] Evans, *Law and Disorder*, pp. 49–51; Murumbi MS; Tom Mboya, *Freedom and After* (London, 1963), p. 34; J. M. Kariuki, *Mau Mau Detainee* (London, 1963), p. 36; Kershaw, *Mau Mau from Below*, p. 248; John Gunther, *Inside Africa* (New York, 1953), p. 348.

That was not Baring's advice. He remained unshaken in his belief that KAU was the fount of tribal subversion. He banned it in June 1953, two months after Kenyatta was sentenced. He would have done so earlier had not that risked contempt; Thacker's judicial imprimatur on the conspiracy thesis cleared the way. Some official wag called the banning 'operation cowslip'. Damningly, KAU had bankrupted itself in defending the criminal six. Baring found it difficult to persuade London; Rogers was concerned lest the ban would lose for the British the battle for the educated African mind. But Kapenguria 'proved' that KAU was too far gone in criminal subversion for rescue. It would be best, Baring thought, to make a clean break with a new African politics. Racial nationalism was in itself anathema in a colony destined for a multi-racial future. The new politics would have to be based on districts and tribes. Kenyatta's plea from the dock for a wiser collaboration had gone unheard.[96]

But the movement of opinion was inexorable. Once the hegemony of the law was accessible to nationalism, colonialism was increasingly seen not to live up to its own ideals. A myth grew up around Kapenguria that the verdict was 'fixed' between the governor and a corruptible judge. Thacker was certainly well paid for his labours – and it was hard labour, with over 900 pages of his longhand notes. Nonetheless, for a pensioner on £474 per annum, £20,000 was a large sum for four months' work. No evidence of the transaction survives. Trench, in central government at the time, explains that Thacker negotiated a large daily fee, citing his risks in hearing the trial and the impossibility of living in Kenya in the event he found Kenyatta guilty. The trial lasted so long, to his financial benefit, not by his intention but because of the brilliance of Pritt's defence. That does not explain why Baring enquired, six weeks into the trial, what an English assize judge was paid; nor did the answer he received, £110 per week, with subsistence and first-class railway fares, support a cumulative total of £20,000. One cannot discover the truth of the myth. He may have winked at Baring, but white officials professed to be nervous of the verdict to the end. Thacker may well have been intimidated by white opinion, as Pritt feared. But it would have been enough for him to trust in his prior knowledge of the African mind to bring in the guilty verdict.[97]

[96] Eric Davies (chief native commissioner), handing over notes to Edward Windley, 31 Jan. 1953, KNA: MAA 8/53. Rogers's minute, 16 Feb. 1953, PRO: CO 822/440/190. The main files are CO 822/699 and, in the KNA: MAA 8/120.

[97] Trench, *Men Who Ruled Kenya*, p. 235; Charles Douglas-Home, *Evelyn Baring, the Last Proconsul* (London, 1978), p. 247; correspondence between Baring and Lyttelton, 14 and 27 Jan. 1953, PRO: CO 822/452/105–6. The two Kenyan defence lawyers, A. R. Kapila and F. de Souza, have differing views: negotiation for the costs of retiring elsewhere (to Rhodesia), and prior agreement to convict, respectively: interviews in 'End of Empire: Kenya', Granada TV, screened 1 July 1985. Sir Geoffrey Ellerton, interviewed 12 Sept. 1996, remembers paying Thacker from the 'Treasury goat bag', the governor's emergency fund. Neither Thacker's files in the KNA nor Baring's papers at Durham University Library offer enlightenment.

Kapenguria's real lesson was that the law was two-edged. The procession of appeals was a drama of remote and impartial, but also ineffectual, power. The British were masters at acting out the hegemony of lawful rule, especially in India where they could build on Mughal ritual rather than invent anew. Kenya, with its chiefless peoples, had few indigenous foundations of ceremonial, and the law was not a royal birthday.[98] It did not restrict native subjects to the audience; it gave them a voice. It brought them on stage, for British and Indian lawyers to argue over in universal terms. Africans were admitted to the core adversarial culture of imperial hegemony; this, long premised on the legal equality of individuals, was now accommodating itself to the sovereignty of peoples.

Kenyatta took the opportunity of the Macharia trial to deliver another political testament in court. Even as he was speaking, eleven Mau Mau convicts were being beaten to death at a prison camp whose name, Hola, came to haunt the British political mind as much as Mau Mau. It was this grisly incident that convinced Iain Macleod, who became colonial secretary a few months later, that all hope of colonial legitimacy had gone. If imperial hegemony was as one with Nineveh and Tyre, all that could be salvaged was British influence. That needed friends not subjects, recognition of what at Kapenguria Kenyatta had called 'Africa's place among the nations'.[99]

Kingsley Martin had been right. He had predicted that, far from being tainted by any conviction, Kenyatta would be 'built into a legendary figure, whose destiny it is to overthrow the European intruders and to lead his people to freedom, independence, and national greatness'. But Martin could not have foreseen how Kenyatta would interpret freedom in court. He distanced himself from Mau Mau, calling it 'anti-society, anti-people' rather than anti-European; he then blamed government for its disorder. The British had ignored the opportunity of co-operating with KAU to keep the peace. Challenged by Somerhough that Mau Mau had taken no heed of his denunciations, Kenyatta snorted, 'You people have the audacity to ask me silly questions. I have done my best and if all other people had done as I have done, Mau Mau would not be as it is now. You made it what it is, not Kenyatta.' To Somerhough this absurdity was the ultimate self-incrimination; he closed his questioning in triumph. But Kenyatta's accusation had epitomised his people's history.[100]

98 Even royal occasions could be ambiguous: John Lonsdale, 'States and Social Processes in Africa', *African Studies Review*, 24 (1981), p. 160.

99 Shepherd, *Iain Macleod*, pp. 155–9.

100 Kingsley Martin, 'The Case against Kenyatta', *New Statesman and Nation*, 22 Nov. 1952. Kenyatta in KTT 5, p. 1227, 5 Feb., and p. 1296, 9 Feb. 1953.

Kenyatta was as much elder as nationalist; elderhood taught his nationalism. Independence was freedom for individuals to do their duty by their community. The individual in his mind's eye was the household head, judged by his peers like any DC, exposed to the colonial onslaught on the moral linkage between people and land. In his book he had criticised colonialism most for destroying the spirit of manhood, tested by decision on behalf of one's dependants. He spoke for that responsibility in court. Denying that his followers would have run after his car or listened to anything he said, he replied with an anger that leaps off the page. 'They do not come running after me like a dog – they are human beings.' And, 'you think those people have no intelligence? They would listen to any rubbish if I spoke rubbish?'[101] These were not direct denials of blame for Mau Mau; indirectly they were. If Mau Mau was 'anti-society', equally anti-social was the racist assumption that Africans were less than human, dogs. Colonialism had caused the crisis in authority which allowed an 'anti-society' movement to grow; the British had made Mau Mau, not Kenyatta. His courtroom repartee would not have been so sharp had it not been deeply felt, inspired by a sense of how African authority could be respected in a different moral world. Had whites paid more heed – had they been capable of hearing – they would not have thought his wise moderation in office, at independence, to be quite so miraculous.[102]

The British had not bought Kenyatta. They did not try. As late as 1961, only two years before independence, they still intended to exclude him from power. They could not do that either; the law had not 'busted' him; its procedures could not fathom deep African politics; it was only there, in the politics of household authority, that one could decide which oaths were legitimate and which were not. British law did not have that authority. But Africans knew Kenya's moral history and hoped Kenyatta could restore the moral couplet of land and people. The landed eldership he had built for himself had earned him that power. They had not been persuaded he was a criminal – criminal though Mau Mau became in many African eyes during years of internecine war. The law had been too blunt a sword of empire to break him; his absent presence in prison had been his making. Churchill had claimed British conquest was legitimised by the shield of due process. In this he was only questionably correct; more certainly, a British attempt to reinforce hegemony had allowed African nationalism its say in open court.

[101] Kenyatta, *Facing Mount Kenya*, pp. 211–13; MTT 7, pp. 1239, 1253, 3 March 1959.

[102] Peter Knauss, 'From Devil to Father-Figure: the Transformation of Jomo Kenyatta by Kenya Whites', *Journal of Modern African Studies*, 9 (1971), pp. 131–7.

12. *Conclusion*

CHRIS WICKHAM

The original aim of this book, and of the conference that gave rise to it, was twofold.[1] First of all, we hoped to develop discussions about the difference between the environment of the courtroom, its moral world and the logic of the processes that go on in it, and the social/moral/processual assumptions of the world outside. This sort of difference can be described, and analysed ethnographically, with considerable nuance. Most of our contributors spent some time on it, with the result that some interesting cross-cultural comparisons and generalisations can be made, as we shall see. Our second aim was to look at this difference from the standpoint of the litigant, in order to see how far his or her expectations of redress and natural justice were satisfied or (more probably) disappointed by the often very different moral world of the court. We were guided here by Edward Thompson's work on the eighteenth century, as Peter Coss has noted already (above, p. 3). We were also influenced by some important work on contemporary US courts by Sally Merry, John Conley and William O'Barr, who have stressed how different the presuppositions and narrative strategies available in court are from what ordinary – working-class – litigants expect from the legal process; plaintiffs, in particular, tend to expect the redress of specific grievances from courts, but what they get is a more distanced justice, the application of rules, which are often unrecognised by or

[1] The Moral World conference was more successful as an intellectual event than many conferences are. There was a startlingly high standard of discussion and debate after each of the papers; listening to the tapes that were made of it is a renewed stimulation even at two years' distance. I have not been able to take full advantage of its complexity – one would have to write a book to do so. But the discussions certainly informed my own concluding remarks at the time, and have informed the framing of this Conclusion now. I thank all the participants for their contributions, particularly Jo Innes, who introduced the final discussion of the conference with me at the time. In what follows, I refer above all to the texts of the articles in the book, rather than to wider literature in the field; the articles themselves, particularly those of Ingram and Ford, contain more general bibliography.

unknown to litigants in advance.[2] We wondered whether it was possible to develop this disjuncture, the alienation, menace and disappointment of the court experience, one familiar to almost everyone who attends a modern western courtroom, in the context of the varying moral worlds of the law in the past, in order to help analysis of the structures of power.

It is fair to say, I think, that this part of our programme was less fully developed by our contributors than was the first question. To an extent, this was a problem of evidence; there are few explicit accounts in most societies of the past of what litigants expected from courts, and how this differed from what they found. (Indeed, it is hard enough in most historical courtroom transcripts to tell what litigants even said, rather than what court scribes or their equivalents thought they should have said.) In part, however, it is because contributors focused on a particular aspect of this question, how courts were chosen and played with strategically by litigants, with greater or lesser success. It might be said that we had anticipated discussion about the alienating effect of court procedure, but what we got was more empowering, with litigants often seeking to exploit an alien moral world, rather than simply being cowed by it. Conferences, like courts, have their own logics, not always predictable in advance. In this conclusion, therefore, I will discuss the different sorts of moral world presented in the articles of this book, and some of the ways they can be distinguished in their practical workings; I will then make some briefer comments as to how legal strategies inform the taking of forensic risks and the construction of stories, returning to power only at the end.

Peter Coss notes in his Introduction that our main theme, *The Moral World of the Law*, 'tended to presuppose the issue in question, i.e. whether or not there were indeed such moral worlds' (p. 3). When *is* a legal system different in its assumptions from that of the civil society it (nominally) serves? There are many variables which, separately or together, will contribute to increasing or lessening that difference: the relative complexity of the written sources of law; the relative professionalisation of legal practice and courtroom procedure; the issue of whether the legal system is generated by the society it serves, as opposed to being imposed on it from outside; the relative social or cultural homogeneity of the society concerned. I will come back to some of these variables in a moment; but it seems to me that their combination tends to produce three rough categories, of legal practices less or more distanced from civil society, which are worth brief characterisation.

[2] S. E. Merry, *Getting Justice and Getting Even* (Chicago, 1990); J. M. Conley and W. M. O'Barr, *Rules versus Relationships* (Chicago, 1990).

The first of these is the relatively unprofessionalised legal system. The clearest examples in this book were those of classical Athens (Todd) and early medieval western Europe (Davies), though there were some parallel elements in early modern England (Ingram) and the native court system in Africa (Jeater, Lonsdale). Here, the major figures in the court process were relatively ordinary people. Some were actually private individuals, as in the mass dikastic juries of Athens or the *adstantes* in early medieval courts, particularly (but not only) the most local ones, or indeed the juries of the English common law. Even 'public' officials, however, like the counts or the like who presided in the early medieval West, or the chiefs of African native courts, were not there because of any legal training. Any specific legal expertise any of these people picked up was exclusively practical, a spin-off of their constant presence at legal proceedings, and by no means necessarily or even often influenced by written norms.[3] The sort of justice such people meted out was likely to be in many respects analogous to the moral world of the society they lived in, or at least of the elites of that society, rather than derived from an autonomous legal realm, as our authors indeed stress.

It must be noted that even these unprofessionalised systems made use of and gave rise to court procedures that were distinct from the more informal or direct processes of social control in civil society at large – hostile gossip, for example, or social exclusion, or informal arbitration, or direct action, including feud. In part, this is because even such wide pools of participation did not by any means reflect the whole of society: they excluded the unfree by definition (a numerous group in many societies), and in almost all cases excluded women too. Effective participation was generally restricted to social elites, even if these elites were in themselves wide. In part, however, it is because of a more general point: if a legal system was *only* a mirror of locally acceptable direct action, it would have no reason to exist as a separately organised sphere at all.[4] The simple act of fencing off systems of collectively sponsored redress that have any chance of working creates an environment with partially separate rituals and procedures. So, in Greece, a specialist legal vocabulary existed, which may not have been fully 'autonomous', in the specific sense that legal historians mean by the

[3] There are anthropological parallels to this, too; two influential accounts are M. Gluckman, *The Judicial Process among the Barotse of Northern Rhodesia (Zambia)*, 2nd edn (Manchester, 1967); J. L. Comaroff and S. Roberts, *Rules and Processes* (Chicago, 1981). In the early medieval period, written law was available as a normative recourse, but was hardly ever dominant in any court case: see for example W. Davies and P. Fouracre, eds, *The Settlement of Disputes in Early Medieval Europe* (Cambridge, 1986).

[4] There are some, fairly simple, societies without a separate sphere for collectively sponsored redress, but they are few in number. See for a survey S. Roberts, *Order and Dispute* (Harmondsworth, 1979), e.g. pp. 80–99.

term (Coss, Lewis), but was at least unlike that used outside the court. Rhetorical strategies were presumably different, too, even though the need to stress one's ordinariness to the audience of the court (one's amateur status, as Todd puts it) would keep legal rhetoric at least recognisable; we know from other societies, for example the southern Tswana studied by John Comaroff and Simon Roberts, or the Iceland of medieval saga narratives, that specific sorts of informed (even if still amateur) forensic skill could be highly valued by courtroom audiences.[5] Actually, all stable environments where people meet – departmental meetings, trade union and political party meetings – generate their own special language, procedural rituals, specialised aesthetics of rhetoric, and the like, usually orally generated (not everyone has read Lord Citrine's Rules), which are most appropriate there and out of place elsewhere. They may not be 'autonomous', but they are on the same spectrum as legal autonomy.

The second category is that of professional legal systems. It can be plausibly argued that these were invented in the early Roman Empire when, for the first time, professional jurists developed who had a specialist knowledge of often arcane procedural points, which could nonetheless make or break a case for a party (Lewis). For the first time, one could win a case merely on the basis of written law, which could well be unrecognisable to litigants. The separate ('autonomous') cultural discourse of law, with its own (largely autonomous) coercive apparatus, became a feature of many post-Roman societies, right up to the present day, as a result – as also of many Islamic societies, though the development of a specialised Shari'a law was a largely separate process. This is the legal environment we live in ourselves, whose moral world is sufficiently different from ours that it can be described as a system entirely separate from that of daily life, or at least the extent of its separation from civil society can be the subject of hot debate (Coss). Historical societies in this category, or aspects of them, were discussed by many of our speakers (Lewis, Hyams, Brand, Ingram, Ford).

There is too much that one can say about this category for it to be possible to do justice to it all in a Conclusion such as this. At this stage, I would like to restrict myself to two broad points. One is that this category is often said to depend on the elaboration of a complex written legal system, like the Roman law of the sixth and twelfth centuries, or the canon law of the twelfth century and later. This is not borne out by our authors, who stress, rather, the role in courts of legal professionals. Andrew Lewis noted that the development of the autonomy of Roman law predated by several centuries its reinvention as a system under Justinian. Paul Brand presented us

[5] Comaroff and Roberts, *Rules and Processes*, e.g. p. 86; W. I. Miller, *Bloodtaking and Peacemaking* (Chicago, 1990), pp. 247–57.

with an extreme example of an autonomous system, in the England of 1300, which was run as an entirely closed network of judges and professional pleaders (serjeants), who frequently acted in the absence of the litigants themselves, and who spoke in a technical language incomprehensible to nearly the whole population; yet this network was largely orally learnt and practice-based. There is an interesting opposition between this world and that of fifteenth-century Florence, as described by Thomas Kuehn. Here we are in a legal system dominated by Roman law, elaborated still further by three centuries of juristic argument. The five jurists who gave their initial *consilia* for one of the parties in his central court case were more learned in their law than, perhaps, any of the other protagonists in this book, even Léon Tillard (Ford) and Denis Pritt (Lonsdale). But it was not they who decided the case; as was common in disputes of this kind, it went to arbitrators, who were not themselves legal professionals. These arbitrators sought further professional opinion, from the college of jurists in Genoa, but this was couched in distinctly less 'learned' terms; even though the final decision of the arbitrators reflected that opinion closely, it was theirs to make – and, it may be noted, that decision reflected a much more 'common-sense' understanding of the rights and wrongs of the case than did the juristic *consilia.* Although the weight of Roman law had an important strategic part to play at several moments in this case, its separate moral world did not have the power to impose itself regardless of the opinions of society at large, simply because it was not only professionals who were administering the dispute. Elaborate written law had less power in this instance than the oral but more hegemonic professionalism of the English case.

This leads us on to a second, but closely related point. It follows from this that the basic question we have to ask, when looking at how law is in practice separate from society, is how much power legal experts, with their fenced-off and sometimes almost secret knowledge (as in early medieval Ireland: Davies), have in any individual procedural system. Experts inevitably create their own separate legal theory, simply by talking to each other, sometimes on the basis of a wealth of written material, but always on the basis of shared knowledge about practice. (So, of course, do all social groups, simply by creating their own local protocols of gossip.[6]) Even opposing lawyers tend to understand each other far better than they understand the parties they nominally represent – a point which is clear in Paul Brand's article, and which reappears in John Lonsdale's analysis of the Kenyatta trial. But not all legal systems put all decision-making into their

6 Cf. C. Wickham, 'Gossip and resistance among the medieval peasantry', *Past and Present,* 160 (1998), pp. 3–24.

hands. The practice of trial by jury, for example, abruptly reintroduces the non-expert values and presuppositions of ordinary (elite, male) social actors. Martin Ingram shows how the dialectic between systemic change and legal decision-making on the one side, and changing values in society on the other, worked in early modern England. It was a complex process, but made more complex by the presuppositions of juries. Juries do not always decide according to the written law judges instruct them about, but rather, at least sometimes, according to their own values and expectations. *Causes célèbres* like the Hardy-Thelwall trial of 1794,[7] or more recent cases such as those of Clive Ponting or O. J. Simpson, keep the point in our minds. Of course, this is not always so; juries are often very respectful of the 'due process of law', whether they share its values or not. The practical hegemony of the law's moral world can be directly tested, indeed, by studying how often this respect fails to work – as with eighteenth-century English juries' reluctance to convict for capital offences such as infanticide, or (less positively) the difficulty Alan Dershowitz has encountered in persuading juries in criminal trials that life, unlike TV drama, is full of irrelevant coincidences.[8] Sometimes, even the law abdicates its power to create a distinct moral universe, as when canon lawyers in the early thirteenth century introduced *publica fama*, common knowledge or reputation, as a criterion for innocence and guilt, along the lines of most actual contemporary legal practice in fact, but against the letter of previous written law (Hyams): the simple introduction of reputation into court meant the wholesale importation of current social attitudes, because only these attitudes could determine what *fama* actually meant in any given place or time.

The increasing professionalism of legal process is the best guide to the real autonomy of law, as I have just argued: law can finally become autonomous when judgements end up in expert hands. But there is, in most systems, quite a complex balance of power between experts and a more 'lay' public: in few legal systems are the latter wholly excluded. Furthermore, law loses legitimacy, radically at times, if it is too distant from 'common-sense' notions of fairness. As Thomas Kuehn said at the conference, 'law has a separateness, an autonomy, from the quotidian; but it has to be related to the quotidian to have meaning'; Rosalind Thomas and Diana Jeater made similar points. It is thus a standard strategy in revolutionary situations to test the position of the legal system by subversive acts which are justifiable

7 E. P. Thompson, *The Making of the English Working Class*, 2nd edn (Harmondsworth, 1969), pp. 132–6.

8 M. Jackson, *New-born Child Murder* (Manchester, 1996), pp. 133–4, 144–5; see further, for the complexities of jury responses, J. M. Beattie, *Crime and the Courts in England 1660–1800* (Oxford 1986), pp. 400–49; A. M. Dershowitz, 'Life is not a dramatic narrative', in P. Brooks and P. Gewirtz, eds., *Law's Stories* (New Haven, 1996), pp. 99–105.

to civil society but which tread the boundary of legality as it is then constituted: either the law will back the current – but contested – social hierarchy, thus weakening its legitimacy, or else it will recognise as legitimate some forms of subversion, thus turning the ideological apparatuses of the state against the classes which are in power, as Santiago Carrillo once put it.[9] John Lonsdale describes just such a test in Kenya in 1952; even if Jomo Kenyatta did not seek that trial of strength, he soon discovered its advantages, as Gandhi, among others, had before him. Law cannot risk being seen, too widely, to be too separate, or else it cannot survive, except by the use of pure force, which is seen as 'legal' by few.

This is the dilemma of the third category discussed in this book, imported legal systems. Both of the articles on colonial societies (Jeater, Lonsdale) showed such systems in operation: law which had no roots at all in the societies it was applied to. Here, one must draw some distinctions. In John Lonsdale's example, law was simply used to coerce, in a highly politicised situation; and unsuccessfully, too, for in the court of public opinion, apart from that of white settler society at least, it appeared unjust and – often more dangerous – comic. In Diana Jeater's article, the lack of mutual comprehension between the colonial administration and the local society of eastern Southern Rhodesia was total, extending to the most fundamental principles of law; although this sometimes led to judgements that were simply meaningless to local society, but were nonetheless enforced, it is also clear that litigants could sometimes subvert that law, in great part because its administrators understood so little about what they were actually talking about. In both these cases, it is clear that even the most alien system of law could not remain entirely separate from the 'quotidian' for long, and that its ideological hegemony could be more easily contested if it did. It is above all colonial situations, with their very obvious coercion of one ethnic group (and legal system) by another, which are most likely to fall into this category; but even these situations can become more mediated, as one group becomes more prepared to adapt to or to instrumentalise the procedures of the other. When alien law is taken over in non-colonial situations, as when whole societies receive the entire system of Roman law – as across most of continental western Europe at some moment between 1150 and 1800, and Scotland as well – mediation is built into the reception of the alien system from the start, because legal experts themselves, and litigants for sure, will tend to look at it through the optic of the values of their own society.[10]

9 S. Carrillo, *'Eurocommunism' and the State* (London, 1977), esp. pp. 44–5. The basic idea behind the point is of course Antonio Gramsci's concept of hegemony.

10 See, for a case study, C. Wickham, 'Derecho y práctica legal en las comunas urbanas italianas del siglo XII: el caso de Pisa', *Hispania*, 57 (1997), pp. 981–1007.

We can thus see that, if non-professional legal systems are not entirely like the societies they serve, totally alien legal systems are not, or do not remain for ever, entirely separate from society either. There is, in other words, in every situation, a dialectic between (in Comaroff and Roberts's words) the 'constitutive order' and the 'lived-in universe': each can influence the other.[11] This is not in itself a completely surprising statement; but looking at how that dialectic works in practice, as the local knowledge, presuppositions about how the world works, values, or strategies of a given society come to terms with a more – or less – independent, effective, all-embracing, internally consistent, complex, or arcane legal system, is one of the best ways of studying any society, whether in the past or in the present. It is the subject of most of the articles of this book, to notable effect; it is clear that it will remain a significant field for historical research.

It is in the framework of this dialectic that the strategies of individual litigants can best be seen. Anthropologists of law these days tend to say that law is 'processual', a framework for bargaining, transaction and compromise. Rules exist, but they themselves are bargained over, between litigants themselves and/or between an individual litigant and the court.[12] Every rule, in every society and every social context, including our own, carries with it a practical awareness of how far one can go in bending or breaking it (and which people can go furthest, and in which context) – laws on speed limits are more acceptably broken than laws on homicide, middle-class whites can get away with more than blacks, and so on. Courts are venues for finding out how far one can go, in practice.

Several of our contributors put considerable stress on strategies: the way early modern English plaintiffs used slander actions to bring quarrels into the public arena (Ingram), or the way native plaintiffs in Rhodesia could use the incomprehensible presuppositions of Roman-Dutch law in order to gain settlements of marriage disputes that did make sense to them (Jeater), or the way early nineteenth-century French lawyers could use public anxieties about confinement as a successful rhetorical trope in their highly publicised *mémoires judiciaires* (Ford). Strategy could also operate on the level of the selection of the appropriate court (Ingram) or the appropriate action to pursue at court (Todd) – those involving more risk, or less. In general, the more distant the court, the higher the stakes: even if the legal

[11] Comaroff and Roberts, *Rules and Processes*, pp. 63–9, 230 (though their 'constitutive order' is wider than the specific legal process); cf. C. Geertz, *Local Knowledge* (New York, 1983), e.g. p. 173.

[12] See e.g. L. Rosen, *The Anthropology of Justice* (Cambridge, 1989); S. F. Moore, *Social Facts and Fabrications* (Cambridge, 1986); and the books cited above, nn. 2, 11. For the procedures of negotiation, see classically P. Bourdieu, *The Logic of Practice* (Oxford, 1990).

procedures were similar, which is not always so, the personnel involved were that much less familiar. There are parallels to this in the use of local or extra-local courts in modern Mexico, as also in the choice whether or not to appeal to the *curia* in Rome in the later middle ages, or, in many contemporary societies, the choice of whether to risk the expense and the arbitrariness of the public legal system at all.[13] These are all, of course, highly heterogeneous types of strategy: some involve choices of the most advantageous venue to pursue a dispute; some involve using the disputing process to gain an end not necessarily contained in the dispute itself; some involve using the law for ends that it does not recognise, maybe with the collusion of the opposing party. All of them, however, show litigants (or their advocates) as creative protagonists, able to use the legal systems available to them to the best of their ability – even if, inevitably, not always successfully.

Part of the construction of any successful legal strategy, in any society, involves the creation of a plausible story-line. The literary analogy appeared several times in our articles. Stephen Todd stressed how Athenian court actions had parallels in contemporary drama; Caroline Ford paralleled her *mémoires judiciaires* to contemporary novels, citing other influential analyses of literary strategies, by Natalie Davis and Ruth Harris, as well. In each case, the strategy employed was to link the dispute to rhetorical skills or plot lines already known to and appreciated by audiences. This can be true today, as well, as Dershowitz's already-cited comments about TV drama remind us: participants in disputes have a ready-made intertextuality of assumptions about how stories work that they will draw on in making legal decisions, or any kind of decision for that matter. Other contributors developed the issue of how story-telling worked rhetorically in court as well (Brand, Ingram, Lonsdale). Here, we should perhaps keep three separate versions of the 'law as story' approach separate. First, we must recognise that a lawsuit is itself a story, attractive for us as historians to reconstruct and describe, with its own plot line and internal rhythms – its social drama, as Victor Turner terms it.[14] Secondly, and most discussed at the conference, there is the forensic power of the stories of plaintiffs, defendants, lawyers and witnesses, each designed to convince in a socially specific rhetorical frame, which is worth analysis for its own sake. Thirdly, there is the widely recognised fact that all our sources for the disputing process are texts, fashioned by notaries or advocates, which themselves distort 'what really happened' for reasons of genre (and of bias and specific audience, as well as ineptness or laziness). All three are the remit of the 'law

[13] See n. 2 above; for Mexico, J. F. Collier, *Law and Social Change in Zinacantan* (Stanford, 1973), pp. 51–74, 251–8; L. Nader, *Harmony Ideology* (Stanford, 1990), pp. 162–81.

[14] V. Turner, *Drama, Fields and Metaphors* (Ithaca, 1974), pp. 23–59.

and literature' school, one of the more recent 'law and . . .' trends to hit legal studies, some of whose best products could usefully be read by historians of the legal process.[15] There seems to be more here that future analysts could pursue: in particular, how stories *actually* work in court, as opposed to how they are intended to work, the best way, perhaps, where there is enough evidence, to get around the relativist edge of narrative analysis. This is not easy, but it has sometimes been tried with some success; it is worth trying it again.[16]

This last comment, on work that could be done rather than work that has been done, brings me back to power and alienation. Law, and the courts, have two functions: to regulate the detail of dispute, and to maintain the social order. Every class society has its own structures of class domination, and every society has its gender hierarchies and its marginal and excluded groups. These dominations are policed in many ways, but courts and other formal patterns of dispute-settlement always play a prominent role in them. The degree to which courts are alienating places is part of that creation of a network of power and hegemony, which dominates and/or excludes the weak. Historians who are interested in analysing power relations (which is most of them) could usefully be interested in how that alienation works. Perhaps Diana Jeater has explored the issue most fully in this book, in her analysis of how Roman-Dutch law, concerned with retribution in its civil law, was utterly unsuited to dealing with local values based on restorative justice. As a device of domination, even if an accidental one, this was as effective as any; it is a tribute to litigants that they got anything out of it, but they did it against the odds. There is more along the same lines that could be done with legal studies. We hope, nonetheless, that any development in this field, along these lines or along the others outlined above, will use this book as one of its starting points.

[15] E.g. W. L. Bennett and M. S. Feldman, *Reconstructing Reality in the Courtroom* (New Brunswick, NJ, 1981); Brooks and Gewirtz, *Law's Stories*.

[16] Examples are R. Harris, *Murders and Madness* (Oxford, 1989), pp. 208–42, 285–312; D. L. Smail, 'Telling tales in Angevin courts', *French Historical Studies*, 20 (1997), pp. 183–215.

Index

Past and Present Publications

Family and Inheritance: Rural Society in Western Europe 1200–1800, edited by Jack Goody, Joan Thirsk and E. P. Thompson*
French Society and the Revolution, edited by Douglas Johnson
Peasants, Knights and Heretics: Studies in Medieval English Social History, edited by R. H. Hilton*
Town in Societies: Essays in Economic History and Historical Sociology, edited by Philip Abrams and E. A. Wrigley*
Desolation of a City: Coventry and the Urban Crisis of the Late Middle Ages, Charles Phythian-Adams
Puritanism and Theatre: Thomas Middleton and Opposition Drama under the Early Stuarts, Margot Heinemann*
Lords and Peasants in a Changing Society: The Estates of the Bishopric of Worcester 680–1450, Christopher Dyer
Life, Marriage and Death in a Medieval Parish: Economy, Society and Demography in Halesowen 1270–1400, Zvi Razi
Biology, Medicine and Society 1740–1940, edited by Charles Webster
The Invention of Tradition, edited by Eric Hobsbawm and Terence Ranger*
Industrialization before Industrialization: Rural Industry and the Genesis of Capitalism, Peter Kriedte, Hans Medick and Jürgen Schlumbohm*
The Republic in the Village: The People of the Var from the French Revolution to the Second Republic, Maurice Agulhon†
Social Relations and Ideas: Essays in Honour of R. H. Hilton, edited by T. H. Aston, P. R. Coss, Christopher Dyer and Joan Thirsk
A Medieval Society: The West Midlands at the End of the Thirteenth Century, R. H. Hilton
Winstanley: 'The Law of Freedom' and Other Writings, edited by Christopher Hill
Crime in Seventeenth-Century England: A County Study, J. A. Sharpe†
The Crisis of Feudalism: Economy and Society in Eastern Normandy c. 1300–1500, Guy Bois†
The Development of the Family and Marriage in Europe, Jack Goody*
Disputes and Settlements: Law and Human Relations in the West, edited by John Bossy
Rebellion, Popular Protest and the Social Order in Early Modern England, edited by Paul Slack
Studies on Byzantine Literature of the Eleventh and Twelfth Centuries, Alexander Kazhdan in collaboration with Simon Franklin†
The English Rising of 1381, edited by R. H. Hilton and T. H. Aston*
Praise and Paradox: Merchants and Craftsmen in Elizabethan Popular Literature, Laura Caroline Stevenson

The Bremner Debate: Agrarian Class Structure and Economic Development in Pre-Industrial Europe, edited by T. H. Aston and C. H. E. Philpin*
Eternal Victory: Triumphant Rulership in Late Antiquity, Byzantium, and the Early Medieval West, Michael McCormick†*
East-Central Europe in Transition: From the Fourteenth to the Seventeenth Century, edited by Antoni Mączak, Henryk Samsonowicz and Peter Burke*
Small Books and Pleasant Histories: Popular Fiction and its Readership in Seventeenth-Century England, Margaret Spufford*
Society, Politics and Culture: Studies in Early Modern England, Mervyn James*
Horses, Oxen and Technological Innovation: The Use of Draught Animals in English Farming 1066–1500, John Langdon
Nationalism and Popular Protest in Ireland, edited by C. H. E. Philpin
Rituals of Royalty: Power and Ceremonial in Traditional Societies, edited by David Cannadine and Simon Price*
The Margins of Society in Late Medieval Paris, Bronisław Geremek†
Landlords, Peasants and Politics in Medieval England, edited by T. H. Aston
Geography, Technology, and War: Studies in the Maritime History of the Mediterranean, 649–1571, John H. Pryor*
Church Courts, Sex and Marriage in England, 1570–1640, Martin Ingram*
Searches for an Imaginary Kingdom: The Legend of the Kingdom of Prester John, L. N. Gumilev
Crowds and History: Mass Phenomena in English Towns, 1790–1835, Mark Harrison
Concepts of Cleanliness: Changing Attitudes in France since the Middle Ages, Georges Vigarello†
The First Modern Society: Essays in English History in Honour of Lawrence Stone, edited by A. L. Beier, David Cannadine and James M. Rosenheim
The Europe of the Devout: The Catholic Reformation and the Formation of a New Society, Louis Châtellier†
English Rural Society, 1500–1800: Essays in Honour of Joan Thirsk, edited by John Chartres and David Hey
From Slavery to Feudalism in South-Western Europe, Pierre Bonnassie†
Lordship, Knighthood ad Locality: A Study in English Socety c. 1180–c. 1280, P. R. Coss
English and French Towns in Feudal Society: A Comparative Study, R. H. Hilton*
An Island for Itself: Economic Development and Social Change in Late Medieval Sicily, Stephan R. Epstein
Epidemics and Ideas: Essays on the Historical Perception of Pestilence, edited by Terence Ranger and Paul Slack*
The Political Economy of Shopkeeping in Milan, 1886–1922, Jonathan Morris
After Chartism: Class and Nation in English Radical Politics, 1848–1874, Margot C. Finn
Commoners: Common Right, Enclosure and Social Change in England, 1700–1820, J. M. Neeson*
Land and Popular Politics in Ireland: county Mayo from the Plantation to the Land War, Donald E. Jordan Jr.*

The Castilian Crisis of the Seventeenth Century: New Perspectives on the Economic and Social History of Seventeenth Century Spain, edited by I. A. A. Thompson and Bartolomé Yun Casalilla
The Culture of Clothing: Dress and Fashion in the Ancien Régime, Daniel Roche†*
The Sense of the People: Politics, Culture and Imperialism in England, 1715–1785, Kathleen Wilson*
Witchcraft in Early Modern Europe: Studies in Culture and Belief, edited by Jonathan Barry, Marianne Hester and Gareth Roberts*
Fair Shares for All: Jacobin Egalitarianism in Practice, Jean-Pierre Gross
The Wild and the Sown: Botany and Agriculture in Western Europe, 1350–1850, Mauro Ambrosoli
Witchcraft Persecutions in Bavaria: Popular Magic, Religious Zealotry and Reason of State in Early Modern Europe, Wolfgang Behringer
Understanding Popular Violence in the English Revolution: The Colchester Plunderers, John Walter
The Moral World of the Law, edited by Peter Coss

* Also published in paperback
† Co-published with the Maison des Sciences de l'Homme, Paris